VARIORUM COLLECTED STUDIES SERIES

Exegesis and Theology
in Early Christianity

Frances Young

Frances Young

Exegesis and Theology
in Early Christianity

ASHGATE
VARIORUM

Published in the Variorum Collected Studies Series by

Ashgate Publishing Limited
Wey Court East
Union Road
Farnham, Surrey
GU9 7PT
England

Ashgate Publishing Company
Suite 420
101 Cherry Street
Burlington, VT 05401–4405
USA

www.ashgate.com

British Library Cataloguing in Publication Data
Young, Frances M. (Frances Margaret)
    Exegesis and theology in early Christianity.
    – (Variorum collected studies series)
    1. Bible – Criticism, interpretation, etc. – History – Early church, ca. 30–600.
    2. Theology – History – Early church, ca. 30–600.
    I. Title II. Series
    220.6'09015–dc23

    ISBN 978–1–4094–4781–8

Library of Congress Control Number: 2012936590

VARIORUM COLLECTED STUDIES SERIES CS1013

The paper used in this publication meets the minimum requirements of the American National Standard for Information Sciences – Permanence of Paper for Printed Library Materials, ANSI Z39.48–1984. ∞ ™

MIX
Paper from
responsible sources
FSC
www.fsc.org   FSC® C018575

Printed and bound in Great Britain by the
MPG Books Group, UK

CONTENTS

This volume contains xvi + 316 pages

PUBLISHER'S NOTE

The articles in this volume, as in all others in the Variorum Collected Studies Series, have not been given a new, continuous pagination. In order to avoid confusion, and to facilitate their use where these same studies have been referred to elsewhere, the original pagination has been maintained wherever possible. Article I has necessarily been reset with a new pagination, with the original page numbers given in square brackets within the text.

Each article has been given a Roman number in order of appearance, as listed in the Contents. This number is repeated on each page and is quoted in the index entries.

ACKNOWLEDGEMENTS

Grateful acknowledgement is made to the following persons, institutions, journals and publishers for their kind permission to reproduce the papers included in this volume: Koninklijke Brill NV, Leiden (for article I); Peeters, Leuven (II, V, VII, VIII, XI, XV, XVIII); the *Australian Biblical Review* (III); Cambridge University Press (IV); SCM Press, London (VI, XII); Oxford University Press (IX, XIII); Baker Publishing Group, Grand Rapids, MI (X); *Augustinian Studies* (XIV); the *Scottish Journal of Theology*, and Cambridge University Press (XVI); the Ecclesiastical History Society and Boydell and Brewer Ltd, Woodbridge (XVII); T & T Clark, Continuum Books (XIX); and Editions Beauchesne, Paris (XX).

Every effort has been made to trace all the copyright holders, but if any have been inadvertently overlooked the publishers will be pleased to make the necessary arrangement at the first opportunity.

Many thanks also go to Dr Andrew Teal, Chaplain, Pembroke College, Oxford, and for compiling the index to this volume, with the assistance of Chris Long.

INTRODUCTION

This collection gathers together twenty previously published papers, all in one way or another concerned with exegesis and/or theology in early Christianity. These have emerged as the principal areas around which my research has clustered.

It was perhaps inevitable that I should end up devoting my mature years to research on patristic exegesis. My original doctoral topic was to have been study of the Fathers' exegesis of the Epistle to the Hebrews, under the direction of Maurice Wiles who was at the time moving from his study of patristic commentaries on *The Spiritual Gospel* to his parallel work on *The Divine Apostle.*[1] My earliest published paper (not included in this volume) was devoted to Christological ideas in the Greek commentaries on Hebrews,[2] but a combination of circumstances and my own core interests had meanwhile shifted the focus of my thesis[3] to enquiry into patristic use of the language of sacrifice, both with respect to atonement and the eucharist. In other words, doctrine exercised a profound pull. It would be some years before work on soteriology and Christology would give way to research directly focused on patristic biblical interpretation, a move by then reinforced by the fact that my teaching post was in New Testament studies. But despite concentration on exegetical method, I was increasingly intrigued by the role of exegesis in theological argument and the profound contribution of the scriptures to the countercultural teachings that emerged as the early Church engaged with its intellectual environment.

The papers collected here mostly belong to the mature period which produced my book, *Biblical Exegesis and the Formation of Christian Culture;*[4] but the rest, some earlier some later, are selected because they also pursue the relationship between doctrine and exegesis, theology and hermeneutics. Together they reflect a fundamental shift in perspective, an abandonment of

---

[1] These were studies of the interpretation of the Gospel of John and the Pauline Epistles in the early Church, published by Cambridge University Press in 1960 and 1967 respectively.

[2] 'Christological Ideas in the Greek Commentaries on the Epistle to the Hebrews', *Journal of Theological Studies* NS 20 (1969), pp. 150–162.

[3] Published as *Sacrificial Ideas in Greek Christian Writers,* Patristic Monograph Series 5 (Cambridge, Mass.: Philadelphia Patristic Foundation, 1979); and in a more popular version, *Sacrifice and the Death of Christ* (London: SPCK, 1975).

[4] Published by CUP in 1997.

the heuristic model of 'doctrinal development', for what might be described as a 'discourse' model – an attempt to trace the lines of theological debate by which Christian thinkers produced increasing clarification and precision in articulating what was perceived as the truth enshrined in the scriptures.

In a number of ways that intellectual progression of mine paralleled, or responded to, major shifts over the course of the past 50 years in the humanities in general and patristics in particular. When I began, study of the Fathers of the Church was a sub-discipline of theology, practised for the sake of understanding the historical development of normative Christian doctrine. Now Early Christian studies have an interdisciplinary feel, overlapping with studies of Late Antiquity or the Early Byzantine period. When I began, tradition and precedent were important motivations for some, while others were drawn to historical explanation of inherited norms for the sake of contemporary critique and rethinking doctrine for the so-called modern world. Such opposing motivations persist, but often now in relation to post-modern interests, such as feminism and the ordination of women, rather than Christology or Trinitarianism. When I began, the discovery of Gnostic texts had stimulated interest in history's underdogs – it was beginning to be recognised that the winners wrote history and heresies were largely known through the hostile reports of their opponents. The consequent rehabilitation of heretics would challenge the notion that doctrinal outcomes were a foregone conclusion, whether determined by providence, or by inherent characteristics of the tradition. So the field has increasingly ceased to be determined by ecclesial interests. The turn to sociological approaches reinforced the emerging focus on power relations, on the social, political and cultural significance of movements, heretical or otherwise, in their particular historical context, while the increasing interdisciplinarity in study of the period meant that topics such as the process of Christianization, or the impact of asceticism modified the extent to which theology exercised primacy in the field. These developments were, of course, related to more widespread post-modern trends. Nevertheless the post-modern challenge to the historico-critical method has, generally speaking, had less impact on patristics than on biblical studies. A key methodological piece, 'From suspicion and sociology to spirituality' (no. VII in this collection) explicitly raises questions about the potential of post-modern literary and hermeneutical perspectives to transform patristic study.[5]

At issue for me remains the question how the theologian is to read patristic texts. That methodological paper is followed by a 'trial run', which calls in

---

[5] Some attempt was made to execute this in *The Cambridge History of Early Christian Literature* (Cambridge: CUP, 2004), a volume which I planned as editor, though it was brought to fruition by Lewis Ayres and Andrew Louth.

question not only the search for precedent but also the treatment of patristic texts as merely collections of historical data, thus opening up the possibility of appropriation. Repeatedly, though not exclusively, the method adopted in these papers is to read closely a particular patristic text or body of texts. The starting point is to seek to understand the Fathers' exegetical and theological thought in terms of the context in which they were operating, focusing particularly on the rhetorical and philosophical discourse available to them given their socio-cultural context, as well as the ways in which scripture modified this, enabling them to articulate a distinctively Christian discourse. But implicit if not explicit are hermeneutical questions about appropriation, about the proper relationship between text and reader.

Necessarily the length and register of the papers selected varies considerably, some arising out of the researcher's own programme though often constrained by the exigencies of a particular conference presentation, others responding to invitations to contribute to someone else's thematic volume. Inevitably there is a somewhat arbitrary element in their ordering. Part A, entitled 'From Exegesis to Hermeneutics', begins with a relatively early article which reshaped the then widely accepted notion that early Christianity's Hellenisation meant a betrayal of its biblical roots by exploring the interaction of biblical and 'scientific' motifs in two fourth century anthropological treatises, medical philosophy providing what would count as scientific knowledge in that period. This is followed by a number of notes and papers (nos. II–V) exploring exegetical practices, including allegory and the reaction against it. Some of these studies indicate the impossibility of separating biblical interpretation from doctrinal and pastoral concerns, so relativising descriptions of patristic exegesis which focus on narrow technical and methodological analyses. Obviously, these were preparatory studies towards my attempt to re-characterise patristic exegesis in the book referred to above. The next group (nos. VI–VIII) raises questions about our assumptions and our own hermeneutical practice with respect to patristic texts, testing this out by consideration of a particularly complex text, the *Apostolic Constitutions*, study of which is carried over into a couple of pieces on reconfiguring received accounts of the development of Church order (IX–X). The final two contributions to this section are transitional, in that they address specifically the relationship of exegetical method to the deduction of doctrine from scripture, so leading into part B's focus on doctrinal and theological matters.

The first issue raised in part B concerns the very nature of 'dogma' and 'heresy' as the Fathers' own usage of those terms is explored (nos. XIII–XV). If the word 'dogma' meant just 'teaching' and the teaching of any philosophical school in antiquity involved not just promulgating propositions, but training in how to live morally and how progressively to enlarge the mind to receive spiritual truths, and if the word 'heresy' meant choosing among the lifestyle 'options' offered by different philosophical schools, then the point is clear that ethics and spirituality could not be divorced from theology. So Augustine's *Confessions*, as well as the exegesis of, for example, Gregory of Nyssa, provide exemplary models of progress in the spiritual and intellectual life, and the formulation of doctrinal propositions was not really what the theologians of the early Church were about – rather it was the formation of Christian souls. To that extent the old 'development of doctrine' approach misrepresents them quite fundamentally. Nevertheless, what we project back as doctrines were clearly articulated in the process of argument, and *creatio ex nihilo* is arguably the first such doctrine to be established. So the next three papers (nos. XVI–XVIII) attend to the way in which Christian thinkers argued, against the prevailing culture, for 'creation out of nothing', and how acceptance of that understanding of the way things are then shaped a Christian discourse quite distinctive in the intellectual environment of antiquity. Space precluded the inclusion of other theological explorations, apart from the final pair of articles, which set key Christological and theological issues in wider contexts, and exemplify the fact that one doctrine is deeply integrated with another in an 'ecology' proper to the character of early Christian theology.

To describe this as the articulation of a distinctive 'discourse' alerts us immediately to the crucial role of language in this endeavour. It is indeed a persistent theme. 'The God of the Greeks and the nature of religious language' (no. XX – the earliest of these articles to be published but here placed at the end as a climax) can be seen in hindsight as quite fundamental to subsequent work, as well as my own emerging theological understanding. Explicitly it addresses the issue of Hellenisation, suggesting that the apophatic concept of God owed more to patristic reading of the Bible than was then generally admitted; but the crucial issue raised is the question how anyone can speak about God at all. Indeed, the way in which finite human discourse points beyond itself becomes a persistent theme in other articles, such as 'Exegetical method and scriptural proof' (no. XI) and those on allegory (nos. III–VI), while issues about meaning pervade discussions of exegesis, doctrine, and even Church order: that we too easily assume that linguistic continuity implies continuity of meaning is the burden of the argument in the note 'On *episcopos* and *presbyteros*' (no. IX) and is an implied question in the short essay, 'Did Epiphanius know what he meant by heresy?' (no. XV).

For discussion of meaning, the discipline of setting the enquiry in the socio-linguistic context of the original texts is fundamental. Hence the importance given to rhetoric in general and the rhetorical schools in particular. Setting the tensions between the so-called Antiochene and Alexandrian schools against the backcloth of long-standing tensions between philosophers and sophists not only sheds light on what the ancient arguments were about, but also provides keys to what exegesis is all about, and how ancient commentary both differs from and parallels the techniques of modern historico-critical methods. At the root of both is the philological method, the close examination of the language used – the vocabulary, syntax and figures of speech which are deployed and the effect produced. Credit must be given to the Fathers for their serious engagement with language through the highly sophisticated analyses of ancient rhetoric. It is because the same thing can be said in different ways, and much everyday language, let alone the language found in literary texts, is metaphorical or allusive, that meaning so often transcends the actual words. For the Fathers, images, associations and symbols were precisely what enabled deeper insight (*theōria*) into what the text was really about. They knew that language is both finite and infinite in its potential, and that communication is an art involving triangular interaction between content, speaker and hearer, or reader, author and text. So parallel post-modern insights do sometimes shed light on what is being discussed, yet the discipline of setting texts from the past in the alien intellectual environment of that past remains essential to the project of understanding what thinkers of the past were up to and, properly pursued, yields surprising dividends.

The legacy of the historico-critical method has thus remained constitutive of my approach. Nevertheless some historico-critical assumptions have been peculiarly unhelpful for assessment of how the Fathers understood things. One example would be the modern search for originality in the work of thinkers who consciously sought to conserve inherited tradition against novelty rather than create anything new. The 'evolutionary model' cannot do justice to what the Fathers thought they were doing, any more than the 'progressive revelation model'; for both are rooted in modernity's thought categories. We need to be as conscious that our own cultural propensities belong to a particular historical environment, as we are aware of the largely Platonising intellectual context within which the Fathers operated. And yet, new ways of articulating the 'truth received' clearly did emerge – the Nicene creed is not to be found in Church teachings of an earlier era nor is it straightforwardly implicit in the scriptures. Crucial to such re-formulation of the 'truth' was reaction to the 'novelty' introduced by 'heresy'. The history of debate, as new questions stimulated new responses, producing a new 'future' for the text of scripture, is exactly what a 'discourse model' facilitates.

A 'discourse model' also facilitates analysis of similarity and difference within a recognisably 'global culture' or thought-world. I may have begun by challenging the once conventional view that Christianity was compromised by its Hellenisation, but exploring the subtle interchanges necessarily involved in the 'enculturation' of the Jewish/biblical heritage into the Hellenised world of the Roman Empire has proved endlessly generative of interesting insights. Not the least of these are, first, the notion that early Christianity was far more like a school, with its own distinctive *paideia* than anything recognisable in the ancient world as religion, and second, the consequent acknowledgement that its triumph would profoundly change how religion is understood. For Jews and Gentiles alike, religion pervaded life at all social levels and had more to do with cultic practice than belief or ethics, until Christians shifted the focus. For, gathered around books with teachers expounding their meaning, including their understanding of the way the world is, the implications for an ethical lifestyle, and the theological warrants for following these teachings, Christian groups rejected the civic cults and other religious practices pursued around them for a more 'philosophical life' and were dubbed 'atheists' by their contemporaries. The process of Christianisation, however, was also a process whereby the Church had to take on the roles expected of religion in antiquity. In fact the convergence of Early Christian studies with work on Late Antique society has significantly refined our understanding of the formation of Christian culture,[6] including (1) our sense of how its art and architecture, liturgy and homily, organisation and charity, even literary forms such as hagiography, both drew from existing norms and incorporated differentiating features, (2) our awareness of subtle shifts of meaning as language and concepts were consciously or unconsciously adopted from contemporary philosophy, and (3) our perception of the role of scripture in modifying cultural norms. Yet it is precisely because we stand outside the ancient cultural *Zeitgeist* that we can engage in this analysis, descrying not only what differentiates emerging Christian practice and discourse, but also how it shared fundamental assumptions. Monotheism and monarchy appear, from our point of view, uncomfortably aligned with one another, while hierarchical norms are pervasive, ecclesial institutions reflecting in turn ancient patriarchal households, municipal structures and imperial organisation. Such features hardly encourage any hope of appropriation or straightforward adoption of precedent in our fundamentally different cultural environment.

And yet, as already acknowledged, the question wherein lies our own interest in all this has always been for me unavoidable. Objectivity and a purely intellectual interest in reconstructing the past, whether events or debates, ideas or social entities, has seemed not only problematic in that our own concerns

---

[6] See e.g. Averil Cameron, *Christianity and the Rhetoric of Empire. The development of Christian discourse*, Berkeley, Los Angeles, Oxford: University of California Press 1991; the second edition of my book, *From Nicaea to Chalcedon. A Guide to the Literature and its Background* (London: SCM press, 2010) records example after example from the scholarship of the past 30 years, as does *The Cambridge History of Early Christianity. Origins to Constantine* (Cambridge: CUP, 2006), which I edited with Margaret M. Mitchell..

and prejudices always affect the questions we ask, but also ultimately barren. I acknowledge, of course, the sheer fascination of engaging with human cultures of different eras, and the importance of that enlargement of one's inevitably limited experience which can only happen by learning the language of 'others' and refusing to reduce their 'world' to categories of one's own perspective. Yet an honest admission that a theologian's engagement in research is driven by the possibility of learning something significant for present understanding seems important, and is explicit, for example, in the little piece on Chrysostom's exegesis of the Corinthian letters. Why shouldn't past exegesis challenge current consensus? And shouldn't a native Greek speaker carry authority in construing problematic Greek sentences? There are, of course, some who would say that such an approach is uncritical, and others who would exploit such considerations simply to confirm tradition. I would certainly not align myself with the latter position, for a serious historian has to admit that the past is another country and it cannot be uncritically appropriated. However, it is surely possible to envisage a kind of ecumenical dialogue over time, taking seriously the need for what I have described as 'ethical reading' (see here nos. VI and VII): this involves respect for one's self, as well as for the 'other', so ensuring that difference is specified, even as one endeavours to engage in empathetic understanding, acknowledging even the possibility of transforming influence.

So for me, patristic study remains a sub-discipline of theology, and its pursuit an element in faith seeking understanding. That being the case, some may be surprised by my apparent lack of interest in women's issues, though in fact questions concerning the ordination of women and Mary Theotokos are in evidence here, and figure large in other published work of mine. The most fundamental reason for eschewing participation in critique of the Fathers' misogyny and refusing to trace precedent for women's leadership in the Church is, firstly, commitment to respecting a past that is different and, secondly, recognition of the complexity of attitudes then, both in society in general and among the Fathers in particular. The issues are less straightforward than some would have it. Nevertheless, the rhetorical triangle involved in communication applies also to our scholarly research – we are interested not just objectively in content or origin or author, but also because what we study bears upon ourselves. So it must be confessed that often particular topics become profoundly interesting to any researcher for personal reasons, and there are, of course, factors in my personal and ecclesial experience that have made other issues paramount. My ongoing interest in creation, anthropology and salvation are without doubt rooted in concern with the persistent questions that arise from being the mother of a son born with profound learning and physical disabilities. The group of papers on creation certainly arose from research motivated by an interest in pursuing more systematically how the reality of impairment is to be understood theologically, if the claim is made that everything is created by a good creator God. They and other studies collected here lie behind the Bampton lectures of 2011, to be published under the title *Credo. A contemporary recapitulation of early Christianity*, in which I have tried to integrate my theological thinking by a process of critical appropriation, entering into dialogue with the Fathers from my own existential perspective, not only as a mother faced with certain practical and theological challenges, but also as an ordained woman with wide ecumenical experience and deep commitment to the congruence of head and heart, mind and spirit, academic and spiritual engagement with God's gracious accommodation of the divine self to our limitations and gone-wrongness. What you have here are the more professional research papers which enabled me to learn certain fundamental and constitutive theological principles from the Fathers, not the least of which concerns that congruence which modern theology and Church life so rarely evidences.

FRANCES M. YOUNG

Birmingham
March 2012

I

Adam and Anthropos
A Study of the Interaction of Science and the Bible in
Two Anthropological Treatises of the Fourth Century*

[110]There are some who today assert that biblical ideas should provide a critique of contemporary presuppositions, that theologians should not pay respect to current scientific knowledge at the expense of distinctively Christian insights. My aim in this paper is to explore the extent to which the Bible actually did perform such a function in the theology of the patristic period, by examining the relationship between science and the Bible in two key anthropological texts of the late Fourth Century. These two texts differ to the extent that one purports to be an exegetical work, while the other is a philosophical or scientific treatise. (It should be remembered that science and philosophy were not then distinguishable disciplines, though one can, and should distinguish between serious philosophy of a professional kind, including medicine, and more popular semi-philosophical assumptions.) Simply because they belong to different genres, the similarities and differences between these two treatises should prove particularly illuminating.

Example 1: An Exegetical Treatise: *De Opificio Hominis*

Gregory Nyssen, the author of this work, took upon himself to further the work of his brother Basil in a number of directions, and this treatise is no exception. Basil had produced the famous nine *Homilies on the Hexaemeron*, but these, at least in their original form, had not covered the creation of man.[1]

---

* This is a revised version of a paper given at the Conference of the Society for the Study of Theology in March 1980 and was first published in *Vigiliae Christianae* 37 (1983), 110–140. (Leiden: E.J. Brill). The original page numbers are given in square brackets within the text.

[1] There are two homilies on the creation of man found in quite different collections of texts, and variously attributed to Basil and Gregory of Nyssa. Their Basilian authorship has recently been defended (A. Smets and M. van Esbroek, *Basile de Césarée. Sur l'origine De l'homme*, Sources Chrétiennes, Paris 1970); but the problems of authenticity are such that we may disregard them. Clearly Gregory did not know of the existence of such homilies from the pen of Basil. Besides the Sources Chrétiennes edition, these homilies appeared in a supplementary

In his preface to the *De Opificio Hominis*,[2] Gregory states that Basil alone had adequately expounded God's creation, but he intends to add to his work, the consideration of man being lacking in his *Hexaemeron*; so Gregory wrote to make up the deficiency, probably soon after Basil's death.

[111] After explaining his purpose, Gregory summarises his intentions. He has taken on a daunting task, for he proposes to examine everything that concerns man, and man is the greatest wonder of the world, the human creation alone having been made *like to God*. Here he anticipates the central theme of the treatise. His principal aim is to integrate the contrasting views of man suggested by the account of creation and his actual state at present, drawing from both scriptural instruction and from the conception of man discovered by the use of reason. In this way he hopes his treatment will be consistent and logical. Gregory aimed then to combine rational knowledge with biblical exegesis. His starting-point was the Genesis narrative of creation, but like Basil in his *Hexaemeron*, he drew upon contemporary science to fill out what scripture had to say. He aimed to produce something systematic. The question is, how successful was he in integrating his scientific knowledge with the Bible. We shall summarise his treatise, and then examine more closely the nature of the biblical and scientific contributions respectively.

A. Outline of Treatise

Gregory first surveys creation in general (I.1–5: MPG 44.128–132), and it is immediately apparent that his cosmological understanding depends upon contemporary assumptions about such things as the laws of motion or the reactions of contrary elements. Yet the Genesis narrative is brought into relation with these, so that God is seen as the creator who providentially ordered everything, and adorned the created world with its appropriate beauty. All this was prepared for man, who was to be its ruler and to enjoy the rich estate provided by the Maker of all. So man was made capable of enjoying both the earthy and the divine (II.1–2: MPG 44.136B–D).

The unique nature and status of man within the created order is then clarified on the basis of Gen. 1.26: the autonomous soul can exercise sovereignty because it is the image of the Sovereign of all (IV.1: MPG 44.136B–D). God

---

volume to Jaeger's edition of Gregory of Nyssa, ed. H. Hörner, 1972. The question of their origin is by no means settled, and for our purposes we may disregard them.

    [2]   Text in Migne, P.G. 44.123–255 (the Forbes edition, Burntisland 1855, is hardly obtainable); translation in NPNF Series II. vol. 5 (this translation is usually quoted in the paper).

is Mind, Word, Love, all-seeing and all-hearing; in man these divine capacities are imitated (V.2: MPG 44.137).

Gregory then turns to the interesting differences between man and other created beings (VII–VIII: MPG 44.140D ff): man's uprightness, his lack of defence from cold and predators, his dexterous hands. These and other characteristics point to man's capacity to tame and co-operate [112] with creatures providentially adapted to serve him; in other words, to man's royal status and skill. Confirmation of Moses' order of creation, beginning with vegetation and ascending via the beasts to rational beings, is found in the fact that there are three orders of soul corresponding to each level: the nutritive, the sensitive and the intellectual. The highest order of bodily life is found in man who combines all these forms of soul (VIII.4: MPG 145A). The mind, itself intelligible and incorporeal, needs a physical medium of communication; man's body is to his mind as a musical instrument to a skilled musician (IX: MPG 44.149B–152A). Mind is not to be identified with the senses, though it depends upon them for information; indeed mind is incomprehensible, and being in the image of God, points to God's incomprehensibility (XI: MPG 44.153C–156B). It cannot be identified with any particular organ in the body, but pervades the whole. It is affected by physical disorders – Gregory here engages in discussion of current debating points, like the reasons for sleep, yawning and dreams (XII–XIII: MPG 44.156C ff); yet in spite of the complex relationship between body, senses and mind, the intellectual is to be identified as soul proper, and its union with the body is stated to be inconceivable (XV: MPG 44.176C–177C).

Gregory now returns to his principal theme in what is probably the key section to his treatise (XVI: MPG 44.177D ff). Heathen writers who call man a μικρὸς κόσμος, he scorns; for that is to dignify man with the attributes of a gnat or a mouse. According to the doctrine of the Church, man's greatness consists not in his likeness to the created world but in his being in the image of the nature of the creator. Gregory then faces the question, how can this mortal, passible, short-lived being be the image of one who is immortal, pure and everlasting? To answer it he turns to Gen. 1.27 and argues that the Bible contains two accounts of man's creation: man-in-the-image is different from man in his present state of wretchedness. The intellectual element in man, man like to God, preceded the irrational which is characterised by its polarisation into male and female. Gregory understands the original creation of man as the creation of man-in-totality, the whole race in one body as it were, not an individual. This archetypal man was not sexually differentiated; sexuality (male and female created he them) was a subsequent concession to

I

the fallen state of man which God foreknew (XVI.17: MPG 44.185C). As a result of sin came fragmentation and death which meant provision had to be made for procreation. So in spite of seeing man as [113] the crown of creation (II–IV), in spite of describing the human body as perfectly adapted for the operations of mind (VII–IX), Gregory is unhappy about the things which man shares with the beasts, especially sexuality. Man, he says, is two-fold, the mean between the divine, incorporeal nature and the irrational life of brutes (MPG 44.181A–C).

Having established this two-stage creation of man, Gregory proceeds to attribute man's predicament to his tendency to be dominated not by his rational soul but by the irrational passions he shares with the beasts. Even man's intellect can be dragged down and rendered brutish. The doctrine of the Fall becomes a key element in his ability to affirm that in spite of man's present state, he is created in the image of God (XVIII–XX; MPG 44.192 ff). Resurrection and eschatology are likewise key elements in his thinking about man; for man's destiny is restoration to his original state and status in Paradise. This process of return Gregory presents as a matter of 'necessity', i.e. it is natural and inevitable (XXI: MPG 44.201B–204A), and he devotes much of the rest of his treatise to a rational defence of resurrection while attacking various other doctrines like the pre-existence and independence of souls. His final section (XXX: MPG 44.240C–256) outlines current understanding of the construction of the human body, a discussion which he justifies on the grounds that "spiritual sheep" would rather get instruction from those inside the Church, instead of having to turn to a "strange voice". But before and after this, Gregory summarises his fundamental position: that man is *one*, a composite unity composed of soul and body, both of which were created together at one and the same time (XXIX: MPG 44.233D ff); that humanity is an animated body (XXX.29: MPG 44.253B) whose soul can mature to perfection and "be renewed after the image of him who created him" (XXX.33: MPG 44.256C).

B. *The Biblical Contribution*

Since the fundamental idea that Gregory pursues is that man was made in the image of God, it is clear that his entire discussion revolves around a biblical idea, and that scripture is seen as a source for basic anthropological concepts. The accompanying Table (Table I on p. 12) indicates that of thirty chapters, there are only four which contain no scriptural quotation or Biblical allusion, and we may add that those four are the shortest chapters in the entire work. Still the use of scripture is somewhat [114] patchy, and a number of occurrences are merely sententious, rhetorical or homiletic flourishes, inessential to the argument. Nevertheless, there are areas of considerable interest, some where scripture is the determining influence, others where scriptural warrant for an idea is deliberately sought.

(i) *The exegesis of Gen. 1.26–7*

Gen. 1.26 occurs in all *eight* times, scattered around the treatise (for references, see Table I). Gregory notes that only in the case of man did God "take counsel" (a point deduced from the form of the text: *let us make* man ...); everything else was produced by a word, but in the case of man, God took careful forethought, relating the human form to its function. Man was made for royalty, Gregory infers from the context; his "purple" is virtue, his "sceptre" immortality, his crown "righteousness". His royal prerogative is that he is "self-governed", ruled by his own will. Man was created last because the ruler could not appear before his subjects – the banquet had to be prepared. Man was to enjoy creation, and so have knowledge of the Creator. Hence, man is two-fold, blending the divine with the earthy, enjoying God by means of his more divine nature and the good things of earth by the sense that is akin to them (II–IV: MPG 44.132D–136D).

As a king, freely pursuing his own ends, man is the image of the one who rules over all. The Godhead is *Nous* and *Logos* (John 1.1), and the prophets, according to Paul, "have the Mind of Christ" which "speaks" in them (I Cor. 2.16; II Cor. 13.3): thus, the Logos and Mind "in you" is an imitation of the divine. Again, God is Love (I John 4.7, 8); and "hereby shall all men know that you are my disciples, if you love one another" (after John 13.35).

In this way Gregory uses other texts to fill out and interpret his basic biblical insight. His argument is by no means exclusively biblical, but scriptural cross-references certainly play a significant role in the development of his fundamental anthropological position.

Gen. 1.27 is discussed in XVI. As already noted, the final phrase of this verse raises the question of sexuality, which was clearly a problem for Gregory; for it is "a thing which is alien to our conception of God" (XVI.8: MPG 44.181). He resolves the problem of sex by appeal to Gal. 3.28: in Christ, there is neither male nor female; and on the basis of Jesus' reply to the Sadducees (Luke 20.35–6), he argues that without the [115] fall, man would have become a plurality in the same way as the angels. Sexuality was therefore God's concession to the fallen state of man which he foreknew, and did not belong to the original creation of man. Again Gregory's use of other scriptural quotations to interpret his key text is a sign of the extent of biblical influence.

(ii) Man as a composite being, based on scriptural material.
(a) Gregory believes that man is composed of "lower" and "higher" elements and has to make choices. He speaks of man as "a man of earth" using I Cor. 15.48 (XXII.3: MPG 44.204D); and uses the text, "He is compared to the beasts that have no understanding and made like to them" (Ps. 48.13, 21 LXX) (XVII.5: MPG 44.189D). The Apostle bids us "Think on those things which are above" (Col. 3.2), adds Gregory (XVIII.5: MPG 44.193C). "Our nature is conceived as twofold, according to the apostolic teaching, made up of visible man and hidden man" (XXIX.2: MPG 44.236). Thus Gregory regards the two poles of man's nature and the opposing attractions of carnal pleasures and spiritual perfection as fundamentally scriptural teaching.

(b) Gregory recognises different faculties of soul, the "nutritive", the "sensitive" and the "intellectual", and he tries to relate this to biblical terminology. He refers to Paul's prayer that the full grace of their "*body and soul and spirit*" may be preserved at the coming of the Lord (I. Thess. 5.23, though Gregory erroneously refers to Ephesians); and he speaks of the Lord instructing the scribe in the Gospel that he should set before every commandment that love to God which is exercised with all the *heart and soul and mind* (VIII.5: MPG 44.145C–D). The Apostle recognises three kinds of dispositions, calling one *carnal*, another *natural* (ψυχικήν) and another *spiritual*; Gregory quotes I Cor. 3.3 and I Cor. 2.14, 15 to support this statement (VIII.6: MPG 44.148A–B). Gregory has hardly derived the tripartite division from this varied scriptural terminology, but he has attempted to find scriptural warrant for an analysis adopted from contemporary science.

(iii) Man as Fallen
While man was created in God's image, an image implies difference as well as likeness; the difference arose from the mere fact of creation. Man came into being; he is therefore subject to change, unlike the eternally existent God. Man's freedom and independence, coupled with his **[116]** mutability, led to his fall; the fall means that man is made like the beasts, inclined to material things and subject to passions (XVIII: MPG 44.192 ff). The fall means a perversion of man's nature:

> … in the compound nature of man, the mind is governed by God, and by the mind is governed our material life, provided the latter remains in its natural state; but if perverted from nature, it is alienated also from mind. (XII.13: MPG 44.164)

Gregory here follows a fundamentally biblical insight, though he works it out in terms of contemporary ideas about the relation between the mind and the passions. He notes that mere temporary gratification of the senses such as animals seek, is made worse in the case of human beings because the passions pervert the mind: thus, anger is akin to the impulse of beasts, but increases when associated with thought into malignity, envy, deceit, hypocrisy; the greed of swine becomes covetousness; and so on. On the other hand, if the impulse of the emotions is harnessed by mind, every motion is conformed to the beauty of the divine image and the image is not obscured, as in the case of Moses and other great figures (XVIII: MPG 44.192–6).

Gregory devotes some consideration to the story of the fall, because it raised some difficulties (XX: MPG 44.197 ff). What was the forbidden tree? How is it that the tree which offered knowledge of good and evil represents the gratification of the senses? How can knowledge or science be condemned? Gregory plunders scripture to ascertain the meaning of its terms. Discernment between good and evil he finds to be a good thing on the basis of Heb. 5.14, 1 Thess. 5.21, and I Cor. 2.15. Knowledge, however, according to scriptural usage, means "the disposition towards what is agreeable": see II Tim. 2.19, Exod. 33.12 (LXX), and Matt. 7.23. The problem with the tree was that it was deceptive – it appeared good but was evil. The nature of evil is mixed; destruction is concealed like a snare. The fruit of the tree is not absolutely evil, though it contains poison. The serpent made it seem glamorous.

Gregory concludes that

> the image (of God) properly belongs to the better part of our attributes; but all that is grievous and wretched in our life is far removed from likeness to the divine. (XX.5: MPG 44.201)

Gregory has taken seriously both the degradation and the glory of man, and on the whole, the biblical expression of the contrast predominates over more philosophical analyses. [117]

(iv) Man's destiny – the resurrection

As we have already seen, Gregory deduces certain features of the archetypal man from statements about the resurrection-life. Man would have lived and is to live like the angels: Luke 20.35, 36; man was created "a little lower than the angels" (Ps. 8.6) (XVII.2: MPG 44.188–9).

That is man's destiny; that is when his character as God's image will be fully realised. If someone is ashamed of the fact that man has to eat like the animals and therefore doubts whether he is made in the image of God, he can rest

assured that one day he will be free of this necessity: for the Kingdom of God
is not meat and drink (Rom. 14.17), and man shall not live by bread alone
(Matt. 4.4) (XVIII.9: MPG 44.196A). But does that mean that the resurrection
life is fundamentally different from man's present life? No, Gregory concludes.
For scripture does not speak only of bodily meat and drink, but of the soul's
nourishment: Prov. 9.5; Jn. 7.37; Is. 12.3; Amos 8.11. God gave man fruit to
eat in Paradise, and whoever is hungry for the good will eat of the tree of life:
Gen. 2.16; Ps. 37.4; Prov. 3.18 (XIX: MPG 44.196C–197B).

Why cannot man enjoy this already? Gregory believes that the full
compliment of man's numbers has to be made up first; but the transformation
will suddenly occur: I Cor. 15.51–2; I Thess. 4.17. Like the patriarchs
and prophets, we have to press on in faith, depending on God's promises:
Heb. 11.40, 13, 11; Ps. 84 passim (XXII.6–7: MPG 44.205–208). The
Gospel miracles are a kind of "foretaste" of God's restoring power, and thus
a confirmation of the promise of resurrection to come; Gregory describes a
number, including Jairus' daughter, the widow's son at Nain, the raising of
Lazarus, and the resurrection of Christ himself. "Thou shalt send forth thy
Spirit and they shall be created and thou shalt renew the face of the earth"
(Ps. 104.29–30) (XXV.3–13: MPG 44.216A–225A). Thus prophetic and
eschatological texts are used to confirm the hope of re-creation.

Oddly, fall and restoration are not related to Christological statements or
to a doctrine of atonement. Christ never appears as "proper man". The cross
is only mentioned because it confirms scriptural predictions; or because it
heightens the miracle of Christ's resurrection and reinforces the proof that
scripture is reliable when it predicts the resurrection of mankind.

However, we may conclude that Gregory not only began from the
scriptural account of creation, but also drew certain key ideas from [118]
scriptural doctrines. His use of texts is not merely arbitrary, and he did try to
establish many of his anthropological ideas on the basis of biblical texts.

C. The Scientific Contribution

Nevertheless, scripture was not sufficient on its own to provide an account of
how the human organism works, nor even to supply a comprehensive analysis
of man's nature and destiny.

(i)   Gregory does not give a great deal of space to medical knowledge
      as it then existed; but he finds it necessary to give some account of
      man's anatomical functioning, and the relationship of his bodily
      activities with the motivating power of soul. The mind, he had

argued in chapters IX–X, works through sense-perception, although it is impossible to identify the location of soul with any particular organ. He had also treated of tears and laughter, sleep and dreams (XII–XIII). Now in a long final chapter (XXX: MPG 44.240 ff), he summarises a mass of information, about respiration, the functions of the heart, liver and brain, the natural combinations of heat and cold, moist and dry, which constitute the parts of the body. He regards such subjects, the typical topics of contemporary discussion, as a digression from his main purpose, which was to show that

> the root cause of our constitution is neither a soul without a body, nor a body without a soul, but that, from ensouled and living bodies, our nature is generated at the first as a living and ensouled being. (XXX.29: MPG 44.253)

The power of soul is interwoven with the body.

Here Gregory is largely uninfluenced by scripture (though he did take the trouble to refute the claim that scripture locates the 'ruling principle' in the heart (XII.7: MPG 44.160D)); insistence on man's psychosomatic unity he derived from current scientific observation, while according to the apostolic teaching, man's nature is two-fold (see above). Gregory believes that the union of corporeal and incorporeal is established scientific truth, but beyond rational conception.

(ii) Gregory was the most distinguished Christian Neoplatonist. This is evident in his treatise. He acknowledges that one can speak of the nutritive and sensitive aspects of soul; but really the word soul should only properly be applied to the intellectual, from which stems a certain 'vital energy' somewhat erroneously referred to as soul (XV.1–2: MPG 44.176–7). The soul finds perfection in what is intellectual and rational; **[119]** mind may use the body as a musical instrument perfectly adapted to express its music (IX: MPG 44.149), but mind itself is invisible and incorporeal (XI: MPG 44.153). Men should not use the more complex analysis of the concept of soul as an excuse for attaching themselves to the phenomena of sense; rather they should busy themselves with their spiritual advantages, as the true soul is found there (XV.2: MPG 44.177A–C). Beauty, Goodness, Intellect, these are the Platonic notions of the Divine which Gregory dwells upon (though acknowledging that God transcends them and is incomprehensible); and these are the characteristics he sees reflected in the divine image in man (e.g. V: MPG 44.137; XII.9–11: MPG

44.161C–4). In any case, ὁμοίωσις Θεῷ, (likeness to God) is a phrase from Plato's *Theaetetus*; so this fundamental idea of his was not exclusively biblical. Gregory is not very happy about man's "animal nature", and, as we have noted, envisages the needs and desires of the flesh – for food, for sex – being in the end transcended. The archetypal man is virtually a Platonic "form" of man.

Gregory resists dualism – but then so did Plotinus. The universe is full of light, and evil but a shadow; evil implies change, evil is limited – so its end is inevitable. The genesis of evil was the withdrawal of the beautiful and the good (XII. 11: MPG 44.164A). Gregory's thought is fundamentally Neoplatonic, though his positive treatment of the goodness of creation has strong Biblical roots, and he firmly rejects the Platonist doctrine of Origen that the soul is bound to the body as a punishment for wickedness. (Plotinus would not have liked that doctrine either).

(iii) Gregory gives a scientific explanation of the "downward drag" that afflicts man – the tendency of sin is heavy and downwards; so our souls are inclined to sink, weighed down by the heavy and earthy element in the irrational nature (XVIII.6: MPG 44.193C). Thus his notion of the fall is by no means entirely inspired by the Bible. Theories of motion and cosmology dominate the description of creation with which his treatise opens, and are even used to establish the 'necessity' of resurrection and restoration in the future (XXI: MPG 44.201–204A). Scientific assumptions dictate the fact that man is treated as a "rational animal" whose hands are adapted for the arts of peace and war, and whose form is an instrument for the use of reason; and current science poses questions like "Why is man helpless compared with the animals?", "Why does man stand upright?" etc. (VII–IX: MPG 44.140–153) These features are typical of a great deal of the treatise. Biblical texts may be interspersed pretty liberally, and may to some [120] extent dictate the framework, but on the whole rational argument predominates. Gregory argues that matter is not co-eternal with God, that motion is not eternal, that creation implies End (XXIII–IV: MPG 44.209–13). Gregory decides that mind pervades the whole body only after surveying the scientific arguments for locating it in the heart or the brain (XII: MPG 44.156–164). His approach is fundamentally rational.

Besides this, a striking characteristic of Gregory's style is his brilliant appeal to political and particularly musical analogies, together with his fine descriptions of natural or aesthetic wonders; these were traditional rhetorical devices, though not the less forceful for that. All this means that the total impact of Gregory's work is much less biblical than our first comments might have led the reader to suppose. Gregory is not only deeply imbued with the culture of the contemporary world, but he also takes very seriously indeed the need to fit scripture with the findings of reason.

What conclusions can we draw from our study of Gregory's treatise concerning the interaction of Bible and philosophy in his anthropology? 1. For Gregory, the Bible is the starting-point, but scientifically speaking it is inadequate. Current philosophical and scientific arguments are used to fill out and explain scripture. Thus the agenda in detail is fundamentally philosophical, and rational arguments are needed to resolve philosophical and scientific problems. Neoplatonism lies behind many of the deductions and inferences drawn from scriptural texts. 2. Gregory has some difficulty in drawing together consistently two opposing concepts of man: (i) that man is the crown and perfection of God's creation which is wholly good, and that therefore, man's enjoyment of the world is part of God's creative purpose; and (ii) that man is twofold, torn between living according to his *Nous* so as to realise God's image in bodily form, and living like the beasts, seeking gratification of his sensual desires. The tension is highlighted by Gregory's positive acceptance of man as a rational animal in the early part of his treatise, and his suggestion later that man is dragged down to the level of the brutes by his passions which arose from subsequent sexual differentiation. It is over-simplifying to suggest that this is a tension between man as psychosomatic unity and man understood in dualist soul-body terms; it is also clear that this difficulty does not arise from a tension between science and the Bible. Gregory believes, not unjustifiably, that both these ideas are drawn from scripture. To some extent the biblical doctrines [121] of fall and redemption help him to ease the conflict; yet not entirely, for the resurrection-life often appears in a highly spiritualised guise. The basis of that spiritualisation is usually found in scriptural argument, for all its Neoplatonic roots.

Gregory's treatise, therefore fulfils remarkably well its basic intention – to marry scripture and reason, the Bible and contemporary scientific knowledge. Where scripture fails, reason prevails, raising the questions and providing the solutions. Yet scripture is seen as the source of fundamental anthropological ideas, and scriptural texts are exploited in masterly fashion. Gregory does not retreat from science, but embraces and Christianises it.

I

Table I   Texts used or alluded to in Gregory's *De Opificio Hominis*

Prologue	Prov. 17.6 (LXX)	'the whole world of money', as Solomon says.
I.1	Gen. 2.4 (LXX)	'This is the book of the generation of heaven and earth ', saith the scripture ...
I.5	Gen. 2.1	'the heaven and the earth', as Moses said, 'were finished' ...
II		No quotes, but the subject is why man was created last, i.e. a question raised by scripture.
III.1	Gen. 1.26 (not exact)	'God said, Let us make man in our image, after our likeness, and let them have dominion over the fish of the sea, and the beasts of the earth, and the fowls of the heaven, and the cattle, and all the earth.'
IV		No quotes, but the subject is man's royalty, derived from scripture.
V.2	Jn. 1.1	'In the beginning was the Word'
	Cf. I Cor. 2.16	the prophets, according to Paul, 'have the
	Cf. II Cor. 13.3	mind of Christ' which 'speaks' in them.
	I Jn. 4.7, 8	'Love is of God'; 'God is love'.
	Jn. 13.35 (not verbally)	'hereby' ... 'shall all men know that ye are my disciples if ye love one another'
VI.2	Ps. 94.9	'He that made the eye' and 'that planteth the ear'
VI.2, 3	Gen. 1.26 twice	See above.
VIII.5	I Thess. 5.23 (Ephesians, acc. to Greg.)	praying that the complete grace of their 'body, soul and spirit' may be preserved at the coming of the Lord.
	Cf. Mk. 12.30	The Lord instructs the scribe in the Gospel that he should set before every commandment that love to God which is exercised with all the heart and soul and mind. [122]
VIII.6		The Apostle recognises three divisions, calling one 'carnal' ... another 'natural' (ψυχικήν) ... and another 'spiritual'
	I Cor. 3.3	'Ye are carnal'
	I Cor. 2.14, 15	'but the natural man receiveth not the things of the Spirit, for they are foolishness unto him. But he that is spiritual judgeth all things, and yet he himself is judged of no man.'
X.2	Cf. Eccles. 1.8	'the ear', as Solomon somewhere says, 'is not filled with continual hearing'

Table I (cont'd)

XI.2	Rom. 11.34	'Who knoweth the mind of the Lord?' the Apostle asks
XI.3	Gen. 1.26	See above.
XII.7	Ps. 7.10	'God trieth the hearts and reins'
XIII. 11	Gen. 40.1ff	the butler presses the cluster for Pharoah's cup; so the baker seemed to carry his baskets; each supposing himself in sleep to be engaged in those services …
XIII.12		Daniel and Joseph etc. v. Interpretation of dreams
XV.2	Gen. 9.3 (not verbally)	'ye shall eat all kinds of flesh even as the green herb'
XVI.1– . XVI.5, 7, 8, 16, 17	Gen. 1.26	See above.
	Gen. 1.27	'and God created man; in the image of God created he him; male and female created he them'
XVI.7	Gal. 3.28	'In Christ Jesus, there is neither male nor female'
XVI.13	Matt. 22.20, 21	As the Gospel calls the stamp upon the coin 'the image of Caesar'
XVI.15	Hist. Susanna 42	He 'knoweth all things before they be'
XVII.2	Lk. 20.35, 36	'For in the resurrection' … 'they neither marry nor are given in marriage, neither can they die any more; for they are equal to the angels, and are the children of God, being children of the resurrection.'
	Ps. 8.6	'made a little lower than the angels'
XVII.5	Ps. 48.13, 21 (LXX)	'Man being in honour knew it not'; therefore he says, 'he is compared to the beasts that have no understanding, and made like unto them.'
XVIII.5	Col. 3.2	the Apostle bids us 'think those things which are above'
XVIII.8		In Moses and men like him, the form of the image is kept pure, according to Gregory.
XVIII.9	Rom. 14.17	'The Kingdom of heaven is not meat and drink'
	Matt. 4.4 *et al. loc.*	'Man shall not live by bread alone but by every word that proceedeth out of the mouth of God'

Table I (cont'd)

XIX.1	Prov. 9.5	'Eat of my bread' is the bidding of Wisdom to the hungry. **[123]**
	Jn. 7.37	'If any man thirst let him come unto me and drink'
	Cf. Is. 12.3	'Drink ye joy' is the great Isaiah's charge to those who are able to hear …
	Amos 8.11	'not a famine of bread, nor a thirst for water, but a famine of hearing the word of the Lord'
XIX.2	Gen. 2.16	'Of every tree of the garden' he says, 'thou mayest freely eat'
XIX.4	Ps. 37.4	'Delight thou in the Lord'
	Prov. 3.18	Solomon names Wisdom herself (which is the Lord) 'a tree of life'
XX.1	The chapter is an exegesis of the 'tree of knowledge of good and evil' (Gen. 2.9) This involves an examination of the scriptural meaning of 'discernment' and 'knowledge'. Texts quoted:	
	Heb. 5.14	to discern .. the Apostle says, is a mark of more perfect condition and of 'trained faculties'
	I Thess. 5.21	and he bids us 'prove all things'
	Cf. I Cor. 2.15	'discernment' belongs to the spiritual man
	II Tim. 2.19	'The Lord knoweth them that are his'
	Ex. 33.12 (LXX)	'I know thee above all'
	Matt. 7.23	'I never knew you'
XX.2	I Tim. 6.10	'The love of money is the root of all evil'
XX.4	Gen. 3.6 (LXX)	'and the woman saw that the tree was good for food, and that it was pleasant to the eyes to behold, and fair to see; and she took of the fruit thereof and did eat'
	Gen. 2.9	See above.
	Ps. 143.4 (LXX)	'like unto vanity'
XXI.4		Paradise to be restored
XXII.3	Gen. 1.26	See above
	I Cor. 15.48	man 'of the earth'
XXII.4		Man in the image of God
	Ps. 95.4	'in his hand are all the corners of the earth'
	Hist. Susanna 42	See above.
	Gen. 1.28	'Increase and multiply and replenish the earth.'

Table I (cont'd)

XXII.6	I Cor. 15, 51, 52	'Behold, I show you a mystery; we shall not all sleep but we shall all be changed, in a moment, in the twinkling of an eye, at the last trump'
	I Thess. 4.17	'we shall be caught up in the clouds to meet the Lord in the air, and so shall we ever be with the Lord'
XXII.7		Abraham and the patriarchs were promised good things:
	Heb. 11.40	'God having provided some better things for us' according to the words of Paul, 'that they without us should not be made perfect'
	Heb. 11.13	they saw 'afar off' and 'embraced them' as the Apostle bears witness, placing their certainty of the **[124]** enjoyment of the things for
	Heb. 11.11 Ps.84.2	which they hoped in the fact that they 'judged him faithful who had promised'; the prophet's 'soul hath a desire and longing to be in the courts of the Lord', even if he must needs be
	(v. 11 LXX)	rejected to a place amongst the lowest, as it is a greater and more desirable thing to be last there than to be first among the ungodly tents of this life ... for he says, 'one day in Thy
	Ps. 84.10	courts is better than thousands'
	Ps. 84.12	wherefore he says at the end of the Psalm. 'O Lord of hosts, blessed is the man that hopeth in thee'
XXII.8	Acts 1.7	'It is not for us to know the times and seasons'
XXIII.1	Heb. 11.3 (not exact)	'By believing we understand that the worlds were framed by the word of God, so that things which are seen were not made of things which do appear'
XXIII.3		Argumentative men might upset our faith in Scripture; therefore Gregory produces arguments.
XXV.3–11	Cf. Mk. 13.1	'What works! What buildings!'
	Gospel stories outlined include:	
	Lk. 23.27–29	Women at cross
	Lk. 4.38–9	Simon's mother-in-law
	Jn. 4.46 ff	the Nobleman's Son
	Mk. 5.22 ff	Jairus' Daughter and the Woman with an issue of blood

I

Table I (cont'd)

	Lk. 7.11 ff	Widow's Son at Nain.
	Jn. 11	The Raising of Lazarus
	Each of the above is re-told, sometimes with quotations from the immediate passage; a quote from elsewhere appears in the following example:	
XXV.11	I Thess. 4.16	For as in the regeneration of the universe, the Apostle tells us that 'the Lord Himself will descend with a shout, with the voice of the archangel', and by a trumpet sound shall raise up the dead to incorruption – so now he who is in the tomb, at the voice of command, shakes off death as if it were a sleep …
XXV.12		In truth the Lord seems tome not to have spoken in vain to them of Capernaum, when
	Lk. 4.23	he said to himself, as in the person of men, 'Ye will surely say unto me this proverb, 'Physician heal thyself.' For it behoved him … to confirm his word in his own humanity. Gregory speaks of Christ's passion and resurrection.
	Cf. Jn. 20.27	Behold him whose hands were pierced with nails; behold him whose side was transfixed with a spear; pass thy fingers through the print of the nails; thrust thy hand into the spear-wound …
	I Cor. 15.12	If then he has been raised, well may we utter the Apostle's exclamation, 'How say some that there is no resurrection of the dead?' [125]
XXV.13	Col. 2.8	Shall we not bid farewell to those who pervert our simple faith by 'philosophy and vain deceit' and hold fast to our confession in its purity …
	Ps. 104.29, 30	'Thou shalt take away their breath and they shall fail and turn to dust. Thou shalt send forth Thy Spirit and they shall be created, and Thou shalt renew the face of the earth'
XXVI.2	Ps. 95.4	Scripture teaches that the world is held in God's hand
XXVII.2	Cf. Lk. 16.19 ff	The Parable of Dives and Lazarus
XXVII.4	2 Kings 5.1 ff (cf. Lk. 4.27)	Healing miracles: Naaman the Syrian and the Gospels.

Table I (cont'd)

XXVIII.1	Cf. Gen. 2.7	Reference to the making of man as stated by Moses ... God first took dust from the earth and formed man, and then animated the being thus formed by his breath. Gregory is anxious to refute the argument based on this text that the flesh is prior and therefore more noble than the soul.
	Matt. 6.25	'the soul is more than meat and the body than raiment
XXIX.1	Hist. Susanna 42	See above.
XXIX.2		Our nature is conceived as two-fold according to the apostolic teaching (but unspecified).
XXIX.9	Deut. 4.28	'Take heed to thyself,' as Moses says.
XXX.1	Cf. Jn. 10.5	spiritual sheep, as the Lord says, ... hear not a strange voice
XXX.31	I Cor. 13.11	'When I was a child I spoke as a child, I understood as a child, I thought as a child, but when I became a man, I put away childish things'
XXX.32	Col. 3.9, 10	Paul ... tells them that they must 'put off the old man' and put on the man 'which is renewed after the image of him that created him'
XXX.34	Gen. 1.26	See above.

Example 2: A Scientific Treatise: *De Natura Hominis* [3]

The manuscript tradition attributes this treatise to one Nemesius of Emesa, about whom we know no more than we can deduce from the work itself. The date is relatively clear from internal evidence: he is the contemporary of Eunomius and Apollinaris, and he is chary of acknowledging his dependence on Origen – so he must have written towards the end of the Fourth Century. He may have used Gregory's work; he certainly seems to have written some ten or twenty years later. However, the work is of a somewhat different character – a kind of [126] philosophical handbook in which the views of various different philosophers are summarised and assessed. It was once plundered

---

[3] Text in Migne, P.G. 40.504–817; translation, commentary and notes by W. Telfer in LCC vol. IV (this translation is usually quoted in this paper).

I

by scholars for evidence concerning Posidonius, the famous Platonic-Stoic
of the first Century BC, but Posidonius' name is not mentioned and in any
case the whole theory that Posidonius was the Father of Middle Platonism is a
hypothesis built on sand.[4] The only reason for mentioning it is to highlight the
fact that this work is an exposition of current scientific ideas about man, and
not fundamentally a work of Christian theology: the most consistently used
source is Galen. At least of its final draft, the author is clearly a Christian, but
he addresses himself not only to a Christian but a pagan audience (§ 42: MPG
40.781B, 792B). The work may have an apologetic intent; certainly it shows
that Christians were not necessarily credulous, illiterate and obscurantist, but
were up with their contemporaries in anthropological studies.

A. Outline of Treatise

The treatise falls naturally into five sections. Following the pattern
recommended in rhetorical schools, it begins with an exordium, introducing
and summarising the subject and endeavouring to engage the reader's interest
(Section A: §§ 1–10: MPG 40.504–536). This section is most important for
understanding Nemesius' overall view, and here we find the most important
references to the Bible. However, it is Plotinus, Aristotle and Plato who appear
first, as Nemesius opens his book with a discussion of the dichotomist versus
trichotomist controversy (the one Christian teacher mentioned, Apollinaris,
is said to be trichotomist following Plotinus). The dichotomist view prevails:
man is composed of soul and body. That man has much in common with
the animals and yet is rational, so that he is on the boundary between the
phenomenal and intelligible, indicates the unity of creation, the interlinking
of every order of reality, and so proves that the whole universe is the creation
of one God (§ 2: MPG 40.508). Nemesius produces proofs from the
observations of natural history (Aristotle is the authority he mentions) that
there is no clear division between the inanimate, the nutritive, the animal
and the rational orders of creation, for one shades into the other; then he
suggests that this justifies the order of the Mosaic story and he appeals to other
scriptural texts to indicate that man is on the border between the rational and
the irrational (§ 4: MPG 40.512–3). Here his theme and the texts he chooses
are reminiscent of Gregory's [127] treatise. Nemesius then proceeds to discuss

---

⁴ W.W. Jaeger, *Nemesios von Emesa*. Quellenforschungen zum Neuplatonismus und
seinen Anfängen bei Poseidonios (Berlin 1914); followed by many others, e.g. Telfer, *Op. cit.*
But see L. Edelstein and I.G. Kidd, *Posidonius* Vol. 1 The Fragments (Cambridge 1972); and the
comments in J. Dillon, *The Middle Platonists* (London 1977).

the story of creation and fall as taught by the Hebrews. It has been suggested that his source here was Origen's commentary on Genesis;[5] wherever he got the ideas from, Nemesius identifies himself with the views expressed (§ 5: MPG 40.516A). He believes man was made poised between being mortal and immortal, or perhaps mortal yet potentially immortal. Until man had reached perfection, his state was to be concealed from him; but man ate of the forbidden tree of knowledge and learned the truth about himself. As a result he became enslaved to bodily needs.

Nemesius now proceeds to explore man's bodily composition out of the four elements and his development of social intercourse; in an interesting section (§ 7: MPG 40.521–4 – to be discussed later), he tries to define the distinguishing marks of man, and then develops the Hebrew idea that the whole world was created for man's benefit (§ 8–9: MPG 40.525–532). His exordium ends with a panegyric of man (§ 10: MPG 40.532C–533A), which seems to summarize his fundamental position while pulling out a number of rhetorical stops: man is not only the crucial link in the hierarchy of created orders of being, but he is in himself a μικρὸς κόσμος, bearing an image of the whole creation in his own nature. (Here Nemesius accepts a commonplace rejected by Gregory, and clearly regards it as compatible with the 'link' idea; precisely this combination of ideas is not found elsewhere, and it was once attributed to Posidonius.) Man, Nemesius believes, is the object of God's special providential care, and the creature for whose sake God became man so that this creature might attain incorruption and escape corruption. He is pre-eminent among creatures in his skills and his authority.

In the next section of the treatise, Nemesius turns to a more technical discussion of the relation between soul and body (Section B: §§ 11–22: MPG 40.536–608). He adopts the method of reviewing a wide range of options, from the pre-socratics to his own time, explores the various proposals suggested, leading up to his own view which will be discussed later.

The centre part, comprising a third of the whole treatise (Sections C–D: §§ 23–45: MPG 40.608–717), consists of further technical discussions concerning the body and the elements of which it is composed; sense-perception, the imagination, the functions of the intellect and the different capacities of soul; the passions and the irrational soul; nutrition, respiration, generation, etc. Here Nemesius again surveys the **[128]** many opinions of philosophers, and for the most part follows the medical writer Galen. All this leads up to the final part of the work which is concerned with morality, the chief preoccupation

---

[5] W. Telfer, *Op. cit.* p. 248, in his commentary on § 7.

of Graeco-Roman philosophy (Section E: §§ 46–70: MPG 40.717–816). The related issues of freewill, fate and providence are given extended treatment before the treatise breaks off, apparently unfinished.

Before considering the contribution of the Bible to this treatise, we will follow up a crucial aspect of Nemesius' discussion, namely, his views on the composition of man.

B. *The Composition of Man*

Nemesius' fundamental interest concerns man's place in the universe and his experience of making moral decisions. He realises, however, that these matters are closely related to an understanding of man's constitution, and understanding man's nature is a very complex matter. For this reason he discusses at length various ways of analysing the components which go to make up man, and their various functions. The soul for Nemesius is no simple entity (§ 34: MPG 40.669) – it has rational and irrational parts, and the interaction of the various faculties of soul with each other and with the body are sometimes conscious, sometimes unconscious. The irrational is partly susceptible to reason's control, partly not. The elements (earth, air, fire and water) which constitute the body have an effect on man's temperament, and emotion provides the driving force of human action. Thus "passions" are necessary to human life (a useful corrective to the widespread ascetic emphasis on ἀπάθεια current at the time when Nemesius was writing). There are good passions as well as evil ones, and pleasures are necessary and natural to the good life which is directed towards divine learning and the virtues (§§ 36–9: MPG 40.676–685). It is only in the light of such a complex analysis of human being that conclusions can be drawn about man's responsibilities and moral potentialities. Man's behaviour is affected by temperament, upbringing, habit; but he has freewill to make choices in certain spheres, and ideally his rationality should be in control of his overall behaviour.

Nemesius recognises, then, very considerable complexity. Yet his underlying conception is that man, as a complex two-fold being, has a footing in two orders of reality. Through the body, he has much in common with the animals – he is indeed the crown of the animal creation; [129] but by being also rational, he shares many things with incorporeal, rational intelligences. So Nemesius accepts the generally agreed analysis that man is composed of soul and body, and it is the relationship between these entities which is most crucial for his understanding of man.

Nemesius' view is no simple dualism. The presupposition of Nemesius' physiological statements is the intimate union of soul and body. The soul is the driving force (ἐνέργεια) of muscular movement:

> Whatever movement takes place by the operation of nerves and muscles involves the intervention of soul, and is accomplished by an act of will. (§ 43: MPG 40.708)

Soul also provides the ἐνέργεια in respiration: panting and sobbing accompany moments of great grief, and soul keeps respiration going during sleep, since it is essential for human life. So the physical and the psychic are intimately woven together: τὸ ψυχικὸν συνεπλάκη τῷ φυσικῷ (§ 44: MPG 40.709). Thus,

> a living creature is composed of soul and body; the body is not a living creature by itself, nor is the soul, but soul and body together. (§ 49: MPG 40.733)

Here is an expression of a true psycho-somatic unity, and it is clearly based upon current scientific observation of how the human organism functions.

The nature of the soul and the manner of its union with the body were not, however, matters easily resolved. Nemesius reviews the following questions: Is the soul corporeal or incorporeal? Is the soul real – that is, some real thing, a substance? Or is it the harmony or temperament or "form" of the body? What is the origin of the soul? Is there more than one kind of soul – rational and irrational, for instance? Are there many individual souls, or is there one "world-soul"? Nemesius concludes that the soul is incorporeal and immortal on the basis of Plato's arguments, yet affirms at the end:

> There are numerous proofs of the soul's immortality offered by Plato and others, but they are difficult and full of obscurities, and can scarcely be understood by those who have been brought up to such studies. But for us the sufficient demonstration of the soul's immortality is the teaching of Holy Scripture, which is self-authenticating because inspired by God. (§ 19: MPG 40.589)

In other words, Nemesius thinks the immortality of the soul is a *scriptural* doctrine which *contrasts* with the views of Aristotle, the Stoics and Galen, whose views he has already discussed and dismissed earlier in this section: he does not, like some modern commentators, regard as **[130]** "typically Greek" the assertion of the soul's immortality. For him, the Bible confirms the dualist analysis, while science demands that some account of man's psychosomatic unity is given.

It is the union of soul and body (§§ 20–22: MPG 40.592–608) which Nemesius finds the most puzzling aspect of the whole subject, and he refuses to consider other analyses of man's constitution partly because three or four constituents (say, body, soul, mind and/or spirit) would complicate the problem of unity still further. The union is a puzzle because there are no satisfactory natural analogies. What comes together to form a single entity is made completely one only if the constituents undergo change. So how is it possible for body and soul to be united without the body losing its corporeity or the soul ceasing to be incorporeal and self-subsistent? Unity can only be achieved by change or juxtaposition, which is not a true unity. Nemesius, having ruled out the possibilities of juxtaposition and mixture, adopts the Platonic view that the soul "puts on" the body; intelligibles, he says, can unite with things adapted to receive them and remain unconfused while in union. So the soul suffers no change through union with the body. The soul is united to the body through "sympathy" – the whole living being συμπαθεῖ ....ὡς ἓν ὄν.

The soul, being itself ἀσώματος, is yet present in every part of the body giving it life and movement, while also being transcendent, that is, not confined to some portion of space (the evidence for this being the occurrence of dreams). Thus, the soul is said to be in the body, not because it is located in it, but because of its habitual relation of presence there. Natural analogies fail, so Nemesius turns to theological ones. The soul is in body *even as God is said to be in us*. How good is that as an account of man's unity? He tries another analogy:

> (the divine Word) continued thus in union without confusion, and without being circumscribed. (§ 22: MPG 40.601)

Christology he uses to cope with his anthropological puzzle, though he does admit that there are difficulties in the analogy since the soul is mutable and the Word immutable. Yet clearly, for the ancients, the transcendence and immanence of the soul, like that of the Word, posed intellectual problems, and it is interesting that just as the anthropological analogy could be used to ease Christology, so the Christological analogy could be used to ease anthropology. In fact, Nemesius makes both moves, rounding off the circle by quoting Porphyry on the [131] union of soul and body in order to confute the mockery of the Greeks who say that the incarnation is impossible.

This fascinating Christological interlude is not of immediate relevance to our theme; yet it is interesting to note that Nemesius presents a remarkable picture of man's psychosomatic unity without being able to offer a very convincing account of it – a situation which is closely paralleled by the Christological position of, say, Theodore of Mopsuestia. To return to our main concerns, however, it is important to observe that for Nemesius it was not the Bible which taught a psychosomatic unity and demanded a resolution of the difficulties raised by a fundamentally dualistic analysis of human nature. Rather, the need for an account of man's unitary being arose from within the scientific philosophy of the time. While Christian doctrine provided possible analogies for solving the problem (though they are really quite peripheral and rather unsatisfactory), the Bible, as Nemesius read it, supported the underlying dualist analysis.

C. *The Biblical Contribution*

The framework and detail of Nemesius' understanding of man comes entirely from current scientific knowledge; Biblical ideas are subtly interwoven with anthropological ideas plundered from Plato, Stoicism and elsewhere. The Bible could provide no alternative science on the basis of which a critique of current assumptions might be constructed. It did confirm Nemesius' preference for one set of conclusions rather than another, but it contributed little that was distinctive.

The actual extent to which the Bible is quoted, alluded to or appealed to is indicated in the accompanying tables (Tables II and III). It is noticeable that its use is extremely patchy, occurring mostly in the general introduction and in the treatment of providence. Plato and many others figure more prominently. The Bible had nothing to say about many of the things discussed, and many of the texts quoted are marginal to the main drift of Nemesius' treatise. Actual use of the Biblical material, then appears very slight. So we may profitably proceed to ask whether any Christian doctrines regarded as deriving from the Bible, have affected his work. What does he make of the stories of fall and salvation? Are there present ideas, like that of resurrection, which are not "christianised" versions of late Roman eclectic philosophy? [132]

One of the most interesting, and yet most unsatisfactory, sections of Nemesius' treatise is § 7: (MPG 40.521–4). Here Nemesius is discussing man's "choice prerogatives" which "are shared by no other creature." He begins by stating that there are two of them:

> Man only on repenting can gain forgiveness; and only man's body, though mortal, is immortalised. This privilege of the body is for the soul's sake. So likewise, the soul's privilege is on account of the body, for it is only man, among rational beings, that has this unique privilege of claiming forgiveness by repenting. Neither demons nor angels repent and are forgiven.

Quite clearly Nemesius has adopted two central Christian doctrines and wedded them to his view of man as the one creature which is a compound of the corporeal and incorporeal. The peculiar character of man's being means that he cannot escape wants and passions, and therefore God is just and merciful in granting him a means of forgiveness; and the soul's immortality means that man alone of the living creatures will experience bodily resurrection. Nemesius' scientific insight into the psychosomatic unity of man could have been developed in a distinctively Christian direction.

The frustrating thing about these comments is that Nemesius develops neither idea in the rest of his work. For the most part, his emphasis elsewhere is on the immortality of the soul rather than the resurrection of the body (contrast Gregory); and his discussions of morality imply the somewhat Pelagian position that man's freewill means that he could succeed in choosing the good life. Furthermore, even in this section, he slips away from the two characteristics with which he begins and introduces other traditional philosophical estimates:

> "Laughter is a peculiar mark of man's being"
> "It is peculiar to man to learn arts and sciences"

– that is, man is rational compared with the irrational beasts. The whole discussion has been described as a "bizarre combination", and Nemesius has not really succeeded in what might have been a promising attempt to introduce into current scientific orthodoxy certain central Biblical insights.

Given this, it is perhaps not surprising to find that overall the fall and redemption play a rather minor role in Nemesius' treatment of man. It is true that Nemesius espouses the view (§ 5: MPG 40.513–6: see Table III), that man was created potentially immortal, and understands the story of Adam as an account of how man discovered his ambiguous **[133]** position and lapsed from the way of perfection. Yet the treatise as a whole suggests that he regarded this story as paradeigmatic rather than as the account of a fatal fall reversible only by an act of redemption. As long as man controlled his passions and the irrational element in him, no other living creature dared to do man harm; sin laid man open to the ravages of wild beasts, but great men like Daniel and Paul proved man's potential authority over animals (§ 9: MPG 40.532). Man in control of his passions is still destined for immortality, but he has to make the choice and strive for virtue. Thus Nemesius' basic view is that man's dual nature means that he has the freewill to make a choice between living like the beasts or aspiring to the heavens. freewill under God's providence is man's prerogative which he could not have exercised if he had not been created mutable (§ 41: MPG 40.776–7). Evil came to all rational creatures through their own choice. On a couple of occasions Nemesius hints that man could not rise from his fall without God's grace and immortality (§ 7: MPG 40.521 and § 10: MPG 40.533); but for the most part he is fundamentally optimistic about human nature and man's moral potentialities, showing little awareness of the need for redemption. Christ is barely mentioned, the cross only appears as an example of how God may permit evil so that good may be vindicated (§ 69: MPG 40.812: see Table III), and Christology merely figures as an analogy (already noted) to ease the conceptual problems of Nemesius' Two-in-One anthropology. Only in the panegyric on man is anything made of the incarnation:

> He is the creature for whose sake God became man, so that this creature might attain incorruption and escape corruption, might reign on high, being made after the image and likeness of God, dwelling with Christ as a child of God, and might be throned above all rule and all authority. (§ 10: MPG 40.533).

From this survey a number of conclusions suggest themselves concerning the interplay of science and the Bible in the anthropological thought of Nemesius:

1. Anthropology was a subject in which pagan and Christian shared a common interest and a common stock of knowledge. Pagan and Christian intellectuals are referred to side by side in this treatise; for both were engaged in a common enterprise and both used the same intellectual tools.

2. The Bible had nothing distinctive to contribute to scientific discussion. Nemesius understood it to confirm what seemed to him the most **[134]** reasonable account of man's being advanced by current scientific orthodoxy. It provided useful examples to add to the commonplaces of literature and moral philosophy, but the only distinctive item it added was the doctrine of *creatio ex nihilo*.

3. The main focus of interest was man's behaviour and destiny. Ethics, freewill, providence and immortality were issues raised by contemporary discussion, not the result of reflection on the Biblical material.

4. Contrary to the impression given in some modern discussions, the idea of man as a psychosomatic unity more obviously arose from current science than from the Bible, which was understood

to confirm the soul's transcendence and immortality. On the other hand, the Biblical doctrine of creation is happily married in this treatise with the philosophical understanding of man as a microcosm uniting all orders of Being. The Bible, then, provided no alternative anthropology, nor a critique of current understanding; but it could confirm conclusions already established on other grounds or derived from other sources.

Table II   Plan of Nemesius' treatise *De Natura Hominis* indicating in what sections the Bible is actually used. (The section divisions are my own.)

Section A: General introduction. §§ 1–10.
Several texts quoted or Biblical material alluded to in §§ 4, 5, 8, 9, 10.
Subjects = Creation, Fall, Man's high estate.
See Table II for details.
Section B: On the Soul and its union with the Body. §§ 11–22.
Bible only used in one context § 17, where Nemesius produces a Biblically-based argument against creationism.
General comment v. immortality of soul being scriptural teaching § 19.
Section C: On the Body, the Elements, Sense-perception, the Intellect and other functions of soul. §§ 23–34.
Bible only used in a discussion of creation § 26.
Section D: On the irrational soul, the passions, pleasures, emotions, nutrition, generation, respiration, etc. §§ 35–45.
No use of the Bible at all.
Section E: On voluntary and involuntary acts, choices, deliberation, fate, providence § 46–70.
Reference to Biblical examples of choice § 46.
All things possible to God-Biblical examples § 55.
Texts supporting freewill § 57.
On providence and evil: texts quoted §§ 66, 68, 69.
Use of the Bible largely concentrated in a few paragraphs of Sections A and E. In the bulk of the treatise, no use of the Bible at all. [135]

Table III   Comprehensive list of passages in Nemesius' *De Natura Hominis* where texts are quoted or alluded to, or Biblical examples used

Section A
§ 4 "The foregoing conclusions justify the Mosaic story of creation when it makes man the last to be created …" (i.e. the fact that creatures are made for man's sake). Another reason: man= link between intelligible and phenomenal order. If man "leans towards the things of the body", he becomes "in Paul's words, 'a man of earth' to whom it is said, 'Dust thou art and unto dust thou shalt return' and 'He shall be compared unto the beasts that have no understanding and is likened unto them' …"
If man "advances in the direction of reason", he "deserves to be called a 'heavenly man'

in accordance with the Apostle's words, 'Such as is the earthy, such also are they that are earthy, and such as is the heavenly, such also are they that are heavenly'."

Texts quoted: Gen. 3.19; Ps. 49.20 (LXX); I Cor. 15.48.

§ 5 "The Hebrews say that man was created at first neither avowedly mortal not yet immortal, but rather in a state poised between the two, in the sense that, if he gave himself up to his bodily passions, he should be subject to all the changes of the body, but that if he put the good of his soul foremost, he should be deemed worthy of immortality."

"Until man had attained his perfection, however, it was not at all suitable for him to know how he was constituted. God, for that reason, forbad him to taste the fruit of the Tree of Knowledge … Man disobeyed and learned the truth about himself …

Moses says that the man was naked and now knew it, whereas, until that moment, God had caused him to be entranced with existence and happily unconscious of himself. When man lapsed from the way of perfection, he likewise lost the immortality which, by favour of his creator, he is to recover at the last."

§ 8 "It is the doctrine of the Hebrews that the whole world was made for the sake of man …" Man's authority over irrational animals discussed: "Such as ill-use the irrational beasts, sin, therefore …; as it is written, 'The righteous man hath compassion on the life of his beast'."

Text quoted: Prov. 12.10.

§ 9 "As long as man controlled his passions, no animal dared to harm him. "The truth of this is confirmed by the instances of those who lived the best of lives … Daniel was superior to attack by lions, and Paul to the bite of an adder."

§ 10 "Knowing then the nobility of which we are partakers, and how we are a 'planting from heaven', let us do nothing that would put our nature to shame."

Text quoted: Is. 61.3.

Section B
§ 17 "… everything of which the genesis is in body and time is corruptible and mortal. The words of Moses agree to these things. For when describing the creation of the sensible [136] universe, he did not expressly say that the nature of the intelligibles was also established by that creation." "Moses does not say that the soul was created at that moment at which it was put into the body …"

"But if souls arrive out of non-existence, then creation is still going on in defiance of the words of Moses that 'God rested from all his works' … For the saying, 'My Father worketh' does not refer to creation but to providence."

Texts quoted: Gen. 2.2; John 5.17.

§ 19 Quoted on p. 21 in the text of the paper.

Section C
§ 26 "Those who favour the doctrines of the Hebrews take a different line concerning the heaven and the earth…" "… (they) say that the heaven and the earth were not

made from any pre-existing matter, since Moses said, 'In the beginning, God made the heaven and the earth'. Apollinaris however will have it that it was out of the deep that God made the heaven and the earth, seeing that in his account of the world's creation Moses made no mention of the coming into being of the deep. Nevertheless in Job we have 'who made the deep'. So Apollinaris will have it that it was from the deep as pre-existing matter that all other things were made ..."

Section E
§ 46 "In most cases one ought to choose what is grievous rather than what is shameful, as Susanna and Joseph did."
   Texts referred to: History of Susanna 43; Gen. 39.12.

§ 54 "(Plato) diverges but a little from Holy Writ which teaches that providence alone rules over all."

§ 55 "On the contrary all things are possible to him (God), including those we call impossible. To prove this, he established once for all the courses of the sun and moon, which are borne on their way by inevitable laws ... and at the same time to prove that nothing is to him inevitable ... just once he made a special 'day' that scripture sets forth as a 'sign' ..." "In like manner, he made unending the lives of certain men, Elias and Enoch ..."
   Texts referred to: Joshua 10.13, 14; II Kings 2.11; Gen. 5.24 cf. Heb. 11.5.

§ 57 Defending the doctrine of freewill: "(some) ... refute us by adducing a citation from scripture that 'A man's ways are not in his own power' ... They cite again 'The thoughts of men's hearts are vain' ..." Nemesius acknowledges that we cannot choose whether to be rich or poor, ill or healthy, etc. but we have power to promote either good or evil, and choice is subject to judgment. "This is proved by what it says in the Gospel, 'Everyone that looketh on a woman to lust after her hath committed adultery with her already in his heart.' Also Job sacrificed to God for the trespasses his children had committed in thought."
   Texts quoted or alluded to: Matt. 5.28; Job 1.5. **[137]**

§ 63 "... (man) provides for his children everything that their life requires, of whatever kind or whatever quality ... It has been proved therefore that God is the God of providence."
   Compare Luke 11.11–13.

§ 66 "These things are addressed, however, to those who make themselves God's judges. To them may also fittingly be cited these words of scripture, 'Shall the clay say to the potter' and so forth".
   Texts quoted: Is. 45.9, cf. Rom. 9.20–21.

§ 68 "If the doctrine of providence over particulars exceeds our comprehension – and surely it does that, as it is written, 'How unsearchable are thy judgments and thy ways past finding out'– still we ought not, on that account, to deny that providence exists ..."

Texts quoted: Rom. 11.33.

§ 69 "... oftentimes God gives permission for a man, though righteous, to fall into misfortune, just so that he may reveal to others, as in the case of Job, what virtue is latent in that man. Another example of divine permission is when God allows some monstrous crime to be committed, so that through the perpetration of an evident outrage, some great and admirable vindication of the right may be achieved, as when by means of the cross, man's salvation was attained. Divine permission appears in a different form where God, as he did in the case of Paul, allows a godly man to suffer grievously only lest his clear conscience and the might that has been granted him should cause him to fall into spiritual pride. One man is forsaken of God for a season so that another man may be corrected, and that others again, in witnessing that man's correction, may be warned by it. It was thus in the case of Lazarus and Dives. For it is natural that we should be restrained by the sight of what happens to others, according to that admirable line from Menander: 'The dread of heaven is fallen on us as we behold what has befallen thee.' Again one man is forsaken of God so as to promote the glory of another, as in the case of the man who was born blind not through any fault of his or of his parents, but for the glory of the Son of Man."
N.B. (1) the quotation from Menander in the midst of a list of Biblical examples. (2) the use of the Cross as an example of 'divine permission' of evil.
Biblical references: Job 1.12; N.T. refs. to the passion; II Cor. 12.7–10; Lk. 16.17–31; Jn. 9.1–38.
"... life is a contest and a striving-ground for virtue ... That is why Paul was allowed to fall into countless afflictions ..." "to the end that the crown of victory ... might be the greater, or rather that it might be unsurpassable."
Texts alluded to: II Cor. 11.23–20; II Tim. 4.7–8.

Concluding Remarks

The two treatises we have examined clearly do not present exactly the same position with respect to the interplay of science and scripture; but they do have certain features in common. For one thing anthropological *analysis* is drawn from contemporary philosophy and medical science; [138] the Bible may complement this or put it in a different perspective, but it does not replace it. This different perspective had less to do with specifically anthropological observations, more to do with the overall theological context, that is, with the doctrine of creation and the eschatological hope.

I have argued on the basis of these two treatises that contemporary scientific knowledge played a significantly greater part in patristic anthropology than the Bible. In a few concluding remarks, inevitably sketchy and to some extent deliberately provocative, may I suggest that the patristic material in general seems to signify the possibility that the adequacy of an anthropology, even a

Christian one, is related very little to its dependence on the Bible and a great deal to the weight given to what scientific knowledge is available.

The anthropology of these treatises is not typical. The popular Platonism presupposed by many of the Fathers was clearly more dualistic and less ready to admit the psychosomatic unity of man. Why are these treatises untypical? Some scholars have spoken of Aristotelian or Stoic influences; but my impression is that most intellectuals were pretty eclectic in this period, and that these elements were already integrated into the general Platonic stream of late Roman philosophy. We shall not find the reason why they are untypical by looking at rival philosophical schools or at the Bible; the reason is simple – they were specifically dealing with the subject of anthropology, taking it seriously, not operating uncritically with popular assumptions but paying attention to serious anthropological discussion among the scientists, particularly the medical philosophers, of the day.

Those who accepted popular assumptions uncritically were trapped into inadequate anthropologies. The major difficulty implicit in the Alexandrian Christological tradition arose from such an inadequate anthropology. Unlike Gregory and Nemesius, Cyril believed that the soul was ἀπαθής, though in some way affected by the body's sufferings; thus the soul was more 'separable' and there was a far less adequate grasp of the psychosomatic unity of man. The consequence was an inadequate understanding of the fall – it was the 'flesh' which distracted and weighed down the mind, not the mind which was perverted. Of course, there is a contradiction here – that the soul should be impassible and yet reduced to passibility by its association with the flesh; yet Cyril's Christological paradox – ἀπαθῶς ἔπαθεν – is an exact parallel. It is no wonder that the soul-body analogy was so central to the Alexandrian [139] Christology; for man too was "one nature out of two natures", and incompatible ones at that! Here was no real engagement with anthropological problems and a consequent over-simplification of the Christological problem. No amount of attention to the Bible could compensate for what was a failure to utilise the best of contemporary science.

Excessive attention to the Bible without considering questions of coherence and without regard to current intellectual demands in fact seems to be characteristic of some who came to be condemned as heretics. Apollinaris appears to have derived his anthropological terminology from the Epistles of Paul, and as a result his position is equally unsystematic. Was he a dichotomist or a trichotomist? – the question has been discussed since his own day! What he says is that according to Paul, man is a νοῦς ἐν σαρκί (dichotomist?); so Christ is the Νοῦς ἔνσαρκος or flesh συνουσιωμένη with the divine πνεῦμα. But he also says that the Christ, having God as Spirit, that is Mind, together with soul and body, is reasonably called the 'man from heaven'; he is "of three, Spirit, soul and body, but he is 'heavenly man' or 'divine spirit'" (trichotomist?).[6] Pauline terminology lies behind the inconsistencies of the fragments, the confusion of Apollinaris' opponents, and their accusation (which he stated was false) that he taught that the flesh came from heaven.

The one instance where Biblical ideas did successfully contribute to anthropology seems to me to be that of Theodore of Mopsuestia. The case is well put in the widely known book by R.A. Norris, *Manhood and Christ* (Oxford 1963). The success was at least partly due to Theodore's appreciation of the eschatology of the New Testament and the moral imperatives of the Biblical tradition. But then Theodore, too, was condemned as a heretic!

---

[6] H. Lietzmann, *Apollinaris und seine Schule* (Tübingen 1904), Fragments 36 (p. 212), 116 (p. 235), 69 (p. 220), and the *Tomus Synodalis* (p. 263); also fragments 72 (p. 221), 29 (p. 211), 25 (p. 210), 89 (p. 237), and especially 69 ff (p. 220 ff).

II

JOHN CHRYSOSTOM ON
FIRST AND SECOND CORINTHIANS

Modern biblical criticism has on the whole taken little interest in patristic exegesis. Abroad at the moment, however, is a loss of confidence in the historico-critical method and an interest in hermeneutical theory. Study of Chrysostom's Homilies on the Corinthian correspondence[1] has been undertaken in the context of a collaborative effort to bring hermeneutical concerns to bear upon the exegesis of a particular text, namely 2 Corinthians. I propose to outline here some of the ways in which we might learn from Chrysostom, both in matters of exegetical detail and in our general approach to hermeneutics. Each of the examples discussed will be argued in detail elsewhere. This is by way of an interim report.

Detailed exegetical points.

Chrysostom has confirmed several surmises about the meaning of the Greek and the thrust of Paul's argument, and has aroused doubts about certain current critical assumptions.

My first example concerns the way in which 2 Corinthians 1:17b is construed. Chrysostom read the longer text with ναί and οὔ doubled, and seems to have taken it to mean: 'Or in making plans, do I do so in a fleshly way so that Yes being yes and No being no rests in my hands?' His exegesis[2] indicates that he understood Paul to be hinting that his travel plans did not depend upon him, but were subject to God's direction. Now modern interpreters universally assume that the text implies that Paul is accused of being a vacillating person, liable to say Yes yes and No no at the same time. It is noticeable that if the modern consensus is followed, the next verses about God's faithfulness have to be treated as loosely related theological digression, whereas Chrysostom's understanding of the verses is consistent both with the immediate context and the thrust of the Epistle as a whole.

Two further examples arise from Chrysostom's reading of Paul's sequence of thought. In each case, his way of taking it calls in question the need for modern dissections of the text. One such case concerns 1 Corinthians 8-10.[3] Chrysostom recognises that 1 Corinthians 9 belongs to the discussion which runs through these three chapters: Paul uses his own foregoing of apostolic privileges as an example of the restrained freedom he is enjoining upon his hearers.[4] Furthermore Chrysostom perceives no inconsistency between the view of idolatry taken in chapter 8 and that in chapter 10; clearly he is sure an idol is nothing, yet he is profoundly aware of the power of the daemons. One suspects Paul felt the same. The difficulties about the text's coherence raised by modern critics prove illusory — as I happen to have pointed out myself at the 1973 Oxford Biblical Congress.[5] Another case of the same kind concerns 2 Corinthians 6:14-7:1.[6] So difficult is the relationship of this passage to its context that modern editors often print it as a distinct paragraph, and commentators treat it as an intrusion into the text. The discovery of Qumran parallels has reinforced these suspicions and called in question even the Pauline authorship of these verses. Chrysostom, however, takes the section in the same homily as Paul's emotional appeal to the Corinthians' affections in the preceding verses, and perceives that the target in not outsiders or pagans, but the false apostles who were corrupting the Corinthians. This again confirms my own view that modern commentators are misled as to the meaning of these verses and therefore fail to perceive that they have an important function in their present context.

Time does not permit the enumeration of further examples, but I must briefly indicate, before passing on, that it seems to me that Chrysostom's 'innocent assumptions' about the unity of these epistles and their close interrelationship — both questioned by modern critics — have a great deal more to be said for them than is generally admitted. I believe the instinct that interprets 2 Corinthians as a whole without partition is fundamentally right. Then there are good grounds in the text for Chrysostom's identification of the offender in 2 Corinthians 2 with the offender in 1 Corinthians 5; nor is his commonsense view that the previous letter is 1 Corinthians unjustifiable, given the many striking connections between the two epistles, connections all the more apparent if 1 Corinthians is read in the light of 2 Corinthians rather than vice versa. In the light of these observations, there may be much in his suggestion that the 'false apostles' of 2 Corinthians are already at the root of the problems in 1 Corinthians; and in his view, based on 1 Corinthians 4:6, that Paul is not actually dealing with the relationship between himself and other major apostles in either epistle, but tactfully transfers to himself and Apollos 'in a figure' what he means to say about the Corinthians' relationship with certain others who are honoured above measure.[7] Above all I am inclined to respect Chrysostom's view that the issues are pride, status, attitude, finance and morality, rather than false doctrines, gnostic or otherwise. There are, of course, places where Chrysostom clearly goes astray — he has no idea, for example, what speaking in tongues was. Yet I am more and more convinced that he perceived the Corinthian situation generally along the right lines, by contrast with the convulsive speculations characteristic of much current research.

Hermeneutical Method

The legacy of the historico-critical method has been the so-called 'hermeneutical gap'. For Chrysostom there was no such thing. Yet Chrysostom was not unaware of historical perspectives; for he belonged to the Antiochene reaction against allegorism.

He outlines the situation in Corinth which Paul addressed, even inviting his audience at one point to imagine what it was like being a Christian in the first generation.[8] Is it possible to discern how it was that he understood the text as both historical and contemporary?

Chrysostom, the pastor and preacher, recognised the pastor and preacher in Paul, the paradoxes of authority and love, discipline and persuasion; so the gap was closed by empathy. Constantly he read between the lines to bring out the tone of Paul's voice and his use of tactics to win over his hearers. It seems to me that this proves of enormous value in elucidating the apparently perplexing mood-changes in these epistles: Chrysostom recognised that these belong to the rhetoric of Paul's discourse. So he re-created for his hearers a drama of pastoral handling, observing the way Paul oscillated between praise and blame, mixed severity with tenderness, humility with assertion. In fact at one point[9] he went so far as to comment that Paul's initial praising of the Corinthians is not very close to truth, and he explains that Paul praises them οἰκονομικῶς, preparing the way for reproofs to come. Paul's subtle handling of the Corinthians in their disunity, immorality, pride, disloyalty, etc., he regards as all part of his loving care — one minute he scares them, next he softens his words to win them. Now this creation of a pastoral drama produces direct communication with Chrysostom's congregation. In the exegetical sections of his sermons, there is no explicit drawing of morals — there is no need for any. The empathy of Chrysostom the pastor with Paul the pastor produces a creative but non-explicit interplay between the two different audiences who, by implication, share the same shortcomings. So there is an entirely unconscious 'hermeneutic of retrieval'.

Needless to say there are problems with this. Chrysostom idealises Paul. In our postcritical period, his hagiographically inclined approach is inevitably suspect, and we can see how it impoverishes understanding: Chrysostom is quite unable to enter into Paul's *Angst* over his apostolic status[10] or to detect the latent pride and self-assertion in Paul's protestations of humility.[11] The 'hermeneutic of suspicion' which Chrysostom lacks is necessary for a full appreciation of the material. Besides more accurate historical knowledge would discipline and improve his imaginative approach. Yet granted that, there is still something significant happening in Chrysostom's handling of the text. Tone of voice is lacking in a written text. The attribution of motive and tone is therefore an essential element in discerning its meaning.[12] Chrysostom overdoes it, and yet his mode of empathy has, I think, enormous potential for discerning the fundatmental thrust of what Paul was getting at. Chrysostom was asking the right questions of the text. He was not much interested in piecing together historical jig-saw puzzles of the kind that preoccupy modern critics, but rather in discerning what Paul was saying and why.

Now some may dismiss his method as incurably subjective, but most who have reflected upon hermeneutical issues would now agree that objectivity is impossible, that no exegesis is presuppositionless, and that it makes a considerable difference what the interpreter brings to the text, what questions he asks of it, what expectations he has. Now Chrysostom approaches Paul expectantly, and listens to the text in order to learn. For that very reason, he often discerns Paul's meaning the more clearly.

Lack of expectancy, indeed deliberate distancing of oneself from the text in the interests of historical objectivity, accompanied by concentration on obscure or incompatible statements in the interests of finding clues as to the genesis of the material, has been regarded as essential in modern research: but could it not be an important factor in distorting our reading of the material? Involved listening to what the text has to say may be the only way to hear and understand. Nor should we imagine that that creates a hermeneutical circle from which there is no escape. Rather real engagement with a text involves dialogue and produces a spiral, a subtle combination of the subjective and objective which has the potential to produce better understanding. Maybe Chrysostom sometimes imports his own moral concerns into the text, but on other occasions, on 1 Corinthians 15 for example, his moral concerns enable him to discern the presence of a moral dynamic in the text which is given little attention in modern discussion. Because he is preaching on the Corinthian letters, Chrysostom does more than preach his own doctrine or morals — he enables Paul to address his hearers.

Notes

1. Text: F. Field, *Joannis Chrysostomi Interpretatio omnium epistolarum Paulinarum*, Bibliotheca Patrum (Oxford, 1845). E.T. N.P.N.F. Series I, vol. 12.

2. *In Epist. II ad Cor. Hom. iii.*

3. *In Epist. I ad Cor. Hom. xx-xxv.*

4. *Hom.* xxi. The point is made more than once. Interestingly Chrysostom opens Hom. xx by indicating that the key to Paul's discussion is to be found in the hymn to love in chapter 13. Because he is untroubled by questions of background and coherence, he is free to concentrate upon the thrust of Paul's teaching about seeking the common good rather than individual advantage, with a cross-reference also to Romans 14.

5. 'Notes on the Corinthian correspondence' *Studia Evangelica* vol. 7 (Berlin, 1982) pp. 563–66.

6. *In Epist. II ad Cor. Hom.* xiii.

7. *In Epist. I ad Cor. Hom.* xii.

8. *In Epist. I ad Cor. Hom.* xx.

9. *In Epist. I ad Cor. Hom.* ii.

10. E.g. Chrysostom cannot take 1 Cor 4:3-4 literally because he could not imagine the Corinthians sitting in judgement on Paul or accusing him of arrogance. So he has to take the passage as another example of Paul's diplomacy, shaming them into recognition of their faults by putting the matter in his own person when really referring to the Corinthians' treatment of others.

11. E.g. *In Epist. ad Cor. Hom.* xiii on 1 Cor 4:16: 'Be imitators of me'. Chrysostom emphasises Paul's humility — for all is the work of God.

12. The attribution of motive and tone is inevitably imaginative and somewhat hazardous. Its dangers are well highlighted by the recent book by Grahame Shaw, *The Cost of Authority* (London, 1983), as well as by Chrysostom's excesses. In the case of Shaw the 'hermeneutic of suspicion' has no counterbalancing empathy; in the case of Chrysostom there is no 'hermeneutic of suspicion' to counterbalance the idealisation. The contrast between the two does not, I suggest, invalidate their common approach, but rather indicates the necessity for criticism and historical knowledge to inform the imagination, and vice versa.

III

ALLEGORY AND ATONEMENT

I am glad of the opportunity to express appreciation of the work of Eric Osborn. My time as a patristic scholar has been punctuated by his books, all of which have succeeded in putting material into a novel perspective.

The area of 'atonement' in the Fathers has rarely been adequately treated because the classic studies are all written by 'retrospective historians', to use Eric Osborn's characterization.[1] The histories of the doctrine produced by such as Rashdall and Rivière were designed to advocate the 'anselmian' or 'abelardian' approach, and found support in the Fathers while dismissing those aspects of patristic thinking which were not congenial.[2] Aulen perhaps did better, tracing the forgotten 'classic theory' through the Fathers to Luther; and Turner does try to be descriptive rather than theoretical.[3] But none of these analyses really captures the flavour of the patristic material.

The fact is that the Fathers had no common 'system' or 'theory' of atonement. Yet increasingly scholars are recognizing the vital importance of their soteriological thinking, in that it forms the backcloth of one controversy after another. The different christologies of Arius and Athanasius, Cyril and Nestorius, were informed by different senses of salvation and atonement.[4] Soteriology is significant despite its absence from the front of the stage. Far from being an afterthought or appendix to patristic theology it is the implicit driving force, the set of underlying assumptions that informed debate in other areas.

How then is the subject to be treated? Not, I suggest, by means of a 'problematic' approach, though Eric Osborn has shown the usefulness of that in some areas of discussion. Nor by means of a 'history of development', retrospective or doxographic. The subject is one that can only be properly handled when the focus is shifted from critical analysis and theoretical reason to an appreciation of the role of imagination and synthesis in belief.[5] Allegory, myth and parable are essential to the religious imagination, and the patristic sense of atonement was 'hydra-headed'. It carried conviction, but in its articulation it lay somewhere between 'hard fact and mere fantasy'. There was no consistent 'doctrine' or 'theory', and yet it cannot be dismissed as 'mere feeling' or 'mere simile'. Patristic reflection on atonement is an example of the integration of different levels of truth in a single imaginative language appropriate to its subject-matter.

Insofar as this paper can be said to have an argument, it is this: First, to appreciate what the Fathers have to say about atonement, you have to begin with an awareness of the richness of typology and allegory, the multifaceted unity of imagery and allusion, and its scriptural source. Second, behind all that, the greatest of them had an underlying system, though this is never directly explicit and varies from one writer to another. Third, the adequacy of the system depends upon its capacity to embrace the richness in a synthesis; to turn a single image into a system is to produce an inadequate theory. The imaginative mind steeped in homiletic and liturgical traditions can alone perceive and assent to the truth which lies between 'hard fact and mere fantasy'.

I. My colleague, Neville Birdsall, stimulated some of these thoughts by sharing with me his translation of the exposition of the Name of Jesus found in a sermonic address in *The Martyrdom of St. Abo of Tiflis*, a Georgian work of the Eighth Century.[6] The names of Jesus are Door, Way, Lamb, Shepherd, Stone, Pearl, Flower, Angel, Man, God, Light, Earth, Salt, Worm, Mustard-seed, Sun of Righteousness, Son of the Eternal Father, and One God. The exposition of each name is sometimes confined to quoting the single obvious scripture passage from Old or New Testament, but often involves an imaginative development of the text, usually drawing on other scriptures:

> He is called Shepherd because he said "I am the Good Shepherd". Truly he has turned us wandering sheep back, and has killed our enemy the lion with the rod of the cross and has brought to life again by the power of the Godhead the corpse of the first-formed destroyed by that lion, and has healed by his wound the bite of the venomous wolf and has dissipated the deadly venom by the medicine of his Godhead and has fulfilled the word spoken through the prophet, namely, "He was wounded because of our sins and by his wounds we are healed".

> He is called Pearl because he shines out like a pearl between the two valves of the spirit and the body. Lovers of God, as merchants of the kingdom, seek him with faith, not as God alone and not as mere man, but as God and Man, and they purchase him solely by the expenditure of all a great-priced treasure (variant reading: the great-priced world) and by pouring out of their blood also.

> He is called Salt because he has drawn near to our body corrupted by sin and has removed from us the stench of idol-worship and has prepared our souls with sweet savour by the faith of the worship of God.

> He is called Flower because as a flower he has sprung from the root of Jesse for the Church from the holy virgin Mary in bodily form, and has spread over us the spirit of grace through the sweet smell of Godhead.

> He is called Earth, as David said "The earth has given its fruit, bless us O God, our God". Truly the maker of the earth came to the earth and from the earth is his body of an earthly nature from those who were made from the earth; as a comely shoot he has sprung from the earth, and has produced as fruit his holy apostles and martyrs and righteous, and has filled the accursed earth with the fruit of blessing.

> He is called Mustard-seed because he made himself small and was made like us in our stature so that he might plant himself in the field of our soul and strike the roots deep and might gather us upon the branches of his cross and be exalted and exalt us with him.

> He is called Worm because he said "I am a worm and not a man". By the brightness of the Godhead, as a hook in a worm, thus he hid his own Godhead in his body and cast it into the nether-regions of the world and drew it up like a good fisherman; about

whom he says "He took the dragon with a hook and put a bridle in his mouth and a spike through his nose", that is the devil he took and whose wiles he broke, about whom the Psalmist David bears witness "Thou hast broken the heads of the dragon".

Such are the seven most interesting examples, and the author ends by saying that he has explained nothing at all of himself, but from the witness of the prophetic books, according to the preaching of the apostles, what is written in the holy Gospels and the faith established by the holy Fathers, the teachers. Clearly the material is ancient. It has been traced back to Amphilochius of Iconium, some parallels are already to be found in Justin Martyr, and lists of titles of Christ which overlap with these are found in the *Acts of Peter* and the *Acts of John*, as Birdsall noted.[7] The 'fishhook' image of atonement is found in the Great Catechism of Gregory of Nyssa (chapter 24), though without the scriptural allusions.

Despite this document's late date, then, this kind of material can be regarded as traditional and popular, and far from untypical of homiletic techniques. It depends upon the interweaving of texts, parables, and images into allegories of Christ and his saving work. Any attempt to spell out the allegories as if they were 'theories' is doomed, and the tendency to try and 'translate' the metaphors which has become the natural modern reaction, leads to absurdity. The total effect defies rational analysis, though it is clear that it creates an imaginative whole with considerable persuasive power, particularly within the culture to which it belonged.

II. The interesting thing to note is that the technique and many of the examples appear also in Origen's exposition of the Name of Christ in the first book of his *Commentary on John*.[8] Here we are not dealing with homiletic material, nor with popular mythology, but a self-conscious attempt to analyse the character of religious language as an element in expounding the meaning of *archē* and *logos* as they appear in the Prologue of John's Gospel.

Origen's list of titles includes Wisdom, Word, Life, Truth, Son of God, Righteousness, Saviour, Propitiation, Light of the World, First-born of the Dead, Shepherd (the Good Shepherd), Physician, Healer, Redemption, Resurrection and Life, Way, Truth and Life, Door, Messiah, Christ, Lord, King, Vine, Bread of Life, First, Last, the Living One, Alpha and Omega — First and Last, Beginning and End, Lion of Judah, Jacob/Israel, Shepherd, Rod, Flower, Stone, a Chosen Shaft, Sword, Servant of God, Lamb, Light of the Gentiles, Lamb of God, Paraclete, Power of God, Sanctification, High-Priest. Clearly the source is again scripture, and while Johannine titles have a certain pre-eminence, both Old and New Testaments provide material.

Those that Origen has in common with the more 'popular' list given above include: Door, Way, Lamb, Shepherd, Cornerstone, Flower, Light. Most of them he develops much more elaborately: for example, on Light, our 'popular' text simply quotes "That was the True Light which lights every man who comes into the world". Origen provides an elaborate catalogue of scripture parallels, distinguishes between the 'earthly light' of sun, moon and stars, and the 'spiritual light' with which the Saviour shines, and speaks of the analogy between the Church and the moon and stars which borrow light from the sun, as the apostles and disciples borrow light from the Saviour. Nor is this the end of his enquiry into the 'metaphorical sense' by means of the 'mystical and allegorical method' − there are further explorations still to be made. Comparison of the treatment of Door and Way shows the same features. Origen is conscious of what he is doing, and proceeds by argument; his range of discussion is much wider; but his use of scripture and response to it is fundamentally the same as in the more 'popular' document.

In detail the development is different: as Shepherd, the Saviour is not depicted as the one who overcomes wild beasts, but as the one who cares for the weak even if they have not sufficient Reason to respond to the *Logos*. Yet the conquest idea is not missing since it appears in association with another title: as King he subdues the enemies of Israel. Rather than springing up as Flower from the root of Jesse and producing the spirit of grace like a perfume, he visits those who need chastisement as Rod, while as Flower he rises up and sheds mercy. So the detailed development is different, but the cast of mind is the same − a kind of free imaginative play with the images of scripture.

Origen produces this material because he objects to those who treat the title *Logos* in a different way. The 'tropological' use of *Logos* must be examined too. He is *Logos* because he drives away from us what is irrational. Scripture texts are used to show that the *Logos* was in humanity all along: the incarnation was a kind of concentration of Reason in humanity, where before it had been imperfect and defective. In Origen's view all the titles he treats have to be examined carefully, because they are taken 'for our sakes': you cannot say that the Saviour is metaphorically a Stone and literally Word. They all have meaningful content, and none expresses the 'essence' of the Saviour's nature. We are somewhere between 'hard fact and mere fantasy'.

Behind Origen's discussion is a philosophical understanding which undergirds his soteriology and his Christology, but it is never quite spelt out. All the titles are important because the one Christ is a 'multitude of goods'. Origen's fundamental perception is that the Saviour unites in himself the multiplicity of the creation and the unity of God. In the end it is that 'linkage', a concept which has its background in the long discussion about the One and the Many in Greek philosophy, which expresses Origen's idea of atonement: the transcendent God and his marred creation re-married by means of their mutual consummation in the mediating 'second God'. It is true that this vision of re-integration in Christ was to break down in subsequent controversy, but it was large enough to embrace the wealth of imaginative perception to which I have drawn attention. It is impossible to say whether Origen's approach to atonement is purely revelatory and educational, or whether it is about overcoming mortality, or conquering the devil, or offering a full perfect and sufficient sacrifice for the sins of the whole world. All of these elements contribute to his vision of how the opposition to re-integration is overcome, and the mystical re-union anticipated in the present, realized in the eschaton. And the richness of language, symbol, metaphor, analogy, parable, allegory was essential to the vision: Christ is a 'multitude of goods'.

The thinking of Athanasius is very different from that of Origen. There is no 'second God' or mediating divine being possible for Athanasius. His fundamental theological outlook cannot permit a blurring of the distinction between the Creator and his creation. Hence his battle with Arius, and the end of the Origenist approach. Yet an examination of the *Contra Gentes-De Incarnatione*[9] shows that Athanasius too had a composite vision, a multifaceted approach, a traditional set of images which provided a rich imaginative language in which to sketch his sense of salvation. Much of this he shares with Origen and the 'popular' homiletic material we have drawn upon. It is equally difficult to specify what 'theory' Athanasius espoused:

> Being with him as Wisdom, and as Word seeing the Father, he created the universe, formed it and ordered it; and being the Power of the Father, he gave all things the strength to come into existence. . . His holy disciples teach that everything was created through him and for him, and that being the good offspring of a good Father and true Son, he is the power of the Father and his Wisdom and Word, not by participation. . . .but he is absolute Wisdom, very Word, and himself the Father's own Power, absolute Light, absolute Truth, absolute Justice, absolute Virtue, and indeed stamp, effulgence and image. In short, he is the supremely perfect issue of the Father, and is alone Son, the express Image of the Father. . . .he is the Word and Wisdom of the Father, and at the same time condescends to created beings; to give them knowledge and an idea of the Father, he is absolute Holiness and absolute Life, he is Door, Shepherd and Way, King, Guide and Saviour for all. Life-giver and Light and universal Providence (*C.G.* pp. 46-47).

The climax is a list like the lists we have examined earlier; the basis is another philosophical theory. Origen is the one so often described as 'Platonist', but here we can see Athanasius' dependence upon the Platonic theory of Ideas, at least in popular form. Athanasius thinks that creatures have certain qualities because they participate in the absolute form of that quality. The 'absolute' is essential for that participation to be possible. The 'absolute' is not just another instance of the quality; it is essentially different, being the principle which makes possible the participation of other entities in it. The *Logos* is Saviour because he is not a creature who merely paticipates in divinity or Sonship, not 'another instance' of qualities which creatures may share in; rather he is the very principle of Sonship or divinity which provides the possibility of participation. He must be fully divine, *homoousios tǭ patri*, in order to be the absolute, the source of all these 'virtues' or qualities. *Theopoiēsis* and *huiopoiēsis* are ways of speaking of this participation, which for Athanasius is salvation. The taking up of the creation into God through participation is his understanding of atonement, and this can only be effected through the fully divine *Logos*. We become 'sons of God' by adoption and participation, because he is 'the Son of God' in reality and truth:

> We will begin, then, with the creation of the world and with God its Maker, for the first fact that you must grasp is this: the renewal of creation has been wrought by the Self-same Word who made it in the beginning (*D.I.* 1).

> He became human (Man), that we might become divine (God) (*D.I.* 54).

Such is Athanasius' total vision, and in the *Contra Gentes-De Incarnatione* we can see many other ways of speaking about salvation integrated with this. In the Longer Recension of the *De Incarnatione*, the problem of dealing with the devil is explicitly faced, and used as a justification for the particular mode of Christ's death on the Cross: but conquest of the devil is not the essence of Athanasius' understanding of atonement, *pace* Aulen. It is often said that Athanasius is more concerned about death than sin, and the restoration of life to creatures that were sinking back to the nothingness from which they had come into being is paramount in his exposition of salvation.[10] Up to a point that is true, but death was the wages of sin, and the loss of the *Logos* also meant the loss of reason. So illumination and purification, sanctification and propitiation are also essential aspects of the saving process as Athanasius describes it. The vision is as multifaceted as that of Origen or of the popular preaching tradition, and ultimately derives from the same sources.

For a final example, let us briefly move backwards in time to Irenaeus.[11] In some of his statements he anticipates Athanasius:

> The Logos became Man, that Man united with the Logos and receiving his adoption, might become the Son of God. (*Adv.Haer.* III.19).

> Because of his measureless love, he became what we are in order to enable us to become what he is. (*Adv.Haer.* V praef.).

Like Athanasius, he envisages many different processes being embraced in this:

> The Lord through his passion destroyed death, brought error to an end, abolished corruption, banished ignorance, manifested life, declared truth, and bestowed incorruption. (*Adv.Haer.* II.20.2).

But Irenaeus understands all this in terms of 'recapitulation':

> . . .the sin of the first-created was amended by the chastisement of the first-begotten. . . Therefore he renews all things in himself, uniting Man to the Spirit. (*Adv.Haer.* V. 19-21).

Adam was created in God's image and likeness, but the similarity was lost and marred. The renewal of God's image and likeness, and the fulfillment of God's real intention in creation is Irenaeus' fundamental idea. So the context of his statements is not the same as the context of Athanasius' somewhat similar language. He does not envisage *theopoiēsis* but rather a new creation.

Different though they are, the importance of both models is that they are comprehensive enough to permit 'a density of metaphor' which admits of no 'reduction'—in other words, the wealth of imagery, symbol, myth, parable, typology, etc., which were the vehicle of the Gospel's communication, and indeed provided the multifaceted expression of each model itself. "To be wise I must know all things as one; to be knowing I must perceive the absolutely indivisible as infinitely distinguishable." Religious language consists of "words that convey all their separate meanings at once, no matter how incomprehensible or absurd their collective meaning may be". Instinctively the Fathers knew what Coleridge thus expressed: somehow Christ *is* both shepherd and lamb, priest and victim.[12]

III. Essentially my third point has already been made. Only those conceptions of atonement which can embrace this richness of metaphor are truly successful. Simple transactional theories, whether involving the appeasement of God or the devil, and doctrines which focus exclusively on either the objective or the subjective aspect of atonement, just cannot be found in the patristic literature, and are quite simply destructive of the integrity of their imaginative vision.

Maybe we need to reclaim something of that approach. The Fathers could multiply images: Ephrem spoke of the three wombs of Christ — Mary, Jordan, and Sheol, Gregory Nazianzen of our three births — natural, by baptism, through resurrection. Jonah's emergence from the whale was an expression of Christ's resurrection and our redemption. Modern distinctions between allegory and typology break down as the Paschal Homilies imaginatively bring every detail of Passover and Exodus into relationship with Passion and Easter. The trouble with allegory is that it can sometimes be as flat and uninspired as an explained joke. The glory of both typology and allegory is the possibility of a poetic integration which can only be expressed in imaginative language, and has its own way of compelling conviction. Christian art depended on such symbolism, and iconography is therefore far from idolatry: its non-literal reference was built into its content, and quite explicit.[13].

But maybe we cannot reclaim that imaginative integration. Maybe our culture has become so impoverished in the matter-of-factness of science and history that we can never do justice to the 'tropological' character of religious language. Yet the best science, like the best poetry and the best art, depends upon bursting the restrictions of common sense and imagining new creative possibilities.[14] What we need is the right criteria for testing the insights of imaginative intuition. Vision is in danger of getting lost because of our fear of fantasy. Perhaps we will never appreciate what atonement is about until we dare imagine the marriage of heaven and hell.

Notes

[1] Eric Osborn, *The Beginning of Christian Philosophy* (CUP: 1981).
[2] H. Rashdall, *The Idea of Atonement in Christian Theology* (1919); J. Rivière, *The Doctrine of Atonement* (ET: 1909).
[3] G. Aulen, *Christus Victor* (SPCK: 1931); H.E.W. Turner, *The Patristic Doctrine of Redemption* (Mowbray: 1952).
[4] E.g. R.C. Gregg and D.E. Groh, *Early Arianism* (Fortress: 1981).
[5] For this paragraph I acknowledge a debt to John Coulson, *Religion and Imagination* 'in aid of a grammar of assent' (OUP: 1981).
[6] Published by J. Neville Birdsall in "Diatessaric Readings in the 'Martyrdom of St. Abo of Tiflis'?" in *New Testament Textual Criticism* Essays in Honour of Bruce M. Metzger, edited by E.J. Epp & G.D. Fee (OUP: 1981), pp. 313-324.

III

[7] Loc. cit., p. 320.
[8] Text in *GCS*; ET in the additional volume to *ANCL*.
[9] Text edited and translated by R.W. Thompson in *Oxford Early Christian Texts* (OUP: 1971).
[10] For further discussion see chapter 2 in my *From Nicaea to Chalcedon* (SCM: 1983).
[11] Text in *Sources Chrétiennes*; ET in *ANCL*.
[12] Cf. John Coulson, *op. cit.*, chapter 1, to whom I am indebted for the quotations from Coleridge.
[13] This paragraph arises from points noted in a Birmingham University M.Litt. thesis by Jill Storer, *The Anastasis in Byzantine Iconography* (1986), and reflections upon it.
[14] See Arthur Koestler, *The Act of Creation* (Hutchinson: 1964; Pan: 1970).

IV

The rhetorical schools and their influence on patristic exegesis

To honour Henry Chadwick is to honour the great tradition of British scholarship to which Edwin Hatch belonged. The work of Edwin Hatch was the inspiration of this paper, and it may be regarded as a celebration of the centenary of the publication of his Hibbert lectures of 1888, as well as a tribute to one who, like him, has achieved international acclaim for his erudition.

Some of what Hatch pioneered in those lectures on *The Influence of Greek Ideas on Christianity* has become commonplace, but not all.[1] It was the content of the first three lectures which provided the starting point of this study, those on Greek education and its legacy, on the influence of Greek methods of exegesis on Christian exegesis, and on the debt Christian preaching owed to Greek rhetoric.

By the Christian era, there was long established a system of education based upon the study of literature and practical exercises in speech-making.[2] As Hatch explained, literature from the distant past was powerful speech preserved from a Golden Age, which could act as a model for those who produced literary exercises to be declaimed. The teaching of the grammaticus and the rhetor in each city's gymnasium was the principal agent for the spread of Hellenistic culture throughout the then known world, and for its ongoing transmission through approximately 800 years.[3]

Hatch stressed the hold the educational system had upon the society into which Christianity came, and showed how inevitably it would affect the emerging church. He then went on to explore Greek and Christian exegesis. His conclusion that Christian allegory derives via Philo from the way Greeks treated Homer is now commonplace. Sensitively he helps us to appreciate how the ancients were affected by the mystery of writing, reverence for antiquity and belief in inspiration, as a prelude to

The rhetorical schools

describing the place Homer had in Greek culture: literature, especially ancient and revered literature, was assumed to be universal, to be wisdom for all time. Drawing moral lessons from literature was normal practice.

But Hatch made little of the fact that the humanistic thrust and this-worldly ideals of rhetorical education were frequently in conflict with the ideals of philosophy[4] – tension between two opposed educational ideals is already there in Plato's disputes with the Sophists and his reservations about poetry. It is true that Aristotle and his successors regarded all areas of research as open to the philosopher, and literary criticism, linguistic analysis and rhetorical techniques were placed on the philosopher's agenda. Indeed, the Stoics pioneered the classification and analysis of grammar and figures of speech which was used in the Hellenistic schools. Undoubtedly each had a profound effect upon the other and some important figures would have claimed both traditions: Cicero, Plutarch, Dio Chrysostom, for example. Nevertheless, tension and accommodation oscillated in the relationship between philosophy and rhetoric: philosophy accused rhetoric of being merely an empty technique with no moral purpose, practised by those who wanted to get ahead in the world; rhetoric countered by emphasizing its moral aspects, its aim being to prepare the pupils to play an active and effective role in civic and political life. On rhetoric's side, philosophy was sneered at as withdrawal from the world, or as useless speculation, the profound disagreement between philosophical schools only reinforcing the criticisms. Indeed, rhetoric was certainly the more pervasive and influential: philosophy was the crown of education for a few, but many studied rhetoric, and over those 800 years the character of education changed only in the proliferation of technical terms and more refined formal analyses.

Hatch tends to imply that nearly all interpretation was affected by the search for symbolical meanings. Certainly everyone looked for the moral of the tale, but symbolical allegory was not universal. The tracing of doctrines, or universal truths, or metaphysical and psychological theories by means of allegorical reading was characteristic of the philosophers, especially the Stoics, but was not, I suggest, the universal way of reading literature in the ancient educational system – indeed, hardly characteristic of the grammar and rhetorical schools. Symbolic allegory was characteristic of a philosophical approach to literature; the rival rhetorical approach sought to derive moral principles, useful instruction and ethical models from their study of literature. This approach, I suggest, informed Antiochene exegesis of the Bible with its reaction against Origenist allegory.

EXEGESIS IN THE RHETORICAL SCHOOLS

What then were the methods of exegesis practised in the schools? The biggest problem is the dearth of direct evidence about what went on in the grammaticus' classroom, or indeed how the rhetor would comment on literature. It was, like school teaching in every age, an oral medium. By contrast we know a lot about how speeches were constructed and how school exercises were set and composed, both from papyri and from text-books. Systematic studies of style and construction are readily available. Inevitably it is on the acquiring of such formal rhetorical techniques that most modern studies of Greek education have focussed, because that is what we have evidence for.[5] Apart from some scholia and marginalia, we do not have notes on texts.[6]

But we can glean some information. Quintilian is one of our most informative sources.[7] True he was not a Greek rhetor, but in his position as first official state rhetor in Rome, he certainly practised Greek rhetoric in a Latin medium, and after his retirement wrote a massive book on rhetorical education. Cross-checks with Greek sources where they can be effected confirm that his methods and aims were essentially the same as those that had been and would be practised for centuries. The chief value of Quintilian's work for our purposes is that he does not assume we know what went on in the elementary stages, as most sources do. So he provides the only summary account we have of the use of literature in the school classes of the grammaticus.

Correct reading precedes interpretation, says Quintilian. It is important to remind ourselves that correct reading was itself a process of exegesis, since words were not divided, there was no punctuation and not all hand-written copies in the class would be identical. Teachers had to begin by establishing an agreed text and rejecting spurious material, and by discussing how a text was to be read. All reading in the ancient world was reading aloud. A text was a form of speech which had to be realized to make sense, rather as a musical score means little to many until it is played.

But more than correct reading is involved in interpretation. The linguistic aspect requires considerable scholarship: much literature being very ancient and containing unfamiliar archaic words and forms,

The rhetorical schools

vocabulary and parsing is bound to occupy the class. Quintilian himself dwells upon the problem of distinguishing the consonantal use of the semivowels 'u' and 'i' in Latin, as well as conjugation, parts of speech, the construing of sentences, etc. The situation with respect to the Homeric dialect of Greek would be even more acute. Much of school comment on literature was clearly concerned with basic linguistic correctness. But the good teacher also expounded the origin and meaning of names as part of this grammatical instruction. Tracing etymologies was certainly a very important activity in commenting on texts in schools.

Quintilian regrets that many teachers do not pay enough attention to these preliminary mechanical foundations, but rush on to display the more interesting aspects of their act. Of these, style was clearly of supreme importance. By noticing how great authors produced stylistic effects, the pupil was prepared for producing his own stylistic compositions under the rhetor. Quintilian recognizes that there is a literary vocabulary which in itself gives the impression of the 'sublime', but he insists that it is the combination of appropriate words in connected speech that also produces real excellence. Teachers therefore need to be discriminating as they note barbarisms, grammatical solecisms and ugly combinations of syllables – not the sort of thing to be imitated, unless a particular kind of effect is required. Comment will be made on foreign words, their origins and how to decline them. The use of metaphor and archaisms will be carefully and judiciously considered. 'Language is based on reason, antiquity, authority and usage', says Quintilian. Coining new words or forms or metaphors is less acceptable than following literary usage. Adopting current speech habits, especially those of the uneducated, is to be frowned upon. So noting proper stylistic usage is a most important function of studying literature.

So what the teacher does, as he reads in class with his pupils the great corpus of classical literature Quintilian recommends, is to analyse a verse into parts of speech, metre, etc., to note linguistic usage, especially commenting on acceptable and unacceptable usage and style, to discuss the different meanings which may be given to each word, to expound unusual words, to elucidate figures of speech or ornamental devices, and to 'impress on the minds of the pupils the value of proper arrangement and of graceful treatment of the matter in hand'. In addition to this he will explain the stories – unpack allusions to classical myths, gods, heroes, legends, histories – not in too much detail, advises Quintilian, nor in too many versions. The mind must not be swamped.

Commentaries are full of such erudition. Nevertheless, the exploration of these background points is important, and these two aspects of exegesis are called *methodikē* and *historikē*. The study of literature with the rhetor became even more pragmatic, as the great orators and prose-writers were used principally as models for rhetorical composition. We are now told more about curriculum than method. Yet there are some clues, and the very technicality of the rhetor's analysis of how a speech should be composed is a good indication of the kind of thing they would be looking for in studying literature. Quintilian passes rhetorical judgment on the classical authors he lists, and in the literary essays of Dionysius of Halicarnassus, the search for standard *aretai* and the application of technical rhetorical distinctions provide criteria for critical assessment.[8]

The principal categories are *ho pragmatikos topos* (or *res*), that is the subject-matter; the area determined by the author's *heuresis* or *inventio*, his skill in presenting and manipulating the material; and *ho lektikos topos* (or *onomata*, *verba*), that is, the style and vocabulary, which the rhetor tended to treat not as integral to the subject but as a separate matter. Undoubtedly the latter interest was predominant: whether a thing was in a plain style, a grand style or a middle style would be carefully computed according to choice of words, their arrangement, the figures of speech and the presence or absence of certain *aretai*, which included purity of language, lucidity, brevity, vividness, character-drawing, emotional power, magnificence, vigour and effectiveness, charm and permissiveness, and propriety.[9] Still, for all the emphasis on style, it is clear that the rhetor was also interested in how the author chose, delimited and handled his theme, how he divided up and arranged the subject-matter, how he drew his characters and produced his effects, how the thrust or intention was actually conveyed or concealed by the adoption of certain techniques.[10] If the exegesis practised in the schools appears at first sight to be piecemeal, and principally concerned with the outer dress of diction and style, the commonplace that language was mere clothing meant that the thought enunciated also needed distinguishing. The author, it was assumed, had a subject to cover or thesis to propound, like those set as exercises for the budding rhetor. So comment included discerning this. Rhetorical criticism, however, was always 'audience-orientated': it always looked for the effect produced, and this was one of many features which blocked the development of historical criticism, or an awareness of the difference between what the author intended and what the interpreter might discern. There was some gossipy biographical interest, but no true historical sense.[11] So all interpretation would tend to be anachronistic.

So, as we can confirm from other sources too,[12] school exegesis consisted of: (i) *diorthōsis* – the establishment of agreement about the text to be read; (ii) *anagnōsis* – the construal and correct reading of it; (iii) *exēgēsis* – the *methodikē* and *historikē* described earlier, comments on language and explanatory notes on all kinds of narrative references, not just what we would call history: places, dates, genealogies, characters, actions, events, whether historical or mythological; (iv) *krisis* – the discernment of the good, the judgment of the poets.

Now *krisis* clearly needs more discussion, though our main source, Quintilian, does not treat it. It apparently included literary, or perhaps we should say rhetorical, evaluation; and questions of authenticity, relative dating, etc., were certainly raised.[13] Yet *krisis* seems on the whole to have been less aesthetic or critical in our sense, than moral, the search for *aretē*, virtue, not just for *aretai*, stylistic excellences. The educator sought moral lessons in literature.

As is well known, Plato had raised doubts about the moral influence of the poets, and literature had to be defended against these charges. Plutarch is one of many who advised various methods of extracting moral advice from literature and neutralizing its potentially adverse moral effect.[14] Poetry he regarded as a seductive form of deception: but prospective philosophers he advises to use poetry as an introductory exercise, and to develop their moral sense by exercising critical judgment. The poets tell lies, so text must be weighed against text, and the poet's real intention thus uncovered. Admonition and instruction is implied in the invention of tales and myths as examples of good and bad conduct. Context and circumstances may modify our apprehension of the sense of the words, as may careful attention to the kind of alternative meanings taught by the grammaticus. Poetry is 'true to life' in its inextricable mixture of good and evil: so moral judgment is important, and the young should be urged to emulate the virtuous. Plutarch advocates a kind of moral 'pruning' which lays bare the profitable things that are hidden under the prolific foliage of poetic diction and clustering tales. This kind of moral criticism was adopted by the rhetorical schools enthusiastically, and the discussion of moral virtues was included among the themes adopted for practice declamations. Thus as Plutarch recommended, the student of poetry with the grammaticus would be used to bringing poetry out of the realm of myth and impersonation through discussing ethical doctrines, and moral philosophy would not come as a shock at a later stage in his education.

So the study of literature critically meant the discernment of moral good as much as aesthetic good. Such procedures, and indeed the search for etymologies too, could be conducive to the development of allegory. But symbolic allegory of the kind practised by the Stoics, seems not to have been characteristic in the schools of the grammaticus and rhetor, except in so far as they came under the influence of philosophical schools. Plutarch expected the teachers of literature to discover moral lessons, not cosmological or mystical meanings. He was hostile to Stoic allegorizing of the poets, in spite of his own use of allegory in religious and philosophical treatises. Perhaps we should conclude there was allegory and allegory – reading texts symbolically and mystically was philosophical whereas reading texts to tease out a moral was rhetorical.

So in spite of the mutual influence of rhetoric and philosophy, it seems likely that there were two overlapping yet distinct traditions when it came to treating literature. They had linguistic, textual and etymological interests in common, and philosophy built upon and embraced the techniques of school exegesis. Yet there were two distinct attitudes to a text's fundamental meaning and reference and how these were to be discerned. Where philosophy found abstract doctrines or virtues through verbal allegory, rhetoric looked for concrete ethical examples in a narrative, and for models of excellence both stylistic and moral in the construction and presentation of the whole. Plutarch's discussion also demonstrates, by the way, that when Basil, in his *Address to young men on how they might profit from pagan literature*,[15] advised parents and young people to allow the usual education curriculum to train the mind while discriminating between the morally useful and the harmful, he was drawing upon an ancient commonplace, and not devising some peculiar Christian double-think.

ANTIOCHENE EXEGESIS

The basic thesis being presented is that the Origenist tradition adopted the allegorical techniques of the philosophical schools, and the Antiochene reaction was the protest of rhetoric against such a way of handling texts. In view of what has been said about the absence of interest in history, this suggestion may appear incompatible with the standard characterization of Antiochene exegesis, emphasizing its concern with the 'literal' meaning and historical reference of the Bible.

The rhetorical schools

But this characterization has introduced all kinds of problems into understanding what the Antiochenes were doing. If we look at their work, we find a profoundly dogmatic exegesis, and in most cases, an attitude to typology and prophecy which sits very uncomfortably with their so-called historical approach. Rowan Greer has tried to explain it in exclusively theological terms.[16] What makes the difference between Antiochene and Alexandrian exegesis, he claims, is their different fundamental theological frameworks, rather than a particular methodology: 'theology...shapes exegesis in the sense that it determines the questions asked of the text'. There is a great deal in this. But my suggestion that the exegetical debate reflected a difference within Greco-Roman culture about how to treat texts, means that the question of method remains relevant, and also accounts for those features of Antiochene exegesis which sit so ill at ease with attempts to characterize it as if it were the precursor of modern historico-critical method. There was no genuine historical criticism in antiquity. The Antiochenes do take *historia* seriously, but in the sense of *to historikon*.

Is there any plausibility in the basic idea that rhetoric influenced the Antiochenes? What do we know about their education?[17] Well, John Chrysostom studied with the famous pagan rhetorician, Libanius, who claimed he would have been his successor if the Christians had not stolen him. He received the nickname 'Golden-mouth', like a famous rhetorician before him, and his reputation was for public speaking. Theodore of Mopsuestia is probably to be identified with John Chrysostom's student friend, Theodore, in which case he had the same education. Their Christian biblical teacher was Diodore: let his enemy Julian the Apostate characterize him:

> Diodore, a charlatan priest of the Nazarene...is clearly a sharp-witted sophist of that rustic creed...For he sailed to Athens to the detriment of the public welfare, rashly taking to philosophy and literature, and arming his tongue with rhetorical devices against the heavenly gods.

No wonder Julian banished Christians from the schools – much to the fury of educated church leaders like Gregory of Nazianzus. Diodore was a Christian Sophist, and a dangerous opponent of his pagan revival in Antioch. As for Theodoret, he may insist that he received all his education from monks, he may describe Diodore and Theodore as his teachers, but every word he writes proclaims his training in the classical *paideia*; he quotes Homer, Sophocles, Euripides, Aristophanes, Demosthenes and Thucydides, and his correspondents include distinguished sophists. The Antiochenes had a rhetorical education. Evidence of formal philosophical training is less apparent.

Turning to their exegesis, what do we find? Characteristic of both commentaries and homilies are opening chapters or paragraphs discerning the *hupothesis* of the book to be studied, or of the passage to be treated. Details of the text are then examined point by point. Details commented upon range from discussion of alternative readings and their relative merits, questions of correct punctuation and how the sentences are to be construed, together with problems of translation where applicable, to etymologies, explanations of foreign and unfamiliar words, attention to metaphor and other figures of speech, and mini-treatises, with masses of scriptural cross-references, on the special biblical flavour of particular words or phrases. What is this but the *methodikē* of the schools? The commentaries further explore the context and sequence of thought, test text against text, as Plutarch recommended, and explain or debate the reference of the text, by outlining what is known of the time of the prophet or, say, the events of Paul's life. Here they speak of the *historia*, and they are concerned to get it right: Theodoret maintained that Paul had visited and knew the church at Colossae, though Theodore had denied this. Yet what is this but the *historikē* of the schools? To jump to the conclusion that they had the same kind of historical interest as modern critics is perhaps understandable, but it is not always convincing. After all, Theodore in commenting on the Psalms recognized that 'By the waters of Babylon, there we sat down…' referred to the exile, but that did not mean drawing critical historical conclusions in our sense. The Psalms were all written by David, so David must have been prophesying. Of course, they usually assumed that the reference was to facts – unless the text was metaphorical, parabolic, clearly intended as a fable, or to be taken as prophetic – in which case the text refers to what it prophesies however veiled the reference. It is quite misleading to view their work as some kind of historical criticism, and to assume that it was a historical concern which produced the protest against allegory. What they were concerned to do was to take the thrust of the text seriously, rather than dissipate or distort it in word-by-word allegory. So much is this the case that many readers both ancient and modern have commented upon the dull and pedestrian character of Antiochene commentaries, which rarely rise above the commonsense 'nitty-gritty' of exegesis or simple paraphrase.

Summary and paraphrase is a persistent Antiochene technique for bringing out the gist of the argument, and the *hupothesis* usually includes this, together with historical or circumstantial introductory material. This technique ensures that context and thrust were not lost under the mass of detailed commentary. Without doubt the discussion of subject-matter in the schools, which included the *hupothesis* and sought to discern the underlying 'idea' dressed up in the words of the text, lies behind this. Theodore in particular was concerned with what he called the *skopos* of the text – its aim or intent, setting this up as a principle against piecemeal interpretation, and insisting that a text has only one *skopos*. This had some notorious consequences, like his denial that Psalm 22 referred to the Passion, despite its appearance on the lips of Jesus in the Gospels, on the grounds that the speaker refers elsewhere in the Psalm to his sins. I have not been able to document the use of *skopos* as a technical term in the schools,[18] but certainly the practice of providing *hupotheseis*, which often outline the *skopos*, appears to have its background in the school treatment of literature.

The use of typology by the Antiochenes may well have some background in literary theory, as well. Theodore accepts that Jonah prefigures Jesus because the extraordinary events of his life signify by *mimēsis* Christ's rejection, resurrection and conversion of the Gentiles. Now *mimēsis* was a key term in ancient literary criticism,[19] and carried implications very different from the fables and fantasies of allegorical interpretation. Literature imitates life, and can therefore be instructive, particularly in the moral sphere. This view, coupled with the long-standing Christian tradition of seeing everything in the Old Testament as prophetic, gave Theodore a method of appropriating some typological exegeses, in spite of his very radical views on the difference between Old and New Testaments. Key Old Testament narratives prefigured by *mimēsis* the events of the New. As for dogmatic exegesis, Hatch noted that ancient texts were universally assumed to contain abiding truths, to be useful and instructive. As we have seen, there was no real awareness in antiquity of the difference between what an author intended and what the interpreter might discern, still less of historical distance. Is it surprising that fifth-century theologians could discern no difference between the theology of Paul and their own doctrine, or that Theodore believed that the purpose of a commentary was to deal with problem texts, particularly those twisted by the heretics?

As is well known, Theodore was somewhat extreme in his exegetical principles, even among the Antiochenes. Theodoret allows a text more than one *skopos*, and permits a far greater range of traditional prophetic and typological meanings – indeed, you might call some of them allegorical, like his acceptance from Origen (against Theodore) that the Song of Songs referred to the marriage of Christ and the Church. But there is allegory and allegory – and on the whole the *theōria* he employs is far removed from the kind of thing Alexandrian allegory produced. His methods are fundamentally akin to those of Theodore. It is the 'nitty-gritty' of exegesis which exercises him – the *methodikē* and the *historikē* – the latter embracing more prophetic references. Furthermore, Theodoret generally focusses on morals drawn from the text, rather than imaginative or mystical speculations.

The propensity to draw morals from the text is most dramatically evidenced in Chrysostom's homilies. Chrysostom shares all the methods described, but he is preaching, and he tends not to burden his congregation with too much *methodikē*. However, expounding the *historia* is important, though not because it is historical, but because it becomes exemplary. Whatever he is commenting upon is turned into a moral lesson, an example, an exhortation. The anhistorical character of Chrysostom's exegesis is evident in another feature, namely the way he collapses the time-gap between, say, Paul's church at Corinth and his own congregation, by reading between the lines to bring out the tone of Paul's voice and his use of tactics to win over his hearers.[20] The preacher makes Paul address his own congregation as he elucidates what response he wished to draw out of his readers. Paul's oscillation between praise and blame, severity and tenderness, humility and assertion, is part of his subtle handling of the Corinthians in their disunity, immorality, pride and disloyalty: that one minute Paul scares them and the next minute softens his words to win them belongs to the 'economy' of his discourse – the term 'economy' being one of the terms of rhetorical criticism for 'arrangement' of the subject-matter. What is this then but the audience-oriented criticism of the rhetor, used now not to train budding declaimers to manipulate an audience, but to facilitate the appropriate moral response from the congregation? And where else did the constant moralizing come from but the educator's search for morally edifying examples? It was, after all, morals that Plutarch thought the poets taught.

This moralizing is of a very different flavour from the moral and spiritual meanings discerned by Origen. Chrysostom sees morality in terms of exemplary deeds not abstract virtues, and, whether it is Paul or Abraham, it is to their exemplary character and practice to which he draws attention. A good example of the kind of difference in interest between someone like Chrysostom and someone like Origen can be found in comparison of their respective comments upon Matthew's Feeding-story. Origen,[21] in his Commentary, takes the story as symbolical of spiritual feeding, seeing the desert-place as representing the desert condition of the masses without the Law and the Word of God, and explaining that the disciples are given power to nourish the crowds with rational food. The five loaves and two fish are interpreted in terms of scripture and the Logos. Chrysostom,[22] however, turns the story into proofs of dogma and moral lessons – Christ looks up to heaven to prove he is of the Father, and he uses the loaves and fish rather than creating food out of nothing to stop the mouths of dualistic heretics like Marcion and Manichaeus. He let the crowds become hungry and only gave them loaves and fish, equally distributed, to teach the crowd humility, temperance and charity, and to have all things in common. He wanted to ensure that they did not become slaves of the belly – and that comment allows Chrysostom the chance to preach detachment from worldly pursuits. This is no more historical or literal than Origen's allegory. It has its basis in the search for morals in literature characteristic of the rhetorical schools.

THE REJECTION OF ALLEGORY

So neither literalism nor an interest in history stimulated the Antiochene reaction against Origenist allegory, but rather a different approach to finding meaning in literature which had its background in the rhetorical schools. This suggestion is confirmed by the one complete surviving work of Eustathius of Antioch, *On the Witch of Endor and Against Origen*.[23]

Quasten remarks, 'Eustathius rejects not only Origen's interpretation of this particular passage but his entire allegorical exegesis, because it deprives scripture of its historical character.' To look at the treatise is to discover very quickly that that is a most misleading statement. It is true that Eustathius begins by attacking Origen for paying attention to *onomata* (names, terms) rather than *pragmata* (deeds, events), but the ensuing discussion proves that what he means by the distinction is analogous to the categories *pragmatikos topos* and *lektikos topos* (or *onomata*) that we found in Dionysius of Halicarnassus. Eustathius objects to Origen's verbal or lexical approach to the text, without paying regard to the subject-matter. Origen is in this case *too literal*!

It appears that Origen has made certain deductions about the resurrection on the basis of the statement that the Witch summoned up

Samuel from Hades. Eustathius argues that only God can raise up the dead, therefore the Witch cannot have done it. Samuel was not raised at all: rather the devil used the Witch to play upon the mad mind of Saul and induce him to believe he saw Samuel. The whole treatise is a series of rationalistic arguments to prove that Origen's literal reading of the text is totally along the wrong lines, and so everything he deduces from it is unacceptable. According to Eustathius, the thrust of the whole tells against Origen's view. It is Saul who *thinks* he sees Samuel – there is no statement anywhere that he actually did.

And so it goes on: rationalistic arguments and scripture parallels justifying a more satisfactory but less literal interpretation than that of Origen. Every detail of the conversation between Saul and the Witch is exploited to show that it represents the dissimulations of the devil and makes sense no other way, and the scriptural laws against sorcery and consulting mediums confirm that the words of the Witch must be treated as false. Eustathius even justifies his non-literal interpretation by giving examples of other scriptural narratives where details are not spelled out verbally but left to commonsense inference.

Now clearly we cannot explore every detail of Eustathius' argument, but there are some points worth noting: Eustathius is really worried about the doctrines Origen deduces from the text, not about his allegorical method. He does, in a long aside, object to the fact that Origen allegorizes Moses' accounts of creation, paradise and many other things, including gospel-narratives which Eustathius thinks should be taken literally, but his point is that it is scandalous to allegorize those things and then treat this story literally, especially when it leads one into blasphemous conclusions. Eustathius is objecting to methods which ignore the sequence of the story, the intention of the story-writer and the coherence of the narrative with the rest of scripture. He argues that the very word *eggastrimuthos* shows that the story-writer meant to imply the Witch was false. It is at this point that he takes a particularly interesting line. He refers to the definition of 'myth' in rhetorical textbooks as a fiction made up for pleasure and also for a purpose. Fiction is a plausible *mimēsis* of reality, like painting, but it creates unreal things. Myths are a way of educating children (and Plato's advice to parents is here quoted), but Greek children are eventually taught to distinguish between truth and fiction. Eustathius' purpose is to prove his basic point: the *eggastrimuthos* has myths created in her inward parts, her stomach rather than her mind, by the devil. In the process he uses standard etymological techniques, explicitly refers to literary-critical observations about art being a *mimēsis* of life, makes a learned reference to Plato as any well-educated teacher would, and actually mentions rhetorical textbooks.

Clearly the source of his methods lies in the schools. All through the piece he insists on looking for the actual *historia* of the *gramma*: this is surely not 'history' in the modern sense, but something like the narrative logic of the text – making sense of the whole sequence of events described, is more or less his own phrase. He is looking for a coherent account of things. His objection to Origen is that, whether he takes a text literally or allegorically, he is too concerned with the verbal level of the text, and not with its thrust or subject-matter.

Doubtless Eustathius assumed a correlation between this 'thrust of the text' and 'what really happened'. But he was no historical critic. He was simply using standard literary techniques deriving from the treatment of texts in the rhetorical schools to protest against esoteric philosophical deductions being made in what he regarded as an arbitrary way. One thing he was keen to show is that Origen appeals to other scriptures which were inappropriate and unconvincing while ignoring genuinely relevant passages. In other words Origen's methods were arbitrary and his conclusions unreliable: this story is not about the resurrection. To prove this Eustathius attempts to interpret instead by *methodikē* and *historikē* – not historically in the modern sense, nor literally, but according to the rationalistic literary-critical methods current in the contemporary educational practice of grammaticus and rhetor. In this he was the precursor of Diodore, Theodore, Chrysostom and Theodoret, and perhaps the successor of that shadowy but influential biblical scholar, Lucian of Antioch.

CONCLUSION

If this line of approach is accepted, then it helps to explain some other puzzles about patristic exegesis. Why is it so difficult to 'place' the exegesis of people like the Cappadocians? Often it has been stated that they are closer to the Antiochenes in method than to Origen – yet they were great admirers and students of Origen, and occasionally used allegory in a distinctly Origenist way. How can their exegesis be explained? We now have the key. They had all been trained according to the classical *paideia*, and naturally used rhetorical techniques in commenting upon literature, in spite of their philosophical interests. Basil even taught as a rhetor before abandoning a lucrative career to become a monk and eventually a bishop. In the *Hexaemeron* he discusses and mocks the various theories of philosophers in true rhetorical style. His brother, Gregory of Nyssa, also had a rhetorical career, until rescued by his pious and domineering sister; and Rosemary Ruether has characterized the vacillating career of their friend, Gregory of Nazianzus, as a constant battle between the ideals of rhetoric and philosophy in Christianized forms.[24] It is in the preaching of the Cappadocians that Christian panegyric flowers, orations celebrating saints and martyrs which follow all the stylistic techniques and devices of the rhetorical text-books.[25] It was a form later embraced and perfected by Chrysostom. Is it not clear that their exegetical work came under the same rhetorical influences?

How far back in the history of the church does this influence from the schools go? To take up Hatch's third Hibbert lecture on Greek and Christian rhetoric is scarcely possible at this stage, and must await another occasion. But perhaps I may conclude by hazarding the suggestion that from a very early date the homily was the bishop's lecture on the literature that really mattered, namely the scriptures. Everyone studied week by week with the Christian 'grammaticus'. Origen was an innovator, not because he was the first rhetorical exegete, as Hatch supposed, but because he was the first philosophical exegete, offering higher education somewhat in competition with the bishop's 'school'. The Antiochenes belonged to the older tradition, and in reaction to Origen, deepened it and refined it.

NOTES

1 Edwin Hatch, *The Influence of Greek Ideas on Christianity*, Harper Torchbooks, New York 1957: reprinted by arrangements with Williams and Norgate, London. Note the foreword with notes and bibliography by Frederick C. Grant to be found in this reprint edition.

2 On ancient education see H.-I. Marrou, *L'Education dans l'Antiquité*. Paris 1948, ET New York, 1956; Werner Jaeger, *Paideia: the Ideals of Greek Culture*, 3 vols.; ET Gilbert Highet, Oxford 1943–5; George Kennedy, *The Art of Persuasion in Greek*, Princeton 1963, *The Art of Rhetoric in the Roman World*, Princeton 1972, *Greek Rhetoric under Christian Emperors*, Princeton 1983, and *Classical Rhetoric and its Christian and Secular Tradition from Ancient to Modern Times*, University of North Carolina 1980; R. W. Smith, *The Art of Rhetoric in Alexandria*, The Hague, 1974; D. L. Clark, *Rhetoric in Greco-Roman Education*, New York 1957.

3 On Hellenization see Moses Hadas, *Hellenistic Culture*, New York and Oxford 1959; Martin Hengel, *Judaism and Hellenism*, London 1974; Emil

The rhetorical schools

Schurer, *The History of the Jewish People in the Age of Jesus Christ*, vol. 2, rev. and ed. by Geza Vermes, Fergus Millar and Matthew Black, Edinburgh 1979; A. H. M. Jones, *The Greek City from Alexander to Justinian*, Oxford 1940.

4 On the conflict between rhetoric and philosophy see: Jaeger, *Paideia*; Marrou, *L'Education dans l'Antiquité*; Kennedy, *The Art of Persuasion in Greek*; Rosemary Radford Ruether, *Gregory of Nazianzus. Rhetor and Philosopher*, Oxford, 1969. The classic study is the Introduction, 'Sophistik, Rhetorik, Philosophie, in ihrem Kampf um die Jugendbildung', to H. von Arnim, *Leben und Werke des Dio von Prusa*, Berlin 1898, pp. 1–114.

5 On rhetoric and rhetorical handbooks see: Marrou, *L'Education dans l'Antiquité*; Kennedy, *The Art of Persuasion, The Art of Rhetoric, Greek Rhetoric*; Smith, *The Art of Rhetoric in Alexandria: Menander Rhetor*, ed. with trans. and commentary D. A. Russell and N. G. Wilson, Oxford 1981. Useful texts include Aristotle, *Ars rhetorica*; Cicero, *De oratore, et al.*; Demetrius, *On Style*; Longinus, *On the Sublime*; Quintilian, *Institutio oratoria*; *Rhetorica ad Herennium* – all accessible in the Loeb Classical Library. Marrou is the exception to my comment that modern studies focus mainly on rhetorical composition. George Kennedy, like Hatch, has only a brief couple of paragraphs in *The Art of Persuasion*, and a summary of what Quintilian says in his *Quintilian*, New York 1969. More helpful are the accounts of ancient literary criticism, but these tend to be based on treatises like Aristotle's *Poetics* and Longinus, *On the Sublime*. Exegetical practice in the schools is barely discussed, largely for lack of evidence. See D. A. Russell, *Criticism in Antiquity*, London 1981, and the selection of texts in D. A. Russell and M. Winterbottom, *Ancient Literary Criticism*, Oxford 1972. Good evidence is probably provided by the critical essays of Dionysius of Halicarnassus: see further below.

6 H.-I. Marrou, *L'Education dans l'Antiquité*, p. 229: the scholia in manuscripts and papyri may provide an echo of the classroom, but the evidence is meagre. For examples of scholia, comment and lexica, see *Sammlung griechischer und lateinischer Grammatiker*, ed. Klaus Alpers, Hartment Erbse and Alexander Kleinlogel. Vol. 3 contains *Die Fragmente des Grammatikers Dionysios Thrax. Die Fragmente der Grammatiker Tyrannion und Diokles Apions Glössai Homērikai*. This confirms an interest in alternative readings, definitions, synonyms, etymologies and other lexicographical points.

7 *Institutio oratoria* i.iv–ix – text in Loeb Classical Library. See also George Kennedy, *Quintilian*.

8 Quintilian, *Inst. orat.* x.i and ii; Dionysius of Halicarnassus, *On Literary Composition*, Introduction, translation, and notes by W. Rhys Roberts, London 1910, and *Critical Essays*, vol. 1, Loeb Classical Library 1974 – see especially the *De Thucydide* (the translation and commentary by W. Pritchett, University of California Press 1975, is also useful). The interest in

classification, and ultimately *mimēsis*, pervades these works. Dionysius also wrote a treatise on *mimēsis*, now lost, but known through epitomes and his own description in his letter to Ptolemaeus: see Dionysius of Halicarnassus, *The Three Literary Letters*, ed. and trans. by W. Rhys Roberts, Cambridge 1901.

9   A useful table will be found in S. F. Bonner, *The Literary Treatises of Dionysius of Halicarnassus*, Cambridge 1939, p. 24.

10 Ibid., 84ff., commenting on the *De Thucydide*. Also Pritchett, *De Thucydide*, p. xxxvi, for summary table of the rhetorical system of Dionysius. The *pragmatikos topos* involved discussion of *hupothesis, diairesis, taxis* and *exergasia*.

11 See particularly D. A. Russell, *Criticism in Antiquity*, especially ch.8 on rhetoric, and ch.11 on literary history.

12 See H.-I. Marrou, *L'Education dans l'Antiquité*, pp. 230ff, and particularly Dionysius Thrax, *Ars grammatica*, ed. G. Uhlig, Leipzig 1883. This treatise is principally about grammar in the technical sense, but in the opening paragraph Dionysius distinguishes six components of *grammatikē*, which is defined as '*empeiria tōn para poiētais te kai suggrapheusin hōs epi to polu legomenon*':

anagnōsis entribēs kata prosōdian;
exēgēsis kata tous enuparchontas poiētikous tropous;
glossōn te kai historiōn procheiros apodosis;
etunologias heuresis;
analogias eklogismos;
krisis poiēmatōn, ho dē kalliston esti pantōn tōn en tē(i) technē(i).

13 See e.g. Dionysius of Halicarnassus, *Epistle to Ammaeus* I, in Rhys Roberts (ed.), *Three Literary Letters*.

14 Plutarch, *Moralia* I, Loeb Classical Library, 1927. N.B. *On the Education of Children* and *How the young man should study poetry*.

15 Ed. N. G. Wilson, *St Basil on the value of Greek Literature*, London, 1975. Trans. in Basil of Caesarea, *Letters*, vol. 4, Loeb Classical Library.

16 Rowan A. Greer, *The Captain of our Salvation. A study in the Patristic Exegesis of Hebrews*, Tübingen, 1973.

17 For evidence and bibliography, see my *From Nicaea to Chalcedon*, London 1983.

18 George A. Kennedy, *Greek Rhetoric under Christian Emperors*, pp. 126–32 notes the use of *skopos* in fifth-century neo-platonic Commentaries on Plato. The search for the *skopos* of the dialogue is linked with the theory that the whole work should cohere like a living organism, since the literary artist is analogous to the demiurge and creates a microcosm of reality through the use of symbols. The commentator's function is to discern the artist's unifying intention, or *skopos*. Clearly this is the same usage as we find in

IV

Theodore. Theodore certainly did not get his idea of the *skopos* of the text from later philosophical commentaries. Neo-platonist and Christian are more likely independently to have taken over what was a technical usage in the schools and each adapted it to their own dogmatic concerns.

19 D. A. Russell, *Criticism in Antiquity*, especially ch.7.

20 See my paper 'Chrysostom on I & II Corinthians' delivered at the 1983 Patristic Conference in Oxford, to be published in *Studia Patristica*.

21 *Commentary on Matthew* Book XI. Text in *GCS*. Origen vol. X, pp. 34ff. Trans. Ante-Nicene Christian Library, additional volume, p. 431ff.

22 *Homilies on Matthew* xlix. Text in Migne, *PG* 58.495ff. Trans. *NPNF*, Series I, vol. X, pp. 303ff.

23 Migne, *PG* 18.613–73. The remark quoted is from J. Quasten, *Patrology*, vol. 3, p. 303. Rowan Greer, *The Captain of our Salvation* recognizes the true nature of this work.

24 *Gregory of Nazianus, Rhetor and Philosopher*.

25 *Menander Rhetor* (See above, n. 5). A number of doctoral theses on the influence of the Second Sophistic on various Greek Fathers have been published by the Catholic University of America, Washington D.C. For the influence of rhetorical forms on the Cappadocians, see also R. C. Gregg, *Consolation Philosophy*, Patristic Monograph Series no. 3. Cambridge, Mass. 1975.

V

The Fourth Century Reaction against Allegory

This subject is one that has intrigued me for some time, and I shall both summarize previously published conclusions[1], providing further evidence to support them, and make additional proposals[2].

It has been a mistake to suppose that the Antiochenes reacted against allegory on similar grounds to the rejection of allegory in the modern period. Furthermore, the associated attempt to reclaim their use of typology has been misplaced insofar as it has been dependent upon modern definitions of the difference between allegory and typology in terms of 'history'. This 'negative' argument, involving the rejection of the characteristic descriptions found in most commonly used textbooks and studies, is more fully treated elsewhere[3]; suffice it to say here that Antiochene exegesis is full of 'dogma' deduced from texts, that they constantly seek the 'moral meaning', and that they both recognised the metaphoricity of language and accepted prophetic references. This paper will eventually add the argument that they were primarily concerned with precisely those aspects of the Christian story which modern exegetes tend to regard as 'mythological'. Its principal concern, however, is to enquire further about the grounds and motivation of the attack on allegory.

Previously I have argued for a methodological account, suggesting that the approach to texts in rhetorical and philosophical schools was different, and that the Antiochenes represent rhetorical methods against the philosophical approach of the Alexandrians[4]. In order to demonstrate this I first attempted to reconstruct from Quintilian and others the exegetical moves standardly made in class as pupils studied with first the *grammaticus* and then the *rhetor*. The

---

[1] I refer to the following articles: Frances M. Young, 'The Rhetorical Schools and their influence on Patristic Exegesis', in Rowan Williams (ed.), *The Making of Orthodoxy. Essays in honour of Henry Chadwick* (Cambridge, 1989), pp. 182-199 and 'Typology', in *Crossing the Boundaries. Essays in Biblical Interpretation in Honour of Michael D. Goulder*, ed. Stanley E. Porter, Paul Joyce & David E. Orton (Leiden, 1994), pp. 29-48.

[2] Some are already offered in my book, *Biblical Exegesis and the formation of Christian Culture* (Cambridge, forthcoming); this will be the published version of the Speaker's Lectures given in the University of Oxford, 1992 and 1993.

[3] In the works already noted, especially 'Typology'.

[4] Especially in 'Rhetorical Schools'. It is, of course, true that it is hard to sustain a stark contrast between rhetorical and philosophical schools. There was much mutual influence and many shared interests. But it is a helpful paradigm for delineating certain differences in approach and methodology, and has some basis in the material from Antiquity.

V

standard distinction was between τὸ μεθοδικόν and τὸ ἱστορικόν, the former dealing with matters of language and text, the latter with background material. Τὸ μεθοδικόν was concerned, then, with the correct reading and construal of the sentences, with the proper sense of the words, especially the archaic terms of a classic like Homer, often using etymology in order to tease this out, and also with things like stylistic devices, especially figures of speech; while τὸ ἱστορικόν did not attempt to distinguish historical background as such from other bits of erudite information which might throw light on the text – it embraced astronomy, geography, natural history, music, anything and everything, including myths and legends, that might satisfy the curiosity of the enquirer (ἱστορεῖν is, after all, 'to enquire'). There is no doubt that the Antiochene commentaries are packed with material belonging to τὸ μεθοδικόν and τὸ ἱστορικόν.

My second argument for taking seriously the issue of exegetical methodology was drawn from a close examination of Eustathius' treatise, *The Witch of Endor and against Origen*, the earliest text which attacks the use of allegory. What I found, to my surprise, was that the treatise in fact accuses Origen of being too literal, of paying too much attention to the verbal details of the text, so drawing false conclusions by not attending to the narrative logic of the whole. Eustathius argues that the story does not imply that Samuel came up from Hades at all — rather the witch played upon the mad mind of Saul so that he seemed to see Samuel; one should certainly not make deductions about the resurrection, as Origen had. In an aside, Eustathius suggests that it is scandalous to take this story literally and allegorize other key biblical narratives. But the principal charge apparently concerns piecemeal interpretations.

I now find confirmation that there was a methodological issue provided by the little known handbook by one Adrianos, entitled *Isagoge ad sacras scripturas*[5]. This is a work devoted to methods of scriptural interpretation. It bears no explicit marks of the controversy, so probably post-dates it, but it clearly belongs to the Antiochene tradition. What Adrianos is concerned to do is to analyse the particular literary characteristics and idioms of Hebrew texts. His first section deals with the διάνοια of scripture. Here he is working with the standard rhetorical distinction between the wording and the sense. He enquires, in particular, how God's ἐνέργειαι are represented by human attributes — in other words, he deals with the anthropomorphic language of the Bible and its underlying sense, which is to be distinguished from the λέξις of the text. No more than Origen does he take literally references to God's eyes, mouth, hands, feet, anger or passions, nor indeed to God sitting, walking, or being clothed, but he never employs the term 'allegory' to describe what he is

---

[5] I am indebted to R. Bultmann, *Die Exegese des Theodor von Mopsuestia* (Habilitationsschrift, posthumously published, Stuttgart/Berlin/Koln/Mains, 1984) for drawing my attention to this work, which is found in Migne, *PG* 98.1273-1312.

doing when he suggests that it is God's knowledge which is expressed in the phrase 'God's eyes on us', and God's mercy in the suggestion that God has ears to hear.

Adrianos' second section concentrates on λέξις, the wording and style, noting the use of metonymy, epitasis, parable, simile and metaphor, rhetorical questions, and so on. The third section looks at the principles of σύνθεσις, and after providing examples of ellipsis, tautology, antistrophe, hyperbaton, transposition, epitasis and pleonasm (every point discussed in this treatise is in fact illustrated by quotations from the scriptural text), he turns to τρόποι, covering the great list of figures of speech distinguished in ancient theory. The list begins with metaphor, parable, syncrisis, hypodeigma, goes on through periphrasis, anakephalaiosis, prosopopoia and hyperbole, then irony, sarcasm, ainigma, paraenesis — I forebear providing the full list of around two dozen. In the midst of all this appears allegory, treated to but 4 lines where, for example, hyperbole merits 16. In other words, allegory is recognised as a figure of speech, but not treated as very important. In the classic passages on allegory, particularly those which discuss Paul's use of the word ἀλληγορούμενα in Gal. 4.25[6], the Antiochenes accept allegory as a figure of speech, but maintain the principle that it must only be identified in texts where something in the text itself demands it[7]. Adrianos sees no need to press the point.

Adrianos also confirms that meaning is grounded in the ἀκολουθία of the text. He uses the analogy of a steersman — the interpreter is blown about if not fixed on the goal. One must begin with the normal sense of words, but one gets a sure and certain outcome by paying attention to scriptural idioms, the figures, tropes, etc., which he has detailed, and by taking the ἀκολουθία seriously. The διάνοια of the words must be earthed in the order found in the body of the text, and the θεωρία must be grounded in the shape (σχῆμα) of that body, and thus the limbs and their synthesis can be discerned properly,

---

[6] Theodore of Mopsuestia, On the Minor Epistles of St. Paul, ed. H.B. Swete (Cambridge, 1880-82), vol. 1, pp. 73 ff; Theodoret on Gal.4.24, Migne, PG 82.489; Chrysostom on Gal.4.24, Migne, PG 61.662. Cf. Diodore on the Psalms, Prologue and Preface to Ps. 118; the text of the former is found in CCG, vi, while both were published by L. Mariès, 'Extraits du Commentaire de Diodore de Tarse sur les Psaumes', Recherches de Science Religieuse 9 (1919), pp. 79-101. K. Froehlich, Biblical Interpretation in the Early Church (Sources of Early Christian Thought. Philadelphia, 1984), has performed an important service in making available in translation the key statements on exegesis found in Theodore and Diodore. As he notes (in the introd. p. 21) the attribution of this material on the Psalms to Diodore is highly probable, though the material comes from an 11th century ms. under the name of Anastasius of Nicaea.

[7] According to Robert M. Grant with David Tracy, A Short History of the Interpretation of the Bible (2nd ed. revised and enlarged, London, 1984; chapters 1-15 originally published in 1963), p. 66, 'John Chrysostom observes that "everywhere in scripture there is this law, that when it allegorises, it also gives the explanation of the allegory".' Rudolf Bultmann, Die Exegese des Theodor von Mopsuestia, p. 60, provides the Greek of the quotation and the reference: In Is. v.3, Migne, PG 56.60 (Bultmann's 't.vi.54, 55' corrected — clearly he meant the 6th vol. of Chrysostom in Migne, which is vol. 56, and his col. numbers do not correspond with the edition available to me).

V

and nothing is seen beyond the body. Adrianos seems to be suggesting that any insight into the meaning of the text must inhere in the text looked at in its completeness.

Now clearly this usually means that, as Adrianos puts is, the διάνοια corresponds with the ὑπόθεσις of the wording (ῥήσεων) so that the interpretation is according to the λέξις — examples of the application of this principle to prophetic texts, such as Jer. 31.31 ff, show that the prophetic meaning is the literal meaning. But it also seems to confirm another suggestion I have made[8], namely that the difference between Antiochene and Alexandrian exegesis lies in the way perceived deeper meanings were taken to relate to the surface of the text. The difference may be characterized as that between an 'ikonic' and a 'symbolic' relationship. An 'ikon' represents and images the underlying reality, a 'symbol' is a token, with no necessary likeness. Allegory took words as discrete tokens, and by de-coding the text found a spiritual meaning which bore no relation to the construction of the wording or narrative. Antiochene exegesis embraced typology and prophecy, morals and dogma, but only by allowing that the sequence of the text mirrored or imaged the realities discerned by θεωρία. The whole σχῆμα is important.

There are, then methodological issues, and Adrianos confirms my previous conclusions. But two objections may be raised against the position I have outlined. The first is that the Antiochenes had no exclusive rights to these standard methods of philological analysis: the Cappadocians, and others such as Cyril of Alexandria, so successfully married these literary/rhetorical methods with allegorical exposition that they are often said to be eclectic in their methods, and indeed, Origen himself used all these methods[9], and was as well trained in them as the Antiochenes. The second is that the denial of historical interest overlooks the fact that ancient critics were not only familiar with a literary genre called ἱστορία, but with traditions which taught budding lawyers to present arguments for and against the plausibility of narratives — as Eustathius remarked, Greek children learn to distinguish between fact and fiction.

One thing that somewhat blunts the last point, is the fact that Origen used these critical techniques not to preclude but rather enhance his allegory, for they helped to uncover the ἀπορίαι in the text which signalled the Holy Spirit's intention that a meaning other than the impossible literal one should be sought[10]. But clearly the larger issue of how history was understood in the ancient world cannot be passed over. The fact that Lucian could write a treatise objecting to the rhetorical excesses of writers claiming to produce history[11] confirms both the point that ancient readers of this genre expected to be told 'true

---

[8] In the Speaker's Lectures, to be published, as noted above.

[9] Bernhard Neuschäfer, *Origenes als Philologe* (Basel, 1987).

[10] See R.M. Grant, *The Earliest Lives of Jesus* (London, 1961)

[11] Lucian, *How to Write History*, ed. and Eng. tr. by K. Kilburn, Loeb Classical Library, vol. vi of Lucian's works, pp. 2-72.

stories' in an 'objective' way[12] — though clearly they often got questionable ones; indeed, novelistic romances parodied the conventions of 'history'[13] — and also the point that plain factuality was not regarded as the aim either. Even Lucian suggests that the historian, 'if a myth comes along', should tell it but not believe entirely: his advice is 'make it known for the audience to make of it what they will'. History was a descriptive narrative intended to improve as much as inform. The genre embraced not just past events, but all kinds of other information — geographical, cultural, technical, strategic, you name it; and it was supposed to be useful, to explore moral issues, and the interplay of fate and fortune in the affairs of men. The Antiochenes could not have had the anxiety about historicity that has bothered modern scholars, with their detective model of historical research. Nevertheless, there was ancient discussion about the plausibility of narratives, and it is important to realise that Diodore was as anxious as Origen about a talking serpent[14].

That must suffice as reply to the second objection on this occasion. But the reply has itself confirmed the first, namely that Origen and others shared the same methodology as the Antiochenes but came to different conclusions. It is this which makes my final point the more telling, since we have to ask why the methodological issues were taken up. Few get passionate about mere methodology!

I am increasingly convinced that what developed into a methodological discussion was motivated by doctrinal imperatives, though not principally the theological differences identified by Greer[15]. It is noticeable that the charges against allegory time and again rehearse a catalogue of stories whose allegorization gives offence: this catalogue always includes, on the one hand, the narratives of Creation and Paradise, and on the other, the expectation of the resurrection of the body and the Kingdom of God. This is true already in Eustathius; it is most evident in Epiphanius and Jerome; it recurs in the classic discussions of allegory in the Antiochene material[16]. The Antiochene reaction against allegory occurs in the same century as the first Origenist controversy. I suspect that methodological issues with respect to exegesis were addressed precisely to support a defense of the over-arching narrative of the

---

[12] M.J. Wheeldon, '"True Stories": the reception of historiography in antiquity', in *History as Text*, ed. Averil Cameron (London, 1989), pp. 36-63.

[13] Niklas Holzberg, *The Ancient Novel*, An Introduction (Eng. tr. by Christine Jackson-Holzberg, London, 1995).

[14] Diodore, Pref. to Ps. 118.

[15] Rowan A. Greer, *Theodore of Mopsuestia. Exegete and Theologian* (Westminster, 1961); and *The Captain of our Salvation. A Study in the Patristic Exegesis of Hebrews* (Tübingen, 1973).

[16] For Epiphanius, see my discussion of the work referred to above, *On the Witch of Endor*; for Epiphanius and Jerome, see Elizabeth A. Clarke, *The Origenist Controversy. The Cultural Construction of an Early Christian Debate* (Princeton, 1992), which stimulated this proposal; for the Antiochenes, see the texts referred to above, and my discussion of them in the forthcoming book based on the Speaker's lectures.

V

Rule of Faith, or by then, the creeds, against the excessive spiritualising implicit in Origen's allegory[17].

It was not history as such, nor even simply Christological docetism, that lay at the heart of the attack on allegory, though the threat to realism, materialism and the body was certainly felt. It was largely to do with taking seriously the beginning and ending of the overarching story that gave meaning to the Christian life. This was not to be treated as a mirage or a parable. A talking serpent was not after all fatal, for the speaker was, of course, the devil in serpent's guise. The Antiochenes cared more about the narrative logic of the whole biblical text than about historicity or literalism. Hence their anxiety about the very aspects of the biblical story that modern historians would be most disposed to treat as mythological.

---

[17] One might also explore the impact of the Anthropomorphite issues raised by the Origenist controversy. No doubt it meant that sensitivities about the anthropomorphic language of the Bible had to be addressed, but not by adopting the Origenist solution. Adrianos' treatise would seem to be proposing an alternative methodological approach via the identification of scriptural idioms in speaking of the divine. The Cappadocian and Syrian response was theological: God chose to clothe the divine self in human language in order to communicate with humanity. Cf. the discussion in my Speaker's Lectures.

VI

Allegory and the Ethics of Reading

Modernism and the Demise of Allegory

There seems to be a fundamental distaste for, or even revulsion against, the whole business of allegory. Why is this? Basically, I think because we feel that there is something dishonest about allegory. If you interpret a text by allegorizing it, you seem to be saying that it means something which it patently does not. It is irrelevant, arbitrary: by allegory, it is said, you can make any text mean anything you like.

So Andrew Louth in a chapter entitled 'Return to Allegory'.[1] And we knew what he meant. We too had been brought up to distinguish between *exēgēsis* and *eisēgēsis*, and to accept the discipline of seeking the so-called original meaning. That almost instinctive sense that allegory was dishonest made it difficult to take Patristic exegesis seriously. Allegory was unethical.

It was also perceived to be unscriptural. The twentieth century had seen a radical reaction against the long-standing assumption that the parables were to be taken as allegories.[2] Jülicher had insisted that they had one point not many, turning them into simple moral sermon illustrations. Dodd and Jeremias had laboured to re-create their life-setting so as to demonstrate how they carried Jesus' message of the Kingdom. The parables were challenging and sharp vignettes, directed *ad hominem*, whose cutting edge had been for too long smoothed over by the mistakes of allegorical interpretation.

But there was another presupposition which strengthened those assumptions, namely the dogma our generation was brought up on that Christianity was a 'historical religion'. Against 'other-worldly' understandings of the Christian tradition, there had been a 'this-worldly' reaction, reinforced both by the so-called 'sense of history' as past and different which had emerged in the modern world, and by the apologetic need to defend the history of Christian origins against the charge that it was a myth or contained mythical elements. Allegory was inextricably mixed up with spiritual speculations rather than hard, defensible, historical facts. It was therefore more than dishonest, for in the modern context it was frankly useless – indeed an embarrassment.

The power of these assumptions can be seen in what now seem to me to be rather curious attempts to justify so-called traditional 'typology', and distinguish it from allegory. As Louth notes, the word 'typology' is a recent coinage. It has often been stressed that the writers of the early church use a variety of terms, *tropologia*, *allēgoria*, *anagōgia*, etc., which shade into one another and cannot be clearly distinguished; of these, 'typology' is not one, though there is much talk of *typoi*.

The modern distinction between typology and allegory was formally advanced by Lampe and Woollcombe.[3] Summarizing it in my own way, it went something like this: typology, unlike allegory, could be justified in the modern world because it represented a genuine historical perception, that sacred or revealing events have a family likeness, follow a pattern or type, simply because they are grounded in the consistency of God's providential love. So the typological parallel, much beloved of the early church, between Passover/Exodus and its fulfilment in Christ need not be jettisoned in essence, only the absurd allegorical details exploited to elaborate it. The authority of Daniélou[4] lay behind an essentially similar distinction between events and words, the first being associated with typology, the second with allegory. For Daniélou typology represented a kind of 'sacrament of the future'. The interest in eschatology undergirded a positive response to prefigurative events to which texts gave testimony, even if the notion of texts consisting of symbolic language, riddles to be unpacked by allegorical techniques, was unacceptable.

It all sounded so clear and convincing. There might be a resurgence of interest in Origen, but when it came to his biblical exegesis, it was so obviously a child of its time, fascinating but quite misguided. The title of R.P.C. Hanson's book, *Allegory and Event*,[5] speaks for itself.

Allegory and the Ethics of Reading

Origen was really out of tune with the Bible, he argued, since he had no historical sense. The historical earthing of the biblical material and the historical nature of the Christian religion Hanson took for granted, an unquestioned dogma. So Origen's inability to grasp the importance of event and history for incarnation or Bible is judged unfavourably. Allegory, everyone assumed, permits escape from events and facts, not to mention the constraints of language, or the so-called 'original meaning'. Allegory must be false, deceptive, inappropriate as a method of exegesis.

Reaction against Modernist Historicism

But now the context has dramatically changed. The set of assumptions I have outlined has been challenged. It turns out that the books of scripture are not simply historical documents permitting access to revelatory events behind the text to which the texts give testimony. For it is only the way the story is told in the biblical material that makes the events significant in any sense. That means we are dealing with literature, and response to story, no matter how 'history-like', involves dimensions other than a documentary reading.

The demise of Biblical Theology signalled the coming challenge, and is well described and analysed in the writings of James Barr.[6] Following Maurice Wiles, Barr pointed out that it was by no means clear what it meant to claim that Christianity was a historical religion. In the claim a number of different elements were confused.[7] Different theological options relate to his six alternative meanings. I would add to his analysis the point that in the claim that Christianity is a historical religion, one may discern two distinct but intertwined characteristics of modern biblical scholarship: (1) defensiveness in the face of recognition that if certain events had not happened then Christian claims were vulnerable, giving rise to a strong element of apologetic in the attempt to claim historical factuality; and (2) enthusiasm for a salvation-historical approach which claimed to identify saving events discrete from yet enmeshed in the historical process, and believed to be the subject of the biblical witness. Both served the dogmatic concern to uphold the anti-docetic argument, a concern which the early church would have shared and most certainly endorsed, but without the same anxiety about historicity or 'event' in the modern sense.

Simply to state these confusions reveals the extent to which this historical emphasis was a novelty, recognizably culturally specific to the modern world. The principal aim was proof of a past revelation: whereas the concern and purpose of biblical narrative appears often to be less attesting past events, more throwing light on future meaning.[8] To treat the Bible as the Book of the Acts of God is not only fraught with philosophical difficulties, but fails to acknowledge the extent to which events become a story in which God participates by the way it is told. Coupled with increasing scepticism about the unity or continuity of Biblical Theology, the idea that revelation is not in the words of scripture but in events behind the text, events to which we only have access by reconstructing them from texts handled as historical documents, was increasingly challenged.

> Revelation through history was supposed to be characteristic of Hebrew thought ... [But] Israel's genius was never directed towards the interpretation of history ... In fact a historical mode of perception was never a primary mark of distinction between Israel and her neighbours ...[9]

Thus the claim that revelation in history is the distinctive characteristic of the Bible has begun to feel shaky, though the idea continues to have a long afterlife. The Bible tells a 'history-like' story, but historical categories do not exhaust the possibilities of biblical interpretation. The meaning of the Bible is not imprisoned in archaeology or past events, now almost inaccessible despite massive efforts at investigation and reconstruction.

Now if history, so important for modern readers for a variety of reasons, turns out not to have been so, or at least not in the same way, for ancient readers, clearly it may have been a modern projection to suppose that parable did not mean allegory, a view advanced despite the fact that allegory was acknowledged to be one among those elements covered by *māshāl*, and irrespective of the reality that allegorical reading was a widespread assumption for ancient readers. We shall have to return to close investigation of what exactly was meant by allegory, and whether all allegory is of a similar kind, but from a strictly historical perspective, John Drury was surely right to challenge the Dodd-Jeremias approach to parables in his essay on the origins of Mark's parables in *Ways of Reading the Bible*:[10]

> The parables in Mark are, briefly and clumsily put, historical

106

Allegory and the Ethics of Reading

allegories mixing concealment and revelation in the sort of riddling symbolism which is an ingredient of apocalyptic.

And that is what Drury successfully documents, beginning with the
range of reference of the word *māshāl* in the Hebrew Bible, distinguishing, in particular, prophetic utterances of an allegorical kind
like those in Ezekiel, riddles and fables, and showing how in apocalyptic, current historical situations were symbolically represented in
allegorical form, deliberately obscure yet meant to be 'cracked', and
revealing the secret mystery of the future. The modern anti-allegori-
cal definition of parable distorts the text of Mark. In fact, if we are to
understand how the biblical books were read by those readers for
whom they were written, symbolism and allegory have to be taken
into account – still more if we are to understand those who passed
them down to us as a scriptural canon.

Finally, there has been the hermeneutical revolution. Andrew
Louth's work with which we began drew upon the hermeneutics of
Gadamer to challenge the idea that the meaning of texts is constituted by the original intention of the author. He drew in as ally the
so-called New Criticism, and especially the views of T.S. Eliot: no
explanation can exhaust the meaning of a poem, and an explanation
of its meaning is not provided by a history of how it came to be
written. Louth argues that like poetry, scripture is, as Newman put
it, *mira profunditas*, a depth, a complexity, 'a richness derived from
the mystery to which it is the introduction, of which it is the
unfolding.' For Louth, Gadamer's observation that the 'infinite
intermediary of tradition' lies between us and those who produced
the classic texts of the past also encourages a reconsideration of the
allegorical tradition which drew out different senses of scripture.

Within biblical studies itself, first structuralism, then literary
critical methods of other kinds, not to mention the influence of Paul
Ricoeur, has pressed upon us the sense that a text has a life of its own
over which the original author has no control, nor is the author in
any way privileged with respect to its interpretation. The writing-
reading relation is not the same as the dialogical relation. These
movements seem to permit the possibility that an author, especially a
prophet, may have said more than he/she consciously knew. So the
Bible must be regarded as a 'classic' with a plenitude of meaning,
capable of transcending the immediate context from which its texts
emerged. Its narratives reflect the fundamental structures of all

narratives: its discrete texts acquire new meanings through constant adaptation and reinterpretation, by incorporation into a canon, and by a long tradition of interpretation. No longer could one justify the critical attempt to cut away all this to unearth the original form of the text and its original meaning.

Many have moved even further under the influence of recent literary theory: a text has no meaning in itself – it is merely a series of marks on a page – until a reader takes it up and begins to invest those symbols with meaning. The act of reading, rather than the act of authoring, is the crucial locus in which meaning is generated. Objectivity would therefore seem to be illusory, and exégésis essentially eiségésis. In principle there are many different readings of a text, and the ideological stance which the reader adopts will materially affect the way the text is read.

The whole course of biblical studies in the modern period is thus brought into question, challenged at a fundamental philosophical level. And even if we wanted one, there is no ultimate sanction against allegory. Readers are invited to read themselves into texts, and allegory might be regarded as one way of making a text mean something meaningful to the reader. There is no responsibility to the illusory 'original meaning' or to the absent author. There is therefore no dishonesty in allegory after all. Indeed, might it not be expedient to allegorize 'the Jews' in John's Gospel so as to appropriate a text whose destructive effects have become embarrassing in the post-holocaust world?

The Ethics of Reading

Such a question immediately alerts us to the difficulties with a radical postmodernist position. The fact is that these texts have fostered anti-Semitism, and it is too easy to pretend that they have no history or mean something other than the words they obviously contain. It is simply not possible to pretend that a text is a blank sheet of paper which we can read how we like. Our instinctive feeling is that how we read texts raises moral issues.

The question of the ethics of reception was first raised for me by George Steiner's book, *Real Presences*, and followed up by exploring Wayne Booth's *The Company We Keep – An Ethics of Fiction* and Werner Jeanrond's *Text and Interpretation as Categories of Theological Thinking*.[11] A word from each will set the direction of the

Allegory and the Ethics of Reading

discussion: 'No reading is ethically neutral, since every reading represents an answer to a textual claim, an answer which may be responsible or irresponsible' (Jeanrond, p. 128). '... [N]o serious writer, composer, painter has ever doubted ... that his work bears on good and evil ... A message is being sent; to a purpose' (Steiner, p. 145), and so the presence of the 'other' impinging on us requires our respect and attention, a certain tact, welcome, civility, courtesy. 'To begin with doubt is to destroy the datum' (Booth, p. 32); we read for improvement, and commonly experience being taken over by what we read – so that 'friendship' is the most appropriate metaphor of reading.

The burden of all three discussions is that text and reader interact. 'I serve myself best, as reader, when I both honour an author's offering for what it is, in its full "otherness" from me, and take an active critical stance against what seem to me its errors and excesses' (Booth, p. 135). Courtesy towards the text does not require capitulation, but a responsible reading articulates difference. It is not simply by identifying ourselves with characters in the story, or with the implied author, but by differentiation, whether by sympathetic listening across differences of culture and time, or by critical distancing, that we properly engage with what we read. Wayne Booth's ambiguous response to *Huckleberry Finn*, once the issue of racism was made overt, is not unlike the potentially ambiguous response of Christians to those texts of early Christianity which have fostered anti-Semitism. The actual reader, especially of a text from the past, is not identical with the reader implied by the text, and an ethical reading has to take account of that gap. But critical assessment cannot neutralize the challenge of a classic text to reshape the reader's world. A communication is to be received with respect and attention.

So to take the ethics of reading seriously would appear to reduce the extent to which readers can treat texts arbitrarily. To respect the 'otherness' of the text and to articulate difference would appear, in the case of texts from the distant past, to require some kind of reaffirmation of the importance of placing them in historical context, of recognizing that language is earthed in time, place and culture, and reading involves what the ancients would call *hermeneia* – translation and interpretation. Historical criticism may become subtly different in its character and goal in the context of post-modern pluralism, losing its apologetic interest in the events behind the text, but it must surely have a role in aiding the articulation of identities and differences, so facilitating an appropriately ethical reading. It is, I think, no accident that sociological readings have radicalized the sense of the incarnation of texts in social settings and therefore demanded new attempts to locate them historically, at the very time when hermeneutical theory has purported to loose them from their historical moorings.

Yet the imperialism of the old modernist claim to be able to state the original and therefore the right meaning of the text is clearly on the retreat on three grounds: (1) the fact that 'assured results' have largely proved so ephemeral and contentious; (2) the evident truth that, although some debates about meaning are soluble since language is in the public domain – indeed in some limited areas real progress has been made in New Testament exegesis – there is no end to the process of discussion, for language also enshrines infinite possibilities; (3) the kinds of hermeneutical considerations we have been taking account of, namely, the role of the reader in 'realizing' a text so as to participate in appropriate interaction with it.

So what about allegory? In the light of these remarks it would seem that respect for the text would rule out arbitrary *eisēgēsis*, and the allegorical readings of someone like Origen persistently provoke the suspicion of arbitrariness. Yet there are two reasons for hesitation before dismissing allegory. The first is a historical one, one we have already touched on, namely the prevalence of allegory as a strategy in ancient literature: to that justice must be done if we are to respect the 'otherness' of these texts. The other is our interest in participation in texts by readers, a process which inevitably involves a kind of allegory, a relationship of *mimēsis* (or imitation) as the reader is taken up into the text.[12] To proceed further we must clearly try to discover how allegory might be defined and what allegory has involved.

The Nature of Allegory

Once we set out on this exploration we soon find that allegory covers a multitude of things. Somehow, differentiation of types of allegory would seem to be vital if we are to assess what kinds of allegorical procedures might be drawn into an ethical reading of biblical texts.

I suggest that differentiating types of allegory is not a methodological issue: methods or techniques such as etymology, gematria

Allegory and the Ethics of Reading

and personification are particularly associated with allegory in almost all types, but are not themselves helpful for analysis. Rather, differentiation is a matter of context and strategy. Having disposed of the mirage of typology,[13] I propose the following seven categories of allegory, though one shades into another. Some are especially characteristic of certain Hellenistic movements, but others are ancient and universal, biblical and rabbinic as well as Hellenic:

1. Rhetorical allegory, where allegory is adopted as a figure of speech on a spectrum with irony and metaphor.

2. Parabolic allegory, of a kind found in fables and riddles.

3. Prophetic allegory, hidden and riddling revelation found in oracles, dreams, symbolic visions, or narrative signs.

4. Moral allegory, where the moral of a text is sought for paedeutic or paraenetic reasons, e.g. by particulars being universalized as examples.

5. Natural or psychological allegory, where a mythological text is read as referring to forces interacting in the world according to accepted scientific norms.

6. Philosophical allegory, where the transcendent world is revealed, in veiled fashion, through the material world, and/or a text employing earthly language to convey heavenly meanings.

7. Theological allegory, whereby Christ, or the creative and saving purposes of the Trinity, becomes the true meaning of life, the universe, the text and everything.

What follows does not attempt to illustrate or discuss these types – a task beyond the scope of this paper – but offers some complementary discussion of the allegorical process as it took place in a world where it was less alien than it appears to us.

The word *allēgoria* is derived from a Greek verb meaning 'to speak in public' compounded with the adjective *allos* meaning 'other'.[14] Ancient definitions all ring the changes on the same theme: allegory is 'to mean something other than what one says'. It is distinguished in textbooks on style as a *tropē*, a 'turn' or figure of speech, and lies on a spectrum with metaphor and irony. By the time of Quintillian it was recognized that a continuous metaphor makes an allegory, and personification, e.g. of abstract qualities, became an increasingly common feature of the compositional allegory. In the rhetorical tradition, therefore, it might refer to deliberate obfuscation on the part of the author, implying the adoption of guarded or elite language, things only to be said in secret or unworthy of the crowd: it was at the very least a sophisticated conceit. In apocalyptic, as Drury has shown us, it produced a riddle to be cracked.

One fundamental distinction to be explored is the difference between such compositional allegory and allegorical interpretation.[15] It is one thing, one might think, for an author to adopt a particular figure of speech and develop it, and then for the reader to identify this process in exegetical analysis; it is another thing for a reader or interpreter to suggest that a whole text has an 'undersense' or *hyponoia*, and should not be read according to what might be claimed to be its 'obvious' meaning.

But there are reasons for suspecting that the distinction cannot hold for too long: (1) the weight this puts on authorial intention and the difficulty, in some cases, of identifying the 'plain sense' – a feature of postmodern sensibility in relation to texts; (2) the ancient propensity to attribute meaning to dreams and what we might call unauthored phenomena; (3) the fact that those who engaged in allegorical interpretation certainly thought that the *hyponoia* was what the author intended. Stoics thought that the original philosophical wisdom was known to Homer, and he really meant what they thought he meant. Origen believed that the Holy Spirit had clothed the divine *skopos* (aim or intent) in the dress of the wording, and only those who probed for the deeper meaning understood what the text was about. It was a commonplace in rhetorical education to distinguish between the subject-matter and the style, and the good author was the one who chose the proper stylistic dress in which to clothe his argument. The aim of the author was to convince the hearer. The conceit of allegory would challenge the hearers and divide them into those who saw through it and those who did not. For Origen, the Word of God performs likewise.

So, to progress we should shift the focus from the intention of the author to the response of the reader to the text, and enquire in what sense the reader submitted to constraints in interpretation. The educational process in grammatical and rhetorical schools was learning first to 'realize' the classics by reading them with understanding, then to emulate them in one's own compositions. Identifying figures of speech, recognizing the multivalent creativity of poetic language, was part of that basic educational process. Not only does allegory lie on a spectrum, and cannot be sharply differentiated from other figures of speech, but there is allegory and allegory.

112

Allegory and the Ethics of Reading

Jon Whitman[16] helps us to grasp the dynamics of allegory:

> ... Our language is constantly telling us that something is what it is not....
>
> All fiction ... tries to express a truth by departing from it in some way. It may embellish its subject, rearrange it, or simply verbalize it, but in every case, that ancient dislocation of words from their objects will keep the language at one remove from what it claims to present. Allegory is the extreme case of this divergence ... In its obliquity, allegorical writing thus exposes in an extreme way the foundation of fiction in general.
>
> The more allegory exploits the divergence between corresponding levels of meaning, the less tenable the correspondence becomes. Alternatively, the more it closes ranks and emphasizes the correspondence, the less oblique and therefore the less allegorical, the divergence becomes.

Taking up this perspective, my suggestion would be that the crucial differences between forms of allegorical reading lie in the way in which the correspondences and divergences are conceived.

In analysing forms of speech, it was generally assumed in ancient schools that the author had chosen the linguistic devices employed for a specific rhetorical purpose to do with the intended effect on the audience, though the particular aim might vary within a given work. The text provided clues. It also provided constraints. And it was in this area of clues and constraints that we find the source of different readings, and the underlying issues in debates about language and about allegory in the ancient world. One of our constant perplexities is how to interpret the procedures of an Irenaeus who attacks gnostic allegory, and from our perspective allegorizes himself, or how to characterize the Antiochene reaction against allegory when their own exegetical practice indulges in moral and dogmatic readings of a kind we find difficult to accommodate in the sort of literal and historical readings modernity has approvingly projected on to them. In both cases, the answer seems to lie in the perception of how surface-text and deeper meaning are related – indeed we can see in the debate about allegory in the early church a reflection of debates about language in the ancient intellectual scene.

There were two theories of language discussed in the ancient world: the *physis* (= nature) theory and the *thesis* (= convention) theory. Etymology originated in the first view that there was a natural connection between language and reality, at least of a mimetic kind. So names were more than signifiers – they pointed to significance. Others took the second view, regarding language as a matter of convention, thus accounting for differences between languages. Theophilus of Antioch, interestingly, believed in a pristine natural language which was corrupted and fragmented at Babel – thereafer *thesis* reigned! If conventional signs might become tokens or symbols, natural names would in some sense mimetically image the reality they represented. Thus whatever the theory of language, it was assumed that language represents, or refers to, a reality other than itself, the debate being about the precise relationship between the reality and the linguistic representation.

It is this kind of distinction with respect to language that gives us a clue to different perceptions of how a text might represent or refer to something other than itself. *Mimēsis* (representation) may occur through genuine likeness or analogy, an 'ikon' or image, or it may occur by a symbol, something unlike which stands for the reality. The 'ikon' will resemble what it represents, but symbols are not representations in that sense, having a much more complex relationship with reality as mere 'tokens' whose analogous relationship with what is symbolized is less clear.[17] Ikonic allegory would find a higher degree of correspondence between the various features of the text, the passage or narrative as a whole reflecting or mirroring in the narrative structure the 'undersense' adduced. Symbolic exegesis would tend to focus on particular verbal 'tokens' which consistently signify specific heavenly realities in the scriptures taken as a whole, but at the level of particular passages may produce a more piecemeal and apparently arbitrary meaning.

So, recently[18] I have distinguished three exegetical strategies in the patristic material which might be described as allegorical: the mimetic, the ikonic and the symbolic. In the ancient world, the 'mimetic' nature of all language and literature was taken for granted. Because art imitated life, it had moral value as exemplary or as a dire warning. Plutarch urges the appropriate techniques for ensuring that literature provides a moral paedeutic, with the critique of Plato and other philosophers much in mind. In a similar way, early Christian paraenetic exploited the exemplary value of stories and characters in a new alien body of literature, the Bible. Another mimetic feature

Allegory and the Ethics of Reading

found in scripture arose from its assumed prophetic or oracular character: narratives provided 'types' or patterns of things to come, and so the significance of current events or the outline of future possibilities could be discerned in the 'shadow' found in the biblical material, e.g. the outstretched arms of Moses ensuring victory over the Amalekites prefiguring the cross. It is, of course, this feature which has been utilized in characterizing so-called 'typology', but this example shows that it is the mimetic stamp (*typos*) in the description of Moses' action which is more significant than the 'event'.

Such *mimēsis* contributed to the reading of a text as speaking of some referent other than that which it purported to describe, as did the 'grammatical' procedure of identifying etymologies and metaphors, for both gave linguistic grounds for supposing that deeper or less than straightforward meanings were present. All this was common ground for the ancient reader, and facilitated allegory.

Someone like Origen was a philologist.[19] More than is generally realized he paid attention to the letter or wording of the text, using all the techniques of the grammarian. In the letter, however, he found certain stumbling-blocks, and these he took as textual clues to the fact that the true meaning lay elsewhere. The letter of the text was a collection of conventional signs or symbols. He found the coherence of scripture in its reference to fall and redemption, to the divine purpose in creation and revelation, in the spiritual journey back home, in the communication of God's true Word, everything pointing to Christ. This was the Spirit's *skopos*, and everything related to this divine *paedeusis*. The wording of the text was both vehicle and veil. Names and numbers were symbols, and the correspondence between words and subjects gave access to a narrative or meaning divergent from the earthly story which was nevertheless its vehicle.

But for Origen as for Irenaeus, there were constraints. The overarching story enshrined in the Rule of Faith provided the framework, the core of revelation to which scripture universally testified. The problem with gnostic allegory was that the wording was rearranged to produce a different *hypothesis*. Irenaeus accused gnostics of creating a *cento* of scripture, a *cento* being a new composition built out of lines or half-lines cribbed from Homer or Vergil; as Irenaeus put it, someone who knew Homer would recognize Homer's words but not Homer's *hypothesis*.

Those who reacted against Origen, namely the Antiochenes,[20] were no less sure that scripture pointed to moral and spiritual truths, but they found such truths imaged in the narrative coherence of the text, rather than lying outside the text and merely symbolized in what seemed a set of arbitrary correspondences. Thus a text offered internal clues to its ikonic intention, whereas the clues to symbolic language lay for Origen in the stumbling-blocks and impossibilities for taking it at its face-value.

Challenging the term allegory, they chose *theōria*, asserting that the allegorist abused Paul's term in Galatians 4.24, treating it as a blank authorization to abolish all meanings of divine scripture. Their understanding of the constraints was different. The story mattered, even if deeper significance lay in its features: Jesus used the boy's loaves and fish rather than creating out of nothing in order to stop the mouths of docetic heretics. So as Heraclitus in his *Homeric Allegories* sought a mirroring of natural and psychological forces in the narrative structure of the *Iliad*, so the Antiochenes sought a mirroring of moral and spiritual truth in the coherence of narratives and the straightforward connections in the text. I have deliberately avoided using the word 'literal', because they certainly did not produce what we would call 'literal' interpretations, and they knew like everyone else that 'the letter' might be quite misleading since texts contain figures of speech like metaphor and irony. Their *theōria* like Origen's allegory was intended to probe for deeper meanings, but without destroying the coherence of the text's surface, whereas in their view Origen's allegory led to piecemeal and dis-integrative readings.

Allegory and the Ethics of Reading

This survey has given us some sense of the extent to which allegory is on a spectrum and hard to distinguish from other readings which assume the possibility of linguistic multivalence, but it also reveals that any reading which seeks a hermeneutic is bound to have features in common with allegory. In fact, the most recent study of allegory by David Dawson[21] is an attempt to show that allegorical reading is an important contributor to cultural revision. Allegory essentially says, 'You have read the text this way, but it should be read like this.' To that extent the development of ideological readings, like liberation theology or feminist theology, are forms of allegory. Even the once dominant historico-critical reading, against which such read-

116

Allegory and the Ethics of Reading

ings have reacted, may be regarded as in some sense allegorical in that it enabled the domestication of ancient texts to modern apologetic needs. It said, 'You used to read these texts as being obviously about dogma, but really they are about something else.' Every critical reading shares something with allegory; every attempt at entering the world of the text, or seeing the text as mirroring our world and reflecting it back to us, involves some degree of allegory.

And the supposed repudiation of allegory has been a dramatic loss to the Christian tradition. Andrew Louth, with whom we began, attempted to reclaim the traditional allegory of the church, drawing particularly on de Lubac's exposition in *Exégèse Mediévale*. For this tradition, Louth argued, symbolism enabled participation in the mystery of Christ, and it was in the liturgy that allegory came into its own. This was not the arbitrary *allēgoria verbi*, or what I have called symbolic allegory, but rather *allēgoria facti*. Louth explores an example, tracing the ways in which allegory opened up the theological significance of the story of the baptism of Christ, drawing the participant into response, 'a response of innocence and a soaring desire for God' like that of the dove. Allusion to the story of Noah draws in further correspondences to show that the storm is over, there is release from evil and peace with God. Allegory lets the echoes be heard, and so invites the hearer into the story of redemption.

I am increasingly sure that the modernist concern with historicity has cut us off from a living tradition of complex multivalent images which have resonated in Christian art and poetry as well as liturgy. The renewed interest in metaphor, in intertextual association, in spirituality, should, I suggest, open our eyes once more to the creative potential of at least mimetic and ikonic readings. Perhaps we may still feel some reservations about the symbolic allegory that seemed to encourage piecemeal reading, but recent work on both Origen and Didymus suggests that their procedures have not as yet been properly understood; and in any case I would not like to be heard pleading for their results, so much as for recognition that we need to become self-conscious of our own actual and potential allegorical reading. For some kind of allegory is involved in any hermeneutic, and the curious Two-Nature or sacramental possibilities that emerge from treating the biblical texts as Word of God seem to me to have been submerged by most modern readings.[22]

And so there are three reasons why an allegorical reading might also be an ethical reading:

1. It enables the reader to grapple constructively with the dynamic between divergences and connections, differences and similarities, as the reader allows the text to impinge on the self and/or the world of the present. It becomes unethical if it simply permits domestication of the text to the reader's perspectives so that the text merely reinforces identities already achieved or authorizes positions already held. But if it allows the right kind of engagement and response, it has potential for creative cultural challenge.

2. It enables associative links of poetic images, symbolic actions, parables, metaphors, stories, to be discerned, so that the rich inter-textuality of the Bible can be reclaimed. It becomes unethical if it spawns a gnostic loss of the biblical hypothesis. But whether the associations were consciously or unconsciously intended by the earthly authors of these texts, the potential of the linguistic realities was surely better reflected in traditional moral and spiritual exegesis which exploited such allegorical associations than it has ever been in the era of historical and documentary reading. Such reading is ethical precisely because it does better justice to the qualities of the texts themselves and the cultures from which they came.

3. Allegory self-consciously makes play with the inadequacies of human language for expressing the divine. Apophatic theology and allegory go together. Positivist views of language have impoverished theological reading of the Bible by reducing God to an item in the world of the biblical text. Allegorical reading can set free the soul for creative engagement with transcendence, and such spiritual reading with a certain open-endedness can alone do justice to the textual claim which the Bible makes, and so provide a truly ethical reading.

Postscript: this has been a ground-clearing exercise, and does not yet claim to have reached the stage of proposals for criteria or con-straints appropriate to a modern allegorical reading.

Notes

1. Andrew Louth, *Discerning the Mystery*, Oxford: Oxford University Press 1983.
2. The classic studies following Jülicher, *Die Gleichnisreden Jesu* (1899–

Allegory and the Ethics of Reading

1910), are C.H. Dodd. *The Parables of the Kingdom*, London: Collins 1934. and J. Jeremias, *The Parables of Jesus*, ET London: SCM Press 1954.

3. G.W.H. Lampe and K.J. Woollcombe, *Essays in Typology*, London: SCM Press 1957.

4. Louth, op. cit., 118; cf. J. Daniélou, *From Shadows to Reality*, ET London: Burns & Oates 1960.

5. R.P.C. Hanson, *Allegory and Event*, London: SCM Press 1959.

6. James Barr, *The Bible in the Modern World*, London: SCM Press 1973, and the essays reprinted in *Explorations in Theology 7*, London: SCM Press 1980; cf. Maurice Wiles, 'In what sense is Christianity a "Historical Religion"?', in *Explorations in Theology 4*, London: SCM Press 1989.

7. Barr (*Explorations*, 31) suggests at least the following list: it meant that the 'historical course Christianity has followed is thereby right and normative'; or that 'because the religion is a historical one, its documents must be subject to the same kind of historical scrutiny as those of any other ideology'; or that 'the historical assertions made in its documents must be considered as historically accurate'; or that Christianity is not a system of timeless truths but a movement with a past and a future, only understood if you have a historical sense and explore its theology historically; or it implies existentialist encounter in historical existence; or that Christianity must be 'made to rest on that limited element in the sources which can stand as historically probable or reliable.' Elsewhere in his writings he examines the features of modern biblical scholarship which I highlight in the following sentences.

8. A point stressed by Barr, *Explorations*, 36.

9. *Explorations*, 37.

10. *Ways of Reading the Bible*, ed. Michael Wadsworth, Brighton: Harvester 1981.

11. George Steiner, *Real Presences*, London: Faber & Faber 1989: Wayne Booth, *The Company We Keep – An Ethics of Fiction*, California: University of California Press 1988: Werner Jeanrond, *Text and Interpretation as Categories of Theological thinking*, ET Dublin: Gill & Macmillan 1988. See further my paper, 'The Pastorals Epistles and the Ethics of Reception,' *JSNT* 45 (1992), 105–20.

12. See further my discussion in *The Art of Performance – towards a theology of Holy Scripture*, London: Darton, Longman & Todd 1990, chapter 7.

13. This matter was more fully discussed in my recent series of Speaker's Lectures in Oxford; the second series will be completed in 1993, and then hopefully publication will follow.

14. For the points in this paragraph I am particularly indebted to Jon

Whitman, *Allegory: the dynamics of an ancient and mediaeval technique*, Oxford: Oxford University Press 1987, Appendix I.

15. See Whitman, op. cit.
16. Ibid., 1–2.
17. For this distinction see James A. Coulter, *The Literary Microcosm: Theories of Interpretation in the Later Neoplatonists*, Leiden: Brill 1976.
18. Cf. note 13.
19. Cf. note 13. I understand my own discussion has been anticipated by Bernhard Neuschafer, *Origenes als Philologe*, Basle 1987, but I have not yet obtained this work.
20. See further my paper, 'The Rhetorical Schools and their influence on Patristic Exegesis', in the Chadwick Festschrift, *The Making of Orthodoxy*, ed. Rowan Williams, Cambridge: Cambridge University Press 1989, 182–199.
21. David Dawson, *Allegorical Readers and Cultural Revision in Ancient Alexandria*, California: University of California Press 1992.
22. See further, *The Art of Performance*.

VII

From Suspicion and Sociology to Spirituality:
on Method, Hermeneutics and Appropriation with
Respect to Patristic Material[1]

Suspicion of received accounts is characteristic of the historico-critical method. It is part of that reassessment of primary sources and that reconstruction of the 'facts' which has, in the Twentieth Century, rehabilitated thinkers once dismissed as heretics, and exposed feet of clay beneath the gilded images of saints and heroes of the faith. Our understanding of the past has been transformed; no longer can we give an account of the Church of the Fathers as if there were from the beginning a pristine orthodoxy from which heretics diverged. Though it has sometimes sat a little uneasily with faith commitments, we owe much to modern suspicion. Hence its place in my title. It is the starting-point, because it is where most of us have started. But the thesis of this paper is that we need to move on.

First, though, let us pause a little longer to identify the presuppositions with which we have all learned to work. We have shared them with biblical scholars. We have shared them with historians in general. Once we shared most of them with literary critics too. They may be teased out by reviewing a major classic of historico-critical research, namely, R.P.C. Hanson's *The Search for the Christian Understanding of God*. Let us observe what is going on in this volume.

1. The title is the first clue. The Christian doctrine of God is not regarded as a given. It is taken for granted that development took place. The underlying assumption would seem to be that the events and experiences of the first Christians were not simply transmitted to later followers, but inevitably interpreted, and in a Greek environment, conceptualized philosophically. The process whereby ideas were proposed, tested, found wanting, revised, refined and eventually established can be reconstructed as a 'search'. Thus, historical contingencies, and indeed the personalities of the major players, must be understood as essentially contributing to the generation of that 'idea' which is

[1] After much consideration I have decided not to attempt to footnote this paper, which was written for oral delivery and to provoke discussion rather than to document a case. I have simply appended a bibliography which includes details (1) of all works specifically referred to, (2) of some which I have found particularly useful in preparing this paper, and (3) of some for the convenience of anyone wishing to follow up the issues addressed.

the Christian understanding of God. One is reminded of the idea of 'progressive revelation' which enabled biblical scholars to see how 'primitive' ideas of God developed into 'ethical monotheism'. The notion of evolution or development, of the history of a doctrine, is fundamental.

2. The subtitle specifies the fact that, within this broader set of assumptions, the book is about a particular period, indeed a particular controversy: *The Arian Controversy, 318-381*, and the volume's first section looks at the origins of this controversy. This is our second clue. It is taken for granted that the first task must be to rediscover the historical Arius, which means separating out authentic information from later projections, or later developments. One is reminded of the quest for the historical Moses, or the historical Jesus. It is also taken for granted that explanation is to be found in two major ways: first, through tracing cause and effect, in getting right the sequence of events, and second, by discovering the background, the influences, the sources of the major claims which became controversial. One is again reminded of biblical studies, both of the one time dominance of histories, whether of Israel or the Apostolic Age, and also of the 'History of Religions School' seeking explanation through background, through parallels with the religion of the Ancient Near East or the Hellenistic World.

3. The first chapter raises a question which provides a third clue: what did Arius teach? To discover authentic information means exercising critical judgement with respect to the data. Few of the 'traces' from past controversies are neutral, most accounts having an interest one way or another. Not only is much material missing, but much material has also been suppressed. Accident may occasionally rectify the distortions of prejudiced reporting, but that is relatively rare luck for the historian. More often the detective must second-guess, abstracting what seem to be quotations, restoring them where they seem mutilated, putting a different construction on them from that provided by the context in which they are found. Similar issues remain pressing as we move into later parts of Hanson's book, and are faced with the complexities of the Athanasian material: some of it is of doubtful authenticity, some poorly attested in the manuscript tradition. Dating it is a crucial and often hazardous enterprise. Thus the objective researcher inevitably becomes imaginatively creative so as to restore the most plausible possible picture. For that's what it's all about. Biblical criticism, with its interest in the originals behind the texts that have come down to us as canonical, and its equally imaginative reconstructions, again parallels this endeavour.

4. Another clue is provided by the documentation adduced in the text, and by the footnotes. The scholar is like a lawyer substantiating a case. The scholarly narrative cannot simply be offered as an alternative to those already existing, but must confirm itself by reference to primary sources, justify its interpretation of those primary sources, acknowledge and refute alternative views, whether of the course of events or of the motivations behind the actions or

From Suspicion and Sociology to Spirituality   423

teachings being described. Like the detective, the scholar seeks to answer the questions who did what and why, who said what and what was meant. It takes persuasive argument to establish one view against others. But everyone assumes that the argument is about the facts, about the truth of the matter. Furthermore, it is assumed that even though the protagonists may have misunderstood one another, the God's eye view of the objective scholar can explain how the misunderstandings occurred, and even adjudicate. The past is, as it were, a foreign country. The researcher both stands outside it, and by empathy seeks to enter it, so being in a position to make fair judgements. But little awareness is shown of the researcher's own cultural and historical contingency.

5. The final feature of this kind of scholarship to which I would draw your attention on this occasion is the emphasis on the contribution made by individuals, the assessment of their originality. The chapter on Athanasius' doctrine provides a clear example, not only of the need to descry the evolution of his ideas and the stages of development in his thought, but also to ascertain its importance. To Athanasius is attributed an approach to 'the central theological problem of his day from a soteriological, not from a cosmological, viewpoint' (p. 423). 'This was a new, indeed revolutionary, theological idea and one entirely consonant with scripture', we are confidently told (p. 424). 'The consequence of this far-reaching innovation introduced by Athanasius is that the doctrine of the Trinity is not just a necessary corollary of the Christian view of God's relation to the world, but at the heart of his theology of the Incarnation, as it ought to be'. Other examples could be adduced. The discernment of the scholar can identify the genius of the key player. The texts are a window through which the mind of the great theologian can be observed. Of course, the great man did not always get it right: 'Athanasius is often wholly astray on the details of the Bible', we are told, despite his 'remarkably firm grip... on its main message'.

One could go on, but perhaps this is the moment to pause and reflect for a moment. From what standpoint is it that such judgments can be made? Would Athanasius have welcomed the idea that he contributed innovations, let alone revolutionary theological ideas? One doubts it. From a patristic standpoint, this kind of scholarship, so far from being true to the outlook of the Fathers themselves, has the arrogance of modernity written all over it. What I suggest in this paper is that from a postmodern point of view, a similar judgment might be made. The whole set of presuppositions which govern this kind of scholarship can now seem positivist and passé. But, to be just a bit provocative, most patristic scholarship has not yet noticed that it resides in an intellectual backwater. For some decades now, biblical studies has been struggling with so-called 'new methods', but in patristic studies only a few have noticed. Still less have most of us realised how profound are the recent philosophical challenges to our methods.

But before we turn to the wider intellectual scene, let us consider another approach to the material with which Hanson deals. For my own reflections on method were initiated some years ago by one of those coincidences which so often prove fruitful in research. I was reading that weighty Hanson volume, when I was presented with a copy of Torrance's work on *The Trinitarian Faith*. Reading these two works side by side had a profound impact. Prior to making an analysis of the differences, I found myself sympathetic to Torrance. It is interesting to consider the reasons why, and then also to note the cause of subsequent frustrations.

Torrance offers something quite different from Hanson. The work is in a sense an exposition of the Nicene faith — the Creed, beautifully inscribed by an Oblate of Stanbrook Abbey, stands at the head of the text, backed by an icon of St. Athanasius. The chapter headings move from 'Faith and Godliness', through such themes as 'Access to the Father', 'The Incarnate Saviour' and 'The Eternal Spirit' to 'The Triunity of God'. Athanasius is no longer an original genius, but typical of those Torrance designates as 'the Nicene theologians'. His works are quoted, but by way of illustrating an attitude of mind, a set of theological motivations and an underlying theological shape, which is not peculiar to him —rather he is the representative of a whole tradition, and others, such as the Cappadocians, Irenaeus, Hilary, the Alexandrians, are cited alongside Torrance's principal source. The focus is on concepts and motifs. It is not chronology but logic that determines the sequence.

Here, background material is used to provide sketches of alternative or influential schemas, as vehicles to highlight the particular characteristics of the theology being presented. Similarly opposing theological views become 'counters' useful for specifying the 'difference' of Nicene orthodoxy. Historical circumstances are barely considered at all, still less the possibility that Athanasius' opponents might have a point! The use of scripture is not grounded in actual controversies at the time — about the use of non-scriptural language, say, or about the exegesis of particular texts; rather it is earthed in 'trembling and prayer', in the need to protect scripture from distortion. Altogether, we are never sure whether we are talking about 'them' or 'us'. Patristic texts are simply exploited to create and endorse a kind of classical doctrinal stance, and this particular theological exposition of scripture is simply appropriated.

That attempt to describe Torrance's approach illuminates the reactions noted earlier. Torrance invites the reader into contemplation of God. Theology and spirituality are indistinguishable as one enters that world, and there is a deep sense of consonance with the mind of the Fathers, a reverence for truth which is given. This, this is the God we adore. But it only works if you let yourself be carried along by it. The style is dogmatic, with no discussion about interpretation. Chronology seems not to matter. The diagrammatic contrasts, such as that between Judaism and Hellenism, or the Hebraic and Hellenic, may

once have had currency, but that one at least has long since collapsed in the
face of historical research. On examination we find Athanasius or Hilary
treated as sources for what might be described as 'proof-texts', authoritative
statements which are never set in context or analysed; true they are usually
identified by a footnote reference, but if you want to follow something up, it
not infrequently turns out to be impossible. Details can often be faulted. There
are inevitable areas of overlap with Hanson, such as the recognised soteriological thrust of Athanasius' theology, but the Hanson in me is uncomfortable
with the implicit claim that this is both historical and somehow of eternal
validity.

What reads like an account of patristic thought turns out, then, to be a thesis about the nature of Christian theology. But its importance lies in the fact
that it challenges us with the questions of hermeneutics. Are we just reconstructing a past the results of which we somehow have to live with, or not, as
the case may be? Or are we reading texts which in some sense we need to
appropriate? For Eastern Christianity, all theology is to be found in the
Fathers, and it is this tradition which Torrance adopts. Western scholars have
devoted much effort to the hermeneutics of scripture, and for the churches of
the Reformation it may seem as if the canon alone has the kind of authority
that requires attention to these questions. But that is to be less than ecumenical
in one's vision, and blind to the continuing importance of traditional doctrines
like that of the Trinity, or indeed of the creeds, as the hermeneutical keys to
scripture itself. We have to do more than reconstruct the story of the past. A
history of doctrine is not enough. But a systematic theology based on patristic
proof-texts is not enough either. The issues of interpretation and appropriation
need to be brought into the open.

Against that background, I turn to the wider question of the isolation of
most patristic study from those current intellectual movements which have
challenged the presuppositions of the historico-critical method. In order to
open the discussion, what I shall present is a series of points which seem to me
to be important, and which contribute to the distinctions between modernity
and so-called 'post-modernism'. This is a risky strategy for several reasons:
firstly, for some of you the ground will probably be familiar and my summaries otiose; secondly, any overview is likely to be out-of-date even as it is
produced; thirdly, I cannot possibly do justice to the process of discussion
which has brought about this situation — what I present runs the risk of being
a *pot-pourri* of Gadamer, Saussure, Foucault, Derrida, Ricoeur, Stanley Fish
and others. But my purpose is not to do a kind of historico-critical review of
modern intellectual trends, putting each contributor in their proper context.
Rather I want to sort out the key challenges to the methods most of us have
taken for granted without examining our presuppositions.

Still, before I embark on my series of points, it is worth clarifying the fact
that I have in mind two separate and yet related intellectual movements which

have, at least to some extent, been influencing biblical studies, though not without controversy. These are the worlds of philosophical hermeneutics and of literary theory. Some exponents of philosophical hermeneutics, such as Gadamer, would disclaim any practical or methodological intent, but a figure such as Ricoeur is oriented rather more to the actual business of determining meaning in reading texts, and is responsive to literary theorists. Literary theory has meanwhile moved through structuralism and deconstruction to reader response theories, and the rediscovery of rhetoric and poetics. There are discrete and highly specialized discussions going on. From all this I confess that I offer merely an inexpert selection of what seem to be the most significant ingredients.

1. A famous essay by Roland Barthes was entitled, 'The Death of the Author'. This highlights a general trend. Authorial intention is no longer considered to have primacy in determining the meaning of any text, even if it were possible to ascertain it. All the labour expended by Hanson on the attempt to elucidate Athanasius' motivations is irrelevant to the interpretation of the meaning of the texts that bear his name. Under the influence of structuralism, the autonomy of the text held the field; more recently the reader's reception of the text has been put in the forefront. At the crudest level, one can say that the text is simply marks on a page until a reader seeks to decipher it, and it has no meaning until it is invested with meaning by the reader's activity. The privileging of originality, the notion of authorial genius, the assumption that an author's biography might have bearing on the interpretation of the literary deposit that bears his name, all this has been characterized as belonging to 'romanticism'. The text is not a window into another mind or indeed another world, but a mirror in which we see ourselves.

2. So meaning is not determined by the world behind the text. Historical background has ceased to have explanatory power. Hanson's researches tell us little, for the history of ideas has become as unilluminating as etymology. Present meaning does not necessarily carry past meaning. This observation goes back to Saussure's linguistics which emphasizes the synchronic rather than the diachronic, and is easily illustrated by the current meaning of the English word, 'gay' — it no longer means what it did when I was a child. Historical analysis, then, only produces an archaeological reading, and fails to connect the text with the reader. This critique has been particularly telling with respect to the Bible: the historico-critical method has produced no hermeneutic, it is said — the Word-of-God-then is useless if you cannot show how it is Word-of-God-now. But it also applies more generally: Gadamer's early hermeneutics concerned the interpretation of Plato, and he concluded that the kind of classical philology practiced by Jaeger was inadequate. For us this sharply raises the question: What difference does a history of their genesis make to our acceptance of the creeds?

3. Indeed, future meaning is more important than past meaning. In other words it is the capacity of a text to generate fresh response which justifies its

preservation. Future meaning is never simply a repeat of past meaning, but arises from the potential of the autonomous text, over which the author has no control once it is published, to produce multiple meanings in the multiple contexts in which it is read. Great literature is plurivocal — it has no fixed or determinate meaning. There is a surplus of possibility in its language and figures of speech. In the case of literary texts, if not others, there is a plurality of voices to be heard, different points of view arising, for example, from the perspective of different characters within the narrative, as well as that of the implied narrator.

So the search for the meaning breaks down. The argument that Arius or Athanasius meant this or that is like shadow-boxing. It is even true that a particular reader finds different meanings in a particular text each time it is re-read. This is partly because the reader has to use imagination informed by infinite linguistic associations to fill in the inevitable gaps — as was discovered by those who found a five-year-old had a far more complex and sophisticated understanding of the meaning of the word 'birthday' than they could possibly programme into a computer. Indeed, gaps are essential to literary texts, generating suspense, interest and surprise: a complete account of the meaning is neither possible nor desirable. A multiplicity of readings is inevitable. The 'aporias' in a text are to be seen as fruitful, rather than problems to be resolved in some grand consistency. The tendency to systematise and homogenise is to be resisted.

4. Nevertheless, language is a system that is earthed in a socio-cultural community. 'Birthday' is a cultural construct, grasped by the five-year old whose understanding is shaped by the socio-linguistic world to which the child belongs. While inside a given system, one may be unquestioning, the world may seem self-consistent, and the self meaningful within the totalizing discourse which has been socially generated and assimilated. Texts belong to traditions, and as long as there is continuity in society, or in the interpretative community which owns the texts, the meaning will seem self-evident and consistent. Here, even as the author dies, we have to recognise an 'author-function', as Foucault suggested. The very attribution of certain texts to 'Athanasius' says something about the authority of those texts for the community which owns them. The social location of language and texts is essential to meaning.

Recognition of the social construction of meaning cannot but affect the interpretation of texts from the past. For, there are bound to be discontinuities arising from historical change, and competing constructs may challenge a once dominant tradition. On the one hand, then, the discontinuities produce cognitive dissonances which mean that for the texts to go on having any meaning or significance, a hermeneutic of retrieval or appropriation is required. This point is well exploited by David Dawson in his book, *Allegorical Readers and Cultural Revision in Ancient Alexandria*, one of the few studies which show themselves aware of some of these issues. The process of appropriation he traces then requires a parallel process now. On the other hand, such changes may expose the underlying power relations inherent in the language and texts generated by a particular system. This is the theoretical basis of feminist hermeneutics: patriarchal societies produced literature that reinforces the social structures it reflects. The power of authoritative texts from the past means that they have political effects which need to be challenged by a hermeneutic of suspicion, and this is rather different from the suspicion of the historico-critic with which we started, even if the trend to rehabilitate heretics may be regarded as an unconscious reflection of the contemporary commitment to do justice to the marginalised of history.

Ironically, then, the recognition of the social location of meaning demands a return to concern with historical contingencies, and with the recognition of the social and cultural differences between the original location of the texts and the location of the readers of those texts. This is why Torrance's approach is in the end unsatisfactory. This is also why sociological approaches to the material from antiquity have found relatively easy acceptance, both in biblical studies and in the study of the patristic and early Byzantine periods. It is an important additional tool, both for explanation and for distinguishing the foreign country of the past from present societies. It fits into and refines the methods of the historico-critic, while enabling new perspectives on the historical data. It can enable the search for the world behind the text.

However, it also challenges the God's eye objective researcher to recognise that that very stance belongs to a historically contingent social setting with its own power relations, namely modern academia. The social formation of the interpreter is also a factor to be taken seriously.

5. Hermeneutics, then, must involve recognition of 'two horizons': the horizon of the reader and the horizon of the text will not concur, according to Gadamer. For Gadamer, dialogue is what enables the process of fusing these two horizons; the text is questioned, and the reader finds response. For Ricoeur, however, dialogue is an inappropriate model. Once a text has left its author, it cannot answer: the hearing-speaking relation is not the same as the reading-writing relation. In other words, this is one fundamental issue over which leading hermeneuticians are not agreed: is it possible to have a dialogue with a text?

Whatever the response to that debate, there is one work of patristic scholarship which does endeavour to have a dialogue with the past, recognising the difference between the two horizons. It also conveniently happens to tackle the same material as our earlier specimens and was published around the same date: I refer to Rowan Williams' book on *Arius*. Awareness of the issues just raised is already evident in the opening chapter, which by reviewing previous scholarship exposes the historical contingency of the scholars, and the tendency to project onto the past images which are shaped by contemporary concerns. The book then attempts a more rigorous endeavour to understand Arius and his followers in their own terms, recognising that 'there is no absolute *locus standi* above the struggle', but 'a continuing conversation' in which 'orthodoxy continues to be made'. The fourth century horizon has to be attended to as different from the scholar's horizon, but that does not necessarily privilege the scholar's viewpoint.

The postscript recognises that, though 'this book has attempted to view Arius without the distorting glass of Athanasian polemic' (p. 234), such an enterprise is unlikely to be entirely successful, and acknowledges again how easy it is to settle on misleading contemporary parallels. Yet it also seeks to go beyond the question which so easily arises from this kind of investigation: If the history was like that, why not simply reject conclusions that are self-evidently problematic in our very different conext, and just 're-make' Christian doctrine? The importance of continuities, and therefore the necessity of a hermeneutic, is implicit. But one thing the fourth century struggle suggests is that 'the loyal and uncritical repetition of formulae' is 'inadequate as means of securing continuity' (p. 236). 'Scripture and tradition require to be read in a way that brings out their strangeness, their non-obvious and non-contemporary qualities, in order that they may be read both freshly and truthfully from one generation to another'. The problem of 'two horizons', the issue of dialogue across difference, has made its mark on this work, so that it is neither so arrogantly modernist as Hanson, nor so certain as Torrance that what was said then is meaningful now.

6. Ricoeur's preferred approach is to say that texts generate 'worlds', and they invite the reader to enter a world other than that which the reader consciously inhabits. Since, as we have seen, each world is constituted by a whole range of 'cultural codes' earthed in the society which generated the language of the text, research may be needed to facilitate entry to that world. But for Ricoeur, the world of the text is not such a reconstruction of past meaning, but the offer of new possibilities for the reader. The world of the text is not just a reflection of the world behind it, but is the construction of a world which the reader may potentially inhabit.

The modern novel might at first sight seem the kind of text in view — one thinks of the way a work like *Watership Down* creates its own complex society of rabbits which does and does not mimic human society, but which presents human readers who enter that world imaginatively with possibilities for transforming their own world. However, it is clear that Ricoeur's view is not restricted to that kind of scenario: the Bible, Athanasius, the Cappadocians, present us with a world which we are invited to inhabit. It makes sense to ask the question whether believers and unbelievers dwell in the same world. For Ricoeur, a reader's 'world' is made up of all the texts read, because the world of the reader is configured by the models offered by those texts.

There has been increasing interest in 'intertextuality', the way in which texts refer to one another, quote, allude, and, consciously or unconsciously, reconfigure previous texts. Already the significance of this for the use of the so-called Old Testament in the New has been observed, but its potential for transforming the agenda with respect to entering the world of patristic texts has hardly been observed. The point is that the language we use, the stories by which we are formed, the texts we read, the discourse of our socio-linguistic community, in fact shapes the world we inhabit.

In other words, language and texts do not merely reflect reality but configure it. Discourse determines the conditions in which we live, the power relations which determine our activities. Liberation involves deconstructing the systems set up by accepted linguistic description. It makes a real difference, for example, what categories we use to describe those whose behaviour is unconventional: are they possessed by demons or mentally ill? Does society medicalize or sacralize their condition? The answer will affect the way they are treated and the reality of their lives. But that very observation raises the fundamental issue: what is the relationship between the language used and the phenomenon? To what extent does the language create the phenomenon?

When it comes to this issue, one fine contribution to study of our material must be mentioned. The subtitle of Averil Cameron's book *Christianity and the Rhetoric of Empire*, 'The Development of Christian Discourse', indicates its significance. What she seeks to plot is the process whereby Christianity developed a 'totalizing discourse' and then the discourse of Christianity shaped late antique society, changing the reality in which most people dwelt. This exploration of the nature of the rhetoric, the metaphors, the models and 'types', which persuaded the adoption of particular beliefs and practices, builds on older scholarship, but profoundly changes the perspective from which the whole period is viewed. Though the work of a historian, it is deeply illuminating theologically, not least because it focusses directly on the issues of language, text and literary analysis.

7. As so often in developing one point we have anticipated others. The focus on textuality has meant renewed interest in how discourse is shaped, how it creates its effects, how narrative configures a world, so that rhetoric and poetics have been rediscovered. Structuralist analysis of universal narrative forms based on binary oppositions has given way to renewed interest in the particular effects, produced by particular narratives — on plot and characterization, point of view, irony, empathy, style. Figures of speech, particularly metaphor, have become an important focus of literary theory and philosophical discussion. The question of how genre affects the reception of texts has re-emerged, both in terms of literary analysis and in terms of what has been called 'reading genre'. The historico-critical method tends to treat all texts from the past as historical documents, simply providing the data for reconstruction, but the texts do not present themselves in that guise. They may be histories or romances, epistles or dialogues, apologies or homilies.

This renewed interest in the rhetoric and the poetics of texts might be particularly fruitful for patristic scholarship. Since the texts we study come from a society shaped by rhetoric and the study of the classics was at the heart of the educational system, our understanding of this literature must surely be enhanced by taking questions of genre, rhetoric, style, and poetics seriously. Literary analysis of these texts has hardly begun, and the potential for exploration of their intertextuality must be enormous; I hope my forthcoming book on the bible in the early Church may at least initiate the latter endeavour, and the *Cambridge History of Early Christian Literature* the former.

Despite the rejection of dialogue, Ricoeur does take seriously the fact that texts are forms of communication, and others have taken communication theory as an important model for literary theory. Some of the best of recent discussion has not simply privileged modern communication theory, or modern discussion of metaphor; rather it has taken seriously the claim of antiquity to have engaged in this analysis in a highly sophisticated way. Perhaps we should look again at the careful analysis of communication to be found in classical rhetoric. Modernism privileged the author, postmodernism the reader; on the way, the autonomy of the text was affirmed. But a communication model demands a dialectical dynamic between all three, as classical rhetoric knew. For persuasion to achieve conviction (πίστις), the ἦθος of the speaker had to instil confidence, the sound reasoning of the content (λόγος) had to be convincing, and the response (πάθος) of the hearer had to be engaged. That is the hermeneutical triangle which would have been assumed by those who wrote and read in the period from which our texts emerged. And perhaps proper attention to that dialectic is the best starting-point for future attempts to grapple with these texts.

Implied in much current theory is a gap between the word and the world. Structuralism encouraged the notion that language is a self-referential system of signs, like mathematics; myths and literary texts might be taken to be manifestations of this system, divorced from any necessary connection with anything outside themselves. Poststructuralist views have often reinforced this gap between reality and language. Naive views of literary realism have been rejected. The referential aspect of language and the mimetic quality of texts has become problematic. Some would speak of the essential metaphoricity of all language, so evacuating literalness of any sense. Thus the historical reference of texts cannot be construed as naively as has been the case, and contemporary challenges to theological realism are grounded in a critique of realism in general.

The down-to-earth historico-critic might well ask whether some of these theorists have any grip on reality, whether history can be distinguished from fiction, whether there is anything in what we say, whether a fact can ever be a fact. If there is nothing but the shifting paradigms of successive societies, no rationality which is not culturally relative, only a plurality of meanings, where is truth? What criteria can distinguish between valid and invalid interpretation? I have to confess that I suffer too from the insecurities generated by these questions... There are those who have welcomed postmodern perspectives because they seem to provide a more hospitable environment for religious belief than the hostile certainties of modern rationality. But there are ways in which pluralism and relativism ultimately undermine every claim to truth, and thus devalue all our researches along with any religious commitments we may have. It is not for nothing that there is so much talk of 'play', for all we can do is 'play' with texts, 'play' with ideas, choosing the game we enjoy, joining the consumer society in the supermarket of life's options.

Yet I wonder if that is all there is to it.

In any case, I am increasingly sure that we cannot simply remain on the siding into which these developments have shunted all historico-critics. For whether we like it or not, scholarship of all kinds creates discourse. The subject-matter of scholarly discourse is texts, and its form is also fundamentally textual. Though some scholarly discourse has the immediacy of dialogue, most of it is written, even if prepared for oral delivery as on this occasion. So the so-called 'secondary literature' of scholarship is itself textual, and since its constructions emerge from engagement with other texts, one might say that scholarship generates 'metatexts'. All texts belong to genres, and this includes the metatexts of scholarship. So I suppose one of the questions I am posing is about the appropriate genres of patristic scholarship. I suspect they must be plural. I do not doubt for one moment that much has been gained by modern historical scholarship, I welcome wholeheartedly the increasing common ground between those of us whose formation has been through biblical and patristic study and Classicists, scholars of Late Antiquity, and Byzantinists, and I endorse the insights that have been gained by borrowing the methods of sociology and social anthropology. But I wonder whether other genres are yet to be created, and whether theologians may not have a particular responsibility towards these theological texts.

Let me tell you a story — a μῦθος, and let those who have ears to hear, hear.

Once upon a time there was a young patristic scholar. As she read these texts from the past, she found herself both attracted and repelled. She was repelled by the wordiness, the labouring of arguments — they really did go on and on so unnecessarily. She was repelled by the intolerance, the hostility to Jews and heretics — the invective seemed deeply alien to the liberal Christian traditions by which she had been formed. She was repelled by the negative attitudes to the body, to marriage and the good things of life, which she had been taught to value sacramentally. Intellectually formed by a very traditional Classics curriculum and the theological study typical of the mid-Twentieth Century, she was fascinated by the evolution of Platonic Christianity and perplexed by its cavalier and unhistorical approach to scripture. Annoyed by allegory, she was nevertheless imaginatively attracted by a work like Gregory of Nyssa's *Life of Moses*, and longed to make a similar journey, a journey both intellectual and spiritual, towards knowledge of God.

But there was no-one to suggest how such a text might be appropriated in the modern world. The unspoken convention kept scholarship and devotion in separate pigeon-holes. You engaged with these texts historically, you mastered them, you made them make sense in terms of their historical context. You might question the historical process, tracing the cultural influences which produced the classic doctrines of Christianity, and arguing, for example, that Chalcedon used out-of-date substance-language, or was simply a paradox. You might construct a coherent account of Fourth Century Trinitarianism, but that was that — only the social pressures of the labels 'orthodox' or 'heretic' required any identification with the resultant formulae. How one might identify with them was largely left to the prviate conscience — as long as you didn't contribute to *The Myth of God Incarnate*.

Now it happened that three angels appeared to this maturing patristic scholar. The first said: 'You should let the Word of God master you, not try to master it'. The second said: 'Why do you imagine that you understand the scriptures better than people who used the same language and were much nearer in time and culture to these texts than you are?' The third said: 'If God is infinite, no language, no concepts are adequate: don't confine God to the limits of the human mind'.

Meanwhile the mid-Twentieth century world became the late-Twentieth century world, and the young patristic scholar was growing old. But the angels' words were seeds. Her world was increasingly shaped by the world of the patristic texts. Her theological language was increasingly metaphorical and yet referential: for, as the Fathers had said, God had clothed the divine self in the many types, symbols and images of the scriptures. Her journey was a journey towards the infinite and incomprehensible reality, the Word to which all human language relates, but which is never confined by it. Her mind was opened to the 'otherness' of all kinds of 'others', those of the past, those of the present in an increasingly pluralist environement, and that 'otherness', though alien, was no longer a threat. For somehow God, to be God, must embrace and challenge all, and judgement must lie in God's hands alone.

So the agenda for this ageing patristic scholar could no longer be merely historical. Somehow the wisdom to be found in texts from the past had to be reclaimed, even as its strangeness was recognised. Respect for these texts and respect for the present were somehow both involved in an 'ethical reading'. There had to be a confluence of theological intellectualising and humble attention to spiritual truth such as the Fathers had known. Did this mean a new scholarly genre? If so, what would it be like? Would it be a kind of systematic theology in dialogue, where the ἀπορίαι would constantly challenge the system and there would be no end to the journey, where the historical contingencies and differences would contribute to a dynamic enquiry about the transcendent, where the reality of Two Natures would inform not merely christology, but creation, sacraments, scripture, church and life commitments, where the hermeneutical issues were to the fore, and the creeds were but the gates of the heavenly mystery, and their language, together with the language of scripture, would be, like the language of poetry, open-ended, capable of generating ever more and more truth...? Could such a glimmer in the eye ever become a reality?

I guess we can only wait and see.

BIBLIOGRAPHY

Wayne Booth, *The Company We Keep — An Ethics of Fiction* (Berkeley and Los Angeles, 1988).

Averil Cameron, *Christianity and the Rhetoric of Empire. The Development of Christian Discourse* (Berkeley, Los Angeles and Oxford, 1991).

Averil Cameron, *History as Text* (London, 1989).

David Dawson, *Allegorical Readers and Cultural Revision in Ancient Alexandria* (Berkeley, Los Angeles and Oxford, 1992).

Terry Eagleton, *Literary Theory. An Introduction* (Oxford, 1983).

Hans-Georg Gadamer, *Truth and Method*, Eng tr. (London, 1975).

R.P.C. Hanson, *The Search for the Christian Doctrine of God* (Edinburgh, 1988).

Richard B. Hays, *Echoes of Scripture in the Letters of Paul* (New Haven and London, 1989).

Werner G. Jeanrond, *Text and interpretation as categories of theological thinking* (Dublin, 1988).

David Lodge (ed.), *Modern Criticism and Theory. A Reader* (London and New York, 1988).

Edgar V. McKnight, *Postmodern Use of the Bible. The Emergence of Reader-Oriented Criticism* (Nashville, 1988).

Mark Allen Powell, *What is Narrative Criticism? A New Approach to the Bible* (London, 1993).

Paul Ricoeur, *Hermeneutics and the Human Sciences* (Cambridge, etc., 1981).

Paul Ricoeur, *Time and Narrative* (3 vols., Eng. tr., Chicago, 1984, -85, -88).

A Ricoeur Reader: Reflection and Imagination, ed. Mario J. Valdes (New York, etc., 1991).

Madan Sarup, *An Introductory Guide to Poststructuralism and Postmodernism* (Athens, Georgia, 1993).

Hugh J. Silverman, *Gadamer and Hermeneutics* (New York and London, 1991).

Janet Martin Soskice, *Metaphor and Religious Language* (Oxford, 1985).

George Steiner, *Real Presences. Is there anything in what we read?* (London, 1989).

T.F. Torrance, *The Trinitarian Faith* (Edinburgh, 1988).

Brian Vickers, *In Defence of Rhetoric* (Oxford, 1988).

Francis Watson, *The Open Text. New Directions for Biblical Study?* (London, 1993).
Joel Weinsheimer, *Philosophical Hermeneutics and Literary Theory* (New Haven and London, 1991).
Rowan Williams, *Arius. Heresy and Tradition* (London, 1987).
Frances M. Young, 'The Pastorals and the Ethics of Reading', *JSNT* 45 (1992), pp. 105-120.
Frances M. Young, *Biblical Exegesis and the Formation of Christian Culture*. The Speaker's Lectures in the University of Oxford (Cambridge, forthcoming).
Frances M. Young, (ed.), *The Cambridge History of Early Christian Literature* (in preparation).

VIII

The *Apostolic Constitutions*: a methodological case-study

My intention in this lecture is to try and work out, in practical engagement with a particular text, some of the theoretical issues raised when I addressed the Patristic Conference four years ago — in other words, to read the *Apostolic Constitutions* with an awareness of that constellation of things referred to as post-modern critical theory. The perhaps surprising choice of text will, I hope, be justified by the outcome — for of all patristic material, this kind of work has surely been most exploited by historico-critics for ends foreign to the rhetoric of the text itself. I shall try to outline only enough theory to be intelligible; otherwise we shall never get down to the brass tacks of the text.

I. The Reader Response Approach and Beyond

The last half century of critical theory has moved through structuralism to reader-oriented criticisms. In the period of high modernity the task of critical reading was conceived as thinking the author's thoughts after him. But then it was observed that authors had no control over the text's meaning once it was published; so the focus shifted from authorial intention to what was inherent in the text's very structures. However, it rapidly became clear that texts only live on because readers realise the marks on the page, mentally filling in the gaps, so conceiving the meaning. Furthermore, the reader, innocent on first reading, will realise the text differently the next time it's read — an observation demonstrating the inevitability of a plurality of readings. That groups of people might after all share the same interpretation of a text was explained by the notion of interpretative communities. Still the reader was king.

To think of an innocent reader tackling the *Apostolic Constitutions* out of sheer curiosity is to stretch credulity. Modern readers of this and like material have invariably had an ulterior motive! Most have been interested in liturgy or clerical hierarchy, reading selectively with the intention of mounting a historical argument documented by the textual evidence, an operation to which I plead guilty myself! In fact, before readers can begin to tackle a text of this kind they need competence in the original language and some preliminary information of the kind provided in the standard 'introduction'. Yet that colours the reading. That this work is a compilation of material described as 'legislative and liturgical' is the usual sort of description. But suppose we attempt to re-read it without such presuppositions, what do we find?

First of all an epistolary greeting, a fact that immediately raises interesting questions about genre. Of that more later. Meanwhile the work proper opens with a description of the Church as God's vineyard, containing believers who are heirs of God's eternal kingdom, partakers of God's Holy Spirit, sprinkled by Christ's precious blood, and so on; followed by the warning to do everything in obedience to God. General commandments drawn from scripture are then assembled, after which men and women are given advice appropriate to each. Much of this material is about moral attitudes: not coveting, blessing those who curse you, loving enemies; the husband pleasing his wife and being compassionate to her; the wife obeying her husband. The practical outworking of this is spelled out for each in terms of not gadding about, not dressing up so as to attract others, sticking to proper tasks, reading the Bible not pagan literature, avoiding bathing in mixed company, and strengthening each other in the faith. The style is more homiletic than anything else, and reminiscent of ethical injunctions found in the New Testament and Apostolic Fathers.

At this point we move into what is conventionally designated the second book, uneven subdivisions making this the most substantial part of the work. The focus is now on the bishop, with some relatively brief mention part way through of others who perform functions in the church, including singers and porters along with deacons and presbyters. Indeed, in the succeeding books III — VI the bishop is never far out of sight, for he holds responsibility for the various things discussed, groups such as widows and activities such as charitable works, the support of Christians who are persecuted and dealing with heresy. The subjects covered are many and various and the treatment far from systematic. But if this description makes it suggestive of legislative material, let's look again.

The character of the bishop is the first thing to be sketched, the characteristics required mirroring those in the Pastoral Epistles. Scriptural quotes and examples back up the picture of one who rules and guides the community with wisdom, fairness and patience. Someone in this position should not be fond of money, ambitious, double-minded, partial or given to anger. Rather his character should be sober, prudent, decent, stable, generous, humble. In fact the bishop represents God to the people, and has God's authority to judge, to exclude, to govern, to reform the penitent, to be the good shepherd of the flock. Other functionaries in the church are mentioned because the bishop is to see that each receive their fair share of the tithes and offerings, for all these officers are to be respected and provided for. The members of the community should treat them as spiritual parents — indeed, the bishop is their father, king and master, deserving of tribute and offerings.

The more one attempts to read without standard critical presuppositions and seeking an overview of the text, the more one realises that this community is analogous to a household and that the character, duties and obligations of household members and servants are being outlined. Doubtless the original readers would have recognised the commonplace analogy between ruling a household and ruling the state as the description of the bishop oscillates from one model to the other. This is moral discourse rather than legislation, moral discourse with a profoundly important intertextual character, and a very specific sociological setting, both of these features having continuity with the so-called 'household codes' of the New Testament Epistles.

Such observations move us on in terms of methodology. For evidently there is a gap between us reading this text in the late 20th century and the reader(s) the text implies. This notion of reader(s) implied by the text puts a more sophisticated spin on the reader response approach. The present reader may become more competent to understand the text the closer that reader approximates to the knowledge and assumptions of those readers which the text presumes. So the question we should now put to the *Apostolic Constitutions* is this: can we characterise the reader(s) this work expects? By this question I do not mean the old historical one: can we deduce their date and identity, where they were living, what the issues were with which they were concerned, what their relationship was with the author, and so on. Rather it is the literary question I want to highlight here. How would one characterise the implied reader?

Clues aplenty lie in the outline already sketched, but the most obvious answer lies elsewhere. The implied reader(s) of the *Apostolic Constitutions* would recognise the authorial voice in passages like the following:

For I, Matthew, one of the twelve addressing you in this teaching — I am an apostle, and once having been a tax-gatherer, now through believing I've received mercy, I've repented of my former deeds and I've been deemed worthy of being an apostle and herald of the Word. (II.39)

Christians ought also mutually to pardon injustices…; as the Lord indicated when I, Peter, asked him, 'How often shall my brother sin against me and I let him off?' He said, 'I tell you not seven but seventy times seven.' (II. 46)

In other words the reader(s) are expected to be person(s) who accept the apostolic authority claimed.

This point is confirmed by the observation that paragraph after paragraph quotes from scripture. The text presents itself as a compendium of biblical injunctions, but only to reader(s) who will recognise the intertextuality — in other words, spot the quotations. Furthermore the very opening of the first book reflects the epistolary greeting of New Testament apostolic writing:

The apostles and elders to all of the Gentiles who believe in the Lord Jesus Christ, grace and peace from Almighty God through our Lord Jesus Christ be abundant for you through acknowledgement of him.

It would seem that this form of greeting was forged by St. Paul and became conventional for Christian letters. The implied reader(s) would receive this as an apostolic communication.

In response to the claim of Roland Barthes that the author was dead, Foucault insisted on the importance of what he called the author function. Here the authority of the implied author(s) is constitutive of the very nature of the text. The fact that the authenticity of this authorial claim has been contested separates the critical reader of the modern world from the implied reader written into the text. So attention has turned away from the communication the implied reader would receive to the issues of pseudonymity, provenance, and so on. If read at all, rather than selectively plundered for clues, the text is misread. An hermeneutic of suspicion may be required at some stage, but the first approach should surely be shaped by an ethic of respect. This text lays claim to authority, at least for the intended recipients, namely believers among the Gentiles.

Interestingly the evolution of postmodern theory has taken some critics through communication theory back to the rhetorical analyses of Antiquity. By focusing on readers of this text we have been subtly driven to talk also about author and content. Ancient rhetoric took seriously all three poles of the triangle of communication. Discourse, oral or written, was meant to persuade. Conviction (πίστις) was achieved if the argument (λόγος) was sound, the author's person and character (ἦθος) commanded respect and the audience was moved to respond (πάθος). That meaning emerges from the interaction of author, text and reader seems almost too obvious to be worth saying. Yet against the background of recent debates it is necessary to reclaim the insights of ancient rhetoric, and it is the more appropriate to do so when dealing with a text written at a time when rhetorical theory was implicit as well as explicit in the culture. But we need to go further and take seriously the persuasive intent of such a text — it is, as we have observed, moral discourse intended to have living outcomes.

Reacting against historico-critical approaches to texts, Ricoeur stated that the meaning of a text lies not in its background, but in its future — for texts create worlds. The implied readers of this text are persons who will listen and shape their lives and their community according to its precepts. This text is future-oriented, its intended consequence being the generation of a particular moral and social order marked by the characteristics embedded in the advice assembled in the document. To that extent the text needs to be read, not as evidence of a once existing communal order, but as an ideal held out to those readers who would respond to what it says and seek to live it out. Thus the implied reader(s) would receive reinforcement in their commitment or challenge to their current behaviour.

Furthermore the impact of the text on its implied readers would have been enhanced by its inherent appeal to tradition. These are readers who would not be impressed by novelty. They would understand themselves as being called back to their roots. The apostles would seem to be issuing this call, but they are not present — indeed they seem to belong to a past that is genuinely passed. In the ancient world, it was a cliché that a letter made the absent person present, and that is what this text seeks to effect.

This impression of distance from the apostolic age is enhanced for the modern critical reader by the fact that this work is a compendium, incorporating known older texts. We need to take into consideration the principal points made in standard analyses: the first six books largely reproduce the *Didascalia*; the seventh incorporates the *Didache*, to which are appended prayers, liturgical texts and other odds and ends; the eighth includes the text known as the *Apostolic Tradition* of Hippolytus. So this work is the end-product of a long evolving tradition. Older texts are not simply copied: the redactor had certain interests of which the most evident is the constant insertion of scriptural quotations to reinforce the canonical authority of every point made. So what are the implications of this source-critical analysis? The *Apostolic Constitutions* must have been compiled in order to preserve and supersede previous documents carrying apostolic authority. Traditions were gathered and given scriptural backing so as to create a community more in line with what was perceived to be apostolic intention.

For the implied reader(s), who were doubtless unaware of all this, features abound which would strengthen the sense of rootedness in the apostolic world. As noted already, the shaping and style, the vocabulary and values recall what we know as the 'household codes' in the New Testament Epistles. So the rhetoric of this moral discourse points to the realisation in present and future of an idealised past, and it issues from a particular socio-linguistic community claiming continuity with that established by the apostles. Such observations about the readers implied by the text lead me naturally into another postmodern interest, namely sociological approaches to interpretation.

II. Sociological Readings

To avoid slipping into social history, so reverting to a historical approach though with some shift of perspective, we must keep recalling that the basis of a sociological approach to interpretation lies in the fact that discourse creates social worlds. It is not just that the language of any text is only fully appreciated when placed in its social context, it is also that a text, especially an authoritative and prescriptive one like the *Apostolic Constitutions*, contributes to the shaping of societies. The implied readers are expected to live out the lifestyles they find in the text — indeed to relate to one another so as to embody the hierarchies represented in the text.

Postmodern theory would quickly identify these as hierarchical and patriarchal. The *Apostolic Constitutions*, like the Pastoral Epistles, would be regarded by feminist critics as a text to be approached with deep suspicion. Texts like this, it would be said, have created social worlds which are deeply hostile to the egalitarianism of pluralist democracies — indeed the tendency for the church to model its structures on the monarchical model is as deeply problematic as the more frequently raised issue about gender. Of course, this particular text may have had little direct influence on the Church because it was soon dismissed as Arian in tendency yet, whether or not scholarly debate about the theology of this compendium has reached resolution in Metzger's view that the work is not explicitly interested in dogma and its implied theology is simply archaic, indeed pre-Arian, without a doubt this text does reflect the social world which shaped the institution. So the suspicions alluded to would seem to be justified.

However, this text is potentially more interesting than that, especially if we approach it in terms of the social assumptions of the implied readers and note how they are modified. The world they inhabited is, of course, taken for granted and affects the discourse. That world is a hierarchical and patriarchal one: as the father rules a household, so the emperor rules the world, and God rules the universe. People have roles within those structures. All this is unquestioned and shared with surrounding society. But how does the church map onto this world? The text suggests that there are a series of overlapping discourses that contribute to the answer, while themselves being transformed.

The most obvious discourse is that of the household. Sociological studies of the New Testament have demonstrated the significance of this for the church in its earliest phase. Not only did Christian groups meet in households, but they clearly used familial language in relation to God the Father, to themselves as adopted sons and heirs (whether male or female) through Christ the Son of God and to each other as brothers and sisters in Christ. If Colossians, Ephesians and I Peter deliver ethical teaching in a form dubbed 'household codes' and comparable with similar ethical discourse in the Graeco-Roman world, the so-called Pastorals display a kind of adapted 'household code' for the needs of the Household of God.

It has been reckoned that the typical household in the Graeco-Roman world consisted of about 50 persons: the immediate kin would constitute an extended family over at least three generations, but in addition there would be servants, slaves, tenants, clients and others. There would be male and female servants, all of whom might be called διάκονοι even though they would undoubtedly have differing duties. Does that help us with the question about women deacons? I suspect so. Starting from everyday usage may shift perspectives on what would become the technical terms of Christian ministry. Deacons were simply servants in God's household with a range of services to provide, some appropriately assigned to men, some to women. The ἐπίσκοπος is simply the head steward, the top servant. But being a managerial slave in charge of others and representing the master could bring great authority in the households of antiquity: it could even mean holding the master's seal and being able to enter into business contracts on his behalf. When St. Paul speaks of himself as God's δοῦλος, it's double-edged — he adopts the humility of a slave while proudly claiming to speak and act on God's behalf. It is hardly surprising that the ἐπίσκοπος appears as representing God in early texts, including the *Apostolic Constitutions*. God is, as it were, the *Pater familias* in whose service bishops and deacons are employed. The discourse of the household is adopted, but undergoes theological transformation.

This makes it intriguing that Book I of the *Apostolic Constitutions* deals with what later editors have called the laity as if difference from clergy were the most important point! Rather the work begins with the whole church, constituted of people who both belong to God's household and also run households of their own. The analogy between them implies parallels in appropriate behaviour and qualities of character. The shape of the text rapidly becomes that of a 'household code' reviewing what is required of first the husband and then the wife. Ordinary life is to be morally reordered in the light of relationships established within the Household of God. Oscillation between God's Household and the everyday households to which people belong on earth becomes even clearer when the following books turn to the character and responsibilities of the ἐπίσκοπος, the *servant* who both represents God the Householder and serves the members of the household, administering the funds and seeing to the family's needs, temporal and spiritual.

Such oscillation reflects the New Testament, as does the oscillation between the language of family and the language of service. And maybe the latter becomes particularly significant when considering terms such as 'widow' or indeed 'presbyter'. These, I suggest, belong to the realm of the family, whereas service is the context from which 'bishop' and 'deacon' were drawn; and this compendium of older texts perhaps preserves the memory of that distinction in discourse. Widows simply seem to be those on a register to receive charity; they are frequently bracketed with orphans, they have to be needy and of a certain age, and they are expected to reciprocate with prayers and proper behaviour — the notion that they (and indeed orphans) are the 'church's altar' (III.6.3) fits with the view that almsgiving replaced sacrifice. What we find here is an extension of the responsibilities of households to provide for their dependents.

So what about presbyters? Most remarkable is *Apostolic Constitutions* II.28. The general context concerns the distribution of tithes and offerings, and soon we read that a double portion should be set aside for presbyters. But first there appear πρεσβύτεραι, and the issue concerns inviting older women to feasts — they should be people the deacons know to be in need. Should we imagine then that presbyters are more than 'older men' who need support? Well, they are described as busy with the 'word' and 'teaching', as standing in the place of the apostles and as the counsellors of the bishop. Are the presbyters, then, the revered elderly in the household of God, those who are the bishop's advisers because they carry the community memory? For researchers into the history of the threefold ministry the dearth of reference to presbyters in the *Apostolic Constitutions*, at least prior to the final book, has been puzzlingly conspicuous by contrast with the repeated attention paid to bishops and deacons. Perhaps this compilation allows us to discern a shift in the discourse whereby everyday terms drawn from household and family become technical terms within a novel social organisation.

But wait: we are in danger of reverting to historical reconstruction. Our purpose here is to consider the extent to which the implicit though modified discourse of the 'household' informs the social world this text seeks to create. I submit that, if there is here a sense of the church as an 'institution', it's more akin to the so-called 'institution of the family' than anything else. Assumptions then current about patriarchy and hierarchy are perforce carried with the discourse, yet the moral values of respect, compassion, care, charity, humility and many others ideally transform these relationships. Indeed, here is sharp critique of family values generally abroad, such as acceptance of abortion or that unwanted or malformed infants should be exposed (widespread in the literature of Antiquity if not often actually put into practice); alongside strong recommendations to Christian householders that they should adopt and educate orphans with their sons and heirs, thus practising in their own households the charitable values evident in the life of God's household.

But the household discourse is not the only one shaping this work. As already noted, households were treated as analogous to kingdoms and *vice versa*: the members of the civil service were known as 'Caesar's Household'; the philosopher king was to be mirrored in the good householder who directed, cared for and even educated and trained everyone for whom he was responsible. Belonging to God's Household easily slid into a sense of being God's people, a nation over whom God rules through earthly ministers. This wider discourse pervades the work and undergirds its use of the scriptures. The institutions of ancient Israel as depicted in the Bible are taken to have their counterparts in the church, which is now God's people; Old Testament texts shape the duties and obligations of members and office-holders, for they are as it were officers of God's State.

This perspective is fundamental and would repay further investigation, not least because it has shaped a discourse which allowed for first a parallel between, then a conflation of traditional state religion as practised by imperial Rome and an alternative state religion as presented by the church. In Book VII, one noticeable modification made to the *Didache* is a long insert about fearing the emperor because he represents Christ; by the time this text was compiled, the analogies between household and state were clearly projected onto the universe, and Christianity was becoming the state religion.

But the discourse of religion was, interestingly enough, not the most obvious to pursue in adopting a sociological approach to the *Apostolic Constitu-*

tions. One persistent difficulty in handling religious texts from Antiquity has lain in the tendency to project back a notion of religion essentially formed by the church's peculiar amalgam of discourses in shaping its identity. In Antiquity religion was not a matter of belief, nor the preserve of a single institution. Religion was woven into everyday life, habitual marks of respect to household gods at one level, civic festivals at another — all expressions of *pietas* towards the traditions of the ancestors, the fulfilling of obligations to gods who protected family and nation. The text with which we are concerned projects Christianised versions of this, but this is because its fundamental discourse is that of household and people.

The church was quickly characterised as a *collegium*, a religious club, or a burial club with its usual religious features — a description doubtless confirmed by meetings in catacombs. Insiders and outsiders soon drew analogies with mystery-cults. But the church was for the most part unlike a recognisable religious organisation. When places of worship were established, Christians adapted houses and built basilicas, public meeting-places where teaching could take place, not palaces for gods served by priests while the people remained in the outside courts.

The description of a church gathering in the *Apostolic Constitutions* (II.57) sharpens up the oddities. The bishop is first described as the commander of a great ship. The building is to be long, with its head to the east, and the seating arrangements such as to reflect the tasks of captain and ship's company — everyone in their proper place. This prepares for the reading of scripture and the exhortation of the presbyters, culminating in the discourse of the bishop who sits centrally as the commander. Then the church is likened to a sheepfold: and again the proper ordering of women, young people, children in the assembly captures the headlines. Only now does attention turn to prayer, followed by the offering of the eucharist. We have reached a climax which is analogous to religious rituals, and the language of sacrifice and priesthood permeates much of this work, but it is placed in a strange context. This text retains the sense of a community which has distanced itself from common religious practices under the influence of a more rational understanding of the universe and its relation to God the Creator, and has instruction at its heart.

Which hints at another fruitful sociological model, namely the school. One of the most important themes in the *Apostolic Constitutions* is knowledge. The very existence of 'heresy' is an indication that the analogy with philosophical schools ran deep, for it was the schools which offered various 'options' (αἱρέσεις), it was the schools that delivered 'teachings' or 'dogmata'; and in this text, the *Apostolic Constitutions*, it is the bishop who is responsible for seeing that members conform to the teachings of the Christian 'school' tradition. Nor should we overlook the fact that placing a body of literature at the heart of the community, and delivering exegetical discourses of those approved texts was analogous to school activity as practised in the cities of the Roman Empire.

What then of the liturgical texts incorporated into this compendium? Most work on these has been done by liturgiologists, whose interest has been to date the prayers in relation to other evidence and trace the development of liturgy. It has been widely accepted that the prayers of Book VII have a strongly Jewish character, and doubtless this is another important clue if we start to ask sociological questions: for certainly another discourse that shaped early Christian institutions was the synagogue. Indeed the precedent of the synagogue could account for many of the overlapping discourses we have been exploring — for the Jewish people had lost their temple and land, but scattered across the world had preserved their culture, including its religious traditions, through community institutions and regular gatherings for reading texts and praying without sacrifice. Jews, too, seemed like a school, and some respected them for having a philosophical religion of a higher order than the rest of society since it was focused on monotheism and morality.

The interesting thing about the *Apostolic Constitutions* is what it takes for granted: namely that these overlapping discourses make sense, despite their oddity in terms of the actual institutions of the Graeco-Roman world. And this exploration confirms the fact that this text belongs to a process in which a new discourse was emerging which would contribute to the formation of a new world, a world in which imperial and hierarchical authority would be given apostolic and theological warrant. Christian discourse transformed ancient religion by adopting and conflating other discourses, its novel intertextuality contributing particularly to this reconfiguration.

Conclusion

I had hoped to explore this text informed by some other aspects of critical theory. But as was predictable, the subject is too vast to be covered in a brief lecture. The coverage of reader response theory and sociological approaches has allowed some passing remarks on other topics, such as rhetoric and genre. Shaped by modernity, we are likely to retain our sense of historical distance and of a quest for reconstructing the past. But I hope this brief journey has shown that asking new questions and challenging methodological presuppositions can sometimes enhance that very quest.

Bibliographical Note

Specific acknowledgement is due to the Sources Chrétiennes edition of the *Apostolic Constitutions* and the introductory essays by Marcel Metzger:

Les Constitutions Apostoliques, Marcel Metzger (ed.), 3 vols. (Paris: les Editions du Cerf, 1985, -86, -87).

Otherwise this lecture draws upon around 20 years of reading, research and reflection; it would be excessive to acknowledge every contributing influence by comprehensive footnoting.

As far as critical theory is concerned, I refer readers to my paper, 'From Suspicion and Sociology to Spirituality: on Method, Hermeneutics and Appropriation with Respect to Patristic Material', *Studia Patristica* vol.xxix (1997), pp.421-35, especially the Bibliography at the end.

For access to work on households in the New Testament, I draw attention to my book *The Theology of the Pastoral Letters* (Cambridge: CUP, 1994).

For further development of my argument about the ministry, I refer to my article 'On 'Επίσκοπος and Πρεσβύτερος', *JTS* NS 45 (1994), pp. 142-8; and acknowledge the work of Dale B. Martin, *Slavery as Salvation: The Metaphor of Slavery in Pauline Christianity* (New Haven and London: YUP, 1990).

For work on the early church as a school, I draw attention to my book *Biblical Exegesis and the Formation of Christian Culture* (Cambridge: CUP, 1997); and to previous articles referred to therein.

IX

ΟΝ ΕΠΙΣΚΟΠΟΣ AND ΠΡΕΣΒΥΤΕΡΟΣ

IGNATIUS twice produces a puzzling image of the Christian ministry. In both *Magnesians VI* and *Trallians III*, he likens the ἐπίσκοπος to God, the πρεσβύτεροι to the Apostles and the διάκονοι to Christ. Reading this in the light of the developed clerical hierarchy, it seems odd that the deacons should be ranked higher than the presbyters.[1] Nor is this to be lightly explained away, for we find exactly the same oddity in the *Didascalia Apostolorum* IX,[2] indeed compounded, since deaconesses are likened to the Holy Spirit, and therefore presumably are also considered above the presbyters! This note offers an explanation which may radically revise our conception of how Christian clerical orders developed.

As is well known, πρεσβύτεροι do not appear in the principal Pauline material, though they do emerge in Acts and the Pastoral Epistles. In the latter, their relationship with the ἐπίσκοπος is notoriously unclear. In Titus 1: 5ff., we are given to understand that Titus was to appoint presbyters in each city in Crete, their character is briefly sketched, and then the text continues: δεῖ γὰρ τὸν ἐπίσκοπον ἀνέγκλητον εἶναι ὡς θεοῦ οἰκονόμον. . . . The resumptive γὰρ has suggested that ἐπίσκοπος may simply be an alternative term for πρεσβύτερος, giving rise to the popular suggestion that a 'college' of πρεσβύτεροι was presided over by the ἐπίσκοπος. Then, it is suggested, in Ignatius we see the situation developing, as he insists upon the authority of the monepiscopate.

This explanation works quite well for this passage, and also fits with the facts that in the Pastorals, whereas ἐπίσκοπος always appears in the singular, πρεσβύτεροι almost always is plural, and where their qualities are listed, the same appear for both. But we should note that the same qualities appear listed also for deacons and others, and they are not functions but aspects of character. So the last point may not be significant, and there are other pieces of data which need to be considered, and which do not fit that simple picture so neatly.

In 1 Timothy 3, which appears a bit like an ecclesiastical code, two, and only two, kinds of 'officers' appear, namely the ἐπίσκοπος and the διάκονοι. This accords with the reference to ἐπίσκοποι

---

[1] As is noted by Andrew Louth in the Penguin Classics translation, *Early Christian Writings*, revised edition, 1987, p. 82, with the bracketed comment: 'That Ignatius has inadvertently given the deacons a higher position than the presbyters shows the danger of carrying a figure too far.'

[2] Syriac translated, with Latin fragments, R. H. Connolly, Oxford 1929, pp. 88–90.

and διάκονοι in Phil. 1: 1, where such officers are simply taken for granted, presumably by both author and readers, for no explanation or discussion is offered. Πρεσβύτεροι do not appear in this context in 1 Timothy, any more than they do in Philippians and the Paulines generally accepted as authentic.

Elsewhere in the Pastoral Epistles, where they do appear, the duty-lists are still very close to 'household codes'. In Titus 2, we find πρεσβύτεις and πρεσβύτιδες, νέαι, νεώτεροι, and δοῦλοι; clearly none of these are in any sense 'officers'—we are talking about old men and women contrasted with young people and slaves within the household community. The situation in 1 Timothy is a bit more complex. The πρεσβύτερος appears in chapter 5, and in the opening sentence of the chapter, the natural sense of 'senior' appears correct, since he is to be treated as a father, young men as brothers, πρεσβύτεραι as mothers, and younger women as sisters. However, there follows an extended passage on widows, the status of whom has been much debated,[3] and then οἱ καλῶς προεστῶτες πρεσβύτεροι appear as worthy of a double τιμή, especially those who labour in the word and teach-

---

[3] The issue concerns whether widows constituted an order with ministerial duties such as praying, house-to-house visiting, and pastoral and charitable work. Suffice it to say here that, just as πρεσβύτερος is ambiguous, so there is an ambiguity about the natural and technical sense of 'widow', not only here but in other early Christian texts. I remain unconvinced that we should project back an 'order' of the kind that developed later, whether clerical or monastic. The widows are often bracketed with 'orphans' (e.g. James 1: 27, Didascalia IX, Connolly p. 88), which suggests they were principally the recipients of charitable support. The regulations about age and need (1 Tim. 5; Didascalia XIV, Connolly pp. 130–1) confirm that, and the widespread suggestion (e.g. Polycarp, IV.3, Didascalia IX, Connolly, p. 88) that they are the church's 'altar' surely means simply that almsgiving has replaced sacrifices—indeed in the latter passage orphans are to be regarded as the altar as well as widows! Furthermore the statements about their supposed pastoral activities are explicable in other ways: (i) Christian women were generally expected to engage in charitable works and the widows presumably to set an example—indeed in the Pastorals, such activities seem to be qualifications for being enrolled as a widow rather than duties afterwards; (ii) in each passage house-to-house visiting is associated with tittle-tattle and is frowned on—it is likely it is being associated with false teaching and leading people astray; and finally, (iii) the conventions of reciprocity in ancient society (see e.g. S. C. Mott, 'Reciprocity in Hellenistic Benevolence', in Current Issues in Biblical and Patristic Interpretation, ed. Hawthorne, Tenney Festschrift, Grand Rapids 1975) meant that recipients of gifts had to make a return of honour, gratitude and support—in a Christian community this would naturally be prayer and, certainly in John Chrysostom, the rich and poor have a reciprocal relationship, the rich supporting the poor materially, the poor supporting the rich spiritually, by prayer. Thus Bonnie Bowman Thurston, The Widows. A Women's Ministry in the Early Church, Fortress 1989, wildly overstates the case for a clerical order of widows. Their position is ambiguous.

144

ing. Presumably, given the following justification in vv. 18–19, the τιμή must be an honorarium or pay for their teaching activities. Besides teaching, they also 'preside'. This, as well as the succeeding discussion of discipline, suggests we are no longer talking simply about 'older men', and the reference in 1 Tim. 4: 14 to the πρεσβυτέριον as laying on hands, presumably in some sense 'ordaining', confirms this.

How is this complex evidence to be understood? I suggest that none of the solutions proposed so far really accounts for these texts, and that the clue is found in the curious statements of Ignatius and the *Didascalia* with which we began.

The ἐπίσκοπος and the διάκονοι were, I suggest, the only original appointed 'officers' of the congregation. The organization was established as 'God's household' (οἶκος θεοῦ, 1 Tim. 3: 15),[4] the ἐπίσκοπος was the 'steward' (θεοῦ οἰκονόμος, Titus 1: 7), and the διάκονοι the servants. Οἰκονόμος is the term most frequently found on tombstones, dedications, and honorary inscriptions set up by slaves to describe their position. Only slaves with means could set up such memorials. They were the trusted business managers and administrators who had the power to act on behalf of their master. The owner's authority was vested in them, yet they had considerable freedom of manoeuvre and some acquired private funds and business interests of their own.[5] A household could be a complex administrative responsibility: the civil service was known as 'Caesar's household'. It is hardly surprising that the θεοῦ οἰκονόμος would acquire authority and be seen as representing God.

In a household in the ancient world, there would be many διάκονοι and many δοῦλοι. They would be under the authority of the οἰκονόμος. The *Didascalia*[6] specifically states that the διάκονοι, both male and female, are answerable to the ἐπίσκοπος and should fulfil whatever tasks he gives them. The likeness to Christ, who had said, 'Whoso among you desireth to be chief, let

---

[4] The importance of this understanding of the church in recent sociological analyses, and particularly study of the Pastoral Epistles, can scarcely be over-estimated. See for example, D. C. Verner, *The Household of God. The Social World of the Pastoral Epistles*, SBL Dissertation Series 71, Scholars Press, Chico, California 1983; Margaret Y. Macdonald, *The Pauline Churches. A Socio-historical Study of Institutionalization in the Pauline and Deutero-Pauline Writings*, SNTS Monograph Series 60, Cambridge 1988; Reggie M. Kidd, *Wealth and Beneficence in the Pastoral Epistles. A "Bourgeois" Form of Early Christianity?* SBL Dissertation Series, Scholars Press, Atlanta, Georgia 1990.

[5] Dale B. Martin, *Slavery as Salvation. The Metaphor of Slavery in Pauline Christianity*, Yale University Press 1990, pp. 13–22.

[6] Chapter XVI, Connolly, pp. 146–50.

him be your servant: even as the Son of Man came not to be ministered unto, but to minister, and to give his life a ransom for many,' and who 'girded a linen cloth about his loins and cast water into a wash-basin. . .and washed the feet of us all and wiped them with the cloth,' was natural, and specifically spelt out in this later text.[7] The fact that 'spirit' is a feminine word in semitic languages may have encouraged the interesting further development of the Trinitarian analogy in the Syriac *Didascalia*.

In the Pastoral Epistles, the term διάκονος is used nontechnically also: Timothy is by implication called both διάκονος Χριστοῦ Ιησοῦ (1 Tim. 4: 6) and δοῦλος Κυρίου (2 Tim. 2: 24); Paul is introduced as δοῦλος θεοῦ (Titus 1: 1). This usage has precedents in Paul's own language about his own ministry (e.g. Rom. 1: 1; Gal. 1: 10; Phil. 1: 1; 2 Cor. 3: 6, 6: 4). In the Pauline material there is a tension between becoming sons and heirs through Christ, and being in Christ's service. That tension remains in the Pastorals. In a sense all members of God's household are brothers and sisters (see, for example, 1 Tim: 6: 2), in another sense they are all 'in service' and charged with the task of washing others' feet. Yet clearly, the term διάκονος also has a more specific use for particular 'officers' in the church from very early on, as does ἐπίσκοπος. These are the functionaries responsible for the household and its service.

Whence then the presbyterate? Interestingly, the *Didascalia*, like the Pastorals, does not have a specific section on πρεσβύτεροι. Their position is not therefore parallel to that of ἐπίσκοποι and διάκονοι. They appear as receiving hospitality and bounties like the widows, which suggests they are literally 'old', and a double portion is recommended because they are to be honoured as the 'apostles and counsellors of the bishop, and as the crown of the church; for they are the moderators and councillors of the church'.[8] Then later we read that the bishop appoints 'presbyters as counsellors and assessors', as well as the deacons he needs for the ministry of the house.[9] Thus they appear as an advisory council, rather than as 'officers'. Two factors tend to confirm that this was the original function of the presbyterate, and that it emerged later than the 'officers' we have already discussed.

1. The terminology is from the beginning ambiguous, and basically suggests seniority. Confusion as to whether the term is used in a natural or technical sense is already present in the Pastorals, as we have seen. The household of God is a family

---

[7] Texts quoted as in Connolly's translation.
[8] Chapter IX, Connolly, p. 90.
[9] Ibid. p. 96.

146

community made up of older and younger people, men and women. As the Pastorals indicate, seniority came with age, and should be respected. It seems entirely plausible that the 'senior citizen' carried what we might call the community memory, and was therefore commissioned to teach the tradition.

That the term was associated with tradition is clear from the fragments of Papias, whose use of the term is notoriously unclear:

I shall not hesitate to furnish you, along with the interpretations, with all that in days gone by I carefully learnt from the πρεσβύτεροι and have carefully recalled, for I can guarantee its truth. . . And whenever anyone came who had been a follower of the πρεσβύτεροι, I enquired into the words of the πρεσβύτεροι, what Andrew or Peter had said, or Philip or Thomas or James or John or Matthew, or any other disciple of the Lord, and what Aristion and the πρεσβύτερος John, disciples of the Lord, were still saying. . . .[10]

The problem with this passage is that the term πρεσβύτερος is used in two, if not three, different ways: to the surprise of many, it refers to the Apostles, then to people who appear to be the second generation, where the phrase 'the presbyter John' may or may not indicate that the term was used in a technical sense, and perhaps also initially for 'seniors' in general who authentically bear the tradition. The importance of the passage, however, is that it shows that the term was not simply used in a technical way for an 'office' in the second century, and that it was apparently used to mean the senior members of the community who carried the community memory, indeed even for the Apostles themselves. This explains the curious link between presbyters and Apostles with which we began.

It makes sense that as the generations passed the ἐπίσκοπος should appoint older, more senior members to act as an advisory council. It also fits with the problem in Corinth with which *1 Clement* is dealing, and with the response made: younger people should not rise in revolt against the senior people who carry the community memory and to whom the ἐπίσκοπος turns for advice. They form the church 'council'. Perhaps Ignatius, and possibly the Pastorals also, reflect a situation in which the (new? young?) ἐπίσκοπος needs to assert his authority, and maybe *vis à vis* the council of presbyters which appointed and advises him (see, for instance, *Magnesians* III, 1 Tim. 4: 12–5: 2).

2. Another factor may also have contributed to the emergence of such a presbyteral council alongside the functionaries already established, namely an increasing tendency to model the church

[10] As quoted by Eusebius, *HE* III.39, *ET*, G. A. Williamson, Penguin Classics, Harmondsworth, 1965.

on Jewish forms of organization. This analogy is offered tentatively, since the development of the synagogue and the situation of Jewish communities in the Diaspora is notoriously unclear.[11] But the picture is suggestive. Πρεσβύτεροι do not appear in the earliest Christian texts. They do appear in the Gospels, however, because there were Jewish 'elders'. The πρεσβύτεροι τοῦ λαοῦ appear with the high priests, constituting the συνέδριον, or the body described in other texts, such as Josephus, as the Γερουσία. Josephus refers to the members of this council as πρεσβύτεροι from the first century. They are community leaders, not synagogue officials, and such πρεσβύτεροι appear to have constituted similar councils for other Jewish communities around Palestine, besides Jerusalem, whether the city be wholly Jewish or mixed. This 'local government' probably had among its duties the overseeing of synagogues and the appointment of synagogue officials, such as the *rosh ha-knesset*, or ἀρχισυνάγωγος, and the other officers, such as the person responsible for the alms contributed by the congregation, and the *chazan ha-knesset*, the διάκονος or ὑπηρέτης, the servant who performed those practical offices such as fetching the rolls of scripture from the Ark, blowing the *shofar*, and so on.

It seems likely that somewhat similar conditions prevailed in the Diaspora, though there were certainly local variations. Roughly speaking, a Jewish community in a Greek city would be governed by a council of ἄρχοντες empowered to exercise certain constitutional functions in relation to their own ethnic community. That the councillors were called πρεσβύτεροι in Diaspora communities cannot be confirmed, but is not implausible. Such councillors were not synagogue officials, but community leaders who appointed the synagogue officials.

When we turn to the early Christian evidence, we find that the presbyterate ordained the ἐπίσκοπος, though the ἐπίσκοπος appointed the presbyters. My admittedly tentative hypothesis is as follows: the administrator of the church, called ἐπίσκοπος by long-standing Christian habit, began to acquire the functions of the ἀρχισυνάγωγος, and the existing διάκονοι those of the syn-

---

[11] Despite Paul Trebilco, *Jewish Communities in Asia Minor*, SNTS Monograph Series 69, Cambridge 1991, it remains so concerning the crucial points in my suggested analogy. My succeeding statements are based upon the New Schurer, *A history of the Jewish People in the time of Jesus Christ*, vol. II, revised and edited by Geza Vermes, Fergus Millar and Matthew Black, T. & T. Clark, Edinburgh 1979, pp. 423–63; and vol. III.1, revised and edited by Geza Vermes, Fergus Millar and Martin Goodman, 1986, pp. 87–107. The need for caution is reinforced by James Tunstead Burtchaell, *From Synagogue to Church. Public services and offices in the earliest Christian Communities*, Cambridge University Press 1992.

148

agogue almoner and attendant, besides those associated with the Christian Eucharistic meal. Meanwhile, Christians, being excluded like Jews by their religious scruples from many normal civic functions, began to organize themselves as a kind of distinct 'ethnic' community, later to be known as the 'third race', neither Jew nor Gentile, and confessing to 'heavenly citizenship'. So their 'seniors' were constituted into a kind of governing council for the community, with authority to appoint and advise the ἐπίσκοπος. Whereas Jewish community leaders would often obtain some constitutional recognition from the city, presumably Christians lacked that privilege, but internally endeavoured to organize themselves in a parallel way. The Apologists are perhaps beginning to try to claim the same right to recognition. So there is a perceptible shift in the way Christians are identifying themselves socially—from 'God's household' to 'God's people'.[12]

The origins of the presbyterate are therefore distinct from those of the episcopate and the diaconate. They were originally a council of senior Christians recognized as the bearers of the apostolic tradition. Thus, their association with the apostles was natural— indeed the very term πρεσβύτεροι could be used of the apostles themselves. Is it surprising then that Ignatius and the Syriac *Didascalia* can speak as they do? Ignatius' order would seem to evidence what became the conventional clerical hierarchy of ἐπίσκοπος, πρεσβύτεροι and διάκονοι, but his images betray an earlier relationship:

... hasten to do all things in harmony with God, with the ἐπίσκοπος presiding in the place of God and the πρεσβύτεροι in the place of the συνέδριον of the Apostles, and the διάκονοι, who are most dear to me, entrusted with the διακονία of Jesus Christ, who was from eternity with the Father and was made manifest at the end of time. (*Magnesians* VI)
Likewise, let all respect the διάκονοι as Jesus Christ, even as the ἐπίσκοπος is the 'type' of the Father, and the πρεσβύτεροι God's συνέδριον and as the συνέδριον of the Apostles. (*Trallians* III)

---

[12] This observation would cohere with the growing supercessionist claim which is a mark of the exegesis of the second century; e.g. Melito and Justin. To pursue that issue would take a further paper.

X

Ministerial Forms and Functions in the Church Communities of the Greek Fathers

Investigation of ministerial forms and functions in the early church is a subject that cannot escape revealing the interests of those who interpret the evidence. Historico-critical scholarship has sought to trace objectively the development of offices in the church. But what has most often emerged is a reflection of the investigator's own denominational face at the bottom of a deep well. More recently interest in the ordination of women has produced further debate, but with evidence all too often interpreted to suit the argument being made.

This more recent debate on the ordination of women, however, evidences a significant shift. For a search for precedents has tended to dominate these discussions. Yet discontinuity with a discredited patriarchal system may be as important for feminists as the discovery of particular continuities. And, indeed, interest in the early church as a social organization set in a very different kind of social order than we live in today has highlighted such discontinuities. The conclusions of older investigators, therefore, must be modified by taking seriously the "otherness" of the cultural world in which people then officiated—even if they held titles of which our titles "bishop," "presbyter" and "deacon" are direct descendants.

On this occasion a further factor encourages taking a less than conventional line, namely the explicit request to focus on the Greek fathers. It has been unusual in patristic studies of this question to distinguish between East and West, Greek and Latin. Once the so-called threefold ministry emerged early in the second century, with Ignatius providing the first clear evidence, parallel developments across the Roman Empire have been assumed. The contentious period has been that for which late canonical and early noncanonical texts overlap, and the argument has been mainly concerned with how early the episcopate emerged and whether certain offices can be proven from Scripture. Then Cyprian, the mid-third-century Latin father, has been seen as the key figure who shifted the "ministry" of the earlier period into a "priesthood" offering the "sacrifice" of the

Originally published in *Community Formation in the Early Church and in the Church Today*, ed. Richard N. Longenecker (Peabody, Mass., 2002). © 2002 Richard N. Longenecker. Used by permission of Baker Academic, a division of Baker Publishing Group.

X

Eucharist. To concentrate on the Greek fathers exclusively, therefore, is a challenge. And to do so effectively I will not confine myself to the pre-Nicene church fathers, for the relevant continuities and discontinuities are best highlighted by examining the better-documented period between the Council of Nicaea in 325 and the Council of Chalcedon in 451.

So what I aim to do in this chapter is to address old questions from newer perspectives, and, drawing on some of my previous work, to challenge conclusions that reflect both old and new interests.

1. BASIL OF CAESAREA: PORTRAIT OF A FOURTH-CENTURY GREEK BISHOP

I begin by offering a portrait of a bishop in the latter part of the fourth century. The area is Cappadocia, a Roman province located in what we now call Turkey. The bishop is Basil of Caesarea, who purports to be the compiler of one of the liturgies used to this day by the Greek Orthodox Church. He was also founder of the dominant form of monasticism in the same ecclesial tradition. The portrait is drawn by his lifelong friend, Gregory of Nazianzus, which is a place also in Cappadocia. The two met as students at Athens. So the speech composed by Gregory in Basil's honor, *Oration* 43, probably for the anniversary of his death, provides a good first source. It will give us some insight into how Basil was perceived.

Family Background

Gregory was a well-trained orator and his speech follows the conventions of panegyric (i.e., "eulogistic" or "elaborate praise") rhetoric. Allowance has to be made for very different cultural expectations, and we will certainly not follow Gregory's speech blow by blow. Much of it rehearses Basil's ancestry, education, and career up to the time when he became bishop—highlighting the facts that this fourth-century bishop, like many another, came from a leading local family and had a first-class education according to the norms of the day. Gregory's recital of Basil's pedigree is nuanced with an emphasis on his martyr ancestors and saintly parents, who are depicted in terms of Christianized virtues and values. Nonetheless, the social superiority of Basil's background glints through the sackcloth, the biblical allusions, and the scriptural exemplars.

Unlike some other Christian leaders of this time, however, Basil grew up in a Christian family and was a baptized Christian and ordained to the presbyterate at the time of his election as bishop. Gregory expresses approval of the fact that Basil had not been advanced to "the holy thrones of the priesthood" too rapidly (43.25)—which provides Gregory the occasion for lamenting the "danger of the holiest of all offices" becoming, as he expresses it, "the most ridiculous among us. For promotion depends not on virtue, but on villainy; and the sacred thrones fall not to the most worthy, but to the most powerful" (43.26).

These words of Gregory were written just over half a century after the conversion of Constantine. Together with many other bits of evidence drawn from the period, they reflect the fact that offices in the church had come to be prized by the ambitious as well as to fall naturally to the local aristocracy. Imperial patronage had dramatically changed the social position of church leaders. Gregory and others recognized that this was a kind of betrayal. Yet they also prized the Christianizing of the elite culture to which they belonged.

Clerical Progression and Politics

Basil progressed through the ranks properly, being first lector, then presbyter, and eventually bishop—receiving this honor "not as human favor but as from God and divine" (43.27). But Gregory has jumped forward in his narrative, and so in what follows he retreats to describe Basil's withdrawal to live as a monk rather than get into an open dispute with the bishop who was his predecessor. At this stage Valens came to the imperial throne. From the point of view of Basil and Gregory, however, Valens was a heretic, and Gregory spares no rhetoric. Hostile rulers of the churches, as well as governors of the provinces, were out for political gain. So Basil returned to church politics (43.31). He was reconciled with his bishop and provided the mind and energy for resistance to the increasingly heretical world. Effectively, he already had episcopal control (43.34).

But what did resistance and episcopal control mean for Basil? It meant standing up to governors and powerful men in the city. It meant deciding disputes, supporting the needy, entertaining strangers, overseeing the care of virgins, challenging exploiters in times of famine, and providing the nourishment of God's Word (43.34–36). Little surprise, then, that Basil was the natural successor when Eusebius, his bishop, died. Gregory praises the virtue of Basil's private life and the way he increased in wisdom and favor, as well as stature—alluding in these expressions, of course, to Luke 2:52. Basil would now exercise his virtue on a wider stage and with greater power (43.38).

But Basil had opponents within the church that he had to appease. Gregory indicates that they surrendered to the superiority of his intellect and to the fact that his virtue was unmatchable. With internal rivalries suppressed, Basil became patron of the wider community, which was under pressure from the civil authorities. His first weapon was the pen; his second, what we would call networking. He also had profound differences with the state.

Statesmanship, Character, Roles

The emperor was using exile, banishment, confiscation, plots, persuasion, violence—and whatever else he could devise—against all those church leaders who would not tow his line. Gregory tells of Basil's famous refusal to kowtow to the emperor's prefect, and then of the way he outfaced the emperor himself on his appearance for the liturgy in Basil's cathedral (43.52). Other anecdotes indicate the pressures to which Basil was subjected because of his differences with the state, and these differences were reinforced by the rivalry of episcopal colleagues.

Indeed, the interlocking of state and church is revealed by a telling incident that Gregory handles with a certain degree of care. The emperor had decided to split the province of Cappadocia—the motive almost certainly being to curb Basil's power, for metropolitan boundaries followed those of the imperial provinces. (The word "diocese" originally had a secular connotation.) Basil's reply was to create a whole lot of new bishoprics. In so doing, he consecrated his friend Gregory to a diocese that Gregory himself regarded as a potty little place—a move that had considerable consequences for Gregory's later career and permanently damaged their relationship. Gregory admits to his pain, even as he commends Basil's political astuteness.

The rest of Gregory's speech is a rhetorical celebration of Basil's qualities—his holiness displayed in temperance and simplicity, his celibacy and leadership in the monastic movement, his philanthropy and support of the poor. Gregory defends Basil against the charge of pride, celebrating acts of condescension and suggesting that "what they [his defectors] term pride is, I fancy, the firmness and steadfastness and stability of his character" (43.64).

Basil is turned by Gregory into the ideal bishop, with the description reaching a climax in telling of his eloquence as a preacher and composer of discourses, his ability to move from scriptural exegesis to moral and practical homilies, and his panegyrics on saints and martyrs in the defense of orthodox doctrine. The ideal picture is confirmed by an extraordinary example of the rhetorical trick of *synkrisis*, in which Basil is compared to Adam, Enoch, Noah, Abraham, Isaac, Joseph, Job, Moses, Aaron, the judges, David and Solomon, Elijah and Elisha, the Maccabees, John the Baptist, Peter, Paul, the sons of Zebedee, and Stephen—with Basil often, according to Gregory, outdoing the biblical hero to whom he is likened.

For our purposes I need not dwell on the details of the deathbed scene with which Gregory's *Oration* 43 ends, except to draw attention to how all sectors of the community were called on to honor Basil as one of them. This list indicates the roles that were projected onto the bishop of the day—that he was to be lawgiver, politician and statesman, popular leader, educator, monk and ascetic, example to contemplatives, pastor and comforter, support to the aged, guide to the simple and the young, reliever of poverty and steward of abundance, protector of widows and father of orphans, friend of the poor, entertainer of strangers, physician to the sick, brother to all, and all things to all men (43.81). It all sounds very good. But even in the hands of the saintly Basil, such power over others could become imperious and damaging—as Gregory himself knew to his own cost.

The Monepiscopate: Basil and Ignatius

Gregory's portrait of Basil is not exactly the medieval prince-bishop of the West. But neither is it the bishop that Ignatius had in mind at the beginning of the second century. Ignatius, bishop of Antioch, was arrested and transported to Rome around 110, where he suffered martyrdom. On the way he wrote letters to various church communities in western Asia Minor. The burden of his message to the Ephesians is that they should be in harmony with their bishop, for he "speaks the mind of Christ." The presbytery are said to be "attuned to their bishop like the strings of a harp," with the result of such tuning being a hymn of praise (*Ephesians* 4). The Magnesians are to have respect for their bishop, despite his lack of years, and never to act independently of him (*Magnesians* 3, 7). The Trallians must be obedient to the bishop (*Trallians* 2). The Philadelphians are to follow their bishop like sheep (*Philadelphians* 2), while the Smyrnaeans will avoid faction by holding to the bishop's Eucharist (*Smyrnaeans* 8).

Ignatius's letters, being full of such advice, have usually been taken as evidence that the "monepiscopate" already existed before the time of this early bishop of Antioch, whereas they actually show that he was its first proponent. It seems likely that he urged the authority of the bishop precisely because it was contested rather than achieved. "To do everything in accordance with the bishop," therefore, should probably be seen as Ignatius's own solution to divisions and heresy in the churches to which he wrote. And so, in his view, the bishop was effectively the congregational leader.

But the social and political position of Basil within the Cappadocian church—let alone in relation to the Roman state—can hardly be compared with that of Ignatius, who was writing letters to obscure local communities as he journeyed on to Rome to die for Christ. We cannot generalize the forms and functions of ministry over several centuries without oversimplification.

2. THE APOSTOLIC CONSTITUTIONS: A FOURTH-CENTURY CHURCH MANUAL

Gregory's portrait of Basil combines temporal power in church and society with certain ideals of character drawn from Scripture. Another text from approximately the same period, the so-called *Apostolic Constitutions,* does much the same thing in ways that provide intriguing clues about both the origins of the forms of ministry that we find in the Greek fathers and the ideological milieu that produced a fourth-century Basil. Some understanding of this text, however, is required before we can explore what it has to say about the church and ministry (for a more extensive treatment, cf. my "*The Apostolic Constitutions:* A Methodological Case-Study").

Provenance and Value

The Apostolic Constitutions is, in reality, the end-point of a long process of development. It is a compendium that incorporates older texts and may loosely be described as collections of rules and canons about church order, ministry, and liturgy. The seventh book incorporates one of the earliest texts of this genre, the *Didache* or *Teaching of the Twelve Apostles* from the second century, which, since its rediscovery in 1873, is usually reckoned among the Apostolic Fathers—to which prayers, liturgical texts, and other odds and ends have been appended. The eighth book includes a third-century text known as the *Apostolic Tradition*, which was erroneously attributed to Hippolytus of Rome. The first six books largely reproduce another third-century writing extant in Syriac and known as the *Didascalia apostolorum*.

These older texts were not simply copied. Previous documents, which were thought to have apostolic authority, have been gathered together and reinforced with scriptural backing so as to create a community more in line with what was perceived to be apostolic intention. Scholars have plundered *The Apostolic Constitutions* to reconstruct what the church was like in the fourth century, and possibly before that to some extent. But the text is more prescriptive than descriptive. Furthermore, *The Apostolic Constitutions* rapidly lost influence, since the work in its final form was thought to be Arian.

Despite these reservations, however, *The Apostolic Constitutions* doubtless reflects the social world from which it came. It provides, therefore, a conservative and ideologically driven picture of a bishop's character and role to be set alongside Gregory's portrait of Basil. It also correlates the bishop's role with other ministerial offices in the context of the community as a whole.

The Church Community

The whole church in general is the opening subject of *The Apostolic Constitutions*. It is introduced as God's vineyard, containing the heirs of God's eternal kingdom—that is, those who are partakers of God's Holy Spirit, sprinkled by Christ's precious blood, and fellow heirs with God's beloved Son. Those who enjoy these promises are to do everything in obedience to God, so general commandments are assembled from Scripture, after which men and women are given advice appropriate to each.

Much of this material is about attitudes: not coveting, blessing those who curse you, loving enemies; the husband pleasing his wife and being compassionate to her; and the wife obeying her husband. The practical outworking of these exhortations is spelled out for each of those addressed in terms of not gadding about, not dressing up so as to attract others, sticking to proper tasks, reading the Bible rather than pagan literature, avoiding bathing in mixed company, and strengthening each other in the faith. The style is homiletic and reminiscent of ethical injunctions found in the New Testament and the Apostolic Fathers. Although often characterized as legislation for the laity, such a description hardly fits. Rather, these are exhortations intended to form a community with particular moral characteristics.

The Bishop and Other Officials

Uneven subdivisions make book 2 of *The Apostolic Constitutions* the most substantial part of the work. The focus is now on the bishop, with some relatively brief mention part way through of all those who perform functions in the church and share the tithes and offerings. These other officials include readers, singers, porters, deaconesses, widows, virgins, and orphans—along with bishops (as already mentioned), presbyters, and deacons. The latter three officials are designated high priests, priests, and Levites, respectively, and so a threefold ministry is here differentiated from other orders.

But emphasis on a threefold ministry is exceptional in *The Apostolic Constitutions*. The multiplicity of functions is more noticeable, as is the dominance of the bishop. In fact, the succeeding four books, books 3–6, revolve around the episcopal office, for the bishop holds responsibility for all the various things discussed—whether groups such as widows, or activities such as charitable works, or dealing with heresy and support of the persecuted.

Prime attention, however, is not given to the bishop's role or functions, but to his character. The characteristics required of a bishop mirror those stated in the Pastoral Epistles: he should not be fond of money, ambitious, double-minded, partial, or given to anger; rather, his character should be sober, prudent, decent, stable, generous, and humble. Scriptural quotes and examples enhance the picture of the one who rules and guides the community with wisdom, fairness, and patience. The bishop, in fact, represents God to the people. And he has God's authority to judge, exclude, govern, reform the penitent, and be the good shepherd of the flock.

In the words of book 2 of *The Apostolic Constitutions:*

> The bishop, he is the minister of the word, the keeper of knowledge, the mediator between God and you in the several parts of your divine worship. He is the teacher of piety; and, next after God, he is your father, who has begotten you again to the adoption of sons by water and the Spirit. He is your ruler and governor; he is your king and potentate; he is, next after God, your earthly god, who has a right to be honoured by you. (2.26)

Clearly, the bishop dominates the community. The social world that the author and his readers inhabited is taken for granted. That world was hierarchical and patriarchal. For as the father ruled a household, so the emperor ruled the world and God ruled the universe. People had roles within those structures under monarchical rule. In *The Apostolic Constitutions* all this is unquestioned. The text, in fact, suggests a series of overlapping discourses that indicate how the church mapped onto that world. The principal discourse would appear to be that of the household.

Servants in the Household of God

Sociological studies of the New Testament have demonstrated the significance of the household for understanding the church in its earliest phase. Not only did Christian groups meet in households, they also used familial language in designating God as Father and themselves as adopted sons and heirs through Christ, the Son of God, and in referring to each other as brothers and sisters in Christ. If Colossians, Ephesians, and 1 Peter deliver teaching in a form comparable with similar ethical discourse in the Greco-Roman world and dubbed

X

"household codes," the so-called Pastoral Epistles display a kind of adapted "household code" for the needs of the Household of God.

Book 1 of *The Apostolic Constitutions*, as we have noted, begins with the whole church, which is constituted of people who belong to God's household and who also run households of their own. The analogy between God's household and their own households implies parallels in appropriate behavior and qualities of character. The very shape of the text rapidly becomes that of a "household code" in reviewing what is required of first the husband and then the wife. Thus the ordinary life of Christians is to be morally ordered in light of relationships established within the Household of God. The analogy between God's household and everyday households to which people belong also illuminates ministerial forms and functions.

It has been reckoned that the typical household in the Greco-Roman world consisted of about fifty persons. The immediate kin would constitute an extended family of at least three generations, in addition to which there would be servants, slaves, tenants, clients, and others. There would be male and female servants, all of whom might be called *diakonoi*—even though they would undoubtedly have had differing duties. Does that bear on the question about women deacons? I suspect it does. For starting from everyday household usage, our understanding of what will later become technical terms of Christian ministry must undergo some shift of perspective. Deacons were simply servants in God's household with a range of services to provide—some appropriately assigned to men, others to women. It is, however, somewhat misleading to look here for precedents when arguing for women's ordination in a very different social world.

Following the same principle, the *episkopos* would simply be the head steward, the top servant. But being a managerial slave in charge of others and representing the master could bring great authority in the households of antiquity. It could even mean holding the master's seal and being able to enter into business contracts on his behalf. When Paul speaks of himself as God's *doulos*, it is, as Dale Martin points out, a double-edged expression that adopts the humility of a slave while proudly claiming to speak and act on God's behalf (cf. Martin, *Slavery as Salvation*). It is hardly surprising, therefore, that the *episkopos* appears as representing God in early ecclesiastical texts, including *The Apostolic Constitutions*. God is, as it were, the *pater familias* in whose service bishops and deacons are employed. So the bishop is to be obeyed as one would obey God, for he is the steward who both represents God the Householder and serves the members of the household—administering funds and seeing to the family's needs, both temporal and spiritual.

Widows and Presbyters

The New Testament oscillates between the language of family and the language of service. So does *The Apostolic Constitutions*. Service would seem to be the context from which the titles "bishop" and "deacon" were drawn. But what about "widow" and "presbyter"? Were these terms drawn from the realm of family discourse?

Commentators have long been puzzled as to why, compared with bishops and deacons, presbyters hardly appear in *The Apostolic Constitutions*. It is worth considering whether this difference preserves the memory of a distinction in discourse that would clarify different ministerial roles. My suggestion is that "widows" and "presbyters" take their designations from the discourse of the family, by contrast with the discourse of service from which "bishops" and "deacons" received theirs.

Some seeking precedent for women's ordination have tried to prove that "widows" formed a kind of ministerial order in the early church (as, e.g., Thurston, *The Widows*). But widows in the relevant texts seem primarily to be those on a register to receive charity. Frequently they are bracketed with orphans, have to be needy and of a certain age, and are expected to reciprocate with prayers and proper behavior. This offering of prayers and their designation as "the church's altar" (*Apostolic Constitutions* 3.6.3, and elsewhere) have suggested, at least to some interpreters, a holy office of some kind. Yet the phrase "the church's altar" is also used of orphans, and so must surely have arisen from the view that almsgiving replaced sacrifice. What we find here, therefore, is not a ministerial "order" but an extension of the responsibilities of households and families to provide for their dependants.

But what about the elusive presbyters? Most remarkable is *Apostolic Constitutions* 2.28. The general context concerns the distribution of tithes and offerings, and soon we read that a double portion should be set aside for the presbyters. But first there appear *presbyterai*. The question is: Are these female presbyters or just old women? The matter at issue in the text concerns inviting these women to feasts—that is, that they should be women the deacons know to be in need.

So are male "presbyters" any more than "older men" who need support? Well, they are described as busy with the "word" and "teaching," as standing in the place of the apostles, and as counselors of the bishop. Are the presbyters, then, the revered elderly in the household of God—in particular, those who are the bishop's advisers because they carry the community memory? My suggestion is that these references in *The Apostolic Constitutions* allow us to discern a shift in the discourse whereby everyday terms drawn from the household and family become technical terms in a surrogate family community, which functions like a voluntary association.

God's People

In the Greco-Roman world, households were generally treated as analogous to kingdoms, and vice versa. So the members of the civil service, for example, were known as "Caesar's household," and the ideal philosopher-king was instructed to mirror the good householder who directed, cared for, even educated and trained everyone for whom he was responsible. Belonging to God's household, therefore, could easily slide into a sense of being God's people—a nation over whom God rules through earthly ministers.

This wider discourse, in fact, pervades *The Apostolic Constitutions* and undergirds its use of Scripture. For in *The Apostolic Constitutions* the institutions of ancient Israel are taken to have their counterparts in the church, which is now God's people, and Old Testament texts are used to shape the duties and obligations of the church's officeholders, who are now, as it were, officers of God's state. And the analogy between household and state is projected onto the universe.

Clearly, this perspective had already shaped a discourse that had already encouraged the conflation of Christianity with traditional state religion as practiced by imperial Rome. In book 7 of *The Apostolic Constitutions* one noticeable modification made to the *Didache* is the long insertion about fearing the emperor because he represents Christ. Yet the discourse of religion does not appear to be the most obvious for us to pursue in adopting a sociological approach to *The Apostolic Constitutions.*

Religion in antiquity was neither a matter of belief nor the preserve of a single institution. Rather, religion was woven into everyday life. At one level, it consisted of respect to the household gods; at another, civic festivals—all of which were seen as expressions of "piety" toward the traditions of the ancestors and obligations to the gods who protected the family and the nation. *The Apostolic Constitutions*, of course, projects a Christianized version of this general religious orientation. But that is because its fundamental discourse is that of household and people.

When Christians established places of worship, they adapted houses and built basilicas. Basilicas were public meeting places and places where teaching took place—not palaces for the gods, which were served by priests while the people remained in the courts outside. The voluntary associations or philosophical schools of the day are closer precedents for early Christian gatherings. These associations and schools had religious aspects, but they also provided precedent for a critique of religion, both public and private. For Christians, that critique was married with biblical opposition to sacrifice, such as is found in the Old Testament prophets (as we will see below).

The Community as "School"

The fact that the Christian community was a religious oddity is sharpened by the description of a church gathering in *Apostolic Constitutions* 2.57. The bishop is first described as the commander of a great ship. The building is to be long, with its head to the east, and the seating arrangements are to be such as to reflect the tasks of a captain and a ship's company—everyone in his or her own proper place. This prepares for the reading of Scripture and the exhortation of the presbyters, which are culminated with the discourse of the bishop who sits centrally as the commander.

The church is then likened to a sheepfold—with, again, the proper ordering of women, young people, and children capturing the headlines. Only now does attention turn to prayer, which is followed by the offering of the Eucharist. This climax may be analogous to religious rituals, but it is placed in a rather strange context. For while the language of sacrifice and priesthood permeates much of this text, it retains the sense of a community that has distanced itself from common religious practices. Furthermore, it has instruction at its heart and claims a more rational understanding of the universe and its relation to God the Creator.

All of this hints at another fruitful sociological model, namely the school. One of the most important themes in *The Apostolic Constitutions*, in fact, is knowledge. The very existence of "heresy" is an indication that the analogy with philosophical schools ran deep, for it was the schools that offered various "options" *(haereses)* and delivered rival "teachings" *(dogmata)*. Indeed, placing a body of literature at the heart of the community and delivering exegetical discourses on such approved texts was analogous to school activity as practiced in the cities of the Roman Empire. *The Apostolic Constitutions*, in fact, presents the bishop as responsible for seeing that members conform to the teachings of the Christian "school" tradition.

What, then, of the liturgical texts incorporated into this compendium? Most work on these texts has been done by liturgiologists, whose interest has been primarily with the prayers themselves and tracing out the development of liturgy. It has been widely accepted that the prayers of book 7 have a strongly Jewish character, and doubtless that is an important clue with regard to origins. For certainly another discourse that shaped early Christian institutions was that of the Jewish synagogue.

Indeed, the precedent of the synagogue could account for many of the overlapping discourses we have been exploring. The Jewish people had lost their temple and land but, though scattered across the world, preserved their culture—including its religious traditions—through community institutions and regular gatherings for reading their sacred texts and praying without sacrifice. The Jewish community to many in the ancient world seemed like a school. Some, in fact, respected them for having a philosophical religion of a higher order than the rest of society since it was focused on monotheism and morality.

The interesting thing about *The Apostolic Constitutions* is what it takes for granted—that is, that these overlapping discourses make sense. A new discourse was emerging that would contribute to the formation of a new world in which imperial and hierarchical authority would be given apostolic and theological warrant. And it is *The Apostolic Constitutions* that enables us to explore the nature of the community within which ministers performed their functions, provides clues to the origins of the forms of ministry we find in the Greek fathers, and sets out the ideological background that produced such a man in the fourth century as Basil, bishop of Caesarea in the Roman province of Cappadocia.

X

3. OUTSTANDING QUESTIONS

It would seem that by the time Basil mounted the episcopal throne and *The Apostolic Constitutions* was compiled, the threefold ministry had been established. Bishops presided over cities with many congregations, and presbyters were local eucharistic ministers served by deacons. Those offering the Eucharist had become priests presenting a sacrifice. A pattern of hierarchical progression through the ranks of the clergy appears also to have established itself, though irregularities sometimes occurred. Yet, as we have seen, the conservative compendium of older texts called *The Apostolic Constitutions* only partially presents such a picture. For the bishop still appears to preside over a unitary community, being assisted by deacons, while the presbyters' role is mostly obscured.

We are left, then, with several pertinent questions: (1) How do the clues picked up from this text relate to other evidence, and how might they affect classic theories about the origin and development of the threefold ministry? (2) Was there—or, perhaps, at what moment in history did there develop—a rigid distinction between ordained clergy belonging to this threefold order and the many other functionaries and holy offices in the church, especially such as lectors, widows, virgins, and ascetics? (3) How was priesthood associated with church functionaries who apparently did not carry priestly titles, and what were the implications of this development? The remainder of this chapter will pursue these issues.

4. ORIGIN AND DEVELOPMENT OF THE THREEFOLD MINISTRY

As is well known, "elders" *(presbyteroi)* do not appear in the principal Pauline letters, but do emerge in the Acts of the Apostles and the Pastoral Epistles. In the latter, their relationship with an "overseer" or "bishop" *(episkopos)* is notoriously unclear. In Titus 1:5–9, we are given to understand that Titus was to appoint "presbyters" *(presbyteroi)* in each city in Crete, their character is briefly sketched, and then the text continues: "For a bishop *(episkopos)*, as God's steward, must be blameless" (v. 7). The little word "for" has suggested that the same subject is in view and that therefore *episkopos* may simply be an alternative term for *presbyteros*. So the standard theory (which is taken for granted elsewhere in this volume) is that a "college" of *presbyteroi* was presided over by one of their number known as the *episkopos*. Then, it is suggested, in the early second-century writings of Ignatius we see the situation developing, when he insists on the authority of the monepiscopate and reflects a threefold ministry.

Ignatius, however, twice produces a puzzling image of the Christian ministry in exhorting two of the churches he writes to in western Asia Minor:

> Hasten to do all things in harmony with God, with the *episkopos* presiding in the place of God and the *presbyteroi* in the place of the *synedrion* of the Apostles, and the *diakonoi*, who are most dear to me, entrusted with the *diakonia* of Jesus Christ, who was from eternity with the Father and was made manifest at the end of time. (*Magnesians* 6)

Likewise, let all respect the *diakonoi* as Jesus Christ, even as the *episkopos* is the "type" of the Father, and the *presbyteroi* God's *synedrion* and as the *synedrion* of the Apostles. (*Trallians* 3)

Thus, in both *Magnesians* 6 and *Trallians* 3, he likens the *episkopos* to God, the *diakonoi* to Christ, and the *presbyteroi* to the apostles.

Reading Ignatius's comparisons in light of the developed clerical hierarchy, it seems odd that the deacons should apparently be ranked higher than the presbyters—as Andrew Louth has noted (*Early Christian Writings*, 82). This is not to be lightly explained away, for we find exactly the same oddity in *Didascalia* 9—indeed compounded—since deaconesses are there likened to the Holy Spirit! And this phenomenon is reproduced in *Apostolic Constitutions* 2.26, where priority is given to the Trinitarian representation in the ministry of the bishop (God the Father), deacons (Christ), and deaconesses (the Holy Spirit)—with presbyters appearing at the end of the list, almost as an afterthought.

The Pastoral Epistles

If we return to the Pastoral Epistles and read them in the light of this evidence, we can find there a distinction between bishops and deacons on the one hand, and presbyters on the other. In 1 Tim 3:1–13, which appears a bit like an ecclesiastical code, two kinds of "officers" appear, and only two: the *episkopos* and the *diakonoi*. This accords with the reference to *episkopoi* and *diakonoi* in Phil 1:1, where such officers are simply taken for granted—presumably by both the author and his readers, for no explanation or discussion is offered. *Presbyteroi* do not appear in this context in 1 Timothy, any more than they do in Philippians and the other principal Pauline letters. Elsewhere in the Pastoral Epistles, where they do appear, the duty lists are still very close to "household codes." Titus 2:1–15 is clearly talking about old men and women, as contrasted with young people and slaves, within the household community.

The situation elsewhere in 1 Timothy, however, is a bit more complex. The term *presbyteros* appears in chapter 5, and in the opening sentence of that chapter the natural sense of "senior" appears correct—for family relations are the subject and a presbyter is to be treated as a father, just as young men are to be treated as brothers, *presbyterai* (feminine plural) as mothers, and younger women as sisters. There follows, however, an extended passage on widows, after which we read that the *presbyteroi* who preside well are worthy of a double "honor" *(timē)*, especially those who labor in the word and teaching. Presumably, given the following justification in verses 18–19, the honor *(timē)* given is to be understood as pay or an honorarium for their teaching activities. Besides teaching, they also "preside." This, as well as the succeeding discussion of discipline, suggests we are no longer talking simply about "older men." And the reference in 1 Tim 4:14 to the *presbyterion* as laying on hands, presumably in some sense "ordaining," confirms this. Furthermore, we should note how closely the *Apostolic Constitutions* follows this text.

X

I have suggested that none of the solutions proposed so far really accounts for this complex evidence. The clue, however, is to be found in the curious statements of Ignatius, which are followed by the *Didascalia*. And the answer, I suggest, lies in the theory outlined earlier: that the *episkopos* and that the *diakonoi* were originally the only appointed "officers" of the congregation; and that the congregation was established as "God's household" (1 Tim 3:15), the *episkopos* being "God's steward" (Titus 1:7) and the *diakonoi* being the servants.

Presbyters as the Guardians of Tradition

As for the presbyters, the terminology was from the beginning ambiguous and basically suggests seniority. Confusion as to whether the term is to be used in a natural or a technical sense is already present in the Pastoral Epistles, as we have seen. "The Household of God" was a family community made up of older and younger people, both men and women. As the Pastoral Epistles indicate, seniority came with age and was to be respected. It seems entirely plausible that the "senior citizen" carried what we might call the community memory, and so was commissioned to teach the tradition.

That *presbyteros* was associated with tradition is clear from the fragments of the second-century writer Papias—though, of course, Papias' own use of the term is notoriously unclear:

> I shall not hesitate to furnish you, along with the interpretations, with all that in days gone by I carefully learned from the *presbyteroi* and have carefully recalled, for I can guarantee its truth. . . . And whenever anyone came who had been a follower of the *presbyteroi*, I inquired into the words of the *presbyteroi*, what Andrew or Peter had said, or Philip or Thomas or James or John or Matthew, or any other disciple of the Lord, and what Aristion and the *presbyteros* John, disciples of the Lord, were still saying. (Eusebius, *Hist. eccl.* 3.39)

The problem with this much-quoted passage is that *presbyteros* is used in two, if not three, different ways: (1) with reference to the apostles; (2) with reference to people who appear to be second generation Christians, where the phrase "the presbyter John" may or may not indicate that the term was used in a technical sense; and, perhaps also initially, (3) for "seniors" in general who authentically bear the tradition. The importance of the passage, however, is that it shows that in the second century the term was not simply used in a technical way for an "office," but was also used, apparently, to mean the senior members of the community who carried the community memory—indeed, in this sense, even for the apostles themselves. This explains the curious link between presbyters and apostles noted earlier.

It makes sense that as the generations passed the *episkopos* should appoint older, more senior members to act as an advisory council. It also fits with the problem at Corinth dealt with in *1 Clement* and with the response made in that writing—that is, that younger people should not rise in revolt against the senior people who carry the community memory and to whom the *episkopos* turns for advice, for they form the church council.

The Synagogue Analogy

But there is also another possible factor to be considered here, and that is the analogy of the Jewish communities in the Diaspora. It seems that such Jewish communities were governed by a council of elders who appointed the synagogue officials. And the early Christian evidence indicates that the presbyterate ordained the *episkopos*, though the *episkopos* appointed the presbyters.

My own admittedly tentative hypothesis is as follows: that the administrator of the church, who was called an *episkopos* by longstanding Christian habit, began to acquire the functions of a Jewish *archisynagogos* ("ruler/head/administrator of the synagogue"); and that *diakonoi* in the churches began to acquire the functions of the almoners and attendants in the Jewish synagogues—in addition, of course, to those associated with the Christian eucharistic meal. Meanwhile, Christians, who, like Jews, were excluded by their religious scruples from many normal civic functions, began to organize themselves as a kind of distinct "ethnic" community—later to be known as a "third race," which was neither Jew nor Gentile but professed a "heavenly citizenship." So their "seniors" were constituted into a kind of governing council for the community, with authority to appoint and advise the *episkopos*.

Whereas Jewish community leaders often obtained some constitutional recognition from the officials of the various cities, Christians lacked that privilege. Internally, however, they endeavored to organize themselves in a parallel way, and the apologists of the second century tried to claim that same right to recognition. So there is a perceptible shift in the way Christians were beginning to identify themselves socially—from "God's household" to "God's people."

So my suggestion (which I have spelled out more fully in "On *Episkopos* and *Presbyteros*" and *The Theology of the Pastoral Letters*) is that the origins of the presbyterate are distinct from those of the episcopate and the diaconate, the *presbyteroi* were originally a council of senior Christians, who were recognized as the bearers of the apostolic tradition, and, therefore, their association with the apostles was natural—indeed, that the very term *presbyteros* could be used of the apostles themselves.

5. FROM "MINISTRY" TO "PRIESTHOOD"

The shift from God's household to God's people is the key to answering our other questions, for not only did it allow the effective taking over of monarchical institutions from what was by now the Christian Old Testament, but by means of typology it also enabled the assimilation of the orders of ministry to the orders of priesthood under the Old Covenant. As already noted, the *Apostolic Constitutions* likened the bishop to the high priest, presbyters to priests, and deacons to Levites.

X

And this correlation of offices, I suggest, is what finally shaped the threefold hierarchy in its traditional ranking.

The distinction between "ministry" and "priesthood" has been important in post-Reformation debates. The churches of the Protestant Reformation, basing their arguments on key New Testament texts, have insisted that the priesthood belongs, on the one hand, to Christ and Christ alone, but also belongs, on the other, to all believers. The Roman Catholic tradition has associated priesthood with the presidency of the Eucharist, with the priest being a "type" of Christ in that context. If we were here taking into account the Latin fathers as well, we would find in Cyprian the earliest statements encouraging that view (cf. my brief excursus on Cyprian appended at the end of this chapter). Elsewhere I have argued that to use references to the priest as a "type" of Christ as an argument against women's ordination is to misunderstand typology—for all martyrs, whether male or female, were regarded as "types" of Christ. But let me not get diverted further, except to point out that, insofar as it claims to represent Christ's servanthood, this kind of typological modeling of ministry on Christ's ministry also undergirds Protestant ministry. The difference between Catholic and Protestant lies in the nature of the Eucharist as sacrifice.

My principal aim in referring to these matters is to highlight what I think is an important contrast—that is, that originally during the postapostolic period, and in the East predominantly, the priesthood attributed to officers of the church was validated not by an explicit reference to the eucharistic sacrifice, nor by reference to the person of Christ, but by means of Old Testament typology. As noted, the three orders *episkopos, presbyteros,* and *diakonos* were linked with the high priest, the priests, and the Levites of the Old Covenant, respectively. Already in the late first-century work known as *1 Clement* we have hints of what was to come, for in chapters 40–41 the author pleads for due order in the church and backs up his exhortations with allusions to the Scriptures. The church at Corinth, to which *1 Clement* is addressed, had at that time, it seems, a high priest, priests, Levites, and laity—each with particular offices to perform. The Eucharist is implicitly paralleled with the daily sacrifices of the Jerusalem temple. Scriptural typology, in fact, is the undergirding concept for the writer of *1 Clement.* And by the time of the *Apostolic Constitutions,* such a typological understanding was clearly written deeply into Christian tradition.

The Rejection of Sacrifice

To get all of this into perspective, it is important to realize that earliest Christianity had firmly rejected cultic worship, whether pagan or Jewish (cf. my *Use of Sacrificial Ideas in Greek Christian Writers*). Adapting the critique of the philosophers, early Christians claimed to offer a spiritual cult, prayers rather than sacrifices, circumcision of the heart rather than of the flesh, and the indwelling of the Holy Spirit—with the indwelling of the Holy Spirit making their bodies into spiritual temples. The antisacrificial passages of the prophets were cited as evidence, together with such classic texts as Ps 51:17: "The sacrifice acceptable to

God is a broken spirit; a broken and contrite heart, O God, you will not despise." By contrast with both Greeks and Jews, Christians spoke of offering "bloodless sacrifices"—that is, true spiritual praises and thanksgivings. From the earliest days, Mal 1:10–11 had become an important text in the church: "I will not accept an offering from your hands. For from the rising of the sun to its setting my name is great among the nations, and in every place incense is offered to my name and a pure offering." Gentile Christians now offered everywhere the pure spiritual worship that God required. Writing in the mid-second century, Justin, who died a martyr at Rome in 165, notes that this pure offering is made especially, but certainly not exclusively, at the thanksgiving "whereby the passion which the Son of God endured for us is commemorated" (*Dial.* 117).

It is abundantly clear by the time we reach the *Apostolic Tradition* of (Ps.-) Hippolytus that first fruits and other offerings in kind, as well as almsgiving and charity, along with the Eucharist, were expressions of Christian sacrificial worship, and that these offerings were made through Christian "priests." Animal sacrifice was not reinstated, but a purified cult was being recommended as an alternative. Second-century apologists used this Christian understanding of a purified cult as a powerful argument. Pythagoreans had long opposed animal sacrifice and practiced vegetarianism. Now for Christians the philosophical critique and the prophetic condemnation of sacrifice came conveniently together.

Typology and Sacrifice

Nonetheless, even as this critique was being pressed home, the cultic system of Leviticus was taken over as "type" or prefiguration of the Christian purified way of worship. Origen's exegesis validated a typological approach to the Pentateuch. Almost two centuries later, a treatise such as Cyril of Alexandria's *On Worship in Spirit and in Truth* develops and sums up a whole tradition: that Old Testament law points forward to its fulfillment in Christ and that Christian worship exemplifies the characteristics of true worship as foreshadowed in that law.

Already in the second century, this typological reading of sacrifice was leading naturally to the association of the Old Testament priesthood with the leaders of the church, especially the *episkopos*. The Greek fathers, however, show little sign of having associated particularly closely this reconstituted priesthood with the Eucharist as such. There is nothing to suggest it in Gregory's portrait of Basil or in the *Apostolic Constitutions.* Later we find John Chrysostom much exercised by the question as to how there could be one sacrifice of Christ when the Eucharist is repeated in many places and at many times (*Hom. Heb.* 27). In fact, he is adamant that Christ's one sacrifice is never repeated, and he resorts to *anamnēsis* (memorial) as he searches for a way to safeguard that one, completed sacrifice.

Yet Chrysostom also wants to claim a mystic union of the many Eucharists with the one sacrifice where Christ was both priest and victim (cf. my *Use of Sacrificial Ideas*). And in his work *On Priesthood* he emphasizes the awe-inspiring nature of the priest's duties at the Eucharist. Christian worship, it appears, was increasingly assimilating the religious features of a dying paganism. Theologically,

X

however, it was as priests of the New Covenant that first bishops, and then presbyters, received their priestly designations, and not originally because they were eucharistic celebrants. Typology was the ancient and persisting justification for associating priesthood with the officers of the Christian community.

So the separation of the three orders from all the others who had roles in the church community arose from the association of bishops, priests, and deacons with the priests and Levites of the Old Covenant. To treat Cyprian as the one who turned ministers into priests, as is often done (cf., e.g., Hanson, *Christian Priesthood Examined*), is to miss the difference between Cyprian's position and the much more general acceptance of the typological character of the Old Testament Scriptures.

6. CONCLUSION

It is hardly possible to trace a simple linear development through the Greek fathers with respect to models of ministry and community formation. If we take seriously the potential for typological association, it is evident that the projection of Old Testament models of kingship and priesthood was almost inevitable. Monarchy and patriarchy were both biblically and socially sanctioned. They were reinforced by monotheism, as God's sovereignty was mirrored in the head of state, the head of the household, and the episcopal head of the church.

What we are to make of this in a world of democracy and equal opportunities is the challenging question we face today. Was it a sellout to the surrounding culture or a healthy "indigenization"? Should we seek parallel "inculturations" or cling to continuity with the past? Probably it is worth noting, in conclusion, that even the conservative *Apostolic Constitutions* did not avoid updating.

AN EXCURSUS

Cyprian was bishop of Carthage around 250 C.E.. In the Decian persecution he tactically withdrew from the city and left the presbyters in charge. His authority was challenged, particularly over the question of the readmission of "lapsed" Christians to communion. It is now widely thought that these events and Cyprian's response to them were instrumental in his developing of a situation where presbyters acted as local eucharistic ministers under the authority of the bishop, who had wider responsibilities—thereby establishing the monepiscopate and a clerical hierarchy.

Cyprian wrote treatises about the issues of his day, including *On the Unity of the Church*. Perhaps more important, however, are his letters, from which a detailed account of his struggles can be reconstructed. In his writings we find clear statements about priesthood: the priesthood is invested in the bishop, but presbyters share in the "priestly honor" of the bishop (*Epistle* 1.1, 61.3).

Epistle 63 is a key text for understanding what this means. Here Cyprian affirms that "the Lord's passion is the sacrifice we offer." This is prefigured in

Melchizedek's offering of bread and wine in Gen 14:18; it is "postfigured" in the Eucharist, where the priest "images" Christ:

> For if Christ Jesus our Lord and God himself is the High Priest of God the Father and first offered himself as a sacrifice to the Father, and commanded that this take place in his memory, that priest indeed truly functions in the place of Christ who imitates that which Christ did, and consequently offers a true and complete sacrifice in the Church to God the Father. (*Epistle* 63.14)

Because this imitation of Christ is occasionally described in rather literal terms, as if the priest were slaughtering the Lamb of God on the altar, this statement has often been interpreted in a rather literalistic way—that is, that only a man can "image" the man Christ. But typology, like metaphor and simile, is not meant to be taken literally, as if every point of comparison were valid. Martyrs, both women and men, were regarded as "types" of Christ as they suffered with him. No one quite meant that the Eucharist was a kind of "passion play." But Cyprian certainly implies that the terminology of priesthood is to be associated with eucharistic presidency.

My argument in this chapter has been that Cyprian's view was not only a novel view, but also one that remained somewhat marginal among the early Church Fathers. Old Testament typology, rather than Christology, was dominant in the postapostolic church's justification of the use of priestly language for ministerial functions.

BIBLIOGRAPHY

Primary Materials in English Translation

Clementines and *Apostolic Constitutions,* in *Ante-Nicene Christian Library: Translations of the Writings of the Fathers Down to A.D. 325.* Vol. 17. Edited by A. Roberts and J. Donaldson. Edinburgh: T&T Clark, 1870. Reprinted in *Ante-Nicene Fathers.* Vols. 7 and 8. Peabody, Mass.: Hendrickson, 1994.

Correspondence of St. Cyprian. 4 vols. Edited by G. W. Clarke. New York: Newman, 1984–1989.

Cyril of Jerusalem and *Gregory Nazianzen.* Vol. 7 of *The Nicene and Post-Nicene Fathers,* 2d series. Edited by P. Schaff and H. Wace. Peabody, Mass.: Hendrickson, 1994.

Early Christian Writings: The Apostolic Fathers. Translated by M. Staniforth and A. Louth. Rev. ed. Baltimore: Penguin Books, 1987.

Eusebius. *The History of the Church from Christ to Constantine.* Translated by G. A. Williamson. Baltimore: Penguin, 1965.

Secondary Literature

Burtchaell, James T. *From Synagogue to Church: Public Services and Offices in the Earliest Christian Communities.* Cambridge: Cambridge University Press, 1992.

X

Hanson, Richard. *Christian Priesthood Examined.* Guildford: Lutterworth, 1979.

Malherbe, Abraham J. *Social Aspects of Early Christianity.* 2d ed. Philadelphia: Fortress, 1983.

Martin, Dale B. *Slavery as Salvation: The Metaphor of Slavery in Pauline Christianity.* New Haven, Conn.: Yale University Press, 1990.

Thurston, Bonnie Bowman. *The Widows: A Women's Ministry in the Early Church.* Minneapolis: Fortress, 1989.

Torjesen, Karen Jo. *When Women Were Priests: Women's Leadership in the Early Church and the Scandal of Their Subordination in the Rise of Christianity.* San Francisco: HarperCollins, 1993.

Young, Frances. "The *Apostolic Constitutions:* A Methodological Case-Study." Pages 105–18 in *Studia Patristica,* vol. 36. Papers presented at the Thirteenth International Conference on Patristic Studies held in Oxford 1999. Edited by M. F. Wiles and E. J. Yarnold with the assistance of P. M. Parvis. Leuven: Peeters, 2001.

———. "On *Episkopos* and *Presbyteros.*" *Journal of Theological Studies* 45 (1994): 142–48.

———. *Presbyteral Ministry in the Catholic Tradition, or "Why Shouldn't Women be Priests?"* London: Methodist Sacramental Fellowship, 1994.

———. *The Theology of the Pastoral Letters.* Cambridge: Cambridge University Press, 1994.

———. *The Use of Sacrificial Ideas in Greek Christian Writers from the New Testament to John Chrysostom.* Philadelphia: Philadelphia Patristic Foundation, 1979.

XI

Exegetical Method and Scriptural Proof
the Bible in doctrinal debate

Exegesis is a curious art — like religion more often caught than taught. Generations of students of the classics unconsciously picked up what the exegetical process involves. But now, in England at any rate, that educational pattern is declining, and students have not assimilated an understanding of what it means to expound or explicate a text. It has become necessary to articulate what is involved, and clarify the question of method, at the most basic level.

Exegesis is a curious art, and the more experts try to articulate method and theory, the more removed they become from its actual practice. Introductory books on critical methods are legion. Books on hermeneutics abound. The methodological debates fuel more books, and spawn more debates. It all purports to describe and evaluate the exegetical process, but just as practising scientists cannot recognise their own activity in the descriptions offered by philosophers of science, so practising exegetes often fail to recognise their own activity in philosophical descriptions of interpretation.

Exegesis is a curious art — curious because of a certain complexity which almost defies exhaustive description; — curious because the judgement of the exegete in distinguishing what is obvious and what needs explanation is absolutely crucial and yet so elusive as to be indefinable; — curious because the impact of the text on the reader and the impact of the reader on the text is inextricably interwoven; — curious because while it is possible to identify and exclude false exegesis, it is rarely possible to establish a final incontestable interpretation.

So much for my exordium!

Anyone trying to describe or assess patristic exegesis faces all these problems and more. The exegetical task is not fundamentally different, yet the problems of evaluation are compounded by differences between the Fathers and ourselves in assumption, language and culture. I am more and more convinced that standard analyses of patristic exegesis are simply inadequate to the material we are actually presented with, and to characterise their exegesis as dogmatic or symbolic, or describe their methods in terms of typology, allegory, theoria, literalism, or what you will, falls far short of doing justice to their practice. Origen, as is well known, rarely followed strictly the methods he himself commended, and a far more sophisticated description of what he actually did, is necessary. Instinctively he practised methods he had caught as well as techniques he had been taught, and the range of moves he actually made in performing the exegetical task was not clearly articulated even by the practitioner himself.

The inadequacy of the classic descriptions and analyses becomes especially clear when we tackle the question of exegetical method in doctrinal debate. On the whole in trying to characterise patristic exegesis, attention has been paid, not to use of the Bible in debate, but to methods used in scriptural exposition as such, in treatise, commentary or homily. A few important studies have noted the appeal to scripture in the Arian controversy,[1] and explored the general place of scriptural authority in doctrinal debate.[2] Some papers have researched the way in which particular texts were interpreted in the course of the patristic period, a notable example being Simonetti's study of Proverbs 8.22,[3] which documents the process whereby debate shifted understanding of the meaning of the text. But the job done is sheer reporting without raising the question by what exegetical methods the meanings were arrived at. The question might be: did doctrinal debate induce appeal to the literal sense of texts, as if the Fathers instinctively sensed that, while it was legitimate to let the imagination run in spiritual meditation or exhortation, texts had to be treated more seriously when concrete issues of truth were at stake? In other words, did the use of texts as proof produce a divorce between this and the allegorical or theoretic methods used in devotion? Perhaps to our surprise, it seems not. Allegory was not perceived as producing other than truth; nor did they mean by "literal" the same kind of thing as we do. Often the use of texts in doctrinal debate presupposes typological, allegorical or Christological meanings which we would not normally admit as "literal". The understanding of texts presupposed or argued in debate is not apparently wholly other than the approach to exegesis in other contexts — or is it? That is the question with which this paper hopes to deal, and in so doing to throw light on the whole process of exegesis.

As a practical acknowledgement of the complexity of the task of describing or analysing exegetical methods, let us begin by simply observing a particular debate. It is a doctrinal debate, but interestingly focusses on the question of the real meaning of a key text. The discussion we will use is found in the first of Theodoret's dialogues between Eranistes, the Picker-up of odds and ends, and Orthodoxus.[4] The context is the great Christological debate between Antioch and Alexandria in the fifth century, and the topic is the ἄτρεπτος

---

[1] E.g. E. Boularand, *L'Hérésie d'Arius et la "foi" de Nicée* (2 vols. Paris, 1972).

[2] E.g. R.E. Person, *The Mode of Theological Decision Making at the Early Ecumenical Councils* (Basel, 1978) — an enquiry into the function of scripture and tradition at the councils of Nicaea and Ephesus.

[3] M. Simonetti, *Studi sull' Arianesimo* (Rome, 1965), chapter 1.

[4] Text ed. Gerard H. Ettlinger (Oxford, 1975).

(unchangeable) nature of the Logos. To our use of it as an example it may be objected that an Antiochene wrote the dialogue and the representative Alexandrian is unfairly represented as a soft touch, but by the time we have finished I think you will agree that that does not invalidate its use for the purposes of analysis of how the meaning of biblical texts was discussed.

The adversaries begin by agreeing to follow in the tracks of the apostles and prophets and the holy men who came after them. They agree that with respect to God, Father, Son and Holy Spirit, we speak of one οὐσία, "as we have been taught by divine scripture, old and new, and by the Fathers gathered at Nicaea". They agree to distinguish οὐσία and ὑπόστασις, the former referring to τὸ κοινόν or τὸ γένος, the second to τὸ ἴδιον, species rather then genus. Such analytical statements are illustrated and confirmed by the use of scriptural examples; in Gen. 6.7, the singular is used for τὸ κοινόν, when God speaks of removing "the man which I have made" from the face of the earth. Similarly in Psalm 49.20 (LXX 48.21), David speaks not of a particular individual when he uses ἄνθρωπος in the singular, but rather of common humanity. Similarly, they agree, the divine οὐσία in the singular signifies the Holy Triad, but ὑπόστασις indicates the individuality of each πρόσωπον, Father, Son and Holy Spirit. In this discussion, scripture is used to provide instances of linguistic usage, and the meaning of the texts to which reference is made is not in dispute.

The discussion turns to the question of "common" and "particular" titles or attributes. Agreement is easy that θεός, κύριος, δημιουργός, παντο-κράτωρ, etc. are common, while ἀγέννητος belongs to the Father, μονογεγής to the Son and παράκλητος to the Holy Spirit. The question then raised is whether ἄτρεπτος is common or particular. They quickly agree that it must be common, because it would be impossible for a single οὐσία to be partly changeable and partly unchangeable. Then comes the crunch question. Orthodoxus, who represents the Antiochene side, demands to know how his opponent, by adducing the Gospel saying ὁ λόγος σὰρξ ἐγένετο, can attribute τροπή — change — to what is by nature ἄτρεπτος — unchangeable. So the discussion focusses on how the word "became" is to be understood in John 1.14, and it is to this issue that the debate constantly returns.

To begin with, impossible alternatives are presented to the hapless Eranistes: either the Logos underwent change or he "seemed" to. The docetic possibility is immediately ruled out, and the assertion made that God was "enfleshed" — the Greek verb σαρκωθῆναι enters the ring. Orthodoxus demands a definition of its meaning: does it mean "to take flesh" or "to be changed into flesh"? Poor old Eranistes ducks the issue and insists upon the word of scripture. That reintroduces the basic exegetical question: how is ἐγένετο to be understood in John 1.14? Eranistes, driven into a corner over whether it means change or not, resorts to "all things are possible with God", backed up with scriptural examples like the Nile being turned into blood, and scriptural proof-texts like Psalm 135.6 (LXX 134.6): "everything the Lord wills he does", coupled with further allusions to the Gospels. Orthodoxus counters with the argument that, of course the Creator can do what he likes with his creation, but in himself he has a nature which is inalienable, ἄτρεπτον and ἀναλλοίωτον; and he for his part also backs up his contention with appeal to scripture: while Amos speaks of God making all things and changing them, Psalm 102.27 (LXX 101.28) says, "You are the same and your years do not pass", and God says through Malachi: "I am and I am not changed". Here we notice both sides, in attempting to elucidate the disputed text, resorting to other scriptural texts. The meaning of these other texts is taken to be indisputable, and the issue between the contestants is which texts are relevant to the case.

It may well be that Theodoret intended to present Eranistes as outwitted by this, but Eranistes' next move is not without theological legitimacy: "one must not investigate hidden matters", he suggests. The appeal to "mystery" is the resort of theologians in every generation when the going gets rough, and the scorn of their opponents is often justifed: "Nor must one be utterly ignorant of matters that are obvious", retorts Orthodoxus. Yet in the end the whole debate, including the exegetical issue under discussion, revolves around the substance or signification of religious language, and the question of what is the appropriate content or reference of human vocabulary when it refers to being which is not confined to the created order and not ultimately definable. It is important to note that the thrust of the debate is about language and its meaning, and to ask whether texts are treated literally or allegorically is far too crude. Nor do we do justice to what is happening if we simply speak of exegesis serving dogmatic ends, or reflecting the prior theological frameworks of the exegete. In the end exegesis is about the meaning and reference of the language used, and such discussion inexorably raises issues far beyond the immediate statements under discussion. What Eranistes wants to say is that we must take ἐγένετο seriously, and yet we cannot take it in the straightforward sense of everyday usage. It has real meaning, but we cannot say exactly what that meaning is because it is like and yet not like our normal usage. He is in a similar position to Gregory of Nyssa in his debates with Eunomius: the language of scripture, he insisted, has real meaning and content when it uses the word "Son", but we cannot therefore attribute sexual activity to God.[5] In such cases to try and describe the interpretative method as "literal" or "non-literal" is to use an inadequate analytical tool. Questions of meaning raise far more subtle issues when it is religious language with which we have to deal. We may suggest that the appropriate description of this kind of language is analogical, but the Greek Fathers were still feeling after the problem. It is not

---

[5] Frances M. Young, "The God of the Greeks and the Nature of Religious Language", in *Early Christian Literature and the Classical Intellectual Tradition. In honorem R.M. Grant*, ed. W.R. Schoedel and R.L. Wilken (Paris, 1979).

fair to suggest that because they did not describe it adequately they did not sense the reality of the situation.

So Eranistes justifiably insists that the word used by scripture must be attended to and not emptied of meaning; yet to press it in the literalising way that his opponent seems to want is to distort the mystery of the divine reality. "The manner of his enfleshment escapes me", he pleads, "but I have heard that ὁ λόγος σάρξ ἐγένετο". Orthodoxus insists upon pursuing the problem: if he became flesh through changing, he did not remain what he was before. Various physical analogies are adduced. Eranistes justifiably insists that he never claimed that he became flesh κατὰ τροπήν, by change. Resorting to paradox, he claims that the Logos, while remaining what he was, became what he was not.

Orthodoxus now proposes substituting "he took flesh" for "he became flesh", since it is less misleading. Eranistes goes on insisting that the scriptural term should be taken seriously. In fact exegesis has always proceeded by the search for substitutes or by paraphrase: "this" means "that". Though the point is never made explicitly, Orthodoxus is quite properly insisting that you get nowhere in teasing out meaning if you will not entertain any synonyms, equivalents or valid "translations" by substitution. Recognising, however, that Eranistes has grounds for refusing to entertain anything but scriptural language, Orthodoxus sets out to prove that his alternative proposal is plainly scriptural. Eranistes allows that Paul is inspired by the same Spirit as the Evangelist. So Orthodoxus points outs that according to Paul, "he took" (ἐπιλαμβάνεται) the seed of Abraham (actually it was not Paul, of course, but the unknown author of the Epistle to the Hebrews). A rather laboured discussion eventually produces agreement that "the seed of Abraham" implies full humanity, body and soul — for Abraham's descendents were the Israelites, full-bloodied human beings. Eventually Eranistes cottons on to the implication, and makes the standard Alexandrian protest that this implies "Two Sons". Interestingly Orthodoxus immediately reverts to the text under discussion: to speak of the God-Word changing into flesh does not produce one Son — it just produces σάρξ — flesh, not a Son at all. We are the ones who confess one Son, he asserts, one Son who took the seed of Abraham according to the divine Apostle, and effected the salvation of human beings.

Eranistes now raises the issue of the inconsistency of scripture; it seems the Apostle makes statements that oppose those of the Evangelist. Orthodoxus does not regard that as a necessary conclusion. The Apostle teaches us how the Evangelist's statement is to be understood: the God-Word became flesh not by changing but by taking the seed of Abraham. With much scriptural quotation, he describes the promises made to Abraham and shows how they were fulfilled in Christ, and then leads Eranistes to agree that the Saviour was sprung from Judah and born in Bethlehem. Jesus was of Jewish descent as a man, even though as God he was Creator of all.

Eranistes, though responding, has been passively letting the argument proceed, but now he intervenes more positively. What do you say to Jeremiah? Quoting Baruch 3.36-8, he suggests that God was actually seen on earth, and the prophet speaks not of "flesh" or "humanity" or "human being", only of God. What need of syllogisms? So he appeals to what might be called the "plain sense" of scripture.

Orthodoxus soon demolishes that line by a battery of texts indicating that God is invisible, and that without a "body", the invisible nature could not be seen. Eranistes resorts to wooden-headed repetition of the prophetic text: did the prophet lie? Heaven forbid, cries Orthodoxus, but we must investigate *how* the unseen is seen. Eranistes dreads human reasonings and syllogisms; he will only believe Holy Scripture. Orthodoxus agrees to take him on on his own terms. He will show him how the unseen is seen by reference to the inspired writings. This is not, I suggest, simply a text-slinging match, or a weighing of one text against another. It is a reasoned attempt to elucidate scriptural language, which implicitly if not explicitly faces up to the issues mentioned earlier: given that the reality of which scripture speaks transcends the limits of human language, how can we do justice to the language used? How can we avoid the blasphemy of literalism on the one hand, or on the other, the danger of evacuating the language used of all recognisable meaning?

I Timothy 3.16 now takes the centre of the stage, the main point being that God was seen *in flesh*: the divine nature is invisible, but the σάρξ is visible. Through the visible, the invisible is seen. Furthermore the Evangelist insists that no-one has ever seen God except the only-begotten who is in the bosom of the Father. Moses desired to see the unseen but heard God saying, "No-one will see my face and live". When scripture speaks of God appearing, or being seen, by Abraham, Isaiah, Micah, Daniel and Ezekiel — even Moses of whom it is said, "God spoke with Moses face to face as one speaks to his friend" — it cannot mean that they saw the divine nature. The question of the integrity of scripture is now pressed by Orthodoxus: are they lying? No, they saw what they were able to see. Being φιλάνθρωπος, the Lord measures his revelations by the potential of those seeing. Those who have seen revelations of God, even the angels, have not seen his οὐσία, but visions, likenesses, some δόξα measured to their nature. Eranistes cannot dispute this, and Orthodoxus presses home I Timothy 3.16: the flesh is what makes visible the invisible.

But the flesh is a veil. Despite his demurrer, Eranistes has to accept that on the basis of Hebrews 10.19-22. Then Orthodoxus neatly reverts to Genesis 49.10 which previously figured in the discussion of how the promises to Abraham were fulfilled in the Saviour. The ensuing discussion proves yet again that doctrinal debate cannot be said to have produced a greater "literalism". They agree that Genesis 49.10, referring as it does to the sceptre not departing from Judah, speaks of the incarnation, so following unquestioned the ancient traditional path of viewing the Old Testament as having an oracular character and predictive reference which allows a Christological reading of almost any text. Then as they move to the next verse of the Genesis passage, we observe no mere struggle with the proper substance or signification of words, but outright allegory, accepted on both sides, indeed promulgated by the Antiochene, a remarkable fact given the standard descriptions of Antiochene attitudes to Alexandrian allegorisation. We will comment further on this phenomenon at a later stage.

Genesis 49.11, then, receives allegorical treatment, which makes possible its linkage with the point about the flesh being a veil. It reads: "his παρουσία the ἔθνη expect; he washes his own garment in wine, and his own veil in the blood of the grape". What is this text about then? Without discussion it is assumed that παρουσία (presence) refers to the coming of Christ, and ἔθνη (nations) refers to the Gentiles. Discussion focusses on the second half of the verse. Does it refer to clothes? Is it to be read "literally", if also prophetically? Or does it refer to his body? A search for the proper reference is undertaken, and the text associated with "I am the vine", and the flowing of blood and water when the Saviour's side was pierced. Clearly Genesis 49.11 is about the eucharist: "for as we call the mystical fruit of the vine after the holy blood of the Lord, so he named the blood of the true vine the blood of the grape".

There is complete agreement, and neither side feels any embarassement about pursuing a similar line of argument about his body being bread. From allegory we move to "type" or symbol, but this is not meant to be "merely" symbolic, a figment of the imagination. The visible symbols — bread, wine — are honoured by the names "body" and "blood" — not "changing their nature", says Orthodoxus, but "adding grace to nature". He clearly regards the language used in Genesis 49.11 as not dissimilar to eucharistic symbolism. It actually refers to the Lord's body. Allegory it may be, but it denotes an important reality through sign, through symbolic language. This is the true meaning of the text, a meaning on the basis of which doctrinal deduction is possible. And both sides find it acceptable.

But wait! This has been described as allegorical interpretation, but having observed how it functions one might well raise the question whether it is altogether appropriate to apply to it what can so easily be a dismissive label. Methodologically, the sequence of the argument is parallel to earlier arguments we have observed, proceeding as it does through appeal to various biblical texts to try and discern the appropriate meaning or reference of the text in question. Perhaps we should note in passing that once again standard analytical categories, like literalism and allegory, tell us little about the exegetical process. Where modern exegetes differ perhaps is in their estimate of what material can and cannot be used to determine appropriate meaning and reference. Surely they would not differ in estimating the language under discussion as properly understood to be metaphorical?

Eranistes now wakes up to where the argument is leading, and retreats into reassertion of the fundamental text: ὁ λόγος σάρξ ἐγένετο. Orthodoxus summarises the course of the argument, insisting that it is purely scriptural, and introducing appeal to one of the Antiochenes' favourite epistles, that to the Hebrews: God did not desire sacrifice or offering, but prepared a body for the Saviour who as High Priest offered the body he had taken. The text cannot imply he changed into a body when Mary conceived of the Holy Spirit. But Eranistes fears that the argument leads to the view that Mary gave birth *only* to a body. The discussion reaches an impasse. Eranistes bridles at Orthodoxus' mockery of his position. Orthodoxus claims to be fighting for the truth.

The dialogue will shortly culminate in a Florilegium, a battery of patristic quotations assembled to reinforce Orthodoxus' argument, interestingly drawn from many authorities he assumes his opponent will venerate, and not just those who represent his own side. But we will leave that on one side, and simply review the final phase of the discussion which precedes it. Once again, it revolves around the reference of biblical texts: promises made to Solomon must refer to our Saviour, not to Zerubabel — such historical assumptions are dismissed as "Jewish exegesis". Psalm 89 obviously points beyond an earthly kingdom, cannot refer to a "mere man", and must refer to Christ. Yet it clearly implies that the Saviour took humanity from the seed of David. The collage of Messianic texts includes similar treatment of Isaiah 11, and then a string of New Testament passages are adduced. All this material reinforces the claim of Orthodoxus that "to become flesh" *means* "to take flesh together with a rational soul". If the God-Word took nothing from our nature, then all the covenants, promises, etc. are void, and "we" are not raised, nor can "we" sit in heaven. The Word became flesh and dwelt ἐν ἡμῖν, not for Orthodoxus "among us" but "*in us*". The flesh he took was a kind of temple. John 1.14 must be interpreted in the light of Philippians 2.5-8: "become flesh" converges in meaning with "coming in the likeness of man"; "dwelling in us" converges with "taking the form of a servant". Appeal to the taunts of the Jews who later in the Gospel stone Jesus "not for a good work but for blasphemy, that being a man, you make yourself God", is dismissed by Eranistes: the Jews were blind because of their unbelief so you should not take their word for it. But he cannot help agreeing to accept the words of the Apostles: "What kind of a *man* is this, that the winds and waves obey him?" And Orthodoxus presses home his advantage, insisting that "coming in the likeness of men" refers to the nature he took, the μορφὴ δούλου, the form of a slave. At the heart of the debate, right through to the end, lies the question of the sense of scripture, the issue of meaning — i.e. the question of the substance and signification of words and texts. And that is what exegesis is all about. This is fundamentally an exegetical debate.

So what can we learn about exegetical method from this debate? A number of points have been noted along the way. Let us list the main conclusions:

1. The effect of debate was certainly not to produce a greater literalism. Whether a text was to be understood literally or allegorically was not a significant question. Rather debate developed an exegetical process which was essentially a sophisticated and rationalistic enquiry into "meaning" involving much greater subtleties and complexities.

2. Exegesis, like all discussions of meaning, proceeds by means of offering substitutes, paraphrases, equivalents, synonyms, alternative expressions. One phrase may be used to interpret another, whether a phrase in the immediate context, or elsewhere in scripture. Disagreements in exegesis frequently arise from different views about which cross-references are relevant.

3. The exegesis of many texts is taken for granted. Their meaning is treated as self-evident. Such undisputed texts are used to illustrate the force of arguments, confirm exegetical conclusions, or facilitate further deductions. Many of these unquestioned assumptions involved an agreed set of symbols, types, prophecies, etc.

4. The question of the reference of a text is fundamental. An oracle or prophecy was assumed to refer to what it was taken to predict. This might mean interpreting its riddling metaphorical language in an allegorical way, but this did not render it a mere work of the imagination. Since it actually referred to what it predicted and not to some other event or person, it could be argued that its "literal" meaning was contained in that reference. Merely to state that, raises questions about the adequacy of the designations "literal" or "allegorical" as commonly used. To note in addition the way reference to dogmatic realities was assumed, is again to distinguish this whole approach from the "literalism" of the modern historico-critical method. And, by the way, let us not forget that the ancient Church tended to accuse the Jews of "literal" interpretation because they were regarded as literally practising the Law (not that their Halakah was always based on what we would call literal interpretation!) The word "literal" cannot be regarded as univocal.

5. Fundamental theological assumptions (e.g. that God is unchangeable, invisible, etc.) are brought to bear on the text, though rarely without being backed up by other scriptural statements. This enables crude assumptions about meaning to be dismissed, but it does not necessarily mean the abandonment of what we might be prepared to call the "literal" sense. There was a sophisticated awareness of the subtlety of language. A statement may have real meaning without on the one hand being tied to its everyday earthly sense, or on the other hand becoming "merely" symbolic. Nevertheless prior theological frameworks have considerable bearing on the selection of texts perceived to be relevant.

6. The exegesis of metaphorical language involves extremely complex judgments. For metaphorical language clearly lies on a spectrum. At one end, it

can be taken as virtually "literal", though not straightforwardly so when it refers to divine realities. At the other end of the spectrum, it may be entirely "allegorical", words being used, or being taken to be used, to refer to something quite other then their own proper content. In between, however, is a range of symbolic, typological and mystical meanings which are not "merely" symbolic but have real significance. One might almost suggest that a correspondence theory of language has to give way to some kind of sacramental understanding of how language functions. The complexity is not well represented by the rigid definitions of literal, typological and allegorical that have become current. In fact, through debate, a set of ecclesiastically agreed symbols eventually became the basis of a refined allegorical treatment of scripture, so that dogma and spirituality were not divorced, and spirituality was "disciplined" by the "orthodox" understanding of key texts.

The point I wish to urge is that the process accepted certain unquestioned traditional assumptions but was fundamentally rationalist, an exploration of meaning which is inadequately categorised as literal, typological, allegorical or whatever. This can, I think, be confirmed by reference to the exegetical element in other debates. Here I propose to exploit Simonetti's excellent assemblage of material concerning Proverbs 8.22.[6] What is the result if you ask of that material the kind of questions I have been raising in this paper?

Let me remind you of the broad outlines of the history of interpretation of this text. At first, Proverbs 8.22 was taken to be part of a poem spoken by Wisdom, who is identified with the Logos. The apologists picked this up from the apostle Paul and John the evangelist. At this stage, no distinction was made between ἔκτισεν in v. 22 and γεννᾷ in v. 25. Both were taken to refer to the generation of the Logos from the Father. The distinction between the immanent eternal Logos and the Logos projected in creation and redemption, need not detain us, though apparently different Apologists related Proverbs 8.22 to this in different ways. In the early stages, a few identified the Wisdom of Proverbs 8 with the Holy Spirit rather than the Logos, but the Christological tradition rapidly established itself, and was never seriously questioned in subsequent debate. Origen considered that the verbs κτίζειν and γεννᾷν were equivalent, as were the nouns κτίσμα and γέννημα. Dionysius of Rome considered it improper to call the Son a ποίημα: scripture speaks of γέννησις. So he argued against his namesake of Alexandria that κτίζειν has various senses — there is a difference between κτίζειν and ποεῖν; and establishes through cross-references that in Proverbs 8, the ἔκτισεν of v. 22 must be equivalent to the γεννᾷ of v. 25. Arius, of course, took the opposite view, arguing that γεννᾷ should be understood in terms of ἔκτισεν. Once a distinction between being created and being begotten was pressed, there was little in principle or in the context to establish the superiority of one mode of interpretation over the other. The only resort could be appeal to other biblical texts.

The answer to Arius could not therefore be simply a conservative reversion to a previous exegesis. The option of denying the fundamental reference to the Logos was never entertained. Marcellus of Ancyra[7] resorted to the novel expedient of asserting that Prov. 8.22 referred to the incarnation, rather than to the origin of the pre-existent Logos. He acknowledged that the proper meaning of κτίζειν was "to create what did not previously exist", and claimed that the "creature" produced was the human flesh assumed by the Redeemer by means of the Virgin Mary. As Simonetti notes, the novelty of his interpretation he was able to mask by recourse to traditional typology, by use of which he contrived to produce a consistent interpretation of vs. 22-25 as prophetic prediction of the new dispensation, the renewal effected by the Saviour, who said, "I am the Way", and was therefore created "in the beginning of his ways" as the Way of piety for us. Verse 23 "before the age he founded me", Marcellus took to refer to God's foreordaining, foundation being interpreted in terms of the New Testament text: "No other foundation can anyone lay except that which is laid, which is Jesus Christ". To cope with the apparently unequivocal statements in v. 24 referring to a time before the earth, the depths or springs existed, he resorted to allegory, so that the "earth" is taken to refer to the flesh made of the dust of the earth according to Gen. 2.6, returning to dust according to Gen. 3.19, and restored by participation in the Logos; the "depths" is taken to refer to the hearts of the saints, "which in their depths have the gift of the Spirit"; and the "springs" are taken to refer to the apostles on the basis of Exodus 15.27, the twelve springs of Elim, a text traditionally associated with Twelve ... And so it goes on. The continuation of the passage in vs. 27-30, however, he understood of the immanent Wisdom or Logos of God in the creation.

The fundamental move of making Prov. 8.22 refer to the incarnation was followed by Eustathius and Athanasius, though the exegetical details did not always correspond: "in the beginning of his ways", for example, was rather more plausibly treated by Athanasius by reference to the "first-born of all creation" (Col. 1.15): the Logos is "only-begotten" in relation to the Father, "first-born" in respect of his condescension. But Eusebius of Caesarea offered a reply to this whole approach in his works against Marcellus. Prior to the Arian controversy,[8] he had been wrestling with the fact that the generation or creation of the Logos as described in Prov. 8 could not imply separation, diminution or division in respect of the Father. On the other hand, it could not mean that the Logos was created out of nothing like other created things.

---

[7] For both Marcellus' treatment of the text, and that of Eusebius, see *Eusebius Werke* IV Band: Gegen Marcell, Über die Kirchliche Theologie, Die Fragmente Marcells. Ed. E. Klostermann (GCS; Berlin, 1972).

[8] In his *Demonstratio Evangelica*; see Simonetti, *op. cit.*, ch. 1, section 7.

Eusebius is prepared to see the Son as "the fragrance and splendour of the light of the Father", but observes that the mystery of the generation of the Son is hidden. Now in answering Marcellus, he also refrains from following the Arian logic.

How does he do this? In the first place, he attends to the whole context, and refuses piecemeal interpretation. Thus he insists upon taking it to refer to the Wisdom which is the Word, the Son of God, not simply the Wisdom immanent in God. Secondly he insists that there is no description here of *how* this Logos came into being. It is about his pre-existence, his preceding the creation of the whole world, his ruling over all things because set over them by the Lord, his Father. This he supports by attention to the meaning of the verb κτίζειν: it is not used in the sacred text to mean "create", i.e. bring into existence out of nothing, but in the sense to "order" or "unite". He turns to the Hebrew and variant translations to show this: the meaning is more like "possess" — ἐκτήσατο rather than ἔκτισεν. The Father constituted the Logos as the foundation of all things, "to sum up all things in Christ, whether the things of heaven or the things of earth" (Ephes. 1.10). Proverbs 8 is about the providential function of the Logos rather than his origin, the manner of which is in any case a mystery beyond description or understanding. Given this kind of overview of the whole passage, Marcellus' contorted explanations of vs. 22-25 are easily dismissed. Naturally these verses refer to the ordering of creation, though Eusebius tends to think not simply of the material creation, but the creation of the intelligible world of the heavenly powers. This is no "merely literal" approach to the text, though profoundly more satisfactory than the arbitrary expedients of Marcellus.

Now our survey of this material surely confirms the points discovered in Theodoret's dialogue. The categories "literal" and "allegorical" are insufficiently exact to describe what is going on, and neither is excluded or given priority. There are certain unquestioned assumptions made about reference, often on the basis of long-standing tradition, assumptions which from our historicising point of view, imply a non-literal approach to the text. There are rationalistic attempts to discern the meanings of the words which exploit linguistic knowledge where it is available, synonymous usage in the immediate context or elsewhere, parallel usages elsewhere in scripture, or arguments drawn from cross-referencing scriptural statements. There is some concern with context and coherence, much with what the text refers to. Fundamental theological assumptions are brought to bear on what the text may conceivably be allowed to refer to. The process can most adequately be described as a rationalistic enquiry into the meaning and reference of the disputed text in question.

Well, we could go on selecting other examples of doctrinal debates, and examining the exegesis of scripture within those debates. We could move back earlier to consider Tertullian's *Adversus Praxean*. We could tackle the works of the Cappadocians against Eunomius. Many other possibilities present themselves. But *tempus fugit...*, and we must allow this to be simply an initial exploratory exercise. My guess is we would find much the same kind of complexity — indeed even without detailed examination the kind of thing we have noticed in the examples taken, easily springs to mind in the works referred to.

So to my peroration — which will not follow custom and summarise the points already made, but rather raise two final questions, and treat them, I fear, somewhat summarily. The questions are: (1) Can this treatment of texts in debate be regarded as any different in principle from the exegetical activity observable in homily and commentary? and (2) Where did it come from?

The answer to both questions, I suggest, lies in the same direction. As Edwin Hatch argued one hundred years ago, the roots of patristic exegesis lie in the ancient educational system, the schools of *grammaticus* and *rhetor*. There texts were exploited to illustrate grammatical usage and rhetorical devices, rationalistic enquiries sought meanings through etymology, synonyms, literary usage elsewhere, and so on; and exegetical comments elucidated the import of figures of speech and explained allusions to narratives common or uncommon, mythical or historical. Discerning morals, references and deeper meanings, was commonplace, though mystical allegory seems not to have been characteristic of rhetors so much as philosophers, at whose feet some, though by no means the majority, might subsequently sit. In a recent paper, to be published in a forthcoming volume entitled *The Evolution of Orthodoxy*.[9] I have attempted to assemble what we can know about the exegetical practice of the rhetorical schools, in order to show that it was this rather than an anachronistic concern with history or "literalism" that informed the Antiochene reaction against Alexandrian allegory. Of course, the same fundamental methods underlay the allegorical tradition, but that tradition went beyond the rationalistic methods noted to discovering how to read out of texts esoteric philosophical meanings, by taking sentences and phrases piecemeal, and finding coherence in the underlying truths rather than in the text and its context. The Antiochenes were concerned with what we might call the "narrative logic" of the whole text — its σκοπός, its content, its context — and in the "moral" or "dogmatic" meaning which could be discerned in the whole — inhering in it, as it were. They reverted to the "schools" approach to texts. As we have seen, they were not averse to exegetical practices which appear distinctly allegorical to us; but they were averse to arbitrary exegesis which took away from the "plain sense" of scripture. Alexandrian allegory may be regarded as an aberration in which the rhetorical traditions common to all were overlayed by philosophical influence.

---

[9] "The Rhetorical Schools and their influence on patristic Exegesis", in *The Evolution of Orthodoxy* (Cambridge forthcoming).

In the light of the work to which I refer, I would now suggest that the search for meaning and truth in texts, whether overtly exegetical or employing exegesis in debate, followed essentially similar lines, and that in both contexts, exegetical methods were derived from the procedures of the grammatical and rhetorical schools.

Which neatly brings me back to my opening paragraph: for the rhetorical schools also shaped the traditions passed on in the Classical schools of the European tradition. The art of exegesis was partly taught, partly "caught", as pupils read texts with their masters. Scriptural exegetes sought meaning and truth in their texts just as literary exegetes did in classical texts. It is the loss of that tradition which has impoverished modern exegesis, and created a preoccupation with but one element — namely the historical reference — in what is in fact an extremely complex process. We may not always find the conclusions of patristic exegesis satisfactory or plausible, but this is more often because of a different estimate of what constitutes a valid cross-reference than anything else. From their methods and their endeavour we might learn much. The fundamental exegetical question is: what does this mean? The answer may be obvious, or it may be arrived at by a complex process of rational enquiry about word usage, about signification and metaphor, about syntax, about reference and about truth. There is no escape from that complexity.

XII

Proverbs 8 in Interpretation (2): Wisdom Personified

Fourth-century Christian Readings: Assumptions and Debates

In this essay I propose to focus on fourth-century interpretation of Prov. 8.22–31. I do not start from scratch. The basic research into the interpretation of this passage in the Fathers is provided by Simonetti[1] in the opening chapter of a book of studies in Arianism – for this passage was a significant bone of contention in the Arian struggle. Building on Simonetti's work,[2] my aim is to try and identify the principles at work in the way the passage was interpreted, and hint at parallels to postmodern approaches.

An interpretative community

Postmodern literary criticism has identified the significance of interpretative communities, observing that debates about meaning occur within communities which share assumptions about interpretation. If this is pertinent in a world where people read

---

[1] M. Simonetti, *Studi sull' Arianismo*, Rome: Editrice Studium, 1965, ch. 1.

[2] In some places I have borrowed paragraphs with little modification from my previous surveys of Simonetti's work, or my previous treatments of, e.g., Athanasius' discussions. These are to be found in Frances Young, 'Exegetical Method and Scriptural Proof: The Bible in Doctrinal Debate', *Studia Patristica* 24, 1989, pp. 291–304; and eadem, *Biblical Exegesis and the Formation of Christian Culture*, Cambridge: Cambridge University Press, 1997.

novels silently to themselves, how much more so when texts were always read aloud, usually as public performance in a gathered community, such as a school or a church! The reality was that no one in the fourth century challenged the fundamental approach to this text which we can already trace in the work of the second-century apologists. The christological reference of personified wisdom was a tradition never questioned. So let's spell this out by reference to texts prior to the fourth century.

Prov. 8.22 consistently appears when the Apologists are explaining their Logos-theology. Let me give you one example from Athenagoras, *Legatio* 10.3–4:

> If in your great wisdom you would like to know what 'Son' means, I will tell you in a few brief words: it means that he is the first begotten of the Father. The term is used not because he came into existence (for God, who is eternal mind, had in himself his Word or Reason from the beginning, since he was eternally rational) but because he came forth to serve as Ideal Form and Energizing Power for everything material . . . The prophetic Spirit also agrees with this account. 'For the Lord', it says, 'made me the beginning of his ways for his works.' (Proverbs 8.22) Further, this same holy Spirit, which is active in those who speak prophetically, we regard as an effluence of God (cf. Wisdom 7.25) which flows forth from him and returns like a ray of the sun.[3]

That final sentence alludes to another passage where wisdom is personified. The conflation and mutual coherence of such wisdom-passages in the LXX was important in developing the Logos-theology, no doubt aided by the fact that Wisdom 7 has clear traces of Stoic influence. But the principal point is clear. The Son of God is both the eternal Logos or Mind of the Father and the first-begotten, and as such identified with the personified Wisdom through whom God created according to Proverbs 8.

This general approach to Proverbs 8 can be further documented

---

[3] ET from the Oxford Early Christian texts edition, *Athenagoras, Legatio and De Resurrectione*, ed. and trans. W. R. Schoedel, Oxford: Oxford University Press, 1972.

by turning to Theophilus of Antioch, *Ad Autolycum* II.10, where the term 'Sophia' is used alongside Logos, and his statement is a collage of biblical phrases:

> Therefore God, having his own Logos innate in his own bowels [cf. Ps. 109.3], generated him together with his own Sophia, *vomiting* him *forth* [Ps. 44.2] before everything else. He used this Logos as his servant in the things created by him, and through him he made all things [cf. John 1.4]. He is called Beginning because he leads and dominates everything fashioned through him. It was he, Spirit of God [Gen. 1.2] and Beginning [Gen.1.1] and Sophia [Prov. 8.22] and power of the Most High [Luke 1.35], who came down into the prophets and spoke about the creation of the world and all the rest. For the prophets did not exist when the world came into existence; there were the Sophia of God which is in him and his holy Logos who is always present with him. For this reason he speaks thus through Solomon the prophet: 'When he prepared the heaven I was with him, and when he made strong the foundations of the earth I was with him, binding them fast [Prov. 8.27–29].⁴

Is Theophilus speaking of both the pre-existent Word and the Holy Spirit, and which is Sophia? Looked at closely the passage quoted from Athenagoras carries the same ambiguity. Despite this fluidity of language, which makes it hard to be sure whether the picture is Binitarian or Trinitarian, the conclusion pertinent to our current concerns is clear. Prov. 8.22–31 is generally read as a passage about the being who was the instrument through whom God created the universe. Irenaeus, building on Logos-theology, notoriously speaks of the Word and the Spirit as God's two-hands, the instruments through which creation was effected. In *Adversus Haereses* IV.20.3, he reckons that he has demonstrated that the Word, namely the Son, was always with the Father, along with the Spirit – in this passage treating the Spirit, rather than the

---

⁴ ET from the Oxford Early Christian texts edition, *Theophilus of Antioch, Ad Autolycum*, ed. and trans. Robert M. Grant, Oxford: Oxford University Press, 1970.

Logos, as the Wisdom which is described in Proverbs 8 as being involved with the Father in creation. This clarifies the ambiguity we noted in Theophilus and Athenagoras in a way that did not become the norm, for after Irenaeus it is not the Spirit but the Logos which is taken to be the reference of Proverbs 8.[5]

If the focus did not lie elsewhere, this example could be reinforced by many others. But let me just draw attention to three features important for the future:

(1) It generated intertextuality, collages of texts being built up to create a picture of this pre-existent creating Power of God, with whom God conversed when he said, 'Let *us* make . . .' (cf. Genesis 1).[6]

(2) Prov. 8.22 was construed in such a way that Beginning was regarded as one of the titles of the Logos or Son of God. When exercised about the correct construal of the word 'beginning' in Gen. 1.1, Origen and Tertullian both appeal to Proverbs 8 to settle the issue. Origen takes it (*Commentary on John* I. 17) that 'Beginning' is a title for Christ, confirming this on the basis of Prov. 8.22, where he construes ἔκτισεν (he created) as having a double object, as a verb of appointment would: thus, 'the Lord made me Beginning of his ways'. Tertullian is arguing against Hermogenes, who stated that the Genesis text supported the idea that God created out of pre-existent matter. 'Beginning' Hermogenes had interpreted as something substantial, Matter, in other words. Tertullian (*Adversus Hermogenem* 19) argues that 'in the beginning' is comparable to 'at last', is about order not origin, and simply refers to the inception of the activity. Then appealing to the

---

[5] See Clement of Alexandria, *Stromateis* vii.2 and Origen, *De principiis* ii.1 and *Commentary on John* i.11 and 39.

[6] See previous note for an example of cross-referencing and intertextuality. For the link with Genesis see Justin, *Dialogue with Trypho* 61–62 where he quotes Proverbs 8 at length and then argues for a correlation with Genesis, raising the question who was God addressing when he said, 'Let us make . . .' and 'Behold, Adam has become as one of us . . .'. For Justin it is clear that God is addressing his Offspring who is to be identified as the one Solomon calls Wisdom.

Greek, ἀρχή (beginning), he adds that the sense is not only priority of order, but of power as well (ἀρχή meaning 'rule' as well as 'beginning'). He goes on to argue that the word must refer to the initial one, that is, the one who says, 'The Lord established me as the beginning of his ways for the creation of his works' – in other words, Wisdom in Proverbs 8. For him Proverbs makes clear that the beginning of God's ways or works was Wisdom. And Wisdom is the Lord's right-hand, the energy that produced creation (cf. *Adversus Hermogenem* 45, which also quotes Proverbs 8).

(3) The doctrinal importance of this interpretative tradition is already clear from Tertullian's repeated references in *Adversus Praxeam*, his principal attack on the Modal approach to Trinitarianism. Arguing for a real distinction between the Logos and the Father he notes (in *Adv. Prax.* vi, for example) that the 'divine intelligence' is also set forth in the Scriptures under the name of Wisdom, and quotes Proverbs 8 at length.

I hope enough has been observed to confirm the fact that we are dealing with an interpretative community with a consistent approach to the basic reference of this text.

Debating the meaning of a key word

This consensus as to the reference of Prov. 8.22–31 was not shattered by the Arian controversy. Debate centred on a particular word and its appropriate synonyms. Commentary has always focused on elucidating the meaning of particular terms in this way. Against a background of shared assumptions, different theological conclusions about the nature of the Logos were drawn from different understandings of the key word.

That word was ἔκτισεν (he created) – Greek, because of course it was the LXX version that was debated. Prior to the controversy, the use of different words in verse 22 and verse 25 was not generally noticed: ἔκτισεν (he created) and γεννᾷ(ι) (he begets) were assumed to be synonyms and to refer to the generation of

XII

the Logos from the Father. In a fragment of a work against the
Sabellians, preserved for us by Athanasius in the *De Decretis*,
Dionysius of Rome stated that he considered it improper to call
the Son a ποίημα (a creature), for Scripture speaks of his γέννησις
(genesis/begottenness). So he argued that κτίζειν (to create) has
various senses – there is a difference between κτίζειν (to create)
and ποιεῖν (to make). He established through cross-references
that in Proverbs 8, the ἔκτισεν (he created) of verse 22 must be
the equivalent of the γεννᾷ(ι) (he begets) of verse 25, so making
explicit what had been assumed all along.

Arius is notorious for teaching that the Son was a creature,
and Prov. 8.22 was for him a prime proof-text. That implies that
he took the opposite view, that γεννᾷ(ι) (he begets) was to be
understood in terms of ἔκτισεν (he created). Once a distinction
between being created and being begotten was pressed, there was
little in principle or in context to establish the superiority of one
mode of interpretation over the other.

Eusebius of Caesarea was the one person to discuss the meaning
of ἔκτισεν (he created) rather than appealing to novel ways of
construing the passage as a whole. Simonetti observes that, prior
to the Arian controversy, Eusebius had been wrestling with the
fact that the generation or creation of the Logos described in
Proverbs 8 could not simply imply separation, diminution or
division with respect to the Father. On the other hand it could not
mean that the Logos was created out of nothing like other created
beings. Eusebius was prepared to see the Son as 'the fragrance
and splendour of the light of the Father', but observed that the
mystery of the generation of the Son is hidden. Consistently
with this, in his work against Marcellus, Eusebius refrains from
following the Arian interpretation, while also resisting the ploys
we shall explore later. He insists on retaining the context with
its overall picture of Wisdom pre-existing and assisting in the
creation of all else, identifying her with the pre-existent cosmic
Christ. He further insists that here there is no description of how
this Logos came into being. The passage is about his preceding
the creation of the whole world and his ruling over all things
because set over them by the Lord, his Father. Thus he reasserts

the inherited consensus of the interpretative community.[7] His strategy for establishing this is addressing the philological question concerning the meaning of ἔκτισεν (he created).

Eusebius argues that κτίζειν (to create) is not used here to mean 'create' in the sense 'bring into existence out of nothing', but in the sense 'order' or 'unite'. He turns to the Hebrew and variant translations to show this. The meaning is more like ἐκτήσατο – 'he possessed'. The Father constituted the Logos as the foundation of all things, 'to sum up things in Christ, whether the things of heaven or the things of earth' (Eph. 1.10). Proverbs 8, then, is about the providential functions of the Logos rather than his origin, the manner of which is in any case a mystery beyond description or understanding.

The sequence of thought

By taking this position with respect to the word ἔκτισεν (he created) Eusebius is able to maintain the natural sequence of thought in the passage. This observation is important since most of those opposed to Arius introduced an unnatural sequence into the passage by claiming that ἔκτισεν (he created) referred to the incarnation. The originator of this approach seems to have been Marcellus. Acknowledging that the proper meaning of κτίζειν was 'to create what did not previously exist', he claimed that the 'creature' produced was the human flesh assumed by the Redeemer by means of the Virgin Mary.

Simonetti notes that Marcellus was able to mask the novelty of his interpretation by recourse to traditional typology. Through this technique he contrived to produce a consistent interpretation of verses 22–25 as a prophetic prediction of the new dispensation, in particular the renewal effected by the Saviour, who said 'I am the Way', and was therefore created 'in the beginning of his ways' as the Way of piety for us. The whole passage is made coherent by such moves. Here is one more example: 'before the ages he founded me' is taken to refer to God's providential foreordaining,

---

[7] Note how he reflects points in Tertullian's discussion, outlined above.

in the light of the text, 'No other foundation can anyone lay except that which is laid, which is Jesus Christ' (1 Cor. 3.11) Whether 'typology' is the best way of describing this procedure might be questionable, but to give a coherent exegesis of this passage as referring to the incarnation rather than the generation of the Son from the Father certainly required exploitation of such typically patristic techniques for shifting reference. To cope with the question how on earth the incarnation might be implied by the apparently unequivocal statements in verse 24, which refer to a time before the earth, the depths or springs existed, he resorted to allegory. The 'earth' is taken to refer to the flesh – for flesh was made of the dust of the earth according to Gen. 2.6, returns to dust according to Gen. 3.19, and is restored by participation in the Logos; 'the depths' is taken to refer to the hearts of the saints, 'which in their depths have the gift of the Spirit'; and the 'springs' are taken to refer to the apostles on the basis of Exod. 15.27, the twelve springs of Elim, a text traditionally associated with the Twelve . . . And so it goes on, though the focus on the incarnation is blurred when the continuation of the passage in verses 27–30 is understood of the immanent Wisdom or Logos of God in the creation.

Undoubtedly Eusebius produces a more satisfactory and less piecemeal approach to the text as he challenges these arbitrary expedients. Another interpretative strategy has clearly enabled this, namely intertextuality: we will explore this further by turning to Athanasius' interpretation. For Athanasius, like Marcellus, adopted the incarnation as the explanation of the awkward word ἔκτισεν (he created).

Genre and intertextuality

That the exegesis of this text was at the heart of the Arian controversy is proved by its high profile in the anti-Arian works of Athanasius, the *De Decretis* and *Contra Arianos*. In the former, discussing the difference between making something external to the maker, like a house, and begetting a son, Athanasius refers to Prov. 8.25, 'Before all the hills he begat me'. But he cannot then escape dealing with the use of 'create' in Prov. 8.22: he does so by asserting that it refers to the incarnation – for then indeed one can say the Son was created. He calls in scriptural cross-references to witness that he became son of man as well as Son of God.

As far as the *Contra Arianos* is concerned, Athanasius devotes the bulk of book II to this text, exploiting a range of exegetical techniques. First he attends to genre: these are proverbs, expressed in the way of proverbs. Enquiry must be made about the reference and the religious sense of each proverb. The sense of what is said must be unfolded and sought as something hidden. This is done by attending to scriptural usage, and intertextuality plays a big role. With cited texts he establishes that the term ἔκτισεν (he created) is elsewhere used of creatures and not where Scripture is speaking of the generation of the Son, and also that there are two scriptural senses of the word, one concerning origin and the other renewal, as in the text 'Create in me a new heart'. So the proverb in question is to be understood not of the generation of the Word, but rather as relating to renewal, and so as referring not to the essence but to the humanity of the Word.

The next tactic is to consider the syntax. He argues (as others had before him) that 'The Lord created me a beginning of his ways' works in the same way as 'My Father prepared for me a body' – the verb has a double object. So the proverb, according to Athanasius, calls the Son a 'beginning of his ways' and he compares this with 'The Word became flesh and dwelt among us'. Neither of these verses speaks of an absolute becoming or creation, but of one relative to 'us' or to 'his works'. Here Athanasius notes that whereas ἔκτισεν (he created) in verse 22 is modified by an expression of purpose, 'for his works', the use of γεννᾷ(ι) (he begets) in verse 25 does not have a similar modifier. So in verse 25, as elsewhere in Scripture, the 'begetting' is stated absolutely, whereas the word 'created' is relative; it is relative to the οἰκονομία – that is, the created order and the incarnation as an expression of God's providential and saving plan.

This distinction between speaking absolutely of the Son's Being and speaking of him relative to the created order (or the 'Economy') is fundamental to Athanasius' discernment of the mind of Scripture. This overarching perspective, coupled with inter-textual references, enables the interpretation in terms of renewal or re-creation to be elaborated: 'We are his workmanship, created in Jesus Christ', he suggests, using Eph. 2.10 among many other passages. Thus he arrives at a classic distinction which he regards as fundamental to Scripture: God's offspring (γέννημα) was *begotten but then made*, made flesh for our salvation in the Economy, whereas creatures (ποιήματα) were *made and then begotten* through Christ, becoming sons by grace. This distinction he thinks applies to this text. He is 'the first-born of all creation' as being the origin of the new creation; he could not be first-born of God, since he is only-begotten of God.

But now the problem of context demands attention. How can this reading of verse 22 be satisfactory in the light of verse 23, where it states: 'before the world, he founded me in the beginning'? Athanasius appeals again to the proverbial character of the material; then (like Marcellus) he calls in the text from 1 Corinthians 'No other foundation can anyone lay . . .', and indicates that Proverbs is speaking of the providential preparation of this grace for us before the foundation of the world. So the essence of Wisdom was not created; what was created was the impress of Wisdom in the works of God as a copy of the divine image. His triumphant conclusion is that thus the whole world will be filled with the knowledge of God. And it must be admitted that he takes a lot longer to get there than my brief survey of his material would suggest!

We can now look back over his handling of the text and see that is raises questions about a number of interpretative strategies. Clearly deductive argument, employing inter-textuality to determine the over-arching 'mind' of Scripture, then determines the sense of particular passages, no matter how implausible! The way Athanasius approaches the questions posed by Arian exploitation of this passage raises issues about genre, not only about the genre of the text in question, which clearly he properly identifies, but also about the 'reading genre' – it is because this text belongs to Scripture, and is to be read as Scripture, that it can be moulded into a meaning that, it is claimed, coheres with the mind of Scripture. This provides a particular reading horizon, and the perspectives which that produces determined what the words may or may not refer to.

The future of the text

From our postmodern perspective it might seem that this kind of interpretation is particularly focussed on the future of the text, as distinct from its original meaning. As noted at the outset, the traditions of an interpretative community had already determined its reference, and the text's future was to generate doctrinal debate about the nature of God's Word. However, this can only be observed through the hindsight shaped by modernity. For the exegetes of the fourth century the issue of distinguishing the 'original' or authorial meaning of the text from other meanings did not arise. This was because the text of Scripture was regarded as fundamentally prophetic. Even proverbs were prophecy – the important point about παροιμίαι is that they are figurative, as is evident from the fact that Athanasius appealed to Jn 16.25 to show that there is a difference between proverbs and plain speech. As a prophet, the author *meant* what the exegete discerned in the text; or if maybe the author was unconscious of it, the Holy Spirit certainly meant it. The future of the text was no different from its original meaning. The text and its meaning was regarded as having a timeless quality. There was one horizon not two!

So the 'reading genre', which identified the biblical text as unified and prophetic ensured the primacy of the dogmatic reading. Indeed, orthodoxy, or correct opinion, became a criterion of interpretation. The true meaning was regarded as always there to be uncovered, even if not fully recognized previously. The text had neither a past nor a future. In fact patristic interpretation reveals an assumption that Scripture always addresses its readers (or rather hearers) directly, whatever the time or place. The exegetical techniques of the Fathers were developed and deployed to show what the text meant eternally for the readers of every generation. We might compare this with reader-oriented criticism, but we should be careful. For the

Fathers were convinced they were uncovering the true, eternal meaning, not permitting their own concerns to determine how the text was read, or self-consciously recognizing that the text only comes alive when a reader realizes it, inevitably bringing their own horizon to the process of interpretation. Yet from our perspective that would seem to be exactly what the Fathers were doing.

To sum up then: Let us note that this debate has nothing to do with the standard exegetical questions raised in dealing with patristic exegesis – the issue is not about allegory, typology or literalism. The debate is about particular reference, the general reference already being established by tradition and assumed by the common interpretative dogmatic community. In conducting the debate, verbal sense is subjected to intertextual tests, and the final appeal is to the scriptural over-view – the 'mind' of Scripture which transcends the 'verbal expression' in any given sentence.

So for us these are the questions:

• Is this eisegesis?
• Do Athanasius et al. twist the text to suit their own purposes? Indeed, is not this exactly the kind of thing that justified disciplined attention to the text with philology, with historico-critical acumen?
• Do not the assumptions of this interpretative community distort discussion of the text and cry out for the identification of a neutral, objective reappraisal? Or is the claim to any privileged position, whether dogmatic or scholarly, equally flawed?
• So does this confirm and strengthen the reaction against the historico-critical programme in post-modern interpretation? Or does it rather illustrate the dangers?
• What would be an 'ethical' reading? And would an ethical reading invalidate a Christian doctrinal reading as exploitative?

Towards an ethical reading

In previous work[8] I have developed an approach to ethical reading, stimulated by George Steiner's plea[9] for an ethics of reception, by Wayne Booth's suggestion in *The Company We Keep*[10] that friendship is the best metaphor for reading, and Werner Jeanrond's[11] description of reading as a dynamic process to which both text and reader contribute. Strangely these explorations lead to a remarkable concurrence between their hermeneutics and ancient rhetorical theories.

In brief the conclusion is that readers have a responsibility to the text, but also to themselves. Responsible reading means the articulation of distance. To the extent that the historico-critical method facilitates that distance, it is a vital contributor to a responsible reading. To the extent that it may fail to engage the reader, producing a merely archaeological approach to the text, to the extent that it encourages blindness to the reader's presuppositions by offering an illusory objectivity, to the extent that it does not deliver potential meanings in a plurality of situations, it is inadequate.

Ancient rhetorical theory spelt out the need for a three-way dynamic if an audience (or readership) was to be persuaded – in other words, to achieve πίστις (proof, conviction, or in Christian parlance, faith). One point on the triangle was the λόγος (the content, the logic or argument), which should be convincing. Another point was the ἦθος of the speaker (the character, lifestyle and authority of the author) which confirmed what the text said. The third was the πάθος ('suffering' or response) of the audience

---

[8] Frances Young, 'The Pastorals and the Ethics of Reading', *Journal for the Study of the New Testament* 45, 1992, pp. 105–120; and eadem, 'Allegory and the Ethics of Reading', in Francis Watson, (ed.), *The Open Text*, London: SPCK 1993, pp. 103–20.

[9] In George Steiner, *Real Presences*, subtitled *Is there anything in what we say?* London: Faber & Faber, 1989.

[10] Wayne Booth, *The Company We Keep*, Berkeley: University of California Press, 1988.

[11] Werner Jeanrond, *Text and Interpretation as Categories of Theological Thinking*, ET T. J. Wilson; Dublin: Gill & Macmillan, 1988.

or reader, swayed by the convincing character of author and text. The dynamic between these was all important.

I suggest that that remains true. The inspiration of the Holy Spirit the Fathers thought essential not just in the composition of Scripture but in its interpretation. Distance and appropriation are both vital for an ethical reading that does justice to the text. That means there will be a plurality of readings, for readings will take place in many contexts, cultures and communities. There will be justifiable critique of the dubious linguistic and contextual moves Athanasius and others may have made, because being as true as possible to the text matters in an ethical reading. But alongside this there will also be a recognition that a Christian reading of the Bible has to wrestle with issues of its unity and the ways in which it points to a reality beyond itself. For the Fathers, the Rule of Faith provided the crucial criteria, and the creeds were regarded as a summary of the truth of the Bible. A Christian ethical reading has to do justice to 'ourselves', and that includes the tradition of reading in which we stand. The Trinity is not explicit in the New Testament, let alone the Hebrew Bible. But it is implicit in the Christian Bible, and was made explicit through such debates about interpretation as we have sketched. Our hermeneutical theory, while enabling exposure of dubious exegetical moves, surely must also take account of this 'future of the text'.

XIII

Paideia and the Myth of Static Dogma

I

Modern theology often treats patristic doctrine as static on the grounds that it dealt in ontological categories, while modern historical scholarship traces the story of doctrinal development in the patristic period. Prima facie it might seem that these perspectives are contradictory, but in fact 'making and remaking' implies development to a fixed form, together with the suggestion of a need to unpick a finished tapestry so as to re-weave it, thus betraying the influence of both modern assumptions.

In so far as the hermeneutical process involves seeing the past in terms of current models of understanding, such perspectives may have some justification, and they provide the assumptions which have enabled the development of Maurice Wiles's stimulating programme of doctrinal criticism. It is a privilege to honour his challenging contribution to a field which too easily permits retreat into safe text-critical studies or neat but merely historical reconstructions.

However, the thesis of this essay is that both assumptions are modern 'projections', and both reflect a mistake about the nature of Christian dogma. This mistake goes some way towards accounting for the gulf between theology and religious experience, doctrine and spirituality, which is evident in Western Christianity. Both doctrine and theology tend to be regarded as 'second-order' activities, intellectual reflection on first-order religion (such a position is explicit in Richardson 1935). A perspective which is more true to much of the Christian tradition may be discovered if we investigate the patristic approach, reclaiming both the central place of exegesis and preaching for doctrine, and uncovering the roots of Eastern theology where doctrine and spirituality are inseparable.

The clue to this perspective is the realization that *dogmata* are

266

simply teachings, and that teaching involved a whole process of education, a *paideia*, ascetic training in a spiritual way of life which involved both moral and intellectual progress. That is why heretics were treated as morally culpable as well as doctrinally deviant: their whole discipline was wrong. The kind of thing we modern Westerners tend to mean by doctrines emerged within the process of marking diversions from the correct direction as the journey or pilgrimage was pursued. They were never intended to provide the whole truth; nor was the truth a static object which could be possessed.

II

It might seem obvious that Origen's teachings were meant to be such a *paideia*. But that is only so because of the progress of Origen scholarship over the past one hundred years.

When in 1886 Charles Bigg produced his Bampton Lectures entitled *Christian Platonists of Alexandria*, it was still possible to treat the *De principiis* as a compendium of Origen's doctrine. Bigg recognized that Origen accepted a somewhat limited role for 'Tradition which handed down certain facts, certain usages, which were to be received without dispute'. Tradition did not explain 'the why or the whence', and so it was 'the office of the sanctified reason to define, to articulate, to co-ordinate, even to expand, and generally to adapt to human needs the faith once delivered to the Church' (Bigg 1886: 191). But he takes for granted that what Origen offers is his established doctrines, doctrines of God, the Logos, the Trinity, the Soul, etc. All that is necessary is to expound Origen's views on the classic doctrinal questions, taking *De principiis* as a kind of systematic theology in which Platonism has contributed to the intellectual formulation of dogma.

Strikingly different is the position of Henri Crouzel (Crouzel 1985). Crouzel has reached the view that Origen belonged to a time when discussion and hypothesis were still permissible, indeed that Origen as a true intellectual made alternative suggestions and that this is the explanation of our difficulties in knowing whether or not he taught such controversial doctrines as *metempsychōsis* (Crouzel 1985: 166). It was in the Origenist controversy that the attribution of 'doctrines' began, for this was a different era, and Origen's 'orthodoxy' was the issue.

Perhaps even more fundamental, however, has been the shift reflected in Crouzel's estimate of Origen's central concern. In evaluating Origen's thought as a whole, his spirituality had already come into sharper focus. Here too the influence of Platonism was explored, but attention had also been directed to his exegesis of scripture. So it is not doctrine derived from Platonist theorizing that is given priority in Crouzel's account of Origen, but rather his exegetical activity, which was indeed the predominant aspect of his life's work. Even more significant is the new approach to studying Origen's exegesis found in the work of Karen Jo Torjesen (see also Greer 1973).

In *Hermeneutical Procedure and Theological Method in Origen's Exegesis* (Torjesen 1985a) she subjects Origen's exegetical practice to careful analysis, and convincingly shows that for Origen the task of the exegete is to enable scripture to function pedagogically for the hearer, assisting the journey of the soul. The progression discerned in his homilies and commentaries corresponds with Origen's conception of that journey through three stages: the stage of purification, then knowledge of the Logos, finally union with God. This journey is the means of redemption, and the saving work of the Logos is essentially educative, leading from one step to the next, each being interconnected. There is progressive transformation through this process and *paideia* takes place through the ministerial task of the church in the exegesis of scripture.

So the hearer is to be drawn into the text, and the steps observable in Origen's exegesis correspond to the progression of the soul on this journey. The literal sense is the wording of the text and what the words meant to psalmist or prophet; the spiritual sense what it means to the Christian making the journey of faith and participating in the history of salvation. This may involve a simple universalizing of the text, the hearer appropriating the words fairly straightforwardly; or it may involve what we would recognize as allegory.

'The purpose of inspiration is paideia, the progressive perfection of the Christian through assimilation of the saving doctrines' (Torjesen 1985a: 42). Not all Christians are ready for every doctrine, and so a homily has teachings intended for different levels. There are saving doctrines for the beginner, for those advancing, and for those perfect. Through scripture and its exegesis these doctrines are taught and made effective for the hearer's salvation. This progression is for every soul. Torjesen argues (Torjesen 1985*b*) that Origen never intended his threefold classification to apply to different 'senses' of scripture, nor to separate classes of Christian. Rather they correspond to different stages on the journey, and the shape of each homily reflects the threefold advance.

Origen's procedure in dealing with the New Testament, she notes, is different from his handling of the Old. This she attributes to the fact that the Old mediates the Logos, whereas in the New the Logos teaches directly:

The exegesis of the Old Testament prepares the reader or hearer for the exegesis of the gospel; unless he is properly prepared he cannot receive the truths of the gospel. This can also be seen in the arrangement of the liturgical services. A three-year catechumenate, during which the Old Testament was interpreted, prepared Christians for participation in the Eucharistic services in which the interpretation of the Gospel was presented. (Torjesen 1985*a*: 107)

The very diversity of doctrines in scripture makes it a perfect pedagogical instrument for the revelation of the Logos.

For Origen, doctrine is the means whereby the Logos communicates himself to the soul. There is a progressive disclosure of the Logos which makes possible a progressive comprehension of him, and that constitutes progress in the soul of the hearer (ibid. 120). The catechumen is at the beginning stage in which purification from sin, healing from the soul's physician, is required. Then there follows sanctification and redemption whereby, through moral and mystical pedagogy, the soul is prepared for perfection. The particularity of scriptural history becomes universal, as the journey of the soul becomes the allegorical meaning of, for example, the wanderings of Israel, and the text itself is taken to refer to these spiritual realities.

To assess Origen's Christology simply according to the categories supplied by the typical 'History of Doctrine' approach is therefore to lose its real dynamic. If it makes sense to speak of humanity and divinity and the relationship between them, it only does so in the context of the overall pedagogical accommodation of the Logos to the level of those who need healing and sanctification. Understanding the Gospels requires the penetration which discerns the divinity beneath the particularities of the earthly presence. There is a profound continuity between the two, a kind of sacramental relationship. What we would call 'correct doctrine' belongs to an entirely different realm of discourse from the transforming and progressive response to the Logos' teaching envisaged by Origen.

III

Maybe Origen can be dismissed as a kind of free-thinker who could float hypotheses, a philosopher rather than dogmatician whose ideas then became much more problematic several generations later as the Church defined and solidified its doctrinal position. After all his more speculative statements were rejected and he did become regarded as dangerous. But such a view is hardly fair to the later period.

Gregory of Nyssa, it is true, avoids mentioning Origen's name— he lived when the shadows had begun to fall. Yet he was much indebted to Origen, and the fact that the journey of the soul is fundamental to Gregory's spirituality takes little demonstration. Again exegesis provides the *locus* for spelling out the mystical progression to knowledge of God. The classic example is, no doubt, the *Life of Moses*.

Gregory produced this work in response to a request to send counsel on the perfect life, and his initial image is the highly dynamic one of a chariot race: as spectators encourage their favourites, so he cheers on his friend. He suggests that perfection in sensible objects involves limitation or boundaries; but virtue is not like that. Like the nature of the infinite God, perfection is boundless, and there is no stopping-place or final attainment. Growth in goodness constitutes human perfection. So examples to be followed are such as Abraham, or Moses. Gregory promises to outline Moses' life, and then, through contemplation of it, reach an understanding of the perfect life for human beings.

Moses' life was characterized by journeying, by watching the mysterious cloud that guided the people and teaching them to keep it in sight. Food was miraculously provided, enemies were overcome. At Mount Sinai he and the people were initiated, passing through purification to revelation. Moses had to ascend beyond the visible and enter the inner sanctuary of divine mystical doctrine. Gregory has summarized the story, yet 'amplified' it to bring out its spiritual intention (325M: Jaeger 33: 3–6). He goes on to probe its exemplary character more deeply.

Expounding details allegorically Gregory delineates both divine accommodation to the level of human weakness and the continuous progress upwards that constitutes perfection. If at first religious knowledge comes as light, further progress and deeper penetration discovers the invisible and incomprehensible, the darkness in which seeing consists in not seeing, for 'no one has ever seen God'. Moses enters the luminous darkness of the cloud of the presence. He is transformed by God's glory so that no one could look at him; he speaks with God as one speaks to a friend. Yet to see God is not attainable, and God hides him in a cleft in the rock, allowing him only to see his back-parts—the point being not just the absurdity of a literal seeing of the invisible, but the recognition of God's infinity. For 'this truly is the vision of God: never to be satisfied in the desire to see him' (404M: Jaeger 116: 17–19), and Moses 'is now taught how he can behold him: to follow God wherever he might lead is to behold God . . . He who follows will not turn aside from the right way if he always keeps the back of his leader in view' (409M: Jaeger 121: 4–6).

In Gregory's spirituality, then, there are no static conceptions, as many important studies have shown. But the relevant point here is the significance of the journey motif, not just in exegesis and in works we might treat as spiritual guides, but also in those we might regard as Gregory's 'dogmatic' works.

The *Great Catechesis* is intended to equip catechetical teachers for their job of training converts for initiation, so it is an object lesson in Christian *paideia* and leads to a consideration of what baptism is about. The crucial point about it is that there is a likeness between the journey made by Christ through death to life and the journey made by those who follow:

it is necessary for those with equal commitment to the Good, to follow by imitation the one who leads the way to our salvation, bringing into effect what he demonstrated. It is in fact impossible to reach the same goal without travelling by the same route. Should those puzzled as to how to thread the turns of labyrinths, happen to meet someone with experience of them, they pass through those various misleading turnings in the chambers by following him behind, which they could not do, without following their leader step by step; so, please note, the labyrinth of this life cannot be threaded by human nature unless one takes that same path as the one who, once in it, got beyond the difficulties surrounding him. Using labyrinth figuratively, I refer to the inescapable prison of death which encircles the wretched human race. (*Oratio catechetica magna*, s. 35, PG 45. 88B)

In this context Gregory stresses the moral character of this journey: it is not just in 'doctrines' but in actions that the way is to be pursued, as was the case with Christ. However, if we return to the beginning of the work, we find that the very procedure of this introductory account of the Christian faith is to encourage catechetical teachers to lead converts on an intellectual journey from their initial notions to a more transcendent conception. This is done by *anagōgē*, moving from human analogy by induction or abstraction to an appropriate conception of God. But while one who engages in this depth of study gains a certain amount of apprehension of God's nature, secretly in his spirit, yet he will never be able to articulate clearly in words the ineffable depth of this mystery. For Gregory the incomprehensibility of God is a 'doctrinal' necessity (*Oratio catechetica magna*, ss. 1–3, PG 45. 13–20).

This is true also in his controversial works against Eunomius, and that presumably has greater significance for our argument: the *Great Catechesis* is after all a work of *paideia* and we might expect a certain emphasis on the process of salvation. The controversy with Eunomius, however, was about the nature and identity of God and the Being known as God's Son. One might expect the 'static ontological categories' to dominate. But in practice the journey into understanding is as fundamental here as anywhere— it is indeed a doctrinal necessity.

For Eunomius' fundamental flaw is cleverness and over-wise philosophy which fixes a gulf between him and the saving faith of Abraham (*Contra Eunomium*, 2. 84–5: Jaeger 251–2), who

went out by Divine command from his own land and kindred on an 'exodus' befitting a prophet set on understanding God . . . For going out from himself and his country, by which I understand his lowly and earthly mind, he raised his conception as far as possible above the common bounds of nature and forsook the soul's kinship with the senses, so as to be troubled by none of the objects of sense and blind for the purpose of contemplating invisible things, there being neither sight nor sound to distract the mind; so walking, as the Apostle said, by faith not sight, he was lifted so high by the sublimity of his knowledge that he came to be regarded as the acme of human perfection, knowing as much of God as it was possible for finite human capacity at full stretch to attain.

That is why, according to Gregory, God is called the 'God of Abraham'. Abraham was able to soar above sense-objects and the beauty of objects of contemplation to behold the archetype of all beauty. He could use various human conceptions, such as God's power, goodness, being without beginning, infinity, or whatever, as stepping-stones for the upward course, and yet recognize that all fall short of what he was seeking, so that

> when he had outstripped every supposition with respect to the divine nature, every single conception of God suggested by any designation, when he had thus purged his reason of all such fancies and arrived at a faith unalloyed and free from all prejudice, he produced an evident and unmisleading sign of the knowledge of God, namely the conviction that God is greater and more sublime than any known signification. (2. 89)

For Gregory, Abraham is the type of a faith which recognizes it is but dust and ashes, and that the curiosity of human knowledge betrays an inappropriate empirical disposition. 'Knowing, then how widely the Divine nature differs from our own, let us quietly remain within our proper limits' (2. 96). Dogmatic formulations issue from heretics who offer the figments of their own imaginations. 'Whoever searches the whole of the inspired Word will find there no doctrine of the Divine nature' (2. 106).

Indeed, there is accommodation to human understanding through analogies, but 'the object to be aimed at, in discourse about God, is not to produce a pleasant and harmonious melody of words, but to work out a reverent conception, whereby a worthy notion of God is safeguarded' (*Contra Eunomium*, 2. 136: Jaeger 265). For Gregory a discernment that proceeds beyond language, indeed beyond knowledge, is required; but since there is no suitable word to encapsulate the divine being, human expressions need to be manifold, and the process of questioning and discussing and 'word-building' is essential to maintain the necessary relativizing of religious language. This is a kind of pilgrimage:

> we apply such appellations to the divine essence which surpasses all understanding, not seeking to glory in it by the names we employ, but to guide our own selves by the aid of such terms towards the comprehension of the things that are hidden (*Contra Eunomium*, 2. 154: Jaeger 270)

according to my account, conception is the method whereby we discover
things that are unknown by finding further consequences through what
attaches to or proceeds from our first perception of the matter pursued.
(*Contra Eunomium*, 2. 182: Jaeger 277)

For Gregory the intelligence to do this is a gift of God. God is not
the creator of words but of things made known to us through the
signification of words. So 'the scriptural account of the Creation is
the learner's introduction, as it were, to knowledge of God,
representing to our minds the power of the Divine Being through
what is more ready to our comprehension' *(Contra Eunomium*, 2.
228: Jaeger 292). Just as *we* have to build a house, even though the
ability to do so is God's gift, so *we* have to invent particular words,
even though the power of speech is God-given. There are lots of
different languages, precisely because language is a human invention. Gregory's conclusion is that 'if certain of our accustomed
expressions are attributed by Holy Scripture to God's person, it
should be recognized that the Holy Spirit is addressing us in
language of our own' (*Contra Eunomium*, 2. 238: Jaeger 296), and
naturally he refers to the story of Pentecost where each heard the
Gospel in his own language.

So like Origen he paints a picture of a divine accommodation to
our level, which provides guides for us to follow as we progress
towards knowledge of God. He refers to Paul's adaptation of his
speech to the capacity of his hearers, offering milk not solid food
where appropriate. The fundamental image, then, is of a process
of *paideia*, a two-way dynamic, a synergism, in which divine
Teacher and human disciple respond to one another. The very
possibility of this is grounded in God's being as love. What is by
nature finite cannot ascend above its prescribed limits:

on this account, bringing his loving power down to the level of human
weakness, he dispensed on us, so far as it was possible for us to receive it,
grace and assistance from himself . . . though transcending our nature and
inaccessible to human communion, yet like a tender mother joining in the
inarticulate gurglings of her baby, the divine power gives our human
nature what it is capable of receiving; and thus in diverse theophanies, he
adapts himself to humanity and speaks in human language, assuming
wrath and pity and such-like emotions, so that through feelings corresponding to our own infantile life we might be led by the hand, and grasp
the divine nature by means of the words which his foresight has provided.
(*Contra Eunomium*, 2. 417–18: Jaeger 348)

XIII

Doctrine is indistinguishable from spirituality, for both are about 'teaching' and 'learning' in a cosmic process of *paideia*.

The significant point here is that this account of doctrine was vital for the confrontation with what was indeed a static and limited view of truth. The notion of dogma as a set of propositions or a fixed credal formula is entirely foreign to Gregory's thought, though the language of scripture and traditional belief is important for guidance on the journey.

IV

At this point, the voice of the objector may be heard. Granted that this is true for the Origenist tradition, and indeed for the Cappadocians in general, it surely cannot be generalized to the whole Greek patristic tradition, or be taken to mean that there is nothing in the modern attribution of fundamentally static categories to patristic thought. Given that the converse attitudes are reflected in the very opponents Gregory was dealing with, they are unlikely to have been absent from Church tradition—indeed, can surely be documented: do not Eusebius and Epiphanius have a view of pristine original truth from which there was subsequent deviation?

The case of Eusebius is particularly interesting. He too was an Origenist, and the Origenist picture of the soul finding salvation occasionally surfaces in his writings. For Origen, however, the process of fall and return was seen not just at the individual level, but also at the cosmic level: the very creation of the material order was part of God's providential *paideia*, the foundation of a kind of 'school' to educate God's fallen creation back to comtemplative union with God's self. Eusebius transported this fundamental conception to his understanding of history.

In his *Praeparatio evangelica* we can see him working this out. Fundamentally this is an apologetic work, but Eusebius recognizes he is charting a path rather different from that of his predecessors. Like them, however, he has to answer those critics who object to Christianity because it neither upholds the ancient religious traditions of the Graeco-Roman world, nor embraces Judaism properly.

In offering his critique of religion, Eusebius exploits accounts given by Plutarch, Porphyry, and many others, accepting a progressive degeneration from primitive worship of heavenly bodies to the superstitious and idolatrous practices of later times. But all alike were deviations from true religion, since they worshipped the creature rather than the Creator. True religion was practised only by the Hebrews, by which he meant the patriarchs prior to Moses. Moses gives a true account of these pioneers, but then introduces polity and legislation to keep their deviant descendants, the Jews, on the true path, providing symbols and prophecies of the truth once more to be revealed in Jesus Christ. Both Jewish and pagan religion is therefore degenerating. The pattern of fall is traced in world history, and the return begins with the incarnation.

The function of the Logos is educative, restoring true religion, which is proper worship of the one true God, not a set of credal propositions, and teaching the true way of life. The Gospel is about 'friendship' with God, and this is what the Logos came to preach. It had been promised in the prophetic oracles, and the way providentially prepared for its revelation. The truth about the Sovereign of the universe wins the world from its delusive worship of daemons, brings peace and justice, restores rationality. Thus the teaching of Jesus in the Gospel and the providential activity of God cohere in the historical provision of *paideia* for the fallen human race, and Eusebius delights in pointing to the growing success of Christianity in his world as proof of his claims.

Book 7 provides a summary focus of this overall conception. The Hebrews alone deduced from the created order the existence of a Creator, and their own place within creation as rational beings charged with the privilege of rule and royalty over all things on earth. Eusebius credits them with realizing that the soul's rational and intellectual faculty should therefore be cultivated rather than the body, since it bore the likeness of God. Knowledge of God and his friendship they recognized as the consummation of all happiness, and they lived (before Moses) a free and unfettered life according to nature. The models of the righteous beloved by God are then sketched, Enos, Enoch, and Noah, then Abraham, Isaac, Jacob, and Joseph. They are called Hebrews, according to Eusebius, because 'they are a kind of "passengers", who have set out on their journey from this world to pass to the contemplation of the God of the universe. For they are recorded to have travelled the straight path of virtue aright by natural reasoning and by unwritten laws, and to have passed beyond carnal pleasures to the life of perfect wisdom and piety' (*Praep. evang.* 7. 8. 309b–c).

Eusebius may have a conception of a pristine faith, indeed of the original true religion, but it is not framed in terms of credal formulae or static ontological categories.

So what about the anti-Origenist, Epiphanius? What we know of Epiphanius is largely related to his campaign to eradicate heresy on all sides. But what did he mean by 'heresy'? The word is not confined to Christian deviations. It embraces also Greek philosophical schools and Jewish parties like the Pharisees and Sadducees. In other words it retains its original meaning of 'options'. What is wrong with options? As far as Epiphanius is concerned, the existence of options implies division, splinter-groups, factions, and is symptomatic of the breakdown of the original unity purposed by God. This unity is now restored in the one, holy, catholic, and apostolic church. Anything that rends that unity is rebellion, adultery, idolatry. Any kind of deviation belongs *outside*. Hence Epiphanius' hostility to anything he saw as false doctrine.

Adam was neither an idolater nor circumcised, but held the faith of the holy catholic church of God which existed from the beginning and was later to be revealed again. Because of Adam's sin, there appeared the opposite of the true faith. Piety and impiety, faith and unfaith coexisted, with the great biblical figures like Abel, Enoch, Methuselah, and Noah representing the former, which was the image of Christianity; Abraham in particular is presented as the type of the Christian, prefiguring, in his departure from his father's house, the call of the first disciples. To some extent Epiphanius shares Eusebius' historical perspective.

However, Epiphanius' main interest is to produce a genealogy of heresy, and his underlying conception seems to be a contrast between unity and multiplicity, heresy necessarily breeding further heresy, and compounding error. His schemata are not entirely consistent, and his material is artificially contrived to suit certain biblical texts (Young 1982), but the notion of the breakdown of pristine unity is clearly fundamental to his conceptions.

For Epiphanius, unity implies simplicity, and he mistrusts all kinds of 'speculation'. There are some things about which enquiry should not be made. Scripture speaks the truth in everything;

heresy is false because it does not receive the Holy Spirit according to the traditions of the Fathers of the holy catholic church. Wandering from the truth means being tossed on the storms of heresy. So good anchorage is required. So far from voyaging, Epiphanius prefers not to leave safe harbour and the security of truth given.

The well-anchored person (*Ancoratus* is the title of a work which preceded the *Panarion* or *Haereses*) knows the right formulae. When Epiphanius expounds the faith he piles up ecclesiastical jargon, scripture and tradition providing him with his tools: Christ is 'the only-begotten, the perfect, the uncreated, the immutable, the unchangeable, the unknowable, the unseen, become man among us . . . the one who though rich became poor for us . . . one Lord, King, Christ, Son of God, seated in heaven on the right-hand of the Father . . .'. Epiphanius not only quotes creeds, but writes in credal style. His fundamental concern is the avoidance of error.

No doubt this attitude is both perennially tempting and particularly understandable in the confusing maelstrom of fourth-century ecclesiastical controversy. No doubt Epiphanius was not the only one with this approach. But was he really typical?

The thrust towards unity is one thing he and others, even Origenists, had in common, and he was not alone in seeking to achieve it by a process of exclusion. To the extent that every philosophical sect had developed a tradition to be imparted to disciples and followed, Epiphanius' outlook reflected contemporary custom, and Christian practice in training catechumens and drilling them in a creed might seem to envisage the same fundamental outlook. This too was a kind of *paideia*, and it was geared to producing loyal adherents to a common stance. Deviation was suspect. But to deduce that catechetical instruction simply concentrated on imparting what we mean by correct doctrine is soon exposed as inappropriate by examination of examples of Catechetical Lectures which are extant from this period.

Catechumens were preparing for baptism, and Cyril of Jerusalem explains that baptism involved a melting-down and a re-moulding —it was quite realistically seen as transformation, as new life, as a dying and rising with Christ (e.g. *Orat. cat.* 3). Justifying the brevity of the Creed on the grounds that all cannot read the scriptures, some being hindered by lack of education, others by want of leisure, Cyril admits (*Orat. cat.* 5. 12) that the Creed comprises the whole doctrine of the faith in a few lines. It is a summary of scripture, but it needs filling out, it is simply the foundation on which the new convert is to build. Cyril of Jerusalem tells his class that they are standing at the gates of the heavenly mystery.

Memorizing the Creed was ensuring that the new covenant was written on the heart and not on tablets of stone: 'He gave us this new covenant . . . and because of this covenant we receive knowledge of these mysteries so that we should put off the old man and put on the new man who is renewed after the image of him who created him' (*Orat. cat.* 1), claimed Theodore of Mopsuestia. Entry to the future kingdom of heaven depends on adoption as sons of God; as the new-born baby is weak, so the newly baptized one cannot expect to be perfect, and needs suitable food for spiritual nourishment (*Orat. cat.* 16).

The Creed, then, proclaims the new creation, the gift of the Spirit, the future hope; a sense of wonder and mystery permeates Theodore's exposition of it. The Creed belonged to the process of commitment, of response to the Gospel proclaimed. It belonged at the beginning of the Christian life and was no mere assent to certain propositions. Converts were certainly warned against erroneous doctrines, but the teaching they received was more holistic, more transforming and dynamic than either Epiphanius or our preconceptions about doctrine might have suggested.

As for Gregory of Nyssa, so for Theodore, an essential component of doctrine is that 'dogma' is impossible: 'Human minds and human words are altogether unequal to the grandeur of the things I have to talk to you about. No language is really capable of explaining the sacred mysteries of our religion' (*On the Nicene Creed*, 1).

Epiphanius, it would seem, represents one persistent tendency in Christianity, reflecting the need for secure anchorage, but he cannot be regarded as typifying the attitude of his own time. The more persistent symbol of the Christian faith is a spiritual journey, or growth to maturity. Indeed, space permitting, it would be possible to show that this is true even for the participants in the Christological controversy. Both the exegesis, and indeed the Christology, of Cyril of Alexandria falls into the same pattern of *paideia*: for the Pentateuch is essentially understood as exemplifying exile and spiritual famine, followed by repentance and renewal, both Abraham's migration and the exodus being paradigms of God's grace effecting conversion, while the dynamic of *kenōsis*, or divine accommodation to humanity, lies at the heart of his Christological concerns. Furthermore the interest of the Antiochenes in the exemplary synergism of divine and human natures in Christ, who as high priest learned by what he suffered, is well documented (Greer 1973).

V

Yet, our objector might retort, appeal to the Fathers as well as scripture in the fifth-century controversies does seem to suggest that the notion of a 'pure deposit' or an original 'orthodoxy' from which deviation took place was a persistent view. Innovation and novelty were charges brought against heresy. Furthermore, the very Platonic notions behind Origen and Gregory of Nyssa imply that even if we are unable to grasp it or express it in propositional form, even if we have to progress towards it, behind the changes and chances of this life is an eternal unchanging reality. So surely the perception that the Fathers believed in static dogma cannot be wholly misguided. And were not the Christological controversies dominated by 'substance' categories?

The character of Platonism can hardly be tackled within the compass of this essay: suffice it to say that it is too easy to caricature ancient philosophy, understanding its concerns and doctrines in an overly simplistic way. An examination of late fourth-century discussions of human nature soon reveals a much more sophisticated sense of the complexity of the soul–body relationship than is generally attributed to this period—the soul is almost what we call the central nervous system, as well as the 'person' who transcends bodily existence (Young 1983). In the Platonist tradition life and motive power were associated with soul, and even the Ideas were regarded as intelligences, living beings. For Origen the eternal world was peopled by *logikoi*. There is a deep tension in Platonism between the attribution of changelessness and impassibility to spiritual realities like God and the soul, and the recognition that spiritual realities are both living and the source of life, movement, and power. Impassibility was not impassivity.

The 'substance' categories were to do with discussion of identity as enduring reality. In the Trinitarian and Christological controversies the issue of identity, and therefore of substantial reality, became the subject of debate, and it was inevitable that ontological terminology should dominate the discussion. This may give a static 'feel' to much of patristic thinking, but this terminology was employed to identify the living subject(s) of God's *oikonomia*.

By the time of the Cappadocians the dynamic of the divine *oikonomia*, God's creative and redeeming activity as self-revealing love, was recognized to be the known aspect of a triune God whose essential being was unknowable:

> God is Light: the highest, the unapproachable, the ineffable, that can neither be conceived in the mind nor uttered in speech, that gives light to every reasoning creature. He is in the world of thought what the sun is in the world of sense; in proportion as we are cleansed, he presents himself to our minds; in proportion as he is presented to our mind, he is loved; and again in proportion as we love him, he is conceived; himself contemplating and comprehending himself, and pouring himself out upon what is external to him. I mean that Light which is contemplated in the Father and the Son and the Holy Spirit, whose wealth is their unity of nature and the single outburst of their brightness. (Gregory Nazianzen, *Orat.* 40. 5. p. 204)

This is the language of dynamic relationship, of response and quest, of mind and heart. It is the language of liturgy and devotion as well as of doctrine; and doctrine informs the religious life of the community in such a way that it is indistinguishable from spirituality.

There is, of course, a sense in which the truth is there in advance of the journey: for the priority lies with the reality of God and God's self-disclosure. The pride of the intellectual athlete who presumes to use human reasoning to comprehend God is certainly to be exposed. Bold innovation is rebellion against the truth. So, as Gregory insists (*Orat.* 27), the true theologian has to submit in humility and obedience to the discipline of purification and meditation. On the other hand, God, like a schoolteacher facilitating a pupil's progress, has to accommodate the *paideia* to the level of the human recipient: there must be a mutually interacting dynamic for the teaching to effect growth in understanding.

VI

The consequences of this study are, I suggest, threefold:

1. That the current tendency, initiated by Maurice Wiles, to see soteriological concerns as underlying the doctrinal debates of the early centuries should be affirmed, and even radicalized in the sense that the distinction between soteriology and doctrine be recognized as false. Since both are about *paideia*, and the education involved is true religion, our Western distinctions, especially that between the head and the heart, have come to distort what lies at the heart of Christianity, which is a process of personal, social—indeed global —transformation effected by getting to know God and being reunited in the divine life.

For that process to be true to the reality of the way things are requires the nearest approximation possible in human terms to a true perspective on the identity and purpose of God, but this can only be attained through response to God's creative and educative activity (another way of characterizing what used to be called 'revelation'). That means doctrine is more than what we now mean by dogma or credal formula, and more than 'second-order' reflection on religious experience. It constitutes the religious life.

2. That the projection of 'static' received dogma on to the teachers of the early Church should be repudiated as a distortion of their fundamental outlook. It is true that they had sufficient humility to revere the common heritage and to seek to honour what had been received from the past. It is also true that innovation and indeed diversity of opinion was distrusted and associated with heretics. But the Fathers were not afraid to enter into argument to spell out the implications of the revelation received, and they largely envisaged this life in terms of a process of response to God's attempts to educate the human race.

This, I would suggest, is the appropriate way of discerning some sense of 'doctrinal development' or 'progressive revelation' in the thinking of the Fathers. Such notions have been attributed to Gregory Nazianzen, who was forced to respond to the charge that the divinity of the Holy Spirit was an innovation: 'The Old Testament proclaimed the Father openly and the Son more obscurely. The New manifested the Son, and suggested the Deity of the Spirit. Now the Spirit himself dwells among us, and supplies a clearer demonstration of himself' (*Orat.* 31. 26). However, this seems at first sight much closer to 'dispensationalism' than any modern notions of historical evolution.

In fact it is precisely because doctrinal development and progressive revelation are notions of modern culture, triggered by Reformation controversies, nineteenth-century scientific theories, and the development of historical consciousness, that I have not hesitated to call them 'projections'. They are ways of thinking which help us to understand the past, and not ideas we should expect to find in past literature.

But having said that, in the passage referred to Gregory affirms gradual progress from glory to glory, the light of the Trinity shining upon the more illuminated—indeed, he appeals to John 14: 16–17 and speaks of the Spirit gradually coming to dwell with the disciples, measuring himself out according to their capacity to receive him. It is clear that progress in understanding, for the individual, for the human race, and for the cosmos, is envisaged in patristic thinking, and this process of *paideia* is the framework in which the equivalent of our idea of 'development' may be discerned. Gregory was not alone in being conscious of spelling out the implications and discerning new depths in the faith once delivered to the saints. History was seen as the arena of process and change, and as the journey of the soul was progressive apprehension of truth, so under the guidance of God tradition would realize its 'potential' meaning under changing circumstances.

3. That the idea should be laid to rest once and for all that patristic theological discourse was conducted in static ontological categories. We ourselves necessarily use such categories when discussing issues of enduring identity, nature, or even character. Such were the questions Church leaders found themselves debating, and which our histories of doctrine have fastened upon. But 'doctrine' was not confined to those issues, and Christian teaching was obliged to affirm change because it was about fall, repentance, and return, about transformation, indeed about deification.

Exegesis spelled out the doctrine contained in scripture, doctrine was doctrine because it was educative, and so it was about spiritual growth, about God's saving *paideia*.

Paideia *and the Myth of Static Dogma* 283

REFERENCES

Editions

Cyril of Jerusalem, *Catechetical Orations*: Migne, *Patrologia Graeca*, vol. 33. 331–1128.

Eusebii Praeparatio Evangelica, ed. E. H. Gifford, text and trans. in 4 vols., Oxford 1903.

Grégoire de Nazianze: Discours 27–31 (*Discours théologiques* = *Orations*), ed. P. Gallay, text and French trans., Sources Chrétiennes 250, Paris 1978.

Grégoire de Nazianze: Discours 38–41, ed. C. Moreschini, text and French trans., Sources Chrétiennes 358, Paris 1990.

Gregorii Nysseni opera, ed. W. Jaeger and Hermann Langerbeck, Leiden. vol i, *Contra Eunomium libri*. ed. W. Jaeger, 1960; vol. vii. 1, *De vita Moysis*, ed. H. Musurillo, 1964.

Gregorii Nysseni: Oratio catechetica magna: Migne, *Patrologia Graeca*, vol. 45. 9–106.

Theodore of Mopsuestia, *Commentary of Theodore of Mopsuestia on the Nicene Creed*, and *Commentary on the Lord's Prayer and the Sacraments of Baptism and the Eucharist*, ed. A. Mingana, Syriac text and Eng. trans., Woodbrooke Studies v and vi, Cambridge, 1932.

Secondary Literature

Bigg, Charles (1886), *The Christian Platonists of Alexandria*, Oxford.

Crouzel, Henri (1985), *Origène*, Paris (Eng. trans. Edinburgh 1989).

Greer, Rowan (1973), *The Captain of our Salvation: A Study in the Patristic Exegesis of Hebrews*, Tübingen.

Richardson, Alan (1935), *Creeds in the Making*, London.

Torjesen, Karen Jo (1985a), *Hermeneutical Procedure and Theological Method in Origen's Exegesis*, Berlin.

—— (1985b), '"Body", "Soul", and "Spirit" in Origen's Theory of Exegesis', *Anglican Theological Review*, 67/1: 17–30.

Young, Frances M. (1982), 'Did Epiphanius Know what he Meant by Heresy?', *Studia patristica*, 18: 199–205.

—— (1983), 'Adam and Anthropos: A Study of the Interaction of Science and the Bible in Two Anthropological Treatises of the Fourth Century', *Vigiliae Christianae*, 37: 110–40.

XIV

The Confessions of St. Augustine: What is the Genre of this Work?[1]

The aim of this paper is to set *The Confessions* against the wider background of patristic literature, especially Eastern texts, so as to illuminate the character of this work and challenge some easy assumptions.

We begin with Augustine's work itself. Relatively innocent readers of *The Confessions* may be forgiven for assuming it is the first self-conscious autobiography ever written. It is plausible, after all, that this text generated "the introspective conscience of the West,"[2] and the title, "Confessions," would encourage us to

---

1. This paper was first delivered as the 1998 St. Augustine lecture at Villanova University. Footnotes are kept to a minimum. The content owes much though not all to my book *Biblical Exegesis and the Formation of Christian Tradition* (Cambridge: Cambridge University Press, 1997). Latin texts of Augustine are found in *Corpus Christianorum. Series Latina*. English translations quoted here are acknowledged in footnotes.

2. The phrase is borrowed from the title of a famous article by Krister Stendahl, "The Apostle Paul and the Introspective Conscience of the West," originally published in the *Harvard Theological Review* 56 (1963): 199–215; republished in *Paul among Jews and Gentiles* (Fortress, 1976; SCM 1977). It is not entirely irrelevant here since his argument was that Augustine radically changed the way Paul's letters have been read in the West.

think that Augustine set the trend in self-exposure. Readers expect here the individual self displayed reflecting upon its own inner development, and deduce that that self-awareness created autobiographical narrative.

That temptation might, however, be resisted by a more sophisticated readership which knew that in the ancient languages "confession" was about confessing God and meant praising or extolling the divine Name. Indeed, a slightly less innocent reader, one who opened the covers and read the first paragraph, would soon discover that the work is an extended prayer. However, as the work proceeds, confession of God becomes confession of a misspent youth, together with testimony to God's providential rescue and celebration of conversion to a new life. To that extent Augustine anticipates the autobiographical testimony tradition of my own Methodist evangelical forebears, and people may be excused for retaining something of their innocent assumptions even as they read the work.

The attentive and thorough reader, however, will eventually be disabused of those assumptions. For the climax of this thirteen-volume work consists of four books with no autobiographical content at all. On reaching the end, no reader will be surprised to hear that scholars have long since puzzled about the role of those books, or that their existence has retrospectively challenged the attribution of the description "autobiography" to the work as a whole. There is a serious issue about the *genre* of *The Confessions* at a time when the significance of *genre* for the evaluation of a literary work has become paramount.

Literary genres do not spring from nothing. So whether we find the description "autobiographical" convincing or not, it is important to search for precedents. Conveniently for us, Georg Misch of Göttingen produced at the beginning of the century a comprehensive history of autobiography in antiquity.[3] A work of this kind inevitably bears the marks of its own time. Looking back from the so-called postmodern perspective, one of the characteristics of "modernity" we now discern is individualism, its focus on the original mind of an author, on the subjective self, on self-expression in the creative arts. It is not surprising that writing in the period of high modernity the account of ancient autobiography that Misch provides is one that details the development of self-consciousness, with Augustine as the climax. But what is convenient for us is the meticulous collection of relevant material, irrespective of whether we

---

3. Georg Misch, *A History of Autobiography in Antiquity*, 2 vols., ET (London: Routledge and Kegan Paul, 1949–50). Originally published in German in 1907, the English translation is of a later edition.

THE GENRE OF AUGUSTINE'S *CONFESSIONS*

share the same analytical perspective. For Misch is prepared to track down autobiographical elements in all kinds of different literary material, and little that is similar to *The Confessions* can have escaped his attention.

So where are the most significant precedents to be found? Misch's work is strictly chronological, and we can ignore his earliest material, from Egypt, Babylonia and elsewhere. When we come to Plato and Isocrates, however, we are dealing with the beginnings of the literary deposit which directly or indirectly was Augustine's heritage, and there would seem to be two significant kinds of precedents. One is apologetic writing produced to explain and defend from criticism a person's past; the other is the meditative literature that emerges from the philosophic tradition and is most obviously instanced in the work of Marcus Aurelius, the Emperor who was also a Stoic philosopher. Roughly speaking Misch's view seems to be that autobiography flowered in late antiquity as ecclesiastical controversy provoked development of the former and Christian devotion reinforced the mystical tendencies of the latter. Neoplatonic spirituality he saw shading into Christian mysticism in Synesius of Cyrene, and as far as apologetic is concerned the then newly discovered work of Nestorius known as *The Bazaar of Heraclides* provided Misch with an obvious example.

More or less contemporary with Augustine we have the so-called autobiographical poems of Gregory Nazianzen. For Misch, Neoplatonic self-communion is the fundamental characteristic that Gregory and Augustine have in common, though both in different ways marry together elements of the apologetic and philosophic traditions. My view, however, is that the precedents so far adduced are not sufficient to account for the work of either of these authors. Only when we discern another important factor can we achieve an adequate literary analysis and account for the puzzle of Augustine's last four books. The fundamental point is this: even if we agree to describe as autobiographical the telling of one's own story, the object of such narrative was not at all what the modern reader might suppose nor what Misch assumed. It was not about individual self-expression, nor about the search for the inner core of one's particular subjectivity, the supposedly real self to be discerned when the layers are stripped off. So if it had nothing to do with psychological self-analysis, what was it? Radically different from Augustine's *Confessions* though Gregory's work is, I shall use it to tease out this other dimension, then show how recent discussion of Augustine's work points in the same direction, and finally address some potential objections to my thesis.

XIV

Gregory of Nazianzus, *De Vita Sua*,[4] and Typology

Written in retirement toward the end of his life, Gregory's poetic account of his life has a strong apologetic flavour—indeed the Neoplatonic strains are found in other poems, not here. The tone is usually that of self-justification, of attack on enemies, of setting the record straight about his own actions and motivations. He wants to stop the flow of false reports, because he knows that people in power can divert blame onto their victims and whitewash their own actions. The apologetic motive is clear.

Nor is it surprising if we consider the course of Gregory's rise and fall. He had been called to Constantinople, the Eastern capital, when it was dominated by Arians, to form a Nicene congregation. Gradually with his eloquence and orthodoxy he had built up a following in the church of the Anastasis. A new Emperor had arrived, the Arians had been routed and Gregory installed in the Cathedral. But his triumph was short-lived. Enemies exploited his previous consecration as bishop of a nondescript little place in Cappadocia and, recognising that he was in breach of a Nicene canon, he resigned his see as well as the chairmanship of the Council of Constantinople in 381. He retired to fulfill his dream of ascetic withdrawal from the affairs of the world. Gregory's poetic narrative tells of his origins, his family, his education, the days in Athens as a student and his friendship with Basil, their search for the right way of life, how Gregory came to be ordained as priest and consecrated as bishop, episodes which bring out the love-hate relationship he had with his father and his closest friend, but all this is mere background to his defence of what happened in Constantinople. A poem of some 2000 lines devotes three-quarters of its length to the successes and failures of about eighteen months. This is primarily an apologetic work.

And yet in the prologue are other clues. He adopts the verse form as a kind of play and a consolation, and uses the metre of tragedy. He presents himself as one

. . . who is completely devoid of falsehood,

and who has suffered greatly amid many twists of fortune,

out of which there has arisen a greater understanding. (lines 17–19)

He explains that "greater understanding" in terms of an appreciation of the transitoriness of earthly life:

---

4. For text and translation (quoted here), see Gregory of Nazianzus, *Autobiographical Poems*, ed. Caroline White, Cambridge Medieval Classics 6 (Cambridge: Cambridge University Press, 1996).

4

THE GENRE OF AUGUSTINE'S *CONFESSIONS*

Everything ends in disaster: even good things are by time
outworn. Little or nothing remains,
as when the earth is swept away by heavy showers
and pebbles are all that is left. (lines 20–23)

Such clues point to the other element at which I have hinted. The particulars of the narrative may have apologetic aims but the overarching story has in Gregory's mind the universal dimensions of tragedy, and so the poem has a didactic purpose. It is to be a source of instruction and pleasure for the young, says Gregory (line 7); and that means he sees it as all literature was seen in antiquity, as an educational vehicle. He is providing an exemplary narrative, a story that carries moral truths about human life.

To describe it thus is to give it a classical flavour, fully justifiably, but we need to go further. Gregory's poem is saturated with biblical allusions which indicate an extraordinary melding of the narrative of his life with the stories of scripture. His father was a second Abraham and became one of Christ's shepherds. Hannah and other biblical mothers, though unmentioned, provide the model of his own mother's story: his birth was the outcome of her prayers and vows, she had a vision revealing his name, she immediately dedicated him to God, or as Gregory put it,

. . . to God

I was offered like a lamb or a sweet calf,

a noble sacrifice and one endowed with reason—

I would hesitate to say, like a second Samuel,

if I did not have in mind the longing of those who offered me. (lines 88–92)

Rather generalised comments about his youthful passion for language and literature leads Gregory into justifying the selection of events for his narrative and introducing the next episode as an example of youthful hot-headedness. But despite its manner of presentation, its purpose is surely not just to instance impetuous rashness in setting sail from Alexandria at the wrong time of year. Near Cyprus a storm comes up. Gregory draws on all his literary expertise to pen a dramatic description, but the point is that God's providence protected him, and Christ was already his Saviour, despite the fact he had not yet been baptised. This is both explicit and implicit, implicit in the narrative parallels with Jonah, explicit in the prayers he reports. The prayers call on the miracle-working God who destroyed the Egyptians and allowed his chosen people to cross the Red Sea, defeated Israel's enemies through the raised hands of Moses

THE GENRE OF AUGUSTINE'S *CONFESSIONS*

(a long-standing traditional "type" of Christ on the cross), and brought down Jericho's walls by a trumpet-led procession. Recalling his mother's dedication, Gregory claims membership of the band of disciples and begs Christ to awake from sleep and still the storm. Gregory implies that it was his prayers which saved the entire ship's company. We note the intertextuality, the scriptural shaping of the narrative, analogous to what we noted before in the account of his parents and his birth.

We could go on and mention how Gregory's father begs him for his support with allusions to Aaron helping Moses and Samuel assisting Eli; how Gregory describes Christ's support when he had to face the magistrates early in his time in Constantinople by reference to Daniel in the lion's den, to Shadrach, Meshach and Abednego in the fire, to Jonah and the whale; how the Exodus plagues and the waves of the Red Sea provide ways of describing his problems with Maximus, the enemy from Egypt; and many more examples, some so subtle they are less easily detectable. But enough has been said to make the basic point. Biblical narratives provide plots, motifs, exemplars, precedents, in the light of which Gregory is able to make sense of his own life. At the heart of his autobiography lies what I would call a typological imagination.

To understand this we need a little further exploration. Typology is a slippery concept, not least because of the history of its use in this century. It is not an ancient term but was coined in the nineteenth century,[5] at least partly as a result of the post-Reformation reaction against allegory; it is loaded with attempts to define non-allegorical ways of recognising deeper meanings, and associated since the work of Daniélou with a strong emphasis on history. Thus events, such as the Exodus, evidenced providential parallels with aspects of the Christ-event, so that they became prophetic. Prophecies grounded thus in history were supposedly more acceptable to the modern mind than prophecies found by the riddling twists of allegory. In my view all this is simply a red herring. With the postmodern emphasis on the shaping of narrative and intertextuality we are in a position to understand better what the ancients were up to.

Already within the Bible, stories were given significance by relation to other narratives. As Greek became the language of early Christianity, the term

---

5. A. C. Charity, *Events and their Afterlife: The Dialectics of Christian Typology in the Bible and Dante* (Cambridge: Cambridge University Press, 1966), p. 171, note 2. For further discussion of the points made in this paragraph, see my article "Typology," in *Crossing the Boundaries, Essays in Biblical Interpretation in Honour of Michael D.Goulder,* ed. Stanley E. Porter, Paul Joyce and David E. Orton (Leiden: Brill, 1994), pp. 29–48, and my book, *Biblical Exegesis and the Formation of Christian Tradition,* chapters 7 and 9.

THE GENRE OF AUGUSTINE'S *CONFESSIONS*

typos was used for a tale which bore the "stamp" of another. The Fathers were ready enough to adopt this (probably semitic) notion of prophetic "types" in scripture. They also understood scriptural narratives as "types" or "exemplars" of character or moral behaviour, since the latter was a common way of reading Greek literature. Types and parables were never clearly distinguished from allegory, which was itself a recognised literary conceit, a figure of speech, like metaphor. In exegesis such non-direct and allusive ways of expression had to be identified so as to discern the true meaning. As we try to analyse the ways in which ancient exegetes handled this complex of "signs" pointing to deeper meanings, we may find the term "typology" convenient, but we must treat it as encompassing at least two significant elements: firstly, Christ and the Christian dispensation were found foreshadowed in the characters and narratives of what had become the "Old" Testament; secondly, models of Christian living and exemplars of true virtues were found in Biblical "types," that is, in the stories and heroes depicted in scripture and held up to be imitated.

This typology is all-pervasive in the homilies and commentaries of the Fathers; it is fundamental to biography and hagiography.[6] In late Antiquity, as Patricia Cox has shown,[7] biographies, whether pagan or Christian, were generally meant to be "literary celebrations of the virtues of eminent individuals," who were seen "through ideal traits." Wayne Meeks has demonstrated how the double purpose of Plutarch's *Lives*, to demonstrate character and encourage imitation,[8] was adopted by Jewish writers; Philo introduces his stories of the Patriarchs by propounding the notion of persons who are "living laws," "archetypes" of which particular laws and customs are but "copies." Averil Cameron[9] tellingly puts the point:

> In a concrete sense . . . written Lives provided the guidelines for the construction of a Christian life. . . . Written lives were mimetic; real ascetic discipline in turn imitated the written Lives. Like visual art, early Christian discourse presented its audience with a series of images.

It is against this background that we note how Gregory of Nazianzus, in his panegyrical funeral orations for his father, mother and brother, and in his encomia on Basil and Athanasius, had already drawn upon the Bible to provide

---

6. For fuller treatment, see my *Biblical Exegesis and the Formation of Christian Culture*, chapter 11.

7. Patricia Cox, *Biography in Late Antiquity* (University of California Press, 1983), p. 134.

8. Wayne Meeks, *The Origins of Christian Morality* (Yale University Press, 1993), p. 190, quoting from C. P. Jones, *Plutarch and Rome* (Oxford: Oxford University Press, 1971), p. 103.

9. Averil Cameron, *Christianity and the Rhetoric of Empire* (University of California Press, 1991), p. 57.

"archetypes," both of character and of event. Clearly in telling his own life, the same element plays a significant role.

Typology in Augustine's *Confessions*?

So my next questions are these: is Augustine's *Confessions* similarly typological? and does this help to explain the final books?

That *The Confessions* presents Augustine's life as a kind of paradigm of all human life is a thesis advanced in two forms in recent scholarship. Henry Chadwick in introducing his translation in the Oxford World's Classics[10] develops the notion that Augustine presents in this work an account of Neoplatonic descent and return. It is "the story of the soul wandering away from God and then in torment and tears finding its way home through conversion." This "is also the story of the entire created order." "So Augustine's personal quest and pilgrimage are the individual's experience in microcosm of what is true, on the grand scale, of the whole creation," and that explains the presence of the four last books. They demonstrate that "the autobiographical books," are "more than a memoir: they illustrate a universal truth about human nature."

Chadwick admits that "Augustine found his story especially symbolized in St. Luke's account of the parable of the prodigal son"; and that he expresses "Neoplatonic themes in language that sounds like a pastiche of the Psalter." In other words there is an interpenetration of Neoplatonic framework and biblical language. Certainly one cannot deny the Neoplatonic flavour of much of Augustine's work; but the other account of *The Confessions* as paradigm would shift attention more definitely to the influence of the biblical text, noting a change in perspective between the earlier Neoplatonic writings and this later work. This alternative proposal is that Augustine's reading of Paul had profoundly changed his view of the human predicament and here he presented his own life as a paradigm of the life of "everyman" as he now understood it.

Augustine, weighed down with ecclesiastical responsibilities, "had broken completely with the classical ideal of virtue by which he had been reintroduced to Catholicism back in Milan," suggests Paula Fredricksen.[11] A new

---

10. *St. Augustine's Confessions*, ET Henry Chadwick, World's Classics (Oxford: Oxford University Press, 1992).

reading of Paul's life gave him insight into the human moral predicament. She quotes from *Ad Simplicianum*:

> What did Saul will but to attack, seize, bind and slay Christians? What a fierce, savage, blind will was that! Yet he was thrown prostrate by one word from on high, and a vision came to him whereby his mind and will were turned from their fierceness and set on the right way towards faith, so that suddenly out of a marvellous persecutor of the Gospel he was made a still more marvellous preacher of the Gospel.

The Neoplatonic Augustine had defended free will and argued against moral determinism. Convinced now that no one can save themselves, Augustine allowed his reading of Paul's life to shape the telling of his own, which by hindsight becomes a paradigm of Adam's bondage and the saving grace of divine providence. And the last four books may be seen as confirming that reading of his intention.

This view is very attractive: it accounts for the change in his views while highlighting scriptural exegesis as a significant factor. But my suggestion is that we must look beyond Paul and ask to what extent Augustine's work is grounded in the common "typological" frame of early Christian narrative. To explore this we must look East again.

The Syriac poems of Ephrem may be utterly different from anything Augustine wrote, but the patterning of lives on biblical models and the shaping of biblical models so that they reflect the underlying pattern of human existence is beautifully evident in these texts. Let us take as an example the treatment of King David in the XIIIth *Hymn on Paradise*:[12]

> In that king
> did God depict Adam:
> since he provoked God by his exercise of kingship,
> God stripped him of his kingship.
> The Just One was angry and cast him out
> into the region of wild beasts;

---

11. Paula Fredriksen, "Beyond the Body/Soul Dichotomy: Augustine's answer to Mani, Plotinus, and Julian," *Paul and the Legacies of Paul*, ed. William S. Babcock (Southern Methodist University Press, 1990), pp. 227–51. Cf. her article "Paul and Augustine: Conversion Narratives, Orthodox Traditions, and the Retrospective Self," *JTS* NS 37 (1986): 3–34.

12. *St. Ephrem. Hymns on Paradise*, Introd. and trans. Sebastian Brock (New York: St. Vladimir's Press, 1990).

he dwelt there with them
in the wilderness
and only when he repented did he return
to his former abode and kingship.
Blessed is He who has thus taught us to repent
so that we too may return to Paradise.
Because it was not easy
for us to see our fallen state—
how and whence we had fallen
at the very outset—
He depicted it all together
in that king,
portraying our fall
in his fall,
and portraying our return
in his repentant return.
Praise to him who delineated
this likeness for the repentant.

As the hymn goes on, Adam becomes a type of Samson as well as David, a type of "us" and a type of Christ. Jonah and Joseph likewise exemplify the pattern of being cast out and rescued. All are fused into a single narrative of fall and redemption which is the universal story of humankind.

In the Pentateuchal exegesis of Cyril of Alexandria we can discern a similar pattern.[13] The drama of fall and redemption is the true meaning of the Law. Various biblical narratives, such as Abraham's migration and the Exodus, display the pattern of exile, spiritual famine and return to a better life. Thus the human predicament and its solution in Christ is the Law's fundamental theme recapitulated in one narrative after another.

Now Augustine certainly lacks the poetic imagination of a Gregory or an Ephraim. In *The Confessions*, as in other works like *The City of God*, he moves from one philosophical question to another, and for all the collages of scriptural texts, the kind of pastiche of biblical narratives noted in the Eastern material is hardly to be found. Nevertheless interest in an archetypal narrative of

---

13. See further my *Biblical Exegesis and the Formation of Christian Culture*, p. 262.

human existence, played and replayed through history, is transparently clear in *The City of God*, and that account is subtly anticipated in the final book of *The Confessions*, when Augustine speaks of intellectual beings in the heavenly *city* resting in the Spirit, while fallen spirits are restless.

As is well known Augustine's fundamental thesis in *The City of God* is that human history displays the presence of two contrasting cities created by two kinds of love: self-love which reaches the point of contempt for God, love of God carried as far as contempt for self. Those who pursue the latter are strangers and pilgrims on earth, because their citizenship is in heaven. Traced through history, and particularly the narratives of the Bible, are instances of each city and the conflict between them. Individuals find their place within the universal story, and discover that the conflict lies within themselves. Written somewhat earlier than *The City of God*, *The Confessions* works through a similar agenda: as Christ came into the history of the world, so he came into Augustine's life. Thus the later work reinforces the notion that in *The Confessions* Augustine was exploring how his own life instanced the universal pattern. The work is not simply apologetic, certainly not purely psychological or self-oriented, it is fundamentally didactic. It is about reorientation from self-love to love of God. The story instances an archetype.

So let us turn again to the final books, beginning with the last. Often billed as an allegorical interpretation of Genesis, this volume, for all its digressiveness, has as overall theme God's praiseworthiness, particularly for the outworking of divine providence. In tune with the earlier books the opening paragraph is in the first person:

> You made me and, when I forgot you, you did not forget me. I call you into my soul which you are preparing to receive you through the longing which you have inspired in it. . . . Before I called to you, you were there before me. (XIII.i [10])

But from the second paragraph there is a turn to the creation as a whole, and Augustine as always focuses on God's priority, the goodness of God as alone giving worth to the creation, and the need for the whole creation to be converted to God. Both the human soul and all the spiritual creation are restless till they find their rest in God. The one is type of the other. Augustine's "I" prays more than a purely personal and particular plea, and the Genesis text points to more than genesis of the material creation. The whole creation groans and travails, as St. Paul had said, and we who have the Spirit groan too.

Later (XIII. xii–xiv [13–15]), in a remarkable collage of scriptural texts drawn from the prophets, the Gospels, the Psalms, the Apostle Paul, as well as

Genesis, Augustine plays out the same narrative with respect to the Church. Everyone shares in the reality that without the Spirit, existence is formless and dark: weighed down one groans; "his soul thirsts for the living God, like a hart for the springs of waters"; each longs for the heavenly city, and there is constant slipping back into the deep; there is testing, and yet assurance that during this wandering pilgrimage, we are already light; so we are saved by hope. In the midst of this long passage, Augustine slips back into the "I" language, only to revert to "we" again. This yearning and wandering, this internal conflict, this dependence on the grace of God, all is of a type, and the ability to abstract biblical texts for his collages suggests an implicit grasp of the way the same narrative is played and replayed in scripture.

It is hardly surprising then that Book X treats Augustine's *persona* as typical of this universal human experience. This book makes no pretence to continue the narrative which finishes at the end of Book IX with the death of Augustine's mother. Much of the book appears to be a philosophical discussion of memory, but to give that title to the book, as Chadwick does, is misleading. Augustine begins by reflecting on the purpose of writing down his confessions:

> When I am confessing not what I was but what I am now, the benefit lies in this: I am making this confession not only before you (= God) with a secret exaltation and fear and with a secret grief touched by hope, but also in the ear of believing sons of men, sharers in my joy, conjoined with me in mortality, my fellow citizens and pilgrims, some who have gone before, some who follow after, and some who are my companions in this life. . . . You have commanded me to serve them if I wish to live with you and in dependence on you. (X.iv [6])

This implies that the service consists in unveiling the pattern of pilgrimage and struggle typified in Augustine's own life, present and indeed past, as the earlier books have shown.

What follows is another remarkable collage of scripture texts, pointing to the fact that as a human person one is not transparent to oneself, that God alone knows and judges, that God alone is the proper object of love, and God transcends everything else. The discussion of memory (really an exploration of mental capacities) is a foil to wonder at the mystery of human being, and points to the epistemological quest which to my mind undergirds the whole work from beginning to end. The theme of *The Confessions* is the quest for truth, and the discovery that we do not know God; rather God knows us. Book X describes the human condition as ever transitional, ever struggling with temptations and desires, yet illuminated by a God in whom confidence can be placed, not least because Christ has died and medicine has been prepared to restore humanity to health.

With these clues, it is possible to revise one's whole view of Augustine's purpose. The episodes in his life which he earlier chooses to narrate are illustrative of the themes he discusses at length, themes which can appear digressive and tedious if we imagine the principal interest is in giving an autobiographical account. Of course there is an apologetic element, as we found also in Gregory's work. But there is also a didactic thrust, and the overall perspective is reflection on human existence and God's providence. Augustine's points away from himself to God, but to do that he has to demonstrate how God has led him to appreciate the fact that true knowledge is ignorance. By doing this Augustine makes himself an instance of the universal human story, and the work is fundamentally typological.

Objection: Augustine's lack of typology

But is this paradigmatic reading really a tracing of typology? After all, Augustine does not in *The Confessions* mirror biblical narratives in the way Gregory or Ephrem does. He does not, for example, allude to biblical mothers like Hannah in depicting the significant role of his own. When he appeals to Adam, he does so in terms of us all being in Adam, or being "sons of Adam," a view more geneological than typological, one might say. Furthermore he does not discuss typology or "types" when he examines language and signs in the *De Doctrina Christiana*—indeed, it has been suggested that he failed to appreciate one section of Tyconius's work precisely because he did not grasp that Tyconius was discussing typology.[14] So is there any justification in seeing a parallel with the kind of thing noted in the Eastern Fathers, Greek and Syriac?

My response to this is threefold. First, *The City of God* justifies the proposal. There are many passages in this colossal work which show without possibility of contradiction that Augustine inherited and exploited traditional prophetic typology. In the people of God

> were prefigured and foretold all things which were foreseen, by inspiration of the Spirit, as destined to come, relating to the City whose kingdom will be eternal, and to Christ, its king and founder. (XV.8)[15]

---

14. *Augustine, De Doctrina Christiana*, ed. R. P. H. Green (Oxford: Clarendon Press), p. xviii.

15. Augustine, *City of God*, ET Henry Bettenson, ed. David Knowles (Pelican Classics, 1972).

Whether tracing the story of Abraham, Joshua or David, the traditional "types" are drawn out. Paradoxically his use of traditional "types" both reinforces and runs counter to his insistence that somehow we were all "in Adam." For that idea leads him to make a distinction between the disobedience of Adam and Eve and all that followed, despite seeing in Adam and Eve the *archetype* both of harmonious unity in plurality and of human discord, with its roots in pride and self-regard.

The project Augustine undertakes from Book XI on of *The City of God* is essentially comparable with the typological construct of Ephrem and Cyril. He tells the twofold universal story, played and replayed in human history, and as he does so traditional typological associations are drawn deeper and deeper into his narrative. If explicit in *The City of God*, why not implicit in *The Confessions*? The likelihood is the greater if we note the occasional examples there of typological parallels, such as the description of Monica in terms of the widow at Nain (VI.i [1]).

Secondly, I cross-reference Augustine's exegesis of the Psalms. In *Enarrationes in Psalmos*, a collection of pieces produced over a long period (392–418) and ranging from brief notes to full sermonic expositions, Augustine consistently refers the words to Christ and the Church. This is not simply allegorical. Archetypes of the Church are found in the temple or people of God. Exemplars of prayer are found in the psalmist's language, as Augustine identifies with the "I" of the psalmist, who becomes a "type" of the saved community.

Two passages from his comments on Ps.30 (29 LXX) are illuminating:[16]

> (i) I, your church, imitating the first-born from the dead, now sing at the dedication of your house: "You have turned for me my mourning into joy. You have cut off my sackcloth and girded me with gladness." You have ripped away the covering of my sins, the sadness of my mortal existence, in order to clothe me in the best robe, and in never-ending joy.

Then (ii) from a comment on the text "O Lord my God, I will confess to you forever":

> there is confession of praise as well as of sins. Confess then today what you have done against God, and you will confess tomorrow what God has done in return for you. . . . And God? God forgives your sins as soon as you

---

16. Augustine, *Enarrationes in Psalmos*, ET in *Ancient Christian Writers* (New York: Newman Press), vols. 29 and 30.

confess your guilt, to free you from the remorse of sin, that you may confess God's praise hereafter forever and ever.

These passages almost provide the text for *The Confessions*, with the implied allusion to the Prodigal and the double sense of "confess." They illuminate Augustine's constant use of the Psalms in his collages of scripture texts. But more than that, they illustrate the "typological" reading of scripture which undergirds what Augustine is doing.

Thirdly, I remind you that the ancients in general did not identify "typology" as such. They spoke of types and parables, metaphors and allegories, all pointing to the deeper meaning of the text. Augustine deals with these matters not discretely but overall in his discussion of "signs" (cf. *De Doctrina Christiana*). He may not use the word "type" or "figura" all that much; he may not self-consciously distinguish in his analysis what we choose to call "typology." But my argument, deriving from familiarity with other early Christian texts, is this: consciously or unconsciously, alongside the apologetic interest, Augustine's purpose in *The Confessions* is typological. He constructs his own life according to the biblically-shaped pattern by which he has come to understand the weakness of the human quest for God and the power of divine providence and grace, so as to provide a didactic "type" or exemplar from which others will benefit by coming to an understanding of their own lives. The particular is understood by reference to the universal and *vice versa*. Scripture provides the models after which each human story may be sculpted.

Conclusion

Let me conclude by returning to the foil for this study, the work of Misch, and making a few admissions. It is true that Misch states early on that from its outset the highest aim of ancient autobiography was to depict an ideal standard of culture or a definite type of character, cast in the form of a self-portrait (pp. 63–4). It is also true that in his account of the Stoics, Seneca, Epictetus and Marcus Aurelius, he recognises the didactic purpose of their "soul-histories" (pp. 412 ff.). Also he notes that Gregory's life is presented as an illustration of general truths about human existence, specifying this as the tragic depiction of idealistic effort overcome by the triumph of selfishness, with retirement as a return to pure life in God (p. 610). Furthermore he explicitly distinguishes Augustine from a modern autobiographer, stating that his conscious purpose was not the narration of individual experience but the arousing of religious emotions and thoughts (pp. 635–7). Misch thus anticipates the points I have drawn out in this study.

Nevertheless, for Misch the importance of Gregory and Augustine, whether they meant to do it or not, lies in their telling how it was for them—uncovering their experience, their feelings. The fact that the ideal of Marcus Aurelius was the harmony of personal life with the divine symphony of the universe was for Misch a negative observation. His work is a detailed account of how the didactic presentation of "type," of a static exemplar, of a model of a particular character and lifestyle (*ethos*), was superseded by genuine self-consciousness, exposure of the inner life, and of the response of the individual to experience. My argument would be that he has turned the subject upside down, emphasising elements most attractive to high modernity, and in so doing seriously distorting Augustine's fundamental intention, which was to show how one might turn away from the self to become God-centred.

But then my challenge has highlighted the elements most attractive to postmodernism, with its emphasis on the way we ourselves construct our own selfhood, on the cultural and indeed linguistic captivity of all experience, on mediation and intertextuality. But I would claim that these current trends in fact enable us to appreciate again the realities of Augustine's linguistic and literary world, where literary texts and rhetorical commonplaces shaped a way of understanding the world, as well as the pattern of education and intellectual formation, whether in pagan or Christianised form.

Finally, I would hint that we have much to learn from this. For our own Christian consciousness, our own telling of our own story, might likewise with profit be shaped by scripture and by tales of the saints. By conforming to "type" we might discern in our lives the workings of God's grace. In fact, if I dared, I could give an account of my own life, with Samuel, Jeremiah and Paul, Augustine, Gregory and John Wesley, in terms of a mother dedicating a child before birth, of miraculous rescue from death, of strange providential coincidences, of trial and testing through suffering, of Damascus Road, call and commitment. But this is not the place to pursue that further.

XV

Did Epiphanius know what he meant by Heresy?

THE work of Epiphanius is best known because it has proved a quarry for material
needed by the textual critic of the New Testament and the historian of the
early Church. A good deal of effort has been expended on tracing Epiphanius' sources
and estimating their reliability; very little work has treated Epiphanius as interesting in himself. Yet a perusal of the first book of his great work against the
heresies raises a number of interesting questions about his intentions and his overall understanding of what he was about; and these questions become all the more
intriguing when this book is compared with Epiphanius' concluding essay, the περὶ
πίστεως, and the summaries offered in his introductory letter to Acacius and Paul
and his earlier work the *Ancoratus*.[1]

I. The first point of interest concerns Epiphanius' use of the word αἵρεσις. Pétau,
who produced in 1622 the edition reprinted in Migne, commented that Epiphanius does
not use the word in the usual theological sense; and Fraenkel draws attention to the
'neutrality of the terminology' he uses, describing it as striking in the work of a
'successor to Irenaeus and Tertullian who had used the words as technical terms for
denouncing error'. These comments reflect the fact that for Epiphanius the word is
by no means confined to Christian deviations; such things as Greek philosophical
schools and the various Jewish parties like the Pharisees and Sadducees are
described as αἱρέσεις.

Of course, the word αἵρεσις simply means 'division'. Long before it acquired the
technical sense of 'heresy', the word was the classical designation for different
philosophical schools. In the book of Acts it is used of the Sadducees, Pharisees
and Nazarenes[2], and in the Pauline Epistles it is used to describe 'splinter-groups'
or factions.[3] It is these senses which lie behind Epiphanius' usage, and he was by
no means an innovator in speaking of pre-Christian groups as heresies: if R.A. Lipsius[4]
is right, Epiphanius' own sources included among the heresies, the Dositheans,

Sadducees, Pharisees and Herodians.

It is hardly right, however, to call this a 'neutral' use of the word. Whatever he meant by it, Epiphanius was one of the most vehement opponents of heresy in his own time, and his whole work was intended as a counterblast to it. What Epiphanius' usage does imply is that for him, heresy is by no means an internal problem arising from differences of opinion within the Christian fold. Embracing as it does all non-Christian religions and philosophies, heresy is quite clearly identified as *external* to the Church, an interesting pointer to Epiphanius' attitudes. In very general terms, then, we may say that what Epiphanius meant by heresy was everything outside the one, holy, catholic and orthodox Church.

II. However, that general definition does not indicate total clarity on his part. His theory regarding the rise and proliferation of heresy bristles with inconsistencies.

In the opening paragraph of the *Panarion*, Epiphanius makes it clear that his purpose is to map out a genealogy of heresy. This genealogical scheme most clearly affects the first book in which he traces its parentage right back to the origins of history. His account goes thus: In the beginning there was no heresy. There was true faith. Adam was neither an idolater nor circumcised, but held the faith of the holy catholic Church of God which existed from the beginning and was later to be revealed again. Because of Adam's sin, there appeared the opposite of the true faith — adultery, rebellion, idolatry. Piety and impiety, faith and unfaith co-existed, with the great biblical figures like Abel, Enoch, Methuselah and Noah representing the former, which was the image of Christianity; Abraham in particular is presented as the type of the Christian, prefiguring in his departure from his father's house, the call of the first disciples.[5] Several times in the text[6] Epiphanius stresses that there was as yet no heresy, no variety of opinions, nor any contrivance other than adultery or idolatry, the opposite of the true worship and faith of the holy catholic Church. He seems at this stage to identify the origins of heresy with the scattering of mankind after the tower of Babel. In other words, heresy is conceived in terms of the breakdown of mankind's unity, and distinguished from man's rebellion against God.

Onto this early history, however, Epiphanius then proceeds to impose his first heretical divisions: Barbarism he attributes to the period between Adam and Noah; Scythian superstition, to the period between Noah and the tower of Babel; thereafter, with the development of magic and astrology, arose Hellenism; and with the circumcision of Abraham came Judaism. Here heresy seems to be simply identified with false religion, or estrangement from the Truth.

Thus two inconsistencies are so far apparent:

First, Abraham's role is conceived in two fundamentally incompatible ways. At one point he is the paradigm of the true Christian, at another his circumcision marks the origin of the Jewish heresy. Secondly, in one context the existence of heresy in the early stages of Man's history is denied, in another, heresy is dated back to Adam. This seems to reflect two different conceptions of the basic nature of heresy, a point expounded by Moutsoulas at an earlier Patristic conference; he concluded that there was no heresy prior to Babel in the sense of sects each with their particular false teaching, but heresy in the sense of estrangement from true belief existed from the Fall of Adam.

However, it is the further development of the account which raises the most acute difficulties. The fragmentation of the four original divisions into smaller sects is the subject of the subsequent story. That he can only enumerate further splintering in Judaism and Hellenism indicates the artificiality of his analysis; but the main problem is the inconsistency between this account of *four* basic divisions and the *five* 'mothers of heresy' which appear in the summaries Epiphanius gives elsewhere. These summaries appear in the prefatory letter and the *Ancoratus*. In both places Samaritanism is treated as one of the five 'mothers of heresy', and in the *Ancoratus*, it is even carelessly placed 'before the Law'. In the text of Book I, however, the Samaritan schism does not appear as one of the great primary divisions of mankind — it is more correctly treated as a Jewish heresy which produced heresies of its own, and it appears after the description of the sects of Hellenism. It is hardly surprising that Pétau concluded that Epiphanius was confused. Fraenkel's valiant attempt to schematise his underlying ideas surely must not be allowed to obscure the inconsistency of Epiphanius' treatment.[7] The inconsistency admitted, two simple explanations can be advanced: First, the order of his treatment of the individual heresies in the main body of the text seems to be determined by his sources rather than his theoretical schemes; and secondly, Epiphanius' thought is primarily determined by scriptural texts — in Book I he is obsessed with one of his key texts, in the summaries his thought is determined by another.

III. So Epiphanius' family tree of heresy lacks coherence; even more serious is the fact that the principles on which he decided what was or was not to be designated a heresy are totally arbitrary. Why, for example, does he list as heresies of Hellenism, the Stoics, the Platonists, the Pythagoreans and the Epicureans, totally ignoring other schools of Greek philosophy? His mention of the Peripatetics in the letter to Acacius and Paul suggests a certain embarrassment at describing only four heresies of Hellenism, and since elsewhere he lists 44 philosophers from Thales to Epicurus, and mentions the Magi and the mystery-religions, ignorance is certainly not the explanation.

No principles of choice can be detected, except perhaps slavish dependence on sources. The only certain fact is that Epiphanius was obliged to produce a total of 80 heresies, and in order to do this he was quite prepared to omit obvious

XV

candidates, to conflate distinct groups, and even to create new heretical groupings out of minor allusions[8] or out of small incidents in his own life.[9] The predetermined number is all important, and once again scripture is the explanation.

IV. What then were the determinative texts, and what did Epiphanius deduce from them ?

1. Canticles 6.7 provides the overall framework: 'there are 60 queens, and 80 concubines, and maidens without number, but my dove, my perfect one, is only one'. This text Epiphanius quotes and explains in the concluding essay, περὶ πίστεως. The one dove is, of course, the holy catholic Church; the 60 queens are the faithful in every generation before Christ, there being 60 generations of them; the 80 concubines are the heresies; and the maidens without number are the countless philosophers and false teachers. This last category, being open-ended, is the rag-bag into which Epiphanius can put all the other philosophers, schools and sects not treated as heresies and therefore not examined in detail in his compendium.

2. The other text Epiphanius quotes as from Paul: ἐν Χριστῷ 'Ιησοῦ, οὐ βάρβαρος, οὐ Σκύθης, οὐχ ῞Ελλην, οὐκ 'Ιουδαῖος, ἀλλὰ καινὴ κτίσις. This is in fact a conflation of Gal. 3.28, 6.15 and Col. 3.11. It appears in Book I and provides the four basic divisions of mankind: Barbarism, Scythism, Hellenism and Judaism.

What these texts have in common is a fundamental contrast between unity in Christ or the oneness of the Church, and the division and disagreement outside; so they chimed well with Epiphanius' basic contrast between two realities, unity and multiplicity, truth and error, the Church and heresy. But they could not provide Epiphanius with an entirely consistent analysis of the breakdown of humanity into heretical groups.

Conclusion

So did Epihanius know what he meant by heresy ? In very general terms his usage is clear, if various: heresy means division which generates further division, and it is all the result of the initial rebellion of mankind; heresy is false religion and includes all that is outside the unity of the one, holy, catholic and orthodox Church.

Yet in detail it does not seem to me that Epiphanius is successful in establishing a clear and consistent thesis, and his application of the word 'heresy' has a certain arbitrariness which reflects pious bending of the material rather than a careful analysis or coherent theory.

Table of Heresy Lists

Ancoratus	*Prefatory Letter*	*Text of Book I*
Barbarism Scythism Hellenism Judaism Samaritanism } = 5 'mothers'	Barbarism Scythism Hellenism Judaism Samaritanism } (not called 'mothers')	Barbarism Scythism Hellenism Judaism
Pythagoreans/ Peripatetics Platonists Stoics Epicureans } = heresies of Hellenism	Pythagoreans Platonists Stoics Epicureans } = heresies of Hellenism	Stoics Platonists Pythagoreans Epicureans } = heresies of Hellenism
Scribes Pharisees Sadducees Essaeans Nassaraeans Hemerobaptists Herodians } = heresies of Judaism	Gorothenes Sebuaeans Essenes Dositheans } = heresies of Samaritanism	Samaritans Essenes Sebuaeans Gorothenes Dositheans } = heresies of Samaritanism
Gorothenes Sebuaeans Essenes Dositheans } = heresies of Samaritanism	Scribes Pharisees Sadducees Hemerobaptists Ossaeans Nassaraeans Herodians } = heresies of Judaism	Sadducees Scribes Pharisees Hemerobaptists Nassaraeans Ossenes Herodians } = heresies of Judaism
Simonians Menandrians Satornilians etc.	Simonians Menandrians Satornilians etc.	*Book II* Simonians Menandrians etc.
Twenty pre-Christian heresies	*Twenty* pre-Christian heresies	*Twenty* pre-Christian heresies

Note: Two other sources are here ignored since they are unlikely to be Epiphanius' own work: the *Epitome* follows the text of the *Panarion*; the *Anakephalaiosis* follows and partially distorts the order of the prefatory letter to Acacius and Paul.

Genealogy of Heresy

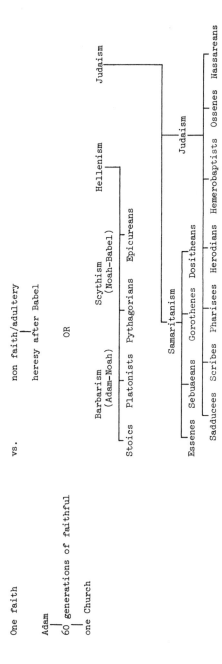

One faith   vs.   non faith/adultery

Adam

60 generations of faithful   heresy after Babel

one Church

OR

Barbarism   Scythism   Hellenism   Judaism
(Adam–Noah)   (Noah–Babel)

Stoics   Platonists   Pythagorians   Epicureans

Samaritanism   Judaism

Essenes   Sebuaeans   Gorothenes   Dositheans

Sadducees   Scribes   Pharisees   Herodians   Hemerobaptists   Ossenes   Nassareans

OR

Barbarism   Scythism   Hellenism   Judaism   Samaritanism
with descendents as above

REFERENCES

1. Since my own interest was aroused, I have traced a couple of earlier pieces of work on the subject: P. Fraenkel, 'Histoire saint et hérésie chez S. Epiphane de Salamine', *Revue de Théologie et Philosophie* 12 (1963), pp. 175-191; and E. Moutsoulas, 'Der Begriff "Häresie" bei Epiphanius von Salamis', *Studia Patristica* VII, pp. 362-371.

2. Acts 5.17, 15.5, 25.5,14, 26.5, 28.22.

3. I Cor. 11.19, Gal. 5,20.

4. R.A. Lipsius, *Zur Quellenkritik des Epiphanius* (Vienna, 1865).

5. *Panarion*, i.8.

6. *Ibid.*, i.5; i.7.

7. Fraenkel, *op. cit.*, pp. 181-182, argues that Epiphanius regarded Samaritanism as syncretistic, and therefore places it and its sects between Hellenism and Judaism in the text. This also means that it is only in the secondary sense one of the basic divisions of mankind, but can still be regarded as one of the 'mothers of heresy'.

8. For example, the Melchizedekians; see F.L. Horton Jr., *The Melchizedek Tradition* (Cambridge, 1976), pp. 90ff.

9. For example, the Antidikomarianitae, a group to whom he wrote defending the perpetual virginity of Mary.

'CREATIO EX NIHILO': A CONTEXT FOR THE EMERGENCE OF THE CHRISTIAN DOCTRINE OF CREATION

C ONFRONTATION with our culture has recently been put on the agenda by Lesslie Newbigin, in *Beyond 1984* and *Foolishness to the Greeks*.[1] Broadly speaking his position is that theology has sold out to Western culture, and the opposing perceptions of the Gospel need to be reclaimed and affirmed against prevailing assumptions.

It is not my purpose to engage in that discussion in this paper, but rather to explore an area where early Christianity did develop an understanding of the world which was self-consciously in confrontation with ancient culture. It is often supposed that Hebraic understanding lost out in the assimilation of the Bible to Greek philosophy, but increasingly this seems to be a false estimate of what was going on in the formation of Christian doctrine. The development of the distinctively Christian doctrine of creation is a clear sign that Christian intellectuals were not 'captured' by Greek philosophy. For *creatio ex nihilo* was affirmed in the face of Greek assumptions: 'nothing comes from nothing' was a Greek commonplace, and implied that anything coming from nothing is a sham! Typical is the view of Plutarch :[2]

> For creation does not take place out of what does not exist at all but rather out of what is in an improper or unfulfilled state, as in the case of a house or a garment or a statue. For the state that things were in before the creation of the ordered may be characterised as 'lack of order' (*akosmia*); and this 'lack of order' was not something incorporeal or immobile or soulless, but rather it possessed a corporeal nature which was formless

[1] WCC publications, 1983 and 1986.
[2] Quoted by John Dillon, *The Middle Platonists*, Duckworth 1977, p. 207.

Originally published in *Scottish Journal of Theology* 44, pp. 139–152. Copyright © Scottish Journal of Theology Ltd ,1991. Reproduced with permission.

and inconstant, and a power of motion which was frantic and irrational. (*On the Creation of the Soul in the Timaeus* 1014B.)

The adoption of the doctrine of creation out of nothing was daring.

It was also the fundamental factor in the development of Christian distinctiveness. By comparison, the first steps in Christology, utilising the concept of the Logos with the precedent of Philo, were far less revolutionary, and indeed Christology became its radically distinctive self only when this creation-doctrine was allowed to affect the perspective within which the questions were debated. For if, as recent work has shown, the 'real' issue behind the development of Christology and Trinitarian doctrine was often soteriology,[3] underlying the most crucial episode in the emergence of the Christian doctrine of God, namely the reply to Arianism, was affirmation of creation out of nothing. The question of the origin of this idea, and indeed its meaning and import, is therefore of particular interest.

Furthermore, the adoption of the idea was of great significance for the future development of European culture. Robin Lane Fox observes[4] that Christianity 'de-sacralised' nature, so allowing the destruction of sacred groves of trees by fanatical monks; but its effects had even more profound consequences for the development of European attitudes. It broke the hold of 'necessity' or 'chance' which crippled other cultures, and substituted the notion of a created order with its own rationality, ultimately permitting the rise of modern science and the exploitation of modern technology.[5] The doctrine of creation out of nothing has had vast consequences, some of which, ironically enough, have contributed to Lesslie Newbigin's perception of the need for confrontation between the Gospel and our culture.

---

[3] E.g. M. F. Wiles, 'In Defense of Arius', *JTS* NS XIII, 1962, 339-47; 'The Nature of the Early Debate about Christ's Human Soul', *JEH* XVI no. 2, 1965, 139-51; and 'The Unassumed is the Unhealed', *Religious Studies* 4, 1968, 47-56; all republished in *Working Papers in Doctrine*, SCM 1976. R. Gregg and E. Groh, *Early Arianism*, SCM 1981; et mult. al.

[4] *Pagans and Christians*, Viking 1986 (Penguin 1988).

[5] Stanley L. Jaki, *Creator and Cosmos*, Scottish Academic Press, 1980, and T. F. Torrance, *Divine and Contingent Order*, OUP 1981.

Where then did the doctrine originate? Contrary to expectations, it does not seem to have been a Jewish idea, though this is often assumed (e.g. by Torrance).[6] The reasons for rejecting this assumption[7] may be summarised as follows:

(i) the sparsity of reference to the doctrine in Jewish texts, and indeed in the earliest Christian material, and the problem of interpreting those references that do exist (see further below);

(ii) the contrary evidence of the *Wisdom of Solomon* and the works of Philo, and in early Christianity, of Justin, Athenagoras, Hermogenes and Clement of Alexandria. All these authors seem quite happy to adopt without question the Platonic view of an active and passive element, namely God plus matter. The fact that Philo can even so speak of things being created *ex ouk onto–n* shows that the term could be understood as consistent with the notion of pre-existent matter which he takes for granted elsewhere.[8] Middle Platonism was married with Jewish tradition without any sense of tension;

(iii) the lack of interest in *creatio ex nihilo* in Jewish tradition prior to the Middle Ages: the Rabbis condemn speculation about creation as much as about the chariot-throne of God! Gamaliel II's discussion with a philosopher, recorded in Midrash Genesis Rabbah, apparently upholds the unlimited creative power of God, suggesting that the primitive stuffs the philosopher thought God used to create are expressly described in the Bible as themselves created by God: but we find no firm doctrine of *creatio ex nihilo* developing, despite the apparent natural logic which would lead to that doctrine evidenced by Gamaliel's discussion.[9]

---

[6] *Loc. cit.* and *The Trinitarian Faith*, T. & T. Clark 1988.
[7] See Gerhard May, *Schöpfung aus dem Nichts*, De Gruyter 1978; following H.-F. Weiss, *Untersuchungen zur Kosmologie des hellenistischen and pleastinischen Judentums*, 1966.
[8] Pace Richard Sorabji, *Time, Creation and the Continuum*, Duckworth 1983.
[9] See May, *Op. cit.* p. 23. This 'apparent natural logic' leads Walter Eichrodt to attribute an absolute beginning to the Priestly authors of Genesis 1: 'In the Beginning: a Contribution to the Interpretation of the First Word of the Bible', first published in *Israel's Prophetic Heritage: Essays in honor of James Muilenburg*, ed. Bernhard W. Anderson and Walter Harrelson; New York 1962; republished in *Creation in the Old Testament*, ed. Bernhard W. Anderson, Issues in Religion and Theology 6, SPCK 1984. However, the article is addressing the fact that Jewish commentators of the Middle Ages, notably Rashi, have understood the text as meaning, 'In the beginning, when God . . .' so as to harmonise the first verse with the chaotic primitive state of the earth in v. 2.

(iv) the lack of emphasis on the idea in early Christian literature of the first and early second centuries, contrasted with its general acceptance by the beginning of the third century.

There are some apparent references to the idea, despite these sweeping generalisations, but their significance depends upon their interpretation. They will be surveyed at a later stage. Meanwhile let us examine the material that indicates positive adoption of the idea.

Tertullian provides the clearest expression of the alternatives: God did not create out of himself, nor out of eternal co-existing matter. So if it was neither out of God's self nor out of something, it must have been out of nothing. These alternatives had been set up and answered differently, it seems, by Hermogenes, a Second Century Christian universally described as a Platonist, and against whom Tertullian was writing (*Adversus Hermogenem*).

Theophilus had reached the same conclusion somewhat earlier, also, it seems, in opposition to Hermogenes, though this is not explicitly the case in the texts which have survived. In the *Ad Autolycum* II.4, he criticises Plato for regarding matter as uncreated and therefore equal to God, arguing for God's unique 'sovereignty' (though *monarchia* could mean something more like 'sole first principle'). A human artisan creates out of pre-existent material, suggests Theophilus; so there is nothing remarkable about God doing likewise. The power of God is evident by his making whatever he wants *ex ouk onto–n*, out of the non-existent.

So Theophilus and Tertullian were both confronting Hellenistic assumptions. Tertullian was also confronting Gnostic views, as indeed Theophilus probably was, though not obviously in the context where we find his comments. Second Century apologetic, together with the struggle against gnosticism, apparently provides the context in which the issue explicitly arises and a clear 'theory' *ex ouk onto–n* emerges: even Gamaliel was arguing with a *philosopher*! It cannot simply be assumed that creation 'out of nothing' is Judaeo-Christian tradition, though the Jewish stress on the unique sovereignty of God would make it a natural step to take once the issue was raised.

The alternative hypotheses opposed, 'out of the divine self' or 'out of matter', indicate a self-conscious differentiation. Speaking very generally one may say that gnostics took the Platonic view of a 'recalcitrant' medium to the extreme of suggesting that matter was evil. But they opened up the possibility of matter not being eternal but coming into existence, by claiming it was produced by the fallen Demiurge. The dualism was no longer an ontological dualism with permanence, but a radical dualism resulting from a fall — their real interest being in the problem of evil and salvation from it. Gnosticism also raised the possibility of the universe emerging by emanation from the divine and by a fall away from its perfection. This is the context of Tertullian's clear statement of the alternatives and his choice of the only one that made sense of the notion of God inherited from Judaism and the Jewish scriptures. Indeed, it helped that such a notion had verbal if not theoretical anticipation in the tradition.

So let us turn to these anticipations and the problem of their interpretation.

1. The first reference to creation out of nothing, it is often claimed, is found in 2 Macc. 7.28:

I implore you, my child, to look at the heavens and the earth; consider all that is in them, and realise that God did not create them from what already existed (*ouk ex onto–n*), and that a human being comes into existence in the same way.

Commenting on this and other such passages, Arnold Ehrhardt[10] noted that martyr literature, Jewish and Christian, tends to regard the present world as a sham; he implies, therefore, that the words here have a very different implication from the later doctrine of creation out of nothing — indeed that they follow the Greek assumption that 'nothing comes from nothing'. This seems unlikely.[11]

More convincing is the exposition of Gerhard May:[12] this is a paraenetic reference to God's power, implying no more than

[10] *The Beginning: a study in the Greek philosophical approach to the concept of Creation from Anaximander to St John*, Manchester University Press 1968.
[11] Jaki, *Op. cit.* p. 75 also finds this explanation unacceptable.
[12] *Op. cit.*, p. 6 ff.

that the world came into existence when it was previously not there; it cannot be characterised as a critical move away from the doctrine of God fashioning the world out of eternal matter. In Xenophon's *Memorabilia* May finds a reference to parents bringing forth their children 'out of non-being', which is clearly a non-philosophical everyday turn of phrase. The reference in II Maccabees, he claims, is no more significant than that.

Attention should be drawn to the context, and in particular the earlier verse 23:

> The Creator of the universe, who designed the beginning of humanity and devised the origin of all, will in his mercy give you back again breath and life . . .

What is envisaged is God's power to bring life out of death, and the comment under discussion merely uses the analogy of birth as a parallel mystery. The text is rooted in Biblical images, and entirely compatible with the creation 'out of clay' found in Genesis 2. Here there is no 'theory' of creation out of nothing — indeed the wording is not the usual later formula, the *ouk* not qualifying the *onto–n* directly. The dogma 'out of nothing' would seem to be a self-conscious rejection of the craftsman analogy presupposed by a Platonism that took the *Timaeus* literally, and that is not in view in Maccabees. Indeed, it seems Philo could take such a Platonic view for granted while using phrases just like those of Maccabees. God could conceivably bring into existence 'things' which do not exist before, without such language excluding a pre-existent 'stuff'.

2. In the New Testament are found two passages which have suggested that a Jewish doctrine was simply assumed by early Christianity:

> Rom. 4.17: In the presence of God, the God who makes the dead live and calls into being things that are not, Abraham had faith.

> Heb. 11.3: By faith we understand that the universe was formed by God's command, so that the visible came forth from the invisible.

Then, in *Hermas* 1.1.6, we find an early confession of faith, which it is claimed, shows the doctrine was part of the tradition long before the debates to which we have drawn attention:

First of all you have to believe that there is one God, who has founded and organised the universe, and has brought the universe out of nothing into existence.

Similar confessions in Justin and Irenaeus have suggested it belongs to the Rule of Faith.

Ehrhardt couples with Maccabees these early Christian references, and offers the same interpretation, drawing attention to the strong tendency of early Christianity to think of the world as 'passing away'.[13] This approach is no more convincing here than before, but that does not mean that the parallel in Maccabees, and our discussion of it, is irrelevant. For given that Justin clearly thought in terms of the Platonist picture, this confession does not represent a 'theory' displacing the Platonist view, and must be understood as already suggested. The thrust of early Christianity is in the direction of a 'new creation' being born out of the old, and cosmogony was not at the forefront. Neither *Hermas* nor indeed Aristides clearly distinguished between creating and 'world-building'.

G. May further surveys early anti-gnostic literature like the Pastoral Epistles. Here the goodness of creation is insisted on, but there is no interest at all in how or from what God created. The assumption generally seems to have been that creation meant ordering without further speculation. The absence of the idea of creation *ex ouk onto–n*, especially if it was, as is often supposed, an established Jewish doctrine, is far more remarkable than the sparse ill-defined cases where the language is apparently used.

Certainly, the Jewish sense of God's sovereignty and almighty power does figure in the tradition from which the 'orthodox' stream of Christianity began when confronted with the questions of the Second Century, and in that context the doctrine of *creatio ex nihilo* became the natural implicate (cf. Gamaliel II above). Theophilus indicates that resistance to an

---

[13] *Op. cit.*, p. 167.

anthropomorphic picture became highly significant in the process of differentiation from Platonism, a process which provides the context in which we first find the explicit doctrine *ex ouk onto–n.* But now we begin to sense that the problem of origin relates to the problem of meaning.

To speak of 'nothing' can be paradoxical, as pointed out in a paper by George S. Hendry concerned with some modern theology.[14] Ancient discussions, though sometimes highly sophisticated, betray considerable confusion, particularly at the more popular level, a confusion only partially eased in Greek by the use of the distinct negatives *ou* and *me–*. Let us simply note some of the problems.

(i) At the commonsense level, to speak of making something 'out of nothing' tends to turn nothing into something.

(ii) In the admittedly later Neoplatonic tradition, matter was taken to be 'non-being' in the sense of being only potentially something. This had earlier roots in philosophical discussion, and it means that there was profound ambivalence in the term. The eternally existing 'stuff' of the universe could be described as 'non-existent'.

(iii) Like Augustine and others influenced by Neoplatonism, Karl Barth has used Nothingness (*Das Nichtige*) as a way to describe the recalcitrant 'Other' with which God struggles in order to produce the Good he wills: so 'nothing' easily slips into being a powerful force for evil. God's activity of bringing good out of evil, order out of chaos, etc., may be correlated with Neoplatonic tendencies to equate evil with non-being, and though explained as the deprivation of good, this inevitably makes the non-existent suspiciously real. Or does it mean that evil does not exist? Or is evil 'non-being' in the same 'potential' sense as matter is 'non-being'? And does this mean matter is evil, a point of view the Christian tradition has firmly resisted since that initial struggle with gnosticism? However we reply to these questions, we are left with some profound 'teasers' about the meaning of the idea of creation out of nothing.

Theophilus, Tertullian and Irenaeus do not seem to be aware of this kind of problem: for them, creation out of

[14] 'Nothing', *Theology Today* vol. xxxix (1982), pp. 275-289.

nothing is simply a logical consequence of the alternatives posed by Hermogenes. It is a way of affirming the dependence and contingency of creation, and the free gracious act of God in creation arising from no necessity. The latter point about necessity was fundamentally important as against the 'automatic', or 'necessary', emanations posited by gnosticism, as was the idea that the Logos was not an emanation but the Reason of God himself becoming active in creation, revelation and redemption. But the point for our purposes is this: the function in Christian theology of the doctrine of creation out of nothing lies in the consequent dependence and contingency of creation, and the question of the 'content' expressed in the verbal formulation is inappropriate. That does not, however, remove the fact that later there is considerable ambivalence in the use of the idea by Athanasius, not to mention Augustine.

However, this discussion of meaning raises the question of Basilides and his possible priority in developing the doctrine. The conclusion that Second Century debates with Gnosticism and philosophy about origins (*archai*, first principles) provided the context in which this doctrine was formulated, has also been reached by G. May. May argues, however, that the idea is first to be found in Basilides.

Basilides, according to Hippolytus (Irenaeus' evidence is different), is atypical among Gnostics in seeing the 'high God' as the ultimate creator rather than a lesser demiurge, and rather than positing emanations, he speaks of the non-existent God producing a non-existent world out of the non-existent. What is produced seems to be a world-seed from which all future developments automatically come about. May suggests that the driving force of Basilides' logic is his notion of radical transcendence, his *via negativa*, his critique of human analogies — the ultimate God is not an anthropomorphic world-builder. At first hearing this seems like Theophilus, and May opens up the possibility of a Syrian tradition influencing both, though with little conviction. The logic of Basilides' thinking makes it more likely he arrived at the idea himself, he suggests. Basilides therefore must be credited with the priority. Here, it seems, is the first thinker to formulate the idea of *creatio ex nihilo*.

May's suggestion cannot be sustained, however. The sheer

ambivalence of the concept of the non-existent seems to be at the heart of what Basilides is saying. Let us look again at Hippolytus' account of his teaching:

There was a time, says he, when there was nothing; not even the nothing was there, but simply, clearly, and without any sophistry there was nothing at all. When I say 'there was', he says, I do not indicate a Being, but in order to signify what I want to express I say, says he, that there was nothing at all (*Ref.* VII.20.2).[15]

Clearly the difficulty about speaking of nothing without making it something is present to Basilides' mind.

For that, says he, is not simply something ineffable which is named; we call it ineffable, but it is not even ineffable. For what is not inexpressible is called 'not even inexpressible', but is above every name that is named . . . (*Ibid.* 3)

Given that the connections in Basilides' thought are far from clear in Hippolytus' report, it certainly seems that May is right. Before Plotinus Basilides was trying to speak of the high God as 'beyond Being' in a radical development of the *via negativa*. The only way he could do this was to speak of 'non-being'. Hence the 'non-existent God'. Platonic thought had not been able to envisage the 'infinite' because it meant 'boundlessness', indefiniteness, lack of Form; so prior to Plotinus, the One and the Good were in some sense finite, and though hard to know, comprehensible to the purified mind since defined.[16] By contrast, for Basilides, as for other gnostics, the ultimate is infinite, ineffable and incomprehensible.

Before a literalising interpretation of the *Timaeus* became fashionable, Platonism saw reality as an eternal interaction of

[15] Quoted from the translation in Werner Foerster, *Gnosis* A Selection of Gnostic Texts, ET ed. R. McL. Wilson, Oxford 1972, vol. 1 Patristic Evidence, p. 64.

[16] See further my paper 'The God of the Greeks and the Nature of Religious Language' in W. R. Schoedel and Robert Wilken, *Early Christian Literature and the Greek Intellectual Tradition*. Festschrift for R. M. Grant, Théologie Historique no. 53, Paris 1979.

Nous, Form and Matter, Matter in a sense being only 'notional', and never 'existing' except 'formed' into something. Infinity, therefore, Platonism tended to attribute to matter which was *apeiron* in the sense of having no 'form' or definiteness, 'existing' only as 'potential', as 'non-being'. Basilides seems to radicalise this perception too, making even 'formed' things indefinable:

> Names do not even suffice, he says, for the world, so multiform is it, but fall short. And I do not have it in me to find correct names for everything; rather it is proper to comprehend ineffably, without using names, the characteristics of the things which are to be named. (*Ibid.*)

As we have seen, Basilides was aware of the problem of using 'non-being' as a way of describing things that are something, and here he insists on the fundamental inadequacies of language. There can be no definitions.

Yet he returns to his first statement about there really being nothing:

> there was nothing, no matter, no substance, nothing insubstantial, nothing simple, nothing composite, nothing non-composite, nothing imperceptible. . . . (*Ibid.* 21.1.)

Recognising the ambivalence of Platonic language, he rejects the notion of a pre-existent matter, as May argues. But out of the non-existent comes a non-existent world. The sense is shifting again, surely. The only world that could come into being was the world of appearance, which is transient and a sham; for 'nothing comes from nothing . . .' and everything we know is only notional.

So, despite Basilides' attempt to affirm an initially real nothingness, the meaning of 'non-existent' as applied to God does not seem to be the same as applied to the world, nor as applied to whatever it is out of which the world is made. Basilides' paradoxical statement would seem to issue from an awareness of the profound ambiguity of language about 'non-being', and yet to be using that language to speak both of the genuinely non-existent and of realities which he took to be beyond articulation in a defined form, though they are indefinable for different reasons. The result is an understanding of everything as incomprehensible and therefore in some sense unreal.

Maybe the Church Fathers were not so far wrong after all in thinking that Gnosticism had affinities with philosophy. Be that as it may, this would appear to be utterly different from the thrust of the argument with Platonism and Gnosticism as outlined above (Theophilus and Tertullian). As May argues, Basilides did not adopt the usual Gnostic resort to emanations, maintaining the sovereign act of a God so transcendent you could say nothing about him. Thereafter, however, as May admits, he slipped into a process of natural necessity, which allowed the use of highly mythological pictures like that of the world-egg. This it was that was produced 'out of nothing'. And if the exegesis of Basilides offered here is accepted, then it provides further proof that his idea of creation out of nothing has a very different function from the idea in Christian theology, and is not so much a confrontation with Greek conceptions as a radicalising of them, everything one says having to be seen as merely notional.

The adoption of the view that the world was created out of nothing was almost universal in Christian circles very quickly. It was not merely a different view of the origin of things, nor just a different estimate of the material world — though that would become more and more significant both in the struggle with otherworldly asceticism, and in the development of a distinctive eschatology: it is instructive to contrast Origen's views on the resurrection with those of Gregory of Nyssa, for restoration of the body rather than mere immortality of the soul informs Gregory's eschatological vision, despite his Neoplatonic leanings. But creation out of nothing was not just a doctrine about the world. It was doctrine about God.

For it meant that God was no longer conceived as ontologically intertwined with the world, as he was in Stoicism, in Pseudo-Aristotle's *De Mundo*, and most other contemporary cosmologies. Nor was he simply the active principle in relation to a passive principle. God became independent of the world as its sole *arche-*, its 'sovereign' as well as its 'beginning'. Furthermore, God was not subject to necessity but free, and that was a better and more biblical grounding for his transcendence and impassibility than a mere adoption of Platonic axioms. He was conceived as containing all things while not being himself contained: thus even before Plotinus, indeed in Irenaeus, the concept of his infinity began to be grasped.

But this was not all. Christological discussions from Arianism on were the result of pressing this theology of God as the sole *arche-*, the one *agene–tos* being, who created *gene–ta* from nothing. Logos-theology had tempered the dichotomy, bridged the gulf between Creator and created: for God's own Reason containing his Ideas produced the material world which the Logos then pervaded as its immanent order and rationality while remaining the Reason of God himself. But the tendency to regard this Logos as a mediating being, in a sense independent of the sovereign, free, impassible, changeless God — indeed, as Tertullian would suggest, the visible form of the invisible or the passible form of the impassible, able to be seen and to suffer, led to the old 'creation' question re-surfacing now in relation to this 'mediator': is the Logos 'out of God' or 'out of nothing'? These are now the only alternatives, and the decision between them had profound consequences for the future of Logos-theology, for the classic formulation of the doctrine of the Trinity as wholly Creator and *arche-*, and for the classic Christological problem: how could one who shared God's invisibility and impassibility be incarnate?

XVII

NAKED OR CLOTHED? ESCHATOLOGY AND THE DOCTRINE OF CREATION

A PAPER on life after death in the early church should probably begin with the underworld: Sheol in the Hebrew Bible, Hades in Greek mythology, with parallels in ancient Mesopotamia, Egypt and Persia. It should reflect on the universally connected theme of judgment and its importance for theodicy, and address the wide variety of beliefs discernible in the New Testament and its background, especially in the apocalyptic literature. It should consider the so-called intermediate state, and the supposed distinction between the Greek concept of the immortality of the soul and the Hebrew idea of resurrection: which takes us full circle, since the latter notion assumes the picture of shades in the underworld brought back to full-bodied living – as indeed the traditional *Anastasis* icon of the Eastern Orthodox tradition makes dramatically clear, Christ springing up from the grave and hauling Adam up with one hand and, often though not invariably, Eve with the other.

But two considerations have led in another direction: (i) all this is well-trodden ground and hardly needs another survey; and (ii) in detail one could hardly cover in a single essay the sheer variety of ideas and the complexity of their relationships, assumed as they are in a whole range of potentially relevant texts, described in apocalyptic tours of the cosmos or adumbrated in accounts of mystical union with the divine. So all that is presumed, especially the remarkable and perennial production (from the third century BC to the Middle Ages) of apocalypses unveiling the fate of the dead, which Bauckham[1] has comprehensively studied. Instead the focus here will be on the one aspect of the afterlife which has in any sense been formally defined by its presence in the creeds, namely, the resurrection of the body; and the significant connection between resurrection and creation will be pursued.

The first part of this paper will advance the thesis that the doctrine of *creatio ex nihilo* so deepened the sense that the union of body and soul

---

[1] Richard Bauckham, *The Fate of the Dead: Studies on the Jewish and Christian Apocalypses,* Supplements to Novum Testamentum 93 (Leiden, 1998).

Eschatology and the Doctrine of Creation

is essential to human nature as a creature made and redeemed by God for eternal life, that Platonizing Fathers of the fourth century, who might have been expected to focus on the immortality of the soul and to have a negative view of the body, in fact defended the resurrection of the body as the hallmark of Christian hope. The second part will turn back to the second century to explore the Christian antecedents of this, and suggest that belief in resurrection may even have contributed to the emergence of the idea that God created out of nothing. It seems clear that it was not until the fourth century, beginning with the Arian controversy, that the corollaries of *creatio ex nihilo* for Christology and anthropology were realized.[2] For completeness, third century ambiguities about the resurrection of the flesh should be considered,[3] along with the way they paralleled ambiguities about *creatio ex nihilo*. However, the main aim is to show how significant for the notion of bodily resurrection was the argument from *creatio ex nihilo*; so the final part of the paper returns to the fourth century to confirm this point from development in the thought of Augustine.

Gregory of Nyssa

Much of the fourth century was dominated by the argument with Arians, who suggested that the pre-existent Logos was a creature – maybe the first and greatest of the creatures, but still a creature. One of the outcomes of this was to clarify the distinction between God, who is uncreated, and everything else that has come into being from nothing, a point that is highlighted by Gregory of Nyssa in his work *De opificio hominis (On the Making of Humankind)*.[4] This means that God is immutable, but created nature cannot exist without change – for its very passage from non-existence to existence is a kind of motion and change.

---

2 This paper is a sequel to the one entitled 'Creation and Human Being: the forging of a distinct Christian discourse', forthcoming in *Studia Patristica*. There I traced the impact of the doctrine of *creatio ex nihilo* on the anthropology of those key fourth-century Fathers who are generally regarded as somewhat Platonist, concentrating particularly on Augustine, and referring across to the Cappadocians. In that paper I also set out reasons for the now commonly accepted view that the notion of *creatio ex nihilo* emerged in the second century in debate with Platonism and Gnosticism.

3 I refer to Origen, misunderstandings of Origen and reactions against views taken to be Origenist; see further Brian E. Daley, *The Hope of the Early Church: A Handbook of Patristic Eschatology* (Cambridge, 1991), esp. ch. 5.

4 Gregory of Nyssa, *De opificio hominis* 16.10, 12 [hereafter: *Op. hom.*]; Greek text in PG 44: 123–256. Paragraph numbers are from the ET in NPNF II, 5: 387–427.

But this mutability is not to be understood as negative:[5] if God's power is sufficient to bring things into existence from nothing, then the transformation of that creation is also within divine power. To press this point Gregory challenges first those who suggest matter is co-eternal with God, then those who deny the resurrection. It is well known that Gregory's spirituality expressed itself in terms of eternal *epektasis* (continual reaching out in the desire for fuller knowledge of God) and progress. He had indeed taken mutability positively in a way that is arguably unprecedented. Scholarship has tended to relate this to his positive evaluation of God's infinity;[6] this work suggests that 'creation out of nothing' was an equally important driver.[7]

So what does Gregory say here specifically about resurrection? He begins his discussion[8] from the inherent mutability of creatures – the great thing about this is that it means human beings will not stay settled even in evil. Since motion is constant, eventually, when the limit of evil is reached, there will be a turn around, and once more human nature will be on course towards good. So paradise will be restored, along with the grace of God's image. Our hope, he says, is for something beyond anything we can envisage. He then turns to those who wonder why this heavy and corporeal existence has to wait for the consummation of all things before the life of human beings is set free for blessedness and *apatheia* (impassibility).[9] Before proceeding with Gregory's argument, we should note that these points – the natural reversion towards good and the weight of the body, like so much else in Gregory's work, bespeak a quasi-scientific or philosophical mode of thought. So will his reply to this question about the delay in consummation, turning as it does on the notion of the pre-existent Form of humankind behind Adam. But this philosophical mode of thought is made to serve another perspective. Gregory attributes the delay to the time it takes for the full number of humankind to be produced by animal generation rather than the method proper to unfallen human nature. When the full complement of human nature has reached its predetermined measure, then the trumpet of the resurrection will sound, awaken the dead and

[5] Gregory of Nyssa, *Op. hom.* 23.5; 25ff.
[6] E.g. E. Mühlenberg, *Die Unendlichkeit Gottes bei Gregor von Nyssa* (Göttingen, 1966); R. E. Heine, *Perfection in the Virtuous Life* (Philadelphia, PA, 1975).
[7] The above paragraph is borrowed, with abbreviations, from 'Creation and Human Being'.
[8] Gregory of Nyssa, *Op. hom.* 21.
[9] Ibid. 22.

transform to incorruptibility those still alive, in the same way as those who have been raised – so that the weight of the flesh is no longer heavy, and its burden no longer holds them down to earth, but they rise up through the air to be with the Lord (here Gregory exploits 1 Corinthians 15: 51–52 and 1 Thessalonians 4: 17).[10] Scripture enjoins hope and confidence in the future.

Gregory associates resurrection with world re-formation (*anastoicheiōsis*), and the next objection he addresses is that it is inconceivable that the processes and the time intervals that are going on now could come to an end.[11] Here we begin to see how Christian insistence on the beginning and end of the world transforms his otherwise somewhat Platonist conceptions. Anyone who takes the view that the universe is eternal cannot also believe that in the beginning the heaven and earth were made by God; and if there was a beginning of motion, so there must be an end – we should therefore believe Scripture on both these matters. It is at this point that he challenges those who suggest that matter is co-eternal with God, and then those who deny the resurrection. Gregory rehearses the standard arguments in his own way: the immaterial God cannot have made matter out of the divine self, nor could the one God have something other than the divine self exist alongside it from eternity; therefore, he asserts, just as we suppose the power of the divine will to be a sufficient cause for the things that exist to have come into being out of nothing, so we are not trusting in something improbable when we refer world re-formation to the same power. Creation out of nothing and resurrection are acts of a kind, and they mutually support each other in challenging certain fundamental philosophical assumptions, namely, that nothing comes from nothing, and that the soul's liberation is to be released from the body.

Gregory turns to the evidence of resurrection in Scripture, and pursues this at some length;[12] but still there are those who doubt that such a thing is possible even for God, pressing such awkward questions as: what about those who have been consumed in fire or eaten by wild beasts? what about ship-wrecked sailors devoured by fish?[13] Gregory dismisses all this questioning as unworthy of God's power and authority. Of course death means dissolution, he acknowledges; the

---

10 Ibid. 22.6.
11 Ibid. 23–24.
12 Ibid. 25.
13 Ibid. 26.

elements return to the elements, earth to earth, moisture to water. But what is possible for God must not be judged by the limits of human capacity or imagination. What once belonged to the person will be restored. The most notable thing about ourselves, he says, is the first beginning of our existence;[14] and here he embarks on a disquisition about the various views of the soul and its relationship with the body. He eventually affirms that as a human being is one, consisting of soul and body, so the beginning of existence is one, common to both parts, neither soul nor body antecedent to the other.[15] The profound interdependence of soul and body is then outlined, drawing on contemporary medical philosophy, and producing a picture of the soul which makes it very like what we would call the central nervous system.[16] For Gregory a human being is a psychosomatic whole. It is this wholeness that is to be restored in the resurrection. The work ends by quoting Paul – we are to put off the old humanity, and put on the one that is renewed after the image of the Creator (Colossians 3: 9–10) – and then praying for us all to return to that divine grace in which humanity was first created when God said, 'Let us make humankind in our image and likeness' (Genesis 1: 26).

This work on *The Making of Humankind* purports to be a continuation of Basil's *Hexaemeron* (*On the Six Days of Creation*). The really striking thing about the *Hexaemeron* is its general tone of sheer wonder at creation, its affirmation that nothing is superfluous or wrong or out of place; indeed, everything contributes to the rich tapestry of the created order and its beauty.[17] Basil draws upon the then current scientific understanding of the cosmos and the natural world to foster this wonder at creation. Yet the development of this 'creation spirituality' is grounded in the assertion that God is the sole source: a dualism with matter is absolutely ruled out.[18] Creation out of nothing means that this wonderful reality is finite; its beginning implies its end,[19] but none of it was conceived by chance or without reason[20] – it must be looked at *sub specie aeternitatis*, Basil implies. The problem with philos-

---

[14] Ibid. 27.9.
[15] Ibid. 29.
[16] Ibid. 30.
[17] e.g. Basil, *Hexaemeron* 1.11; 3.10; 7; 8; 9.
[18] Ibid. 2.
[19] Ibid. 1.3.
[20] Ibid. 1.6.

Eschatology and the Doctrine of Creation

ophy is precisely its inherent atheism – its failure to rise to knowledge of God through its much ado about explaining nature.[21]

In exploring human nature, its formation and re-formation, Gregory follows a similar agenda. His picture of how the dissolved particles of the body are imprinted with an identity and are reconstituted by the soul's knowledge of them might seem quasi-scientific – indeed a parallel with modern notions of the persistence of DNA has been drawn.[22] Yet the fundamental drive is to affirm God's creativity. Gregory explicitly makes an analogy between two miracles, resurrection being no more extraordinary than reproduction:

> The growth of the body with its many parts out of a sperm, which is substance that is both shapeless and formless, is nothing short of miraculous. If God can bring this about, there is no doubt He can restore life and shape to matter ... .[23]

> The features of parents and forefathers appear in their children and grandchildren. We do not understand the 'how' of those extraordinary things. But seeing that God gives those features of rotten and ruined bodies to others, it would be foolish if we would not admit that He can give back to the soul its own elements.[24]

The fact that many changes occur to the human body over time without its losing its identity implies the continuity of change after death. Analogies with sleep or animal hibernation make resurrection plausible. It must be very easy for God who creates out of nothing.

The same sense of someone entering into the inherited parameters of the intellectual debates of antiquity, but with a distinctive counter-cultural position, can be picked up from Gregory's dialogue *De anima et resurrectione*.[25] Here he adopts a genre which invites comparison with Plato's *Phaedo*: his sister Macrina, rather than Socrates, discusses the nature of the soul on her deathbed. She roundly rejects the immortality of the soul as pagan nonsense. A definition is given which picks up the

---

21 Ibid. 1.2. This paragraph is drawn from 'Creation and Human Being'.
22 Vasiliki Limberis, 'Resurrected Body and Immortal Flesh in Gregory of Nyssa', in E. D. Moutsoulas, ed., *Jesus Christ in St. Gregory of Nyssa's Theology: Minutes of the Ninth International Conference on St. Gregory of Nyssa, Athens 7–12 September 2000* (Athens, 2005), 515–28. I am indebted to this article for the quotations from *In sanctum pascha* which appear in this paragraph.
23 Gregory of Nyssa, *Op. hom.* 27.9.
24 Idem, *In sanctum pascha.*
25 Greek text in PG 46: 11–160; ET in NPNF II, 5: 430–68.

detailed presentation of a complex, psychosomatic whole already found in the *Making of Humankind*: 'The soul is an essence created, and living, and intellectual, transmitting from itself to an organised and sentient body the power of living and grasping objects of sense, as long as the natural constitution capable of this holds together.'[26] But to treat death simply as the dissolution of this complex being has already been dismissed: you can only think that if you remove from consideration the Deity who upholds the world. Creation proclaims the Creator. This premise prepares the ground for arguing that reconstitution is less problematic than the initial creation from nothing. Gregory explores at greater depth here the questions about the re-assembly of the dissolved particles, as well as introducing discussion of the emotions, dismissing Plato's famous charioteer analogy, and identifying the emotions as growths, somewhat like warts, on the soul's thinking part, rather than being essential to the soul. Focussing on the biblical idea of humanity being created in God's image, Gregory suggests that in the re-formation of human nature which is the resurrection, all this will be stripped away so that there will be nothing to impede contemplation of the Beautiful, nothing to prevent participation in the Good, both identified with God. To the one purified of its emotions and negative habits, love alone will remain – that is, an inherent affection for the Beautiful, grounded in its simplicity and godlikeness. This Platonic-sounding dream is then confirmed by reference to Paul's hymn to love in 1 Corinthians 13.

Like other Platonists Gregory assumes that the 'body weighs us down', but the important point for this discussion is that even the body, which weighs us down, although woven from the very same particles of matter, will be transformed, its threads worked up into something more subtle and ethereal, restored to us with a brighter and more entrancing beauty. For the soul still wrapped in earthly passions there will be agonized struggle when God is drawing it to the divine self and scraping the foreign matter off by force – the analogy with metal dross being purified in fire creates the impression of a Platonic interpretation of the apocalyptic image of hell. Speculating about the 'how' of creation, or indeed of reconstitution, is to engage in meddlesome prying: the problems of conceiving how a child or old man will be when resurrected are dismissed with other objections. But nature and

---

[26] NPNF II, 5: 433 (PG 46: 29B). The following paragraphs summarize Gregory's lengthy reasoning and there is no attempt to provide detailed references to a text which does not have convenient standard subdivisions.

Eschatology and the Doctrine of Creation

Scripture alike point to the hope that in the resurrection we are born again in our original splendour.

So Gregory of Nyssa surely supports our first thesis: that *creatio ex nihilo* so deepened the sense that the union of body and soul is essential to human nature as a creature made and redeemed by God for life eternal, that bodily resurrection became its inevitable corollary, despite tendencies to a Platonist outlook. Turning to our second thesis, that belief in resurrection generated insistence on the goodness of the material creation and may even have contributed to the very emergence of the idea that God created out of nothing, will allow us to explore the specifically Christian background to Gregory's challenges to Platonism.

Creation and Resurrection in Second-Century Debates

The connection between creation and resurrection goes back beyond the articulation of a specific doctrine of *creatio ex nihilo*. It is already found in 2 Maccabees 7: 28, where the mother pleads with her seventh son to suffer martyrdom:

> I beg you, my child, to look at the heaven and the earth and see everything that is in them, and recognize that God made them not out of things that existed. And in the same way the human race came into being. Do not fear this butcher … Accept death, so that in God's mercy I may get you back again along with your brothers.[27]

This text is often taken to be a reference to creation out of nothing, on the assumption that the idea was already accepted in Jewish circles. Certainly it would have been read that way later; but here it is not advanced as a theoretical argument concerning the presence or absence of a material substrate; rather, implying no more than that the world came into existence when it previously was not there, it is entirely compatible with human creation 'out of clay' found in Genesis 2. The context in 2 Maccabees is God's power to bring life out of death; birth is called in as a parallel mystery: 'The Creator of the world, who shaped the beginning of humankind and devised the origin of all things, will in his mercy give life and breath back to you again' (2 Maccabees 7: 23). Thus it is simply a paraenetical observation that fear can be dismissed

---

[27] All biblical quotations in this paper are taken from the NRSV.

because God brought you into existence when you did not exist *as you before*, and can therefore restore that existence if you put your hope and trust in God.[28]

In Romans 4 a similar connection between creation and resurrection is made. The thrust of Paul's argument concerning Abraham's faith is that he believed that God could bring life out of death, for:

> he did not weaken in faith when he considered his own body, which was already as good as dead ..., or when he considered the barrenness [i.e. *nekrōsis* or deadness] of Sarah's womb .... Now the words, 'it was reckoned to him [as righteousness]', were written not for his sake alone, but for ours also. It will be reckoned to us who believe in him who raised Jesus our Lord from the dead ... (Romans 4: 19, 23–24)

Earlier in the discussion Paul speaks of 'those who share the faith of Abraham' in the God 'who gives life to the dead and calls into existence the things that do not exist' (Romans 4: 17). Again it is unlikely that Paul was making a point about the something or nothing out of which God brought things into existence.

One of the many reasons for contesting the presence of an unambiguous doctrine of creation out of nothing at this early stage is the fact that some second-century writers, such as Justin Martyr and Athenagoras, assume that God as Creator imposed form on a material substrate.[29] The case of Athenagoras is particularly pertinent to our investigation since, assuming he was the author,[30] he provides us with the first treatise on the subject of resurrection. He is clearly facing opponents who disbelieve, and he challenges them about the connection between creation and resurrection: either they must deny to the creation of human beings any cause, or, if they do ascribe creation to God, they must examine what that presupposes and show why they regard resurrection as an untrustworthy doctrine – in other words, they need to demonstrate that God, despite being Creator, either cannot or

---

[28] This paragraph repeats points made in 'Creation and Human Being'.

[29] For Athenagoras, see *Legatio* 15.2; cf. 4.1–2, which is more ambiguous.

[30] W. R. Schoedel takes it to be an anti-Origenist work of the third century in his introduction to the text and translation quoted here: *Athenagoras: Legatio and De Resurrectione* (Oxford, 1972) [hereafter: *De res.*], following R. M. Grant, 'Athenagoras or Pseudo-Athenagoras?', *HThR* 47 (1954) 121–29. The case against authenticity has been subjected to vigorous critiques by L. W. Barnard, *Athenagoras: A Study in Second Century Christian Apologetic* (Paris, 1972), and others. See further Daley, *Hope of the Early Church*, 230 n. 4.

Eschatology and the Doctrine of Creation

will not restore dead bodies so as to reconstitute the human beings they were before.[31] As to God's power to do this, the original creation of our bodies is enough to show that it suffices for their resurrection; if God first gave them form when they did not exist before, he can just as easily raise them up after their dissolution.[32]

So, where 2 Maccabees and Paul used creation as encouragement to faith in God, even in the face of death, this author turns that tradition into a philosophical defence of the notion of resurrection. Whatever the objections raised, such as what happens to those eaten by wild animals or turned into food for fish after drowning, Athenagoras will find a reasoned way through and trump it with the power and wisdom of the Creator.

> Moreover one cannot say that it is a work unworthy of God to raise up and reconstitute a decomposed body; for if the lesser work – the making of a corruptible and passible body – is not unworthy of God, how much more is the greater work – the making of an incorruptible and impassible body – not unworthy of God.[33]

Of course, some at this time did indeed think it was unworthy of God to get mixed up with the creation of physical things. The apparent crudities of collecting all the bits of matter that had belonged to each body is finessed by the notion of a body which transcends what we know in our present existence: Paul's idea of a spiritual body (1 Corinthians 15: 35–57), together with his sense that the soul needs to be clothed rather than naked (2 Corinthians 5: 1–6),[34] undoubtedly contributes to the picture. Without the composition of soul and body you would not have a human being; so even a transformed human being must be such a composite. This necessitates the resurrection.[35]

The connection between creation and resurrection is further developed by the observation that the reason for creating human beings was not God's own need – rather it was for humanity's sake and out of God's wisdom and goodness; and so God 'decreed an unending existence to those who bear his image in themselves, are gifted with intelli-

---

31 Athenagoras, *De res.* 2. 2–3.
32 Ibid. 3.1.
33 Ibid. 10.6. Note the form of argument, often referred to as *Qal wahomer*, or 'from light to heavy', and regarded as a particularly Jewish form of reasoning.
34 The title of this paper was taken from this passage.
35 Cf. Athenagoras, *De res.* 15.2, 5.

gence and share the faculty for rational discernment'. That being the case, the two parts, soul and body, are receptive to the appropriate changes, 'including, along with the other changes affecting age, appearance or size, also the resurrection'.[36] Resurrection from the dead is taken to be 'transformation for the better', or 'survival in a incorruptible form', and Christians expect this because of their confidence in the will of the Creator, who

> made man that he might participate in rational life and, after contemplating God's majesty and universal wisdom, perdure and make them the object of his eternal contemplation, in accordance with the divine will and nature allotted to him. The reason then for man's creation guarantees his eternal survival, and his survival guarantees his resurrection, without which he could not survive *as man*. From what we have said it is clear that the resurrection is demonstrated by the reason for man's creation and the will of the Creator.[37]

Against others the author insists that the resurrection does not take place primarily for judgement but because of the will of the Creator and the nature of those created.[38] Interestingly enough, the author of this treatise eventually notes for himself that all the arguments brought forward to confirm the resurrection are of the same kind and spring from the same basic idea, namely the origin of human beings in the act of creation.[39]

Clearly this treatise anticipates a great deal that we found in Gregory – in fact it maps the *topoi* of discussion that keep recurring in the patristic period.[40] It affirms the goodness of materiality; it insists that the union of body and soul constitutes a created human person; it emphasizes the connection between creation and resurrection; yet so far creation out of nothing is not explicitly articulated.

Justin Martyr had also accepted that God created out of pre-existent matter. His pupil Tatian, however, was already moving on in the argu-

---

[36] Ibid. 12.5–7.
[37] Ibid. 13.2.
[38] Ibid. 14.6.
[39] Ibid. 18.1.
[40] For example, Tertullian's (fl. 200) treatise *On the Resurrection of the Flesh* (*De resurrectione carnis*) and the fourteenth *Catechetical Lecture* of Cyril of Jerusalem (d. 386) cover much the same ground.

Eschatology and the Doctrine of Creation

ment. God was definitely alone, he asserts;[41] matter is not, like God, without beginning; it was brought into existence by the Creator who begat our world, having first created the necessary matter. Tatian goes on to say that it is 'on this account' that 'we believe that there will be a resurrection of bodies'. Tatian confesses that he did not know who or what he was before he was born; but being born, after a former state of nothingness, he obtained a certainty of his existence. In just the same way, having come to be and through death existing no longer, he would exist again. Even if all trace of his physical existence were to be obliterated by fire, dispersed through waters or torn in pieces by wild beasts, there is nothing to stop the creative power of God restoring him to his original pristine condition.

Behind this argument is the utter rejection of the immortality of the soul, which Tatian spells out later.[42] He has recognized that the notion of the soul's immortality is incompatible with the doctrine of creation. The soul is mortal; and yet it is possible for it not to die. If it does not know the truth, it dies, dissolved with the body; but united with Spirit, it ascends. In other words the creative activity of God is at the root of any afterlife. 'Tatian's rejection of natural immortality is fundamentally theocentric', wrote Jaroslav Pelikan:

> Neither for his original birth out of the nothingness of non-being nor for his ultimate rebirth out of the nothingness of death can man take the credit, but it belongs to God's sovereignty and discretion to create a human being in the first place and re-create him after he has been annihilated by death ....
> Whatever immortality a man may obtain is thus by participation in the immortality and incorruptibility of God.

Pelikan speaks of 'a necessary corollary from the confession ... that God is the Maker of heaven and earth'.[43]

And this involves another corollary – that the material aspect of human existence is given due recognition. Tatian is particularly conscious of the complexity of human nature and the inability of the soul to be by itself without the body – both reach dissolution in death, and neither can rise without the other. He is clear, then, that body and

---

41 Tatian, *Oration to the Greeks* 5, 6 [hereafter: *Orat.*]; *Tatian, Oratio ad Graecos and fragments*, ed. and trans. Molly Whittaker, OECT (Oxford, 1982).
42 Tatian, *Orat.* 13.
43 Jaroslav Pelikan, *The Shape of Death* (London, 1962), 17–18.

soul belong together and after death may be reconstituted by the Creator God who created them together in the first place.

So Tatian espoused the notion of *creatio ex nihilo* and asserted its bearing on resurrection,[44] in conscious opposition to philosophy in general and Platonism in particular. But second-century discussion of cosmology and eschatology was also affected by views later to be designated by the term 'Gnostic'. Indeed, it is in an evidently Gnostic work that the consequences of losing the connection between creation and resurrection can be observed, namely, the *Epistle to Rheginos* (or *Treatise on the Resurrection*)[45] found in the Nag Hammadi library, and probably dating from the late second century – in other words, in all likelihood, approximately contemporary with Athenagoras's treatise.

This short work responds to a question about death and the afterlife, but generally seems to treat 'death' and 'resurrection' as having metaphorical connotations only: for while the Lord 'existed in flesh', he lived 'where you remain', a place which 'I call "Death"!' It goes on to assert that he was Son of God so that he might vanquish death, and Son of Man so that 'restoration to the Pleroma' might occur. He was 'originally from above', 'a seed of the Truth'; he 'transformed [himself] into an imperishable Aeon and raised himself up, having swallowed the visible by the invisible, and he gave us the way of our immortality'. The Apostle is quoted (rather roughly, it has to be said): 'we suffered with him, and we arose with him, and we went to heaven with him'. So the elect were revealed: 'We are manifest in this world wearing him', and then 'drawn to heaven by him', unrestrained by anything. 'This is the spiritual resurrection which swallows up the psychic in the same way as the fleshly.' After exploring the need for faith, the question is posed again, 'What is the resurrection?' The answer is: 'It is always the disclosure of those who have arisen.' The appearance of Moses and Elijah in the Transfiguration narrative is alluded to and used as proof that the resurrection is no illusion; rather, the world is an illusion. The resurrection is the 'revelation of what is, and the transformation of things, and a transition into newness'. The recipient of the letter is urged to 'flee from the division and the fetters, and already you have the resurrec-

---

[44] The second-century writer Theophilus of Antioch made similar moves: see *Ad Autolycum* 2.4, where he argues that creation out of pre-existent matter makes God no better than a human craftsman; cf. ibid. 1.4, 7 for the connection between creation and resurrection.
[45] Trans. Malcolm L. Peel, in *The Nag Hammadi Library in English*, ed. James Robinson (Leiden, 1977), 50–53.

Eschatology and the Doctrine of Creation

tion'. This is to 'enter into the wisdom of those who have known the Truth'.

It is hardly surprising, then, that this work has been characterized as 'permeated with Valentinian symbols and imagery', and as spelling out the views of those criticized in 2 Timothy 2: 18 for asserting that 'the resurrection has already taken place'.[46] In the genre of epistle, in its language and its allusions, it could almost pass as Christian, yet it clearly assumes that redemption is escape from matter and evil, and if it apparently speaks of being clothed in the Lord, or even of receiving flesh 'when you ascend into the Aeon', it turns out to be something 'better than flesh', and resurrection is actually rising up to the Pleroma or the All. If nothing else, then, this treatise proves that it is not so straightforward as has been assumed to distinguish resurrection and immortality – both terms could refer to the same thing, though with very different connotations in different contexts.

But its main importance for our argument here lies in the fact that creation is never mentioned – the connection has been lost. It shows how the argument with Gnosticism about the goodness of the material creation would inevitably involve the defence of bodily resurrection, as well as the true enfleshment of Jesus Christ in the incarnation. Creation, incarnation and resurrection all hung together. A brief look at Tertullian's treatise on the *Resurrection of the Flesh*[47] shows how clearly he saw the connections. From both heathen and heretic alike comes invective against the flesh, he asserts,[48] and he proceeds to offer a different view – of the glory of the flesh, created by God out of nothing, redeemed in Christ and to be resurrected. The opening chapters of the treatise suggest that he sees the resurrection as the basis of the whole Christian position; and his cross-references to other treatises, *Against Marcion* and *On the Flesh of Christ*, indicate his awareness of how all these doctrines cohere. 'First they crash in respect of the resurrection of the flesh,' he says, 'and afterwards they crash in respect of the unity of the deity.' He continues: 'Just as the foundations [of the unity of the deity] are shaken by denial of the resurrection of the flesh, so by the vindication of [the resurrection], [the unity of the deity] is established.'[49]

---

[46] Peel's introduction: ibid. 50.
[47] *Tertullian's Treatise on the Resurrection*, ed. and trans. Ernest Evans (London, 1960).
[48] Tertullian, *On the Resurrection* 4.
[49] Ibid. 2; here I have used and corrected Evans's translation and inserted explanations from the context.

It is this point which underlies my claim that resurrection had something to do with the emergence of the doctrine of creation out of nothing. It would be impossible to demonstrate a linear connection: Athenagoras apparently affirms one without the other, and the doctrine's basis undoubtedly lay in the arguments against alternative cosmogonies. On the one hand, God did not create out of the divine self (as Gnostic myths of the fragmentation of the divine might suggest) or everything would be divine; on the other hand, God did not create out of an eternal material substrate (as Platonists argued) or God's *monarchia* (his sovereignty as the single first principle) would be threatened – there would be two first principles. Tertullian was the first to set out these alternatives, rejecting both in favour of *creatio ex nihilo*.[50] Yet it was also Tertullian who saw how the incarnation and resurrection of Christ hang together with God's act of creation out of nothing, and that must surely be significant. His treatise *On the Resurrection of the Flesh* could have been written as an answer to the *Epistle to Rheginos*, it so precisely sets out to deny the positions taken up there. Metaphorical and spiritual interpretations of resurrection were alike heretical in Tertullian's view. The rejection of anti-materialist positions and the assertion of creation out of nothing surely derived a good deal of their punch from faith in the physical resurrection of Christ and the promised general resurrection.[51]

Such, then, is the case for my second thesis: that we can trace such a long-standing connection between creation and resurrection, both alike attesting God's power, that it can plausibly be argued that belief in resurrection, founded on the resurrection of Jesus Christ, not only reinforced insistence on the goodness of the material creation, but also contributed to the emergence of the idea that God created out of nothing.

Augustine of Hippo

To conclude, it is worth returning to the fourth century and Augustine of Hippo. The final book (22) of the *City of God* is his most extended treatment of the resurrection, though earlier books (such as 10, 13, 20 and 21) anticipate some of the material discussed at the climax. Here we

---

[50] Tertullian, *Against Hermogenes.*
[51] A similar argument could be adduced from the works of Irenaeus, who was also, of course, opposing Gnostic heresies.

Eschatology and the Doctrine of Creation

see how his thinking, like that of Gregory of Nyssa, was indebted to the traditions we have been exploring,[52] though developed in his own inimitable way, with much reference to Scripture, as well as asides targeted at the Platonists, whose views, Augustine keeps arguing, should logically lead to Christian truth if they were not misguided about certain crucial matters: for example, despite saying that 'in the celestial sphere there are immortal bodies of beings whose blessedness is immortal', they assert that 'escape from any kind of body is an essential condition for our happiness', whereas Christians affirm that 'the resurrected body will be eternal', 'incorruptible and immortal and will present no obstacle to that contemplation by which the soul is fixed on God'.[53]

The following points provide a summary of Augustine's views:

1. The promises of God are to be relied upon because God is the originator of the creation, with all its marvels and surprises.[54] Belief in the physical resurrection of Christ, the coming resurrection to the new age of humankind and the immortality of the body is now generally accepted, Augustine affirms, because of the persuasive power of prophecy, the fearless proclamation of the martyrs and demonstrations of divine power, including contemporary miracles,[55] though created existence is itself the most powerful testimony.[56] The goodness of creation is rooted in God.[57]

2. There is a resurrection of the soul, from the death of irreligion and wickedness to righteousness and faith; this first resurrection is here and now, and is a resurrection of mercy. The second resurrection is of judgement, and anyone who does not want to be condemned then must rise up in the first. The resurrection to come is of bodies, and through fire their corruptible elements will perish, and 'our substance itself will acquire the qualities ... suited, by a miraculous transformation, to our immortal bodies ... renewed for the better even in their flesh'.[58]

3. The objections to the idea that bodies and material flesh could belong to heaven are met by appeal to the same Creator God – should it

---

52 Latin text in CChr.SL 47–48 (Turnhout, 1955); ET in *Concerning the City of God*, trans. Henry Bettenson, intro. David Knowles, Penguin Classics (Harmondsworth, 1972).
53 Augustine, *City of God* 10.29.
54 Ibid. 22.1–3.
55 Ibid. 22.5, 7–9.
56 e.g. ibid. 22.4, 24.
57 Ibid. 11.24.
58 Ibid. 20. 6, 16.

not be regarded as more amazing that immaterial souls are bound within earthly bodies? For 'the interweaving of material with immaterial substances', the one being 'heavenly' and the other 'terrestrial', 'is surely a greater miracle of divine power than the conjunction of the material with the material'.[59] Platonist appeals to the weight of bodies cannot set limits to the power of Almighty God, as if God were not able to make our bodies capable of dwelling in the heavens.[60]

4. The classic problems of people being consumed by wild beasts or fire, drowned, or born with defects receive the classic answer: nothing is beyond the resources of the Creator. It is unthinkable that the Creator should lack the power to revive them all and restore them to life. Loss of nail-parings and hair-cuttings are not inimical to the general point that nothing will 'perish' from the person at the resurrection. The original substance of the person will be reused rather as an artist reuses or remixes material to produce a work without defects. The Almighty Artist can correct all disharmony and distortion, yet will retain the marks of the glorious wounds of the martyrs. At the resurrection to eternal life the body will most likely have the size and dimensions which it was to attain at maturity, according to the design implanted in the body of each person, with any necessary rearrangements to produce the harmony and beauty of the whole. The same flesh will arise, but re-formed as a spiritual body, the grace of which Augustine cannot describe because he has had no experience of it.[61]

5. Other questions designed to derail the idea – like, 'What about abortions or miscarriages?' or 'What will be the height and size of the resurrection body?' – are met by appeal to the apostolic statement that we shall all attain to the stature of the full maturity of Christ.[62] To reach that stature and be shaped in his likeness, refers not so much to literal size as to the inner person and the condition of immortality.[63] The point is that no weakness will persist, though sexual differentiation will, being regarded as natural, not a defect; but there will be no lust or childbirth, so the female organs will be part of a new beauty arousing praises of God 'for his wisdom and compassion, in that he not only created out of nothing but freed from corruption that which he

---

[59] Ibid. 22.4.
[60] Ibid. 22.11.
[61] Ibid. 22.12–14, 19–20.
[62] Ibid. 22.12.
[63] Ibid. 22.15.

Eschatology and the Doctrine of Creation

created'.[64] The Body of Christ is what is meant by perfect humanity – so the gradual building up of the Church is what will find fulfilment at the resurrection.[65] When Augustine attempts a description,[66] it is of a society in heaven, which is genuinely a body politic, at peace and bound in the closest possible harmony, where God is the goal of all longings, and 'we shall see him for ever, love him without satiety and praise him without weariness'.

To appreciate the significance of all this, it is important to scroll back through Augustine's earlier writings. His first instinct was to place sensible and material reality well below the intellectual in the hierarchy of existence, treating it as a drag downwards, while arguing in Platonic fashion for 'the indestructibility of the soul as a philosophically evident truth',[67] a position he never entirely abandoned, though he would also root the soul's immortality in its creation in the image of God and natural kinship to the transcendent world of Truth and Beauty. As for the body, in the 390s he could suggest that being 'raised a spiritual body', as Paul suggested in 1 Corinthians 15, implied a lack of material flesh and blood, taking seriously the words 'flesh and blood cannot inherit the Kingdom of God' (1 Corinthians 15: 50); whereas later he would speak of spiritual flesh.[68] In the *Confessions* Augustine focused on the vision of God promised to the purified soul, for which he yearns; he also offers praise to his Creator, taking creatureliness very seriously;[69] but he hardly touches on expectations for eternity or what the resurrection might mean. Over the years he had, of course, alluded to resurrection in sermons and other ecclesiastical writings, and in his completed work on *The Literal Meaning of Genesis* he considers the bodily state in the resurrection, but it is not until the *City of God* that he fully sets out his appreciation of the Christian critique of Platonism and explores at length the integration of soul and body as the ultimate human reality to be realized at the resurrection.[70] Here he even integrates this with his

---

[64] Ibid. 22.17.

[65] Ibid. 22.18.

[66] Ibid. 22.30.

[67] Daley, *Hope of the Early Church*, 142. See also Brian E. Daley, 'Resurrection', in Allan D. Fitzgerald, ed., *Augustine through the Ages: An Encyclopedia* (Grand Rapids, MI, 1999); other entries on 'Soul', 'Body' and 'Anthropology' helpfully trace Augustine's developing views.

[68] Augustine, *City of God* 22.21.

[69] In 'Creation and Human Being', I argued that this was the key to the *Confessions* and the much-debated question of its unity.

[70] I am indebted to the work of a graduate student, Rowena Pailing, for demonstrating the exceptional character of the *City of God* in this respect.

more Platonic desire to contemplate God by discussing at length what it means 'to see God in the body',[71] – whether one would see God through the eyes of the body. He adopts the view that in the resurrected state those physical eyes must have some function, even though the incorporeal God cannot be seen in a physical way; he suggests that seeing the physical bodies of the new heaven and new earth will involve seeing God in utter clarity, present everywhere and governing the whole transformed material creation. Hence the power of God the Creator so to transform the whole person that the goal of the original creation is realized, beyond time in eternity, fully informs Augustine's vision. Now, too, despite all the oddities and speculations that discussion of bodily resurrection kept raising, it is possible to appreciate the thrust of that ancient creedal affirmation and its deep connection with the doctrine of creation.

Finally, as a postscript, it may be observed that the argument advanced here suggests that the heuristic model for studies of this kind should shift from the evolutionary notion of doctrinal development – surely a child of modernity – to that of discourse formation through argument and deduction. A deep-seated connection between resurrection and creation contributed to *arguments* that resulted in the idea of creation out of nothing; the implications of that doctrine, which took time to work out, then had a major impact on the formation not only of Christological discourse but also the Christian conception of the nature of the human creature and its eternal destiny. This study points up the importance for that *discourse formation* of dawning recognition of the coinherence of one doctrine with another.

---

[71] Augustine, *City of God* 22.29.

XVIII

Creation and Human Being:
The Forging of a Distinct Christian Discourse

My principal interest on this occasion is to explore what it meant to become conscious of oneself, of humanity in general, the universe as a whole, including the spiritual world, as being essentially creatures of the one true God, Maker of heaven and earth. To put it another way, I propose to trace the way in which the otherwise Platonic discourse of key fourth century Fathers, Eastern and Western, was transformed by the doctrine of *creatio ex nihilo*, and a distinctive Christian spirituality was forged. I shall suggest that it was the process of teasing out the implications of this very unhellenic view of the origins of the universe which contributed substantially to the articulation of Christian doctrine, including its anthropology; and by focussing on this aspect, I shall incidentally make some observations about the conceptual models we scholars use in constructing a history of doctrinal formation.

The Confessions of St. Augustine

I take as my starting-point Augustine's *Confessions*, a work whose climax is a discussion of creation. Otherwise the work is plausibly described as the first autobiography – roughly two-thirds being a work of profound self-consciousness, telling the story of Augustine's childhood and youth, education and intellectual development, up to his conversion to the faith of his mother, and his mother's death. Puzzlingly, however, this is followed by lengthy philosophical explorations of memory, time and eternity, and creation, the final book providing an exposition of *Genesis* chapter 1. Can we give an account of the *Confessions*, which explains the presence of those final four books?

This is not the first time I have attempted to address the problem of the genre of the *Confessions*. In the 1998 St. Augustine lecture at Villanova,[1] I discussed possible ancient precedents and parallels to its autobiographical character. There my conclusion was this:

---

[1] Frances Young, *The Confessions* of St. Augustine: What is the Genre of this Work?: *Augustinian Studies* 30 (1999) 1-16.

Consciously or unconsciously, alongside apologetic interest, Augustine's purpose in *The Confessions* is typological. He constructs his own life according to the biblically-shaped pattern by which he has come to understand the weakness of the human quest for God and the power of divine providence and grace, so as to provide a didactic 'type' or exemplar from which others will benefit by coming to an understanding of their own lives. The particular is understood by reference to the universal and *vice versa*. Scripture provides the models after which each human story may be sculpted.

Thus it was that I then hoped to provide an integrated view of the whole work. I accepted the parallels with Neoplatonic ideas of Fall and Return,[2] but suggested that a more significant contribution was made by Augustine's reading of Paul and the over-arching story of Fall and Redemption whereby the wider Church read the Bible as a whole. Augustine's own life becomes a 'type' demonstrating the outworking of God's providence and grace, anticipating in individual terms the agenda worked out on the plane of history in *The City of God*, namely, reorientation from self-love to love of God. Now, however, I want to retain those insights but integrate them into a new perspective: Augustine, I suggest, is working out the implications for human being of *creatio ex nihilo*, and it is this which more than anything else shifts his earlier Platonic assumptions.

The opening words of the *Confessions* suggest a re-reading of the first book in terms of a reflection on creatureliness. God is to be praised, and humanity, described twice within the opening lines as 'a little piece of your creation', is stirred to praise, 'because you have made us for yourself, and our heart is restless until it rests in you'. Chadwick notes[3] that 'For Plotinus (VI 7.23.4) the soul finds rest only in the One'; but, to adapt Mark Edwards' words,[4] 'Unlike the God of Origen [or for that matter Augustine], the One can make no choices; it causes without creating, presides without governing, superabounds without love.' The context focuses on creation, and Augustine invokes a God who causes, but does so as Lord of heaven and earth:

You are God and Lord of all you have created. In you are the constant causes of inconstant things (I.vi(9)); Lord, I must give thanks to you, the most excellent and supremely good Creator and Governor of the universe, my God... (I.xx(31)).

Augustine tells of his own birth and early years as a way of celebrating his existence and the gifts given him by God:

I thank you for your gifts. Keep them for me, for in that way you will keep me. The talents you have given will increase and be perfected, and I will be with you since it was your gift to me that I exist (I.xx(31)).

---

[2] See *e.g.* the introduction and notes to Henry Chadwick's translation in the World's Classics (Oxford, 1992); all quotations are taken from this ET.

[3] Chadwick (1992), 3.

[4] Mark Edwards, *Origen against Plato* (Aldershot, 2002), 61.

Indeed, the first book may be read as a meditation on the miracle of existence, and the paradox of a God who is 'deeply hidden yet most intimately present', without whom nothing would exist (I.4(4)).

The striking thing is that themes from Book I are taken up in the opening words of Book XIII:

> You made me and, when I forgot you, you did not forget me. I call you into my soul, which you are preparing to receive you through the longing which you have inspired in it.

What Augustine has shown is the way in which God has exerted pressure on him, and continues to do so, constantly calling him further on the journey towards the divine self. 'To you I owe my being and the goodness of my being', he affirms; 'your creation has its being from the fullness of your goodness.' And this utter dependence on God for existence is reinforced by the reflection that neither physical matter nor the spiritual creation would exist unless God had made it; nothing has any claim on God. The climax of the whole work affirms explicitly *creatio ex nihilo*:

> Your works praise you that we may love, and we love you that your works may praise you. They have a beginning and an end in time, a rise and a fall, a start and a finish, beauty and the loss of it. They have in succession an evening and a morning, in part hidden, in part evident. They are made out of nothing by you, not from you, not from some matter not of your making or previously existing, but from matter created by you together with its form – that is simultaneously … You made matter from absolutely nothing, but the beauty of the world from formless matter – and both simultaneously so that the form followed the matter without pause or delay (XIII. xxxiii(48)).

This being made from nothing is precisely what produces instability and restlessness. Augustine may seem to distinguish in classic Platonic style between what is changeable and what is changeless:

> … it was clear to me and certain that what is corruptible is inferior to that which cannot be corrupted; what is immune from injury I unhesitatingly put above that which is not immune; what suffers no change is better than what can change (VII.i(1)).

However, he has shifted the thrust of this. A creature is inherently changeable because it has changed from nothingness into something – the really important thing is that that change goes on in the right direction. His story, like that of the whole human race, is one of restless wandering from the right path, and being brought back on track by God's providential promptings. So the story of creation is also the story of redemption. While according to *Sir.* 18:1 God created everything at once, Genesis records things in a particular order, so revealing the hidden plan whereby order emerges from chaos, and saints from sinners. It is this process that justifies the figural reading of Genesis 1 in terms of new creation in Christ – creation is not just a one-off event, but something that happens within time and in response to God's loving providence. Without the

Word creation is inchoate and unformed, and needs to be converted, conformed to the Word 'by whom it was made, more and more to live by the fount of life, to see light in his light, and to become perfect, radiant with light and in complete happiness' (XIII. ii(3) – iii(5)). Augustine has moved on from his Platonist position, substantially because he understands himself as a creature, brought into being by the Creator God to whom he prays, and sees himself as integrally part of what Rowan Williams describes as 'a living system destined to grow toward beauty and order, even if this beauty and order is not at any given moment apparent'.[5] This acceptance of vulnerability and mutability, in the context of a creation with a beginning and an end, and in response to the creative and providential action of a God who freely loves, distinguishes Augustine's self-understanding from the intellectual mysticism of Neoplatonism, for all its surface similarities.

Those surface similarities he acknowledges by telling the story of his intellectual formation, and his struggles with the great problem of evil. The books of the Platonists rescue him from the Manichaean position (VII. ix(13) – xx(26)). He discovers that evil is not a substance – as long as things exist they remain good (VII. xii(18)). So evil cannot really exist; rather it is privation of good. Sounding rather like a Platonist, he can write (as usual, addressing God), 'the further away from you things are, the more unlike you they become' (XII. vii(7); xi(11)); heaven is 'close to you', while the 'earth' is 'close to being nothing' (XII. vii(9)). But the implicit correlation of evil with nothingness confirms that for Augustine the creative power of God is constantly at work bringing things out of nothingness into existence, and bringing order out of chaos, and good out of evil, redeeming what wanders restlessly and gets corrupted because of its inherent changeability – it is all of a piece. Things, which are liable to corruption because they are created out of nothing, are nevertheless good – even heaven is created and liable to lapse because of its createdness, yet contemplation of God checks its mutability (XII. ix(9); xv(20-1)); so creatureliness and corruptibility do not exclude goodness, and the totality of creation is good (VII. xii(18) – xiii(19)), though finite, time-bound and in need of grace (VII. xv(21)), indeed in need of the completion offered by the incarnation. The incarnation is what Augustine famously confessed he did not find in the Platonists, and the incarnation is indispensable to God's creative purpose because the cause of things is not descent from the One, but ascent from nothingness by the power of God's creative Word.

There is, then, a deep connection between Augustine's reassessment of the problem of evil and his discovery of what it means to be created; that connection lies in the 'nothingness' from which God brought things into being. The doctrine of creation 'out of nothing' is thus fundamental to both Augustine's

---

[5] Rowan Williams, Creation, in: Allan D. Fitzgerald (ed.), *Augustine through the Ages: An Encyclopedia* (Grand Rapids, 1999), 251-4, 252.

rejection of Manichaeism and his journey beyond Platonism. The *Confessions* may tell the story of this intellectual journey, but the point of the story is to celebrate what it means to be a creature in the process of being formed according to the will of the Creator. The presence of the final three books simply confirms that assessment. The work as a whole is about knowing God, as also being known by God (1*Cor.* 13:12), being naked before God, who is also the physician of one's most intimate self, and responding to a God of mercy and grace over the course of one's life and in one's day to day existence. That is the subject of Book X, which is by far the longest and has justifiably been called a 'microcosm of the whole work'.[6] Augustine has developed a distinctive spirituality which is rooted in creatureliness. He has reached a clear if contestable philosophical position: the Trinitarian God alone transcends the created, time-bound, changeable but perfectible order, which is as it is because created out of nothing. Creation out of nothing lies at the heart of what it means to live a human life, and so shapes the subject of Augustine's reflections in the *Confessions*.

Second century arguments about creation

To appreciate the significance of this, it is important to realise just how extraordinary the whole notion of creation out of nothing was in the context of ancient philosophical thinking:[7] 'nothing comes from nothing' was a Greek commonplace, and implied that anything coming from nothing is a sham![8] Something must have been there for creation to happen at all. Typical is the view of Plutarch:[9]

For creation does not take place out of what does not exist at all but rather out of what is in an improper or unfulfilled state ... [This] may be characterised as 'lack of order' (*akosmia*); and this 'lack of order' ... possessed a corporeal nature which was formless and inconstant, and a power of motion which was frantic and irrational.

Everything comes from something, and nothing comes from nothing. So where did this distinctly unhellenic notion of creation out of nothing come from?

Perhaps unexpectedly, it does not seem to have already been an established Jewish idea, simply taken over by Christians. The reasons for rejecting this assumption are, in summary, as follows:

---

[6] Frederick van Fleteren, *Confessiones*, in A.D. Fitzgerald (1999), 227-232, 231.

[7] What follows is adapted from Frances Young, 'Creatio ex nihilo': a context for the emergence of the Christian doctrine of creation: *Scottish Journal of Theology* 44 (1991) 139-51.

[8] Arnold Ehrhardt, *The Beginning: A study in the Greek philosophical approach to the concept of Creation from Anaximander to St. John* (Manchester, 1968), 166.

[9] *On the Creation of the Soul in the Timaeus* 1014B; quoted by John Dillon, *The Middle Platonists* (London, 1977), 207.

340

* The general lack of interest in *creatio ex nihilo* in Jewish tradition prior to the Middle Ages: the Rabbis condemn speculation about creation as much as about the chariot-throne of God![10]
* The sparsity of reference to the doctrine in relevant Jewish texts, and the ambiguity of texts which might seem to anticipate this doctrine.
* The apparently contrary evidence of the Wisdom of Solomon and the works of Philo, confirmed by early Christian writers such as Justin, Athenagoras, Hermogenes and Clement of Alexandria. All seem to adopt without question the Platonic view of an active and passive element, namely God plus matter.[11]
* The lack of emphasis on the idea in Christian literature of the 1st and 2nd centuries, contrasted with its general acceptance from the beginning of the 3rd century, and its increasing impact on other doctrines such as Christology.
* The consistency with which the earliest references to the doctrine, whether Jewish or Christian, appear in the context of debate with philosophy, notably Platonism. Indeed it was clearly on the basis of argument that the doctrine of *creatio ex nihilo* was established.

The classic arguments Augustine rehearses in his own way:

> You made heaven and earth not out of your own self, or it would be equal to your only-Begotten Son and therefore to yourself ... Moreover there was nothing apart from you out of which you could make them ... That is why you made heaven and earth out of nothing (XII. vii(7)).

Tertullian provides the first clear statement of these alternatives: God did not create out of the divine self, nor out of eternal co-existing matter; so if it was neither out of God's self nor out of some-thing, it must have been out of no-thing. The alternatives had been set up and answered differently, it seems, by Hermogenes, a second century Christian described as Platonist, and against whom Tertullian was writing (*Adversus Hermogenem*). Theophilus had reached a similar conclusion somewhat earlier: in *Ad Autolycum* II 4, he criticizes Plato for regarding matter as uncreated, and therefore equal to God, arguing for God's *monarchia*; the word is, of course, ambiguous – it might mean 'sole sovereignty', but could also imply 'sole first principle'. A human artisan creates out of pre-existent material, suggests Theophilus; so there is nothing remarkable about God doing likewise. The power of God is evident in the creation of whatever he wants *ex ouk ontōn*, out of the non-existent. Statements of that kind clearly emerge in debate with Greek philosophy, or with Christians adopting philosophical arguments.

There are, however, verbal anticipations of the formula *ex ouk ontōn*. The question is what did they imply? Is the first reference to creation out of nothing to be found in *2Macc.* 7:28?

---

[10] Gerhard May, *Creatio ex Nihilo: The Doctrine of Creation out of Nothing in Early Christian Thought* (ET A. S. Worrall; Edinburgh, 1994; German original, 1978), 23, notes its presence uniquely in Gamaliel II's discussion with a philosopher, recorded in Midrash Genesis Rabbah.

[11] Philo can speak of things being created *ex ouk ontōn*; but this only shows that such an expression was consistent with the view that matter pre-existed.

I implore you, my child, to look to the heavens and the earth; ... realise that God did not create them from what already existed (*ex ouk ontōn*), and that a human being similarly comes into existence.

Commenting on this and other such passages, Arnold Ehrhardt[12] noted that martyr literature, Jewish and Christian, tended to regard the world as a sham, so implying that the words here follow the Greek assumption that since 'nothing comes from nothing', everything is unreal. More convincing is Gerhard May's exposition:[13] this is a paraenetic reference to God's power, implying no more than that the world came into existence when it previously was not there; it cannot be characterised as a critical move away from the doctrine of God fashioning the world out of eternal matter. Biblical images dominate and the statement is compatible with the human creation 'out of clay' found in *Genesis* 2. The context in 2*Maccabees* is God's power to bring life out of death; birth is called in as a parallel mystery:

The Creator of the universe, who designed the beginning of humanity and devised the origin of all, will in his mercy give you back again breath and life ... (2*Macc.* 7:23)

Here there is no 'theory' of creation out of nothing – indeed the wording is not the usual later formula, *ex ouk ontōn*, but rather *ouk ex ontōn*. Similar observations can be made about the earliest Christian references in the New Testament, Hermas, Justin and Irenaeus. Even Origen is ambivalent.

So the dogma 'out of nothing' would seem to be a self-conscious rejection of the craftsman analogy presupposed by a Platonism that took the *Timaeus* as literally speaking of an initial act of creation by the Demiurge. In passing we should note that most Platonists did not so read the *Timaeus*, seeing the model, or as Plato calls it the 'myth', as a description of how things eternally are as they are. It was attractive to both Jewish and Christian philosophers, however, to correlate the *Timaeus* with Genesis, and it seems that Philo could take for granted the notion of unformed, unstable matter while using phrases just like those under discussion: God could conceivably bring into existence things which did not exist before, without such language excluding pre-existent stuff. Even Augustine still distinguishes between the creation of matter out of no-thing and the creation of some-thing out of matter by the imposition of form, though asserting that God did both simultaneously.

The dogma arose, then, in the second century, when not only was the apologetic enterprise engaging with philosophy, but cosmogony was a key element in the debate with gnosticism. The nature of the Demiurge was the prime issue. It was in this situation that the very unhellenic idea of creation out of nothing was forged. It would have a profound effect on the whole of Christian theology, but it took time for its implications to be teased out.

---

[12] A. Ehrhardt, *The Beginning* (1968), 167.
[13] G. May, *Creatio ex Nihilo* (1994), 6ff.

The forging of a distinct Christian discourse

At this point I digress from my immediate subject to place my approach in the context of debates about the history of Christian doctrine. I belong to the generation that grew up with courses and textbooks on 'the development of Christian doctrine'. That developed Christian doctrine was not to be found in the scriptures read historico-critically, that one could trace a history in which the major doctrines evolved, was an unquestioned assumption. But might this not be an unquestioned cultural presupposition of modernity rather as Platonism was for the Fathers? Evolution is built into the way we think, affecting our understanding of everything – it is an idea easily transferred from biology and genetics to history and society. Constitutional monarchy developed from a system based on the divine right of kings, just as *homo erectus* evolved from their ape-ancestors. Of course I over-simplify, but it is in order to pose the question: is 'development' or 'evolution' applicable to the realm of ideas?

Recently there has been a reaction against this model, notably in the work of John Behr,[14] who makes a good case for the history of Christian doctrine being the gradual articulation of what was there all the time, from the beginning. Thus he is more in tune with the thinking of the Fathers themselves: patristic prejudice was against novelty and originality, and they would not have been flattered, rather horrified, by our tendency to identify creativity in the thinking of particular individuals. Their instinct was to argue from precedent, appeal to tradition and find the truths they were defending written into the very foundation documents of the Church. As is well known, Athanasius had to defend the use of non-scriptural language in the Arian controversy.

But that fact in itself alerts us to the reality on the ground: new issues demanded new linguistic statements, new discourse, which was forged in the fires of controversy. There is no automatic development or evolution in the realm of ideas, but there is change – there is definition, modification, rejection, construction, as the to-and-fro of debate leads to refinement of language, or change of conviction, or the recognition that consistency demands fresh conception. In the case of Christian doctrine, heresy or different opinion is vital to the story. *Creatio ex nihilo* was not simply inherited from Judaism – it was articulated in the second century struggle to produce an acceptable theological account of cosmogony. I concede to John Behr's approach the fact that the Biblical affirmation of the power and sovereignty of the one true God was a driving force there from the beginning, as was the affirmation that creation arose from God's will to create; but I maintain that the implication of that *monarchia*, namely that God is the 'sole first principle', and its specific consequence, that what has come into being other than God can only be attributed to a divine creativity that produced existent things out of no-thing, was only

---

[14] John Behr, *Formation of Christian Theology* (2 vols., Crestwood, NY, 2001, 2004).

articulated in the face of argument with philosophy in a context where gnosticism posed a threat.

Argument produces discourse; which then becomes agreed and accepted as the appropriate statement of doctrine (i.e. what is to be taught). That social acceptance of the right way of putting things is a second key element in the process of formation, for it then acts as a catalyst, setting up the conditions for the new statement or formula to raise questions about other accepted statements or formulae. The Arian controversy was to a large extent driven by the need to correlate the doctrine of *creatio ex nihilo* with Christology. Scripture did not straightforwardly offer a simple answer to what was essentially a new question.

So, debate, both with external and with internal parties, drove doctrines into relationship with one another, demanding that they form a coherent cluster by assimilation to one another. But because this was not simply an intellectual process analogous to individuals arguing with one another in the (post-) modern academy, but rather a social and cultural process, the impact of the acceptance of a new way of expressing a doctrine took time to have effect. *Creatio ex nihilo* seems to have been argued at the turn of the second-third centuries, and then gradually accepted. The Christological consequences became an issue a century later. What I am suggesting here is that it was later still that theologians began to reflect on the consequences of 'creation out of nothing' for a distinctive Christian anthropology and spirituality. So back to my principal subject.

Towards a Christian understanding of Human Being

The Cappadocians first made moves similar to those traced in Augustine's *Confessions*. Gregory of Nyssa in his *De Opificio Hominis* states (XVI 10, 12) that God brings humanity into being for no other reason than that God is good, and that it is from nothing that humanity is created. He insists on the distinction between God who is uncreated and everything else that has come into being, a point highlighted during the course of the Arian controversy. This means that God is immutable, but created nature cannot exist without change – for its very passage from non-existence to existence is a kind of motion and change. But this mutability is not to be understood simply as negative (XXIII 5-XXVff.): if God's power is sufficient to bring things into existence from nothing, then the transformation of that creation is also within divine power. To press this point Gregory challenges first those who suggest matter is co-eternal with God, then those who deny the resurrection. It is well known that Gregory's spirituality expresses itself in terms of eternal *epektasis* and progress. He has indeed taken mutability positively in a way that is arguably unprecedented. Scholarship has tended to relate this to his positive evaluation of God's infinity;[15] the *De Opificio Hominis* suggests that 'creation out of nothing' was an equally important driver, as we saw it to be in Augustine.

For Gregory, however, the radical nature of creatureliness is somewhat offset by other aspects of human nature received from scripture and tradition. He affirms our nature as two-fold (XVI 8-10): on the one hand, like to God, on the other, differentiated from God. That two-fold-ness, he believes, is enshrined in the Genesis text, which speaks both of God creating humanity in God's own image, and also of creating them male and female: that second comment differentiates human creatures from the divine, to whom it is inappropriate to attribute maleness or femaleness. So humanity is the mean between two extremes, the divine and the animal. It is true that this leads him to reflect on human being in terms of a psychosomatic whole, and also to envisage the new creation in the resurrection as embodied; but it also keeps in play the Origenist notion of the intellect's kinship to the divine. The challenge for humanity is to make the choice to follow the angelic or divine aspect of human nature and reject the bestial or irrational tendency which arises from the other side of our nature. So Gregory's perception of human creatureliness appears less radical than the position of Augustine in the *Confessions*. This impression is reinforced by Gregory's affirmation of the position of humanity as the crown or 'king' of creation. It is important not to forget that his work is conceived as the continuation of Basil's *Hexaemeron*. For Gregory humanity represents God within the created order, and is given a kind of delegated sovereignty. But humanity is also set in the context of a creation that God calls good so as to enjoy and appreciate it (II). This was a central theme of Basil's work.

So *creatio ex nihilo* not only shifted perspective on human being itself, but also on the natural world. It stimulated wonder and rejoicing in the beauty and harmony of the created order. We cannot deny Robin Lane Fox's observation[16] that fanatical monks cut down sacred groves of trees as nature was de-sacralised, but that destruction is not the whole of the story. It has been argued that empirical science was made possible by a combination of that de-sacralisation and the urge to understand the mind of the one who created such marvels;[17] and that is anticipated in Basil's work. For the really striking thing about the *Hexaemeron* is its general tone of sheer wonder at creation, its affirmation that nothing is superfluous or wrong or out of place, everything contributes to the rich tapestry of the created order and its beauty (*e.g. Hexaemeron* I 11; III 10; VII *passim*; *etc.*). The development of this creation spirituality is grounded in the assertion that God is the sole source: a dualism with matter, or indeed with

---

[15] *E.g.* Ekkehard Mühlenberg, *Die Unendlichkeit Gottes bei Gregor von Nyssa* (Göttingen, 1966); Ronald E. Heine, *Perfection in the Virtuous Life* (Philadelphia, 1975).

[16] Robin Lane Fox, *Pagans and Christians* (London, 1986), 43-4.

[17] Stanley L. Jaki, *Creator and Cosmos* (Edinburgh, 1980); T.F. Torrance, *Divine and Contingent Order* (Oxford, 1981).

evil, is absolutely ruled out (II). The Creation out of nothing means that this wonderful reality is finite, its beginning implies its end (I 3); but none of it was conceived by chance or without reason (I 6) – it must be looked at *sub specie aeternitatis*, Basil implies. The God who creates and judges is providentially at work in the whole process. The problem with philosophy is precisely its inherent atheism – its failure to rise to knowledge of God through its much ado about explaining nature (I 2). Of Basil's work Gregory Nazianzen affirmed (*Oration* 43.67):

Whenever I take his *Hexaemeron* in hand and quote its words, I am brought face to face with my Creator; I begin to understand the rationale of creation; I feel more awe than ever I did before...

We conclude by returning to Augustine – for we are left with several questions:

* What about Augustine's response to the natural world as God's creation?
* How far can we treat the *Confessions* as typical, and was his view of human creatureliness really more radical than that of Gregory?
* Wasn't Augustine's anthropology ultimately shaped less by *creatio ex nihilo*, more by original sin?

Prior to writing the *Confessions* Augustine had already addressed the question of creation more than once. Clearly creation was as much a major intellectual issue for him as the problem of evil. In *De Genesi adversus Manichaeos*, written at Thagaste and one of his earliest works, he tackled Manichaean objections to Genesis and offered a spiritualised account of creation. Within five years, and after his ordination as priest in Hippo, he tried to tackle it again by offering a so-called 'literal' exegesis of Genesis, but gave up. After completing the *Confessions*, from 401 to 415 he worked on the 12 books *De Genesi ad litteram*. He returned to creation again in the *City of God*, and again around 420 in a work against an anonymous heretic who attributed the creation of the world to an evil demon. Clearly the treatment in the *Confessions* lies on a trajectory of development in his thinking on the subject. Taking all this into account can we respond to the questions raised?

Augustine rarely celebrates creation in the way Basil does. In his works on Genesis he tends to focus on philosophical and ethical problems; but awkward questions about creation sometimes provoke parallel claims about the beauty and harmony of the whole. In his earliest work refuting the Manichees he faces their challenge concerning the creation of so many animals, many of them pernicious and fearful. He simply asserts that the objectors fail to understand how such creatures are beautiful to their Maker, and that there is a use for them in the management of the universe as a whole. He confesses that he has no idea himself why mice and frogs, flies and worms were created; yet he can see they are all beautiful in their own way. Reflection, he is sure, will reveal how everything is fitted together in harmony: you might find 'more genuine satisfaction when you praise God in the tiny little ant down on the ground, than when you are crossing a river high up on an elephant' (I 25(16)-26).[18] To turn to the *City of God*, here Augustine certainly celebrates the natural world, though so much ground is covered that relevant passages get a little submerged. In his long discussions of the faults of paganism, he suddenly affirms (VII 26):[19]

As for us, what we are looking for is a soul which puts its trust in the true religion and does not worship the world as god, but praises the world as the work of God, and for the sake of God,

namely, the God who made the world. Later (XII 4, 5) he claims that the nature of things in itself, without regard to our convenience or inconvenience, gives glory to the Creator; all nature's substances are good, because they exist, have their own mode of being, and peace and harmony among themselves, a point developed at greater length in his long discussion of what peace is (XIX 12-14). And in his final celebration of the divine generosity in Book XXII, the sheer beauty and utility of the natural creation figures, as well as the wonderful fashioning of the human body.

So to the second question: how typical is the *Confessions*? If we look across the trajectory of Augustine's works, there is much in the earliest reflection on Genesis against the Manichaeans that anticipates what we found in that work: besides figural interpretation of the creation-story, insistence on 'out of nothing' was important to refute Manichaean objections, as was rejection of the craftsman analogy (*e.g.* I 10(6); II 43(29)); and even more significant is the importance of the soul and spirit not being part of God, but made by God (II 10(8); II 43(29)). But Genesis was a challenge for Augustine, and in his *Unfinished Literal Commentary on Genesis*, he asserts at the start that these obscure mysteries mean that questions are more appropriate than affirmations. He kept returning to the fundamental question what really happened – that is what he means by speaking of a literal, as distinct from a prophetic, figural or allegorical, interpretation. His focus is on ensuring that the text is understood in a way appropriate to the eternal, transcendent God. So, for example, in the completed *Literal Commentary on Genesis*, he concludes that the first account of creation, despite its organisation in six days, 'tells of the first moment of creation, in which a single creative act of God called all things into existence in an inchoative state', while 'the second account no longer describes an event on the threshold between time and eternity, but an event within time'.[20] Yet occasionally we do find the same kind of 'programme' as in the *Confessions*: the Word calls back to himself the imperfection of creation, so that it should not be formless but formed;

[18] ET Edmund Hill in: *On Genesis*, The Works of Saint Augustine I.13 (New York, 2002), 57, who confesses that 'elephant' replaces 'beast of burden' to bring out the contrast implied; though, I suggest, it does perhaps emphasise size at the cost of obscuring the point about 'usefulness'.

[19] ET quoted by Henry Bettenson (Harmondsworth, 1972), 287.

[20] E. Hill, Introduction to ET of the *Literal Meaning of Genesis* in (2002), 160.

and creation imitates the form of the Word, unless it turns away from the Creator and remains formless, imperfect and incomplete (I. ix(4)). Human beings, in particular, are not the sort of things that, once made and left to themselves, could do well by themselves – their good activity is simply to turn to him by whom they were made (VIII 25(12)). Then it is possible for the Creator to form them fully.

But was this sense of creatureliness more radical than that of Gregory Nyssen? Like Gregory, Augustine can speak of human nature as the mean between angels and beasts (*City of God* XII 22), and relate the bodily difference between animals and humans, namely the fact that humankind stands erect (*On Genesis: A Refutation of the Manichees* I 28 (17); *Unfinished Literal Commentary on Genesis* 60; *Literal Meaning of Genesis* VI 22 (12)), to the call to be upright in mind, the intellect being the thing that differentiates human beings from animals and makes them in the image and likeness of God. Augustine, however, speaks of humanity as the mean specifically in relation to Adam – the rest of humanity cannot escape the consequences of Adam's choice. So, in Augustine's mature anthropology, has the Fall replaced the radical sense of creatureliness we observed in the *Confessions*?

The completed *Literal Meaning of Genesis* covers Genesis 1-3 and so engages in depth with the story of Adam and the Fall. This work and the Pelagian controversy undoubtedly brought the later Augustine to focus more on Adam's disobedience; but does this entirely overshadow the importance of creation out of nothing? After all, the story of Adam is only possible because of the mutability of a creature made out of nothing. I want to suggest briefly that there are three features of the *City of God* which show that *creatio ex nihilo* remains a foundational impetus to Augustine's thinking about human being.

The first is the focus on worship; as in the case of the *Confessions*, prayer and praise are fundamental. The true God is to be worshipped rather than false gods, and often Augustine justifies this on the grounds that this God is the Creator of all that is, indeed the Creator of the soul itself (IV 30; V 11; VII 5, 28, 30). That Platonists do not confine worship to the Creator of all, that they do not recognise the createdness of the soul, and that they have wrong ideas about mediation, for Augustine vitiates their otherwise remarkable perception of the truth about the way thing are (VIII *passim*; X 3ff., 20, 24, 31). Giving thanks for existence and life (VII 31), celebrating the good things in human life, appreciating the wonders of the human body and of nature as a motive for praise, recognising the blessings God bestows through creating and transforming human creatures – all this reaches its climax in the final picture of eternal felicity, rest and peace in the city of God (XXII 24, 30).

The second feature I would point to lies in the implicit parallels between the *Confessions'* story of the individual and the *City of God's* history of the whole human race as it unfolds in time. Images of wandering, of exile and of pilgrimage are pervasive, reflecting the restlessness depicted in the *Confessions*. 'There is only one unchanging Good,' writes Augustine; 'that is the one, true, blessed God. The things he made are good because they were made by him; but they are subject to change, because they were made not out of his being but out of nothing' (XII 1). Failure to adhere to God is a perversion in the rational nature – for, though changeable, it was created to obtain blessedness by adherence to the unchangeable God. The long history of the two cities illustrates the two tendencies: to turn away from God to self-love, and to allow God's grace to renew and transform.

The third is the eschatology. The very fact of creation out of nothing is the guarantee that God's promises will be fulfilled (e.g. XXI 7, 8; XXII 11). All the problems of conceiving a resurrection of the body are answered by reference to the resources of the one who created out of nothing in first place: all things are possible to God – including restoration to the full maturity and completeness of each body, whether one died in infancy, lost stature in old age or limbs in war (XXII 5, 11–7). What is needed is not escape from the body but an imperishable body (XXII 26). The removal of defects will 'arouse the praises of God for his wisdom and compassion, in that he not only created out of nothing but freed from corruption that which he created' (XXII 17). 'We cannot keep silent about the joy of our hope, because of the praise due to God …' (XXII 21).

I submit then that the doctrine of *creatio ex nihilo* was an important factor in shaping the anthropology of the *Cappadocians* and of Augustine. I am not necessarily implying direct influence, though there is a debate to be had there, and one should not overlook the possible mediating influence of Ambrose, who like Basil composed a *Hexaemeron*. What I do affirm is that coincidence in ideas can occur when the time is ripe, a classic example being the moment when Darwin discovered that Alfred Russel Wallace had independently come up with exactly the same theory of the origin of species as he had. *Creatio ex nihilo*, the great gulf between the Trinity and the created order, the positive potential of mutability, these were ideas that, after the Arian controversy, were seeping into deeper consciousness among Christians of both East and West and affecting the way they thought, not just about Christology, but about human nature. The doctrine of creation was thus a crucial factor in forging a distinctively Christian discourse, reflecting a distinctively Christian sensibility in relation to nature, and a distinctively Christian spirituality in relation to God.

Theotokos: Mary and the Pattern of Fall and Redemption in the Theology of Cyril of Alexandria

Cyril is known for his defence of the title *Theotokos* for Mary. What I want to suggest in this chapter is that the position Cyril adopted in the controversy was fundamentally grounded in a reading of the Bible that generated an overarching story of Fall and Redemption. This can be traced in Cyril's pre-controversy biblical exegesis and links his fundamental approach to Christian theology with predecessors such as Irenaeus. The focus on Mary as antitype to Eve is of crucial importance as the broader context for patristic attitudes to women, but even more significant as a vital element in what can be seen as the core narrative constituting the common Christian account of human existence. Cyril's theology not only reflects this tradition but in key ways enables a more profound grasp of its typological roots, its biblical character and its fundamental significance for any truly Christian theology.

Theotokos in the Nestorian controversy

It is universally acknowledged that the Nestorian controversy was fundamentally christological, but because of the occasion which originated it, Mary figured large in the dispute. Nestorius, recently appointed bishop of Constantinople, had reacted to a sermon in which Mary was celebrated as *Theotokos* (i.e., the one who gave birth to God) by saying that such a designation had to be balanced by the term *Anthropotokos* (i.e., the one who gave birth to man):

in fact, strictly speaking, God did not take origin from a creaturely human being, and *Christotokos* would be better all round. Hearing of this Cyril leapt into action with letters all over the place, to the bishop of Rome, to the monks, to Nestorius himself. The controversy had begun. It was the year 429. One of the more notorious things Cyril did was to draw up 12 Anathemas, and the first provides another indication of how *Theotokos* was core to the debate:

> If anyone does not acknowledge Emmanuel to be truly God and therefore the holy Virgin to be *Theotokos* (for she gave birth according to the flesh to the Word of God made flesh), let him be anathema.[1]

These Anathemas formed the basis of treatise and counter-treatise as the battle developed. But the controversy is treated elsewhere. This will suffice as a reminder of the place of the Holy Virgin, *Theotokos*, at the heart of the debate.

Cyril's position as evidenced in the literature associated with the controversy has been well worked over. What I propose to do is to seek the undergirding theological perspective which produced his response, and to do that by looking at some of his pre-controversy biblical exegesis.

Fall and Redemption as key

The text to focus on first is Cyril's massive treatment of the Pentateuch known under the title, *On Worship in Spirit and in Truth*.[2] The work is a dialogue, Cyril responding to an interlocutor called Palladius. The opening question is this: how is the statement in St Matthew's Gospel that not a jot or tittle of the law will pass away to be reconciled with that in the Gospel of St John that the Father will not be worshipped in Jerusalem but in spirit and in truth? This conundrum becomes the occasion for working through the law to show that it is a *typos* (type), a foreshadowing of the proper shaping of devotion to God: the beauty of truth is hidden within it.[3]

---

[1] Cyril's *Explanation of the Twelve Chapters* is found in Russell, pp. 176–89. Anathema 1 appears on p. 178. In order to facilitate students in following up relevant texts, wherever possible quotations are given in the English translation by Russell.

[2] *De Ador.* (PG 68). Quotations given in the author's English translation.

[3] *De Ador.* (PG 68, 137).

The law is a pedagogue – leading infants to maturity, using metaphors and types, delivering truth through stories and pictures which we need to understand spiritually.[4] This general approach becomes specific as the story of humanity's Fall provides the clue to one subsequent narrative after another. It is not just that in later books Cyril will turn Leviticus into spiritual sacrifices and passages on the priesthood into types of Christ and the Church, seeing the bloodless sacrifice of the eucharist and the roles of bishops and presbyters prefigured in the law, but also that the movement from fall into sin, through repentance, to renewal through God's grace becomes a universal paradigm, traced out in particular in one narrative after another and applied to 'us'; for each of us are instances of the universal story of the human race. It is not hard to see that what happened to Adam, happens to each of us, Cyril suggests.[5]

Abraham becomes the first exemplar. Cyril wanders back and forth over the biblical narrative a little so as to construct the Fall and Redemption pattern. He begins with the way Abraham was caught in Egypt by Pharaoh because of Sarah's beauty. The whole story is a paradigm of spiritual enslavement, the physical representing the spiritual, Pharaoh representing the father of sin, who treats us well as long as he can distract us with pleasure. Only God and the divine grace could rescue Abraham.[6] Like Abraham those with Jacob went to Egypt because of famine and suffered God's anger through the yoke of slavery – they were tempted by worldly food when they should have been hungry for God's Word.[7] All through the discussion is a profound inter-textuality with allusions and quotations from across the prophets and the New Testament.

The point Cyril leads to is that we, like Abraham, are called to follow God, to leave behind everything in which we take pleasure, homeland, kindred – after all, Jesus spoke of leaving father and mother to follow him. Abraham leaves what is worldly to build an altar in the Promised Land.[8] So we receive no grace so long as

---

[4] *De Ador.* (PG 68, 140).
[5] *De Ador.* (PG 68, 148).
[6] *De Ador.* (PG 68, 152–3).
[7] *De Ador.* (PG 68, 160–1).
[8] *De Ador.* (PG 68, 168).

we are wedded to the world; but we are called too, and if obedient
will journey to the high country, to knowledge of God, and will
stand before God as a living sacrifice well-pleasing to God. Yet
the story of Sodom and Lot demonstrates the problem for us all of
falling from this state of grace.[9] With immense detail Cyril traces
the symbols in the Lot story which point to the progress of the
soul and its gradual ascent back to where it was.

Cyril eventually returns to Abraham in Egypt: he escapes rich
to build an altar and call on the name of the Lord.[10] Here is a
changed life. Enigmatically, or in riddles, his journey shows the
importance of changing wholeheartedly, of loving the desert, that
is, the purity of mind and heart which humanity enjoyed in the
beginning. And the same basic idea is to be traced in the story of
the Exodus.

So now, from Abraham, Cyril moves to this second great
exemplary story. Both descents into Egypt are seen as the result of
a free choice, but the consequent enslavement is oppression from
Pharaohs who stand for the devil. Human souls are oppressed and
put to hard and useless labours, just like the Israelites. But God
took pity on those harassed by Egyptian excesses, and he lavishes
grace on those dragged into sin. For the Israelites he appointed
Moses, and now writes the law on the heart through the Mediator
who brings free life to us.[11]

That is enough, without further detail, to show basically how
Cyril works. The thrust of his treatment is that God is the Liberator
and Saviour, but we need to go out into the desert to prepare a
holy feast for God apart from the Egyptians, removed from worldly
darkness.[12]

> We are all called to freedom through faith in Christ and ransomed
> from the tyranny of the devil, . . . this being prefigured (*proanatupou-
> menou*) in those of old, especially Moses and Aaron, so that by
> reason of God's gracious arrangements (*oikonomikos*) you may
> discern that Emmanuel is in similar fashion, lawgiver, high priest and
> apostle.[13]

[9] *De Ador.* (PG 68, 169–70).
[10] *De Ador.* (PG 68, 184–5).
[11] *De Ador.* (PG 68, 188).
[12] *De Ador.* (PG 68, 192).
[13] *De Ador.* (PG 68, 200).

Cyril means us to understand, then, that not a jot or tittle of the law is taken away, but the whole matter concerns worship in spirit and in truth. God's intentions are graciously set out in Scripture if we only read the Scriptures aright. But that reading is shaped by a universal paradigm of Fall and Redemption. We have reached the end of Book I, and Books II and III follow a similar pattern, developing Moses as type of Christ, the law as pedagogue, and so on. Let me highlight just one passage[14] to show how Cyril plays with the symbolic connections.

In Exodus 4, Moses expresses his fear that the Israelites will not believe him. He is told to throw his staff on the ground and it becomes a snake. He runs from it. But the story goes on that God then told him to catch it by its tail, and it reverted to a stick. Cyril comments that God provides a 'wonder' to counter disbelief, but the form of the 'wonder' is a figure of salvation in Christ, of our transformation from the condition in which we were in Adam.

Pressed to explain by Palladius, he elucidates. The staff, or sceptre, is a symbol of kingship. Adam was to rule the earth, but through the snake he was deprived of kingship and of his original glory, falling from paradise. Moses fled from the snake, and Cyril quotes from the book of Wisdom 1:5: the Holy Spirit of wisdom will flee from deceit and back off from foolish thoughts. Holiness and impurity, light and darkness, righteousness and unrighteousness are incompatible, he comments. The fact that the staff fell from the hand of Moses would signify that in the beginning there was a sprig of paradise made in God's image, in the glory of kingship, in the hand of the Creator, but he fell to the ground and in the eyes of God was like a snake. But the result of Moses catching him by the tail was reversion into a sceptre, a sprig of paradise. When God was pleased to recapitulate everything in Christ, and create anew what he had made in the beginning, he sent to us the Only-Begotten, his right-hand, the Creator and Saviour of all, Cyril proclaims. He took our humanity, transformed our wildness, our sin, and through sanctification, brought us to royal honour and the tameness that leads to virtue. (The domestication of wild animals provides the metaphor, doubtless because the story focuses on the snake.)

[14] *De Ador.* (PG 68, 240–5).

Cyril expands the theme with many intertextual references, insisting on finding significance in the tail and the head. But his focus is on the transformation through grace of the whole human race, including the head, Adam. Christ died and rose so that he might rule over the living and the dead.

Adam and Eve: 'type' and recapitulation

Throughout the work which we have been considering, Cyril exploits the traditional 'types'. It is easy, though not very subtle, to characterize his exegesis as allegorical. To understand what Cyril was doing, two features of early Christian use of 'types' are important.[15] The first is the discernment of exemplars, a common characteristic of ancient use of literature: in drama and literary texts it was thought possible to see a morally instructive *mimesis* of life, which means more than an 'imitation' – rather a 'representation'. Everything we have said so far is evidence of Cyril's commitment to this approach to Scripture. The other feature is the notion that prophetic 'types', images or patterns were etched into the narratives of what had become the Old Testament, symbols of what was to come. Cyril, like his predecessors, exploited key examples, so that, for example, the crossing of the Red Sea signified baptism, Moses' arms raised in the battle with Amalek signified the cross, and so on. For our purposes we need to dig a little deeper into Cyril's typological understanding of Adam and Eve.

Near the beginning of *On Worship* Book I, as Cyril sketches the themes of the work, he provides an outline of the Adam story, but he never uses the name, nor does he follow the motifs of the Genesis narrative; rather the presentation is almost abstract.[16] He speaks of 'humanity' (*anthropos*) and refers to James 1:13–15: each is tempted, not by God, but by one's own desire, lured and enticed by it, and that generates sin. The woman is a 'type' of pleasure. Satan compounds the problem by his deceit. The soul which had been *atreptos* (unchangeable) and *aphthartos* (immortal) was changed, corrupted by the act of disobedience. The story

[15] See further the author's discussion in *Patristic Exegesis and the Formation of Christian Culture* (Cambridge: Cambridge University Press, 1997).
[16] *De Ador.* (PG 68, 145–9).

Genesis told has given way to this generalized account of the human condition of which Abraham and Moses then become the exemplars, while later reference to Adam constitutes a kind of shorthand for this undergirding theory.

Some would look to contemporary philosophy to explain this approach to anthropology. The Neoplatonic pattern of descent and return is easily pressed into service in discussing the theology of Cyril's near contemporaries, the Cappadocians and Augustine. Assumptions about the immortality and unchangeability of the soul are suggestive of such influence. Cyril's mind was, like the minds of the rest of us, shaped by the intellectual culture in which he had matured. But his self-conscious understanding indicates another significant source, namely the Bible. Doubtless the key scriptural texts were read through the spectacles of a particular mind-set – that is always inevitable. But that the Bible was key to Cyril's thinking is evident. Indeed his direct exegetical engagement with Scripture was key in ways that not even Athanasius' was. For Cyril rarely describes the Fall, in the way Athanasius does in the *De Incarnatione*, as a falling back into the nothingness from which we created; and he tends to speak of salvation less as a restoration of the Logos to humanity, more as a refilling with the Spirit.[17]

If we turn to the *Glaphyra*, Cyril's 'Elegant Comments' on Genesis, we find his more explicit treatment of the Adam story, and what is now striking is the Pauline basis of Cyril's reading of Genesis.[18] Ephesians 1:10 provides the word *anakephalaiosis*, 'recapitulation'. 2 Corinthians 5:17 points to renewal: 'Behold, I make all things new', and 'if anyone is in Christ, there is a new creation'. Galatians 5:24 indicates that the flesh is crucified with Christ, so indicating how the old is done away. For Cyril re-creation in Christ is the thrust of Paul's message, but also the meaning of the Genesis narrative.

So he goes on to describe the original creation, in which humanity was a *mimema*, a copy, of the highest glory, a kind of clay statuette endowed with the living spirit so as to be a rational

---

[17] For this observation I am indebted to Daniel Keating's unpublished D.Phil thesis, 'The Appropriation of Divine Life in Cyril of Alexandria' (Oxford University, 2000).

[18] *Glaphyra* (PG 69, especially 16–32).

and immortal *zoon* ('animal' or 'living being'). Humanity was the image of the divine substance on earth, and sin's deviation did not yet exist. A lengthy exposition of the story of Adam follows, beginning with his loss of 'singleness' with the creation of woman from his side, continuing with the devil's temptation and his expulsion from Paradise. But then Cyril is back to Paul: the grace of salvation was given before the ages began (quoting 2 Tim. 1:8–10 in full), and everything was preordained so that all things work together for good (Rom. 8:28–30 also quoted in full). God knew he would send his Son, and the manner of the incarnation was foreknown. Redemption (*apolutrosis*) would come through the *anakephalaiosis* – the recapitulation.

In elucidating what that recapitulation was Cyril again exploits Paul. 1 Corinthians 15 is key, with cross-reference to Galatians 3:13 and Romans 5. Christ is the last Adam, recapitulating and reversing the fall of the first. By being a 'type' of Christ, Adam is prophetic of the mystery of the Incarnation, of Emmanuel, God with us. The first Adam brought us to death, the curse, judgement; the second to life, blessing and righteousness. Adam brought the woman to himself so as to become one flesh and was destroyed through her; but Christ saves, drawing the Church to himself through the Spirit. Here is an oblique hint that Eve and Mary will become vital to the Fall and Redemption pattern in Cyril's theology.

Apart from his acknowledged debt to St Paul, Cyril owed much to theological traditions of long standing, and in this tradition the typological relationship between Eve and Mary was as crucial as that between Adam and Christ. It was first introduced in the second century by Justin Martyr:

> Christ became man by the Virgin in order that the disobedience which proceeded from the serpent might receive its destruction in the same manner in which it derived its origin. For Eve, who was a virgin and undefiled, having conceived the word of the serpent, brought forth disobedience and death. But the Virgin Mary received faith and joy, when the angel Gabriel announced the good tidings to her that the Spirit of the Lord would come upon her, and the power of the Highest would overshadow her . . . and she replied: 'Be it unto me according to thy word.'[19]

---

[19] *Dialogue with Trypho* 100 (ET *Ante-Nicene Fathers*).

The one born of her was the one by whom God destroyed the serpent, and so reversed Eve's conception of the false word by conceiving the true Word of God.

This typological parallel was developed in further ways by Irenaeus, for whom recapitulation was the key to his anti-gnostic polemic. Adam's creation from the virgin earth was a type of Christ's formation from the Virgin Mary. Mary's obedience undid the knot of Eve's disobedience, so that Mary becomes the cause of salvation for the whole human race, and Eve's advocate.[20] The dissemination of this way of thinking is evidenced in the vivid Syriac poetry of Ephrem (fourth century):

> Just as from the small womb of Eve's ear
> Death entered in and was poured out,
> So through a new ear, that was Mary's,
> Life entered and was poured out.[21]

Restoration to Paradise is the focus of Ephrem's vivid parallels between Fall and Redemption, Adam and Christ.

Given this older and wider tradition it would be surprising if Mary did not come to play a crucial role in Cyril's development of this crucial theme for his theology. Many of Cyril's references to the theme of Fall and Redemption in the pre-controversy exegetical works remain in abstract form, Adam being named no more than Eve. In the *Commentary on John*, for example, we find comments such as the following:

> There was no other way for us who have borne the image of the man of dust to escape corruption, unless the beauty of the image of the man of heaven is imprinted upon us through our having been called to sonship (cf. 1 Cor. 15:49). . . . For scarcely do we thus recover the ancient beauty of our nature, and are conformed to that divine nature, than we become superior to the evils that arose from the Fall.[22]

But Adam is a shorthand – indeed it has been noted that even though Adam appears nowhere in the text of John's Gospel, Cyril's *Commentary on John* is saturated with allusions to Christ as the

---

[20] *Adv. Haer.* 3, 21, 22; 5, 19; *Demonstratio*, 32–4.

[21] *Church*, 49, 7. ET and further discussion in Sebastian Brock, *The Luminous Eye: The Spiritual World Vision of St Ephrem* (Placid Lectures, Rome: C.I.I.S., 1985).

[22] *In Jo.* 1:12 (Russell, p. 100).

second Adam.[23] As we were all in Christ, so we were all in Adam, we might say.

> The common element of humanity is summed up in [Christ's] person, which is also why he was called the last Adam: he enriched our common nature with everything conducive to joy and glory just as the first Adam impoverished it with everything bringing gloom and corruption.[24]

Interestingly it is in this context that the Virgin comes into play. She is the one from whom he took his 'temple':

> You should not think that the Word was transformed into flesh but rather that he dwelt in flesh, using as his own particular body the temple which is from the Holy Virgin.[25]

How important this is is evident also in the *Commentary on Isaiah*, especially with regard to Cyril's comments on 7:14–16. He insists, against Jewish exegetes, that the text does not refer to the birth of Hezekiah, but is a prophecy of the Holy Virgin:

> For he who is from above, and is by nature the only-begotten Son of God the Father, emptied himself and was brought forth from a virginal womb according to the flesh . . . you will call his name Emmanuel, that is, you will acknowledge that God has appeared in human form. For it was when the only-begotten Word of God appeared like us that he became 'God with us'.[26]

The voluntary self-emptying and enduring of birth for us is emphasized again when Cyril discusses the prophecies of Messiah in Isaiah 11.[27] Thus the *kenosis* involved in birth from a Virgin has become a significant element in Cyril's understanding of the recapitulation. So prior to the controversy, the Virgin already had a vital role in the overarching narrative that was foundational for Cyril's reading of Scripture and for his theological thought.

---

[23] By, for example, Robert Wilken in *Judaism and the Early Christian Mind: A Study of Cyril of Alexandria's Exegesis and Theology* (New Haven: Yale University Press, 1971), and Lars Koen, *The Saving Passion: Incarnational and Soteriological Thought in Cyril of Alexandria's Commentary on the Gospel according to St John* (Uppsala: Graphic Systems, 1991).

[24] *In Jo.* 1:14b (Russell, pp. 106–7).

[25] *In Jo.* 1:14b (Russell, p. 106).

[26] *In Is.* 7:14–16 (Russell, p. 79).

[27] *In Is.* 11:1–3 (Russell, pp. 82–3).

Kenosis and the importance of *Theotokos*

Three features of Cyril's theology in the conflict with Nestorius are worth recalling. My argument is that these features derive from the theological reading of Scripture we have outlined, explain the defence of the title *Theotokos* for Mary, and hold together in a single pattern the divine story of incarnation and the human story of Fall and Redemption.

(1) The first feature to note is a characteristic aspect of his argumentation, namely, his refusal to assign different phrases of the Nicene creed to different subjects: it was the same one who was eternally begotten of the Father who came down from heaven and was crucified. Cyril is determined to hold onto a narrative of descent by keeping the unity of subject.

The second and third we have already observed in Cyril's pre-controversy exegesis, but they are repeatedly pressed at the time of the controversy; they are (2) his appeal to the title *Emmanuel* – 'God with us', and (3) his emphasis on *kenosis*. How to interpret Philippians 2:5–11 was much debated, the Antiochenes emphasizing the phrase 'he *took* the form of a servant' as a way of avoiding the implication of change when 'he became flesh', Cyril focussing on the fact that it was the Word, the one in the form of God, who emptied himself. *Kenosis* was a keynote of his theology. Noticeably all three of these features emphasize the motif of descent and ascent, mirroring the overarching pattern of Fall and Restoration. Incarnation and redemption together lie at the root of Cyril's theology, and we can find this long before the controversy erupted.

In his *Commentary on John* Cyril had celebrated the 'deep mystery' by which we are all in Christ: 'the Word dwelt in all of us by dwelling in a single human being'. With a battery of scriptural quotations and allusions, Cyril shows that

> 'in Christ' that which is enslaved is liberated in a real sense and ascends to a mystical union with him who put on the form of a servant, while 'in us' it is liberated by an imitation of the union with the One through our kinship according to the flesh. [28]

That was why Christ had to be made like his brethren in every respect (Heb. 2:16–17). Cyril speaks of him 'giving us himself as a

[28] *In Jo.* 1:14b–15 (Russell, pp. 106ff.).

gift, "so that we by his poverty might become rich"' (2 Cor. 8:9). The ascent of redeemed humanity depends upon the descent, the emptying, of the one who is full of grace and truth.

Later in the commentary, Cyril speaks of 'the blending of two elements into a single reality'.[29]

> For his ineffable generation from God the Father raises him up, in that he is Word and Only-begotten, to the divine essence and to the glory that naturally accompanies it, while his self-emptying draws him down somewhat to our world.

He hastens to say that this self-emptying is not sufficient to overwhelm his divinity – indeed it was self-chosen out of his love for us: he humiliated himself voluntarily. It is only because he humbled himself willingly that we may become sons of God by grace. Though Cyril would probably have shied away from expressing it quite that way, we may almost speak of a chosen 'fall' to our level. He does dare to speak of him 'appearing to fall short of God's majesty by becoming a fully human being', while insisting that the Godhead is in no way diminished by this chosen path of humiliation. 'He brought himself down to that which he was not for our sake.'

These thoughts are perhaps most sharply expressed in the *Commentary on Isaiah*.[30] Cyril is sure that it is a property of human nature to have no trace of the heavenly graces of its own will or nature. Rather humanity was enriched from outside. So it was necessary

> that the only-begotten Word of God who brought himself down to the level of self-emptying, should not repudiate the low estate arising from that self-emptying, but should accept what is full by nature on account of the humanity, not for his sake but for ours, who lack every good thing.

I take that to mean that although full of the Spirit by nature, he had to empty himself in order to receive the Spirit for our sake. So, according to Cyril, he received the Spirit while being the supplier of the Spirit, and that receiving was proportionate to the self-emptying. In the beginning the Spirit was given to Adam; but he was careless and sank into sin. So the Spirit had no resting

[29] *In Jo.* 17:11 (Russell, pp. 125–6).
[30] *In Is.* 11:1–3 (Russell, pp. 83ff.).

place among human beings, until the Word of God became man. Cyril makes much of the loss of the Spirit through the Fall in other texts, such as his discussion of the baptism in his *Commentary on John*; redemption was a re-rooting of the Spirit in the human race.[31] Here he goes on:

> Since he was not consumed by sin even though he became as we are, the Holy Spirit rested once again on human nature ... That grace was not bestowed upon him as a particular gift, in the way that the Spirit is said to have rested on the saints, but that it was the fullness of the Godhead which took up residence in his own flesh as if in his own temple ... the prophet makes clear when he says, 'the spirit of the fear of the Lord shall fill him' (Is. 11:3).[32]

Already in this commentary Cyril is insisting that it is the 'Lord of all' who was born of the Virgin when he 'made the limitations of humanity his own'.

So the pattern of Fall and Redemption is mirrored in Christ's descent and ascent. Self-indulgence is reversed through self-humiliation. For Cyril this narrative movement is fundamental, and he will defend it through thick and thin against the apparently fragmenting analysis of a Nestorius. Our human destiny depends on the truth of the universal pattern whereby Christ redeems Adam, whereby God liberates from enslavement to the world, the flesh and the devil. Willing submission to God is the converse of that *hybris* which brought about the Fall, and is supremely played out in the *kenosis* whereby the Word was made human that we might be made divine.

Now if obedience and humility provide the key to our redemption, the receptivity of Mary as she becomes *Theotokos* is crucial. She is the one through whom God is formed within humanity. She is the 'type' of the Church, of the humanity which is God-receptive and therefore in process of being redeemed. Once the controversy was under way, Cyril would, of course, acknowledge that the Word pre-existed the birth of Christ from Mary – this birth was not, as he puts it, 'the beginning of his being'.[33] But if he is Emmanuel, God with us, then Mary must properly be called

---

[31] This point is made by Koen, *The Saving Passion*; and discussed further in Keating, 'The Appropriation of Divine Life in Cyril of Alexandria'.

[32] *In Is.* 11:1–3 (Russell, pp. 83–4).

[33] *Expl. XII Cap.* 7 (Russell, p. 179).

Theotokos. Mary is the vehicle of the new creation. This is the thinking that underlies Cyril's response in the controversy, and clear continuities are traceable.

Of course, the Lord could have just created a body for himself, just as he did for Adam. But Cyril knows that that would easily encourage docetism. So in his work *Against Nestorius* he comments thus: [34]

> He therefore necessarily observed the laws of human nature, and since his aim was to assure everybody that he had truly become man, he took to himself the seed of Abraham (cf. Heb. 2:16) and with the blessed Virgin acting as a mediator to this end, partook of flesh and blood in the way we do (cf. Heb. 2:14). For this was the only way in which he could become 'God with us'.

He goes on to emphasize the fact that 'if he had not partaken of the same elements as we do, he would not have delivered human nature from the fault we incurred in Adam', and proceeds to rehearse the story of the Fall once again. The Holy Virgin is blessed along with the fruit of her womb because 'in Christ we see human nature, as if experiencing a new beginning of the race, enjoying freedom of access to God'.

At the same time Cyril is adamant that we are talking about 'God the Word who was with his Father before all ages', insisting that the one who came 'to be with us according to the flesh' was truly the divine Logos. 'Emmanuel, the second Adam, did not come forth for us from the earth like the first, but from heaven', he asserts, basing his point on Paul (cf. 1 Cor. 15:47). Nor did he simply descend on some human individual. Rather he 'recapitulated human birth in himself', having 'made his own the body which was from a woman, and having been born from her according to the flesh'. This is why Mary is *Theotokos*. He berates Nestorius: just because you are scared stiff that people will think 'the Word brought forth from God had the beginning of existence from earthly flesh', he charges, 'you destroy utterly the mystery of the economy of the flesh by saying the Holy Virgin should not be called *Theotokos* by us'. Thus Cyril's concern to defend the title *Theotokos* for the holy Virgin Mary is deeply founded on her role in the overarching story of Fall and Redemption.

---

[34] *Adv. Nest.* 1, Proem (Russell, pp. 134ff.).

Container of the Uncontained

The homily on *Theotokos* that Cyril is purported to have preached at Ephesus, Quasten calls 'the most famous Marian sermon of antiquity'. It consists largely of an incantation of honorific epithets – here is some of it:

Mary is
>the sacred treasury of all the world
>the unquenchable light
>the garland of virginity
>the mirror of orthodoxy
>the indestructible temple
>the container of the uncontainable
>mother and virgin.

Moreover, she is the one
>through whom the Trinity is sanctified
>through whom the Cross is called precious and is worshipped
>>throughout the world
>through whom heaven rejoices
>through whom angels and archangels are glad
>through whom demons are made to flee
>through whom the tempting devil falls from heaven
>through whom the fallen creature is received into the
>>heavens
>through whom all creation, held back from idolmania,
>>comes to knowledge of truth
>through whom holy baptism came for those who believe
>through whom came the oil of gladness
>through whom churches were founded in all the world
>through whom the Gentiles came to repentance
>through whom the only-begotten Son of God gave light to
>>those in darkness and the shadow of death
>through whom the prophets prophesied
>through whom the apostles preached salvation to the Gentiles
>through whom the dead are raised
>through whom kings rule through the Holy Trinity
>The Virgin Mother – O marvel! [35]

At first sight one might be forgiven for imagining that here we have a baptized version of some ancient Hymn to Diana of the

---

[35] *Hom.* 4, PG 77.

Ephesians. There are many examples of how Christianity was becoming enculturated in the world of ancient Mediterranean religious patterns as well as contemporary philosophical rationalizations. Here in Ephesus the Holy Virgin naturally replaces the worship of Artemis as Christianity comes to dominate through imperial patronage. A 'History of Religions' account of the development of Mariology would exploit all such parallels with much plausibility. But if we set this Homily in the context of Cyril's theology as outlined in this chapter, we must surely conclude that the matter is more complex. Doubtless all kinds of sociological and psychological factors reinforced the popular propensity to 'divinize' the Mother of God, and Nestorius saw the dangers. But it is unlikely that Cyril had much truck with idolatry given his track record of opposition to surviving paganism in Alexandria and his great apologetic work, *Against Julian*. His veneration of Mary has deeper theological roots.

Again, at first sight one might be tempted to think that Mary has usurped the functions of Christ. She is now the one through whom demons are cast out and the devil falls from heaven; through her 'the fallen creature is received into the heavens', through her 'all creation . . . comes to knowledge of truth' and through her 'the dead are raised'. Even more extraordinary, she is the one 'through whom holy baptism came for those who believe', the one 'through whom churches were founded in all the world'. She is even the one through whom prophets prophesied and apostles preached – as if the Holy Spirit or the pre-existent Logos had been outfaced! One might with plausibility propose that after Nicaea Christ had become so remote, so immortal, invisible, incomprehensible and impassible that a new mediator of salvation was required, and Mary filled the gap. But such an assessment would be untrue to the overall theological perspective we have been tracing, and to the overarching perspective of the homily itself.

Mary is essentially 'the temple' which allows the presence of God the Word to dwell within creation, the essential medium of the Word's *kenosis*. Rarely does Cyril explicitly draw out the Eve–Mary typology, but undergirding his whole understanding is the reversal of the Fall. Where Eve facilitated the entry of sin into the world, Mary allowed herself to be the 'container of the Uncontained' and so the one 'through whom the only-begotten Son of God gave light to those in darkness and the shadow of death'. What is necessary for salvation is the birth of Christ within humanity. So Mary becomes both the unique medium of salvation, the one through whom all is made possible, and also 'type' of each believer, 'type' of the Church. Thus it is that through her 'the Trinity is sanctified' and 'the Cross called precious and worshipped throughout the world'. She is the 'mirror of orthodoxy' because she is inseparable from her son: if you challenge her right to be venerated as *Theotokos* you cannot possibly give due honour to Christ.

Some feminist scholars have dwelt upon the negative views of women found in the majority of patristic writers, tracing these to the widespread acceptance that Eve was the cause of the Fall, a 'type' of the way men are tempted and misled by women. But such a critique only notices half the story. The fact that Protestants have lost the ancient traditional practice of venerating Mary while Catholic women have felt oppressed by the impossible ideal of virgin and mother has meant that feminist theologians have overlooked the profound significance of Mary in the structure of the overarching story of Redemption. Cyril's defence of *Theotokos*, grounded as it is in this core narrative, and enhanced as it is by a sense of Mary's vital necessity for humanity's appropriation of the divine life through Christ, might prove the starting-point for a better appraisal of Mary as a feminist symbol. Indeed the Eastern Orthodox way of honouring Mary as *Theotokos* provides a potentially important critique of Western Mariology.

The crucial thing for Cyril is that the Word dwelt in flesh, 'using as his own particular body the temple that is from the holy Virgin'. And this particular dwelling meant a dwelling in all of us, in the whole of humanity. So

> 'in Christ' that which is enslaved is liberated in a real sense and ascends to a mystical union with him who put on the form of a servant, while 'in us' it is liberated by an imitation of the union with the One through our kinship according to the flesh.[36]

It is time we considered more carefully how Cyril envisaged our reception of this redemption which was achieved by the Word dwelling in the flesh he took from the Holy Virgin.

---

[36] *In Jo.* 1:14b (Russell, p. 107).

Receiving Redemption

Essentially Cyril, like Athanasius before him, believed that what humanity needed was the restoration of divine life and that the incarnation effected this. But particular human beings had to appropriate this and this was made possible through the sacraments.

It has been widely recognized that Cyril's christological position was designed to preserve the reality of divine assimilation through feeding on the flesh of Christ in the Eucharist.[37] Cyril's commentary on the sixth chapter of John's Gospel is crucial. Here he speaks of 'the eucharistic reception of the holy flesh and blood which restores man wholly to incorruption'.

> Accordingly the holy body of Christ endows whose who receive it with life and keeps us incorrupt when it is mingled with our bodies. For it is . . . the body of him who is Life by nature, since it has within itself the entire power of the Word that is united with it, and . . . is filled with his energy, through which all things are given life and maintained in being.[38]

His holy body is life-giving because it is united with the Word that is from God:

> For after the incarnation they are not divisible, except insofar as one knows that the Word that came from the Father and the temple that came from the Virgin are not identical in nature.[39]

So the flesh of the Saviour is life-giving, and 'when we taste of it we have life within ourselves, since we too are united with the flesh of the Saviour in the same way as that flesh is united with the Word that dwells within it'. The Eucharist 'will certainly transform those who partake of it and endow them with its own proper good, that is, immortality'. Cyril again sets this resurrection to life through Christ's flesh against the corruption, decay and death which came through the Fall. The Eucharist dispels both death

---

[37] See Henry Chadwick, 'Eucharist and Christology in the Nestorian Controversy', *Journal of Theological Studies* NS 2 (1951), pp. 145–64; and Ezra Gebremedhin, *Life-Giving Blessing: An Inquiry into the Eucharistic Doctrine of Cyril of Alexandria* (Uppsala: Borgströms, 1977).

[38] *In Jo.* 6:35 (Russell, pp. 110–11).

[39] *In Jo.* 6:53 (Russell, p. 115).

and the diseases that are in us, for Christ comes as a doctor to tend us, his patients.[40]

> It is as if one took a glowing ember and thrust it into a large pile of straw in order to preserve the vital nucleus of the fire. In the same way our Lord Jesus Christ hides away life within us by means of his own flesh, and inserts immortality into us, like some vital nucleus that destroys every trace of corruption in us.[41]

There are many indications that the flesh is vital as the medium of this eternal life. So Mary *Theotokos* is essential as the vehicle of the Word's enfleshment.

The *Commentary on John* shows that baptism is as significant as eucharist. For Cyril redemption is couched in terms of the restoration of the Spirit to human nature; it is by the Spirit that the Pauline move from slavery to sonship (Romans 8) is effected. That is how human beings are born of God (Cyril is commenting on John 1:13) and become partakers of the divine nature (2 Peter 1:4). 'The gift of the indwelling Spirit is the means by which Christ now accomplishes our cleansing and sanctification and imparts to us new life.'[42] Although closely linked to circumcision, for Cyril discusses at length the New Testament phrase 'circumcision in the Spirit', Christian baptism has never been an exclusively male rite. Cyril simply takes for granted that the whole human race is sanctified and renewed.

For Cyril the appropriation of divine life is twofold, both physical and spiritual, for a double healing is required. A person has to be born of water and the Spirit to enter the kingdom. Keating has summed up his perspective as follows: 'We receive Christ into ourselves, participating in him and his life, and thus in the divine nature, through a twofold means: through the indwelling of the Holy Spirit, normally related to baptism, and through the partaking of the flesh and blood of Christ in the Eucharist.'[43] None of this would be possible without Mary *Theotokos*. Later Keating draws out the significance of Christ as 'type' or pattern in the process of our sanctification, and the way in which human beings become

---

[40] *In Jo.* 6:56 (Russell, p. 119).
[41] *In Jo.* 6:54 (Russell, pp. 117–18).
[42] Keating, p. 64.
[43] Keating, p. 95.

participants in the process through imitation. This is possible because of his kinship with us as human being. Christ becomes the pattern of our reception of divine life, the pattern of obedience.

So the pattern of Fall and Redemption undergirds Cyril's biblical exegesis and his stance in the controversy. We can pull the whole argument together with a fuller version of a passage already quoted from the *Commentary on John* where Cyril makes recapitulation in Christ explicit, and the necessity of Christ participating in our nature so that we might participate in his:

> There was no other way for us who have borne the image of the man of dust to escape corruption, unless the beauty of the image of the man of heaven is imprinted upon us through our having been called to sonship (cf. 1 Cor. 15:49). For having become partakers of him through the Spirit (cf. Heb. 3:14, 6:4), we were sealed into likeness to him and mount up to the archetypal form of the image in accordance with which divine scripture says we were also made (cf. Gen. 1:27). For scarcely do we thus recover the ancient beauty of our nature, and are conformed to that divine nature, than we become superior to the evils that arose from the Fall.
>
> We, therefore, ascend to a dignity that transcends our nature on account of Christ . . .[44]

[44] *In Jo.* 1:12 (Russell, pp. 100–1).

XX

THE GOD OF THE GREEKS
AND THE NATURE OF RELIGIOUS LANGUAGE

In his *Miracle and Natural Law in Graeco-Roman and Early Christian Thought,* a book whose scholarship and clarity of exposition is characteristic of its author, Robert Grant showed that a debate, generally assumed to be peculiar to modern thought, in fact had its counterpart in ancient philosophy and in early Christian apologetic and theology. In a paper written in his honour, it seems not inappropriate to take another philosophical problem which looms large in modern discussions and enquire how far it was recognised and discussed by philosophers of the ancient world and in particular by patristic theologians. The problem chosen is that of religous language: to what does such language refer? What sort of meaning does it have? How does it function? My purpose is to show that ancient philosophers and the early Christian Fathers were aware that religious language has peculiarities, and does not function in precisely the same way as ordinary language.

Of course, the intellectual context of the ancient world was markedly different from our contemporary situation; the questions do not always appear to be the same, and the arguments were conducted according to different presuppositions and terms of thought. Underlying modern discussions is the suspicion that God-talk is somehow all a misleading hoax, that in the absence of empirical tests theology can have no claim to be a formal discipline of enquiry into reality; whereas in the ancient world the issue was how to talk about a being defined as inexpressible. It is important that this difference not be obscured, and that we avoid the pitfall of distorting the ancient intellectual tradition in an artificial attempt to solve modern problems. In order to keep the discussion firmly anchored in its proper intellectual context, a patristic text will be taken as a basis from which arguments and presuppositions may be extracted, then to be explained and illustrated from other ancient material. The *Five Theological Orations* of Gregory Nazianzen seem admirably suited to serve as a springboard of this kind, partly because they may be regarded as a concise summary of the patristic theological consensus, but more especially because a central issue in the controversy with Eunomius, the extreme Arian theologian of the time, was the possibility of knowing and talking about God. Selected passages relevant to these issues will provide triggers for our discussion.

1. RELIGIOUS LANGUAGE AND THE BEING OF GOD.

The *Second Theological Oration* (*Or.* 28) is concerned with the question of God's being, and it is here that we find statements about the possibility of using meaningful theological language. Gregory distinguishes two problems, the question of God's *existence* and the problem of his *essence* or nature. His concern is with the latter. At the outset, then, we meet the difference between ancient and modern discussions — though the problem of God's existence is not entirely independent of the question of what sort of a being we are discussing. Gregory, however, assumes an intellectual tradition which required a cosmological first cause in order to avoid an infinite regress, and indentified that first cause with God[1]. Gregory dismisses the whole question of God's existence in a brief paragraph whose very language reflects a long tradition of philosophical thought *(Orat.* 28.6):

> For, that God exists and that he is the creating and sustaining cause, sight and natural law teaches us, sight by encountering visible things beautifully ordered and progressing, immovably moved, so to speak, and carried around, natural law by reasoning back through things seen and ordered to their author. For how could all this be established or constituted unless God brought it all into being and sustains it? For no one who sees a beautifully made lyre, well-tuned and in good order, or who hears its melody, thinks of anything else but the lyre-maker or musician, and

---

1. PROCLUS, *Elements of Theology* Proposition 11: there must be a first cause to avoid an infinite regress (cf. ARISTOTLE, *Metaphysics* 994a). For discussion of the cosmic god as the first principle, see e.g. Arnold EHRHARDT, *The Beginning* (Manchester, 1968); A. J. FESTUGIÈRE, *La Révélation d'Hermès Trismégiste*, Vol. 2: *Le Dieu Cosmique* (Paris, 1949).

inevitably imagines him even if he does not know him by sight; so the creating principle is clear to us also — the one which moves and preserves created things — even if he is not comprehended by mind. Anyone who does not willingly proceed thus far in following natural demonstrations is wilfully ignorant[2].

At first sight it might appear that Gregory is using a form of the cosmological argument and that therefore he did feel it necessary to prove God's existence. However, the argumentative style belongs to the tradition on which he is drawing and is by now no more than shadow-boxing. For he goes on:

"but even this which we have formed in our fancy or imagination, or which reason has sketched for us, is no proof that God is,"

and proceeds to argue that God's being is not demonstrable or comprehensible.

Gregory, then, is concerned with the difficulty of expressing, or indeed of knowing, one whose existence is presumed. For in the background of Gregory's *Second Theological Oration* is the Eunomian claim to define the nature of God. Gregory summarises his position as follows:

To know God is difficult, to speak of him impossible, as one of the Greek theologians taught — quite cleverly it seems to me; for in saying it is difficult, he appears to have comprehended him and yet escapes examination because of his inexpressibility; but in my opinion, to speak of God is impossible and to know him even more impossible. For what is known, some word can perhaps make plain, if not adequately at least obscurely, to anyone who has not completely lost his hearing or is mentally slow. But it is altogether impossible and impracticable mentally ($\tau\hat{\eta}$ $\delta\iota\alpha\nuο\acuteί\alpha$) to encompass so great a subject, not merely for the indolent with lowly inclinations, but even for those who aim high and love God — indeed for all created nature, in that this darkness and this thick fleshiness gets in the way of perceiving the Truth... (*Orat.* 28.4). [A little further on he adds:] It is not just the peace of God which passes understanding and knowledge... but his very nature, which is beyond our grasp and comprehension (*Orat.* 28.5).

---

2. The allusiveness of his words may be quickly observed by turning to the following passages: PLATO, *Timaeus* 37-39, 47; *Laws* 10, 896D-902E; *Laws* 12, 966D ff.; ARISTOTLE, *Metaphysics* 1073a; CICERO, *De natura deorum*, book 2.

48

As Gregory himself hints, a respectable philosophical heritage enables him to indicate the intellectual absurdity and blasphemous character of Eunomius' claims. The Greek theologian to whom he refers is Plato, and the text to which he alludes is Plato's much quoted remark in the *Timaeus* (28e):

> But it is an effort to discover the Father and Maker of all this universe; and it is impossible for the discoverer to speak of him to all men[3].

Gregory clearly takes this to mean that Plato thought that God was inexpressible though not incomprehensible, and he proceeds to argue that it is necessary to go beyond Plato. Thus he asserts both the indescribability and the incomprehensibility of God. He therefore recognizes the problems both of religious language and religious knowledge. Let us examine the background to these assertions.

1. God's indescribability: from anthropomorphism to the apophatic theology of Platonism.

It is important to remember that all through the history of Greek philosophy the gods of literary myths and religious rituals were in the background if not the foreground of theological discussion. Philosophers moved from criticism through toleration to what can only be described as sophisticated credulity in respect of these beings, and their philosophical theology was undoubtedly affected by these reactions to traditional religion. The issue at stake was the character and nature of the god or gods.

Cristicism of popular religion began in the presocratics, and is especially associated with the figure of Xenophanes. Since in their attacks on polytheism and idolatry Christian apologists used criticisms drawn from the philosophers to reinforce motifs borrowed from Judaism, it is not surprising to find several of Xenophanes' fragments preserved in the works of Clement of Alexandria. From these we learn that Xenophanes had observed that men make gods in their own image:

---

3. A list of places where this is quoted will be found in J. GEFFCKEN, *Zwei griechische Apologeten* (Leipzig, 1907). It is found in two passages to be discussed later in this paper: CLEMENT, *Strom*. 5.12; ORIGEN, *Contra Celsum* 7.42.

Ethiopians make their gods black with turned up noses, Thracians make them with red hair and blue eyes; mortals think that gods are born and have their own food, voice and shape; but if oxen or lions had hands and could draw or produce images like men, horses would draw the shapes of the gods like horses, oxen like oxen, and they would produce such bodies as the bodily frame they have themselves[4].

Elsewhere fragments survive in which Homer and Hesiod are criticised for attributing to the gods human faults like stealing, adultery and mutual deception, and those who tell stories of the birth of gods are accused of blasphemy no less serious than the blasphemy of those who say they die (Ritter and Preller, §§ 98, 99). According to Clement, Xenophanes asserted that there must be one god who is quite unlike mortals in form and thought; and elsewhere we find accounts describing this god as eternal, unoriginated (ἀγένητος) and impassible (ἀπαθής), as one and everything, as neither finite nor infinite (ἄπειρος), neither moved nor at rest, but the greatest and best of all things[5]. It is probable that late witnesses have distorted Xenophanes' vocabulary, but it is not insignificant that later tradition thought that his description anticipated Parmenides' One and the apophatic theology of later Platonism; apophatic theology was clearly associated with radical criticism of anthropomorphism.

This criticism of anthropomorphism, coupled with Plato's moral objections to the traditional gods of mythology (*Republic* 2, 363-366; 377-383), made a significant contribution to later Platonic development of a monotheistic doctrine of a transcendent Being with largely negative attributes. That God has no beginning or end, is beyond time and place, has no needs and, being perfect, is unchangeable, are deliberate contrasts to the gods of popular religion and mythology, even if other more philosophical concerns have contributed features of Plato's Ideas and Aristotle's Unmoved Mover to the total picture. The resultant idea of God is summed up for us in Maximus of Tyre s Eleventh Discourse entitled *Who is God according to Plato?* (9 c-d; 11 e):

He is the Mind which is Father and Maker of All, whose name Plato cannot tell because he does not know it, whose appearance

---

4. RITTER and PRELLER, *Historia Philosophiae Graecae* (Gotha, 1913) § 100.
5. For discussion see W. JAEGER, *The Theology of the Early Greek Philosophers* (Oxford, 1947), ch. 3. RITTER and PRELLER, §§ 100, 102, 106a.

he cannot describe because he cannot see it; whose size he cannot estimate, since he cannot touch it. "The divine is invisible to the eyes, unspeakable with the voice, untouchable with the flesh, unknown to the hearing; only by the most beautiful, most pure, most intellectual... aspect of the soul is it seen through its likeness and heard through its kinship, the whole together being present to the whole understanding..." God has no size, no color, no form, nor any other accident (πάθος) of matter, but he has a beauty unlike any other beauty.

Clearly, Maximus interprets Plato in the same way as Gregory did: God is indescribable but he can be perceived by the mind. Such is the position found also in Albinus, Apuleius, Celsus and Numenius, as well as some Christian philosophers[6]. Even though there is a possibility of religious knowledge by means of direct intuition, religious language is not possible, because there is no category by which we can speak of God; Albinus puts it thus, so indicating the influence of Aristotle in the Platonist traditions of this period:

> God is unspeakable (ἄρρητος) and grasped by the mind alone (τῷ νῷ μόνῳ ληπτός) because he has no genus or form, no differentia or accidents; no quality or lack of quality, for he is not deprived of anything nor is he composed of parts; he is neither identical to nor different from anything else; he is not affected by anything; he neither moves nor is moved (*Didaskalikos* 10).

In respect of such a Being, description, analysis and definition are impossible. The categories of human logic are inapplicable.

2. God's incomprehensibility: other influences on apophatic theology.

Given that Gregory's interpretation of Plato is clearly consistent with that of the Middle Platonist tradition, we might suppose that the more far-reaching idea of God's incomprehensibility even by the mind has a different source and background. In fact this very question has been the subject of some debate since the publication of Norden's *Agnostos Theos* in 1913.

It is in Gnosticism that extreme emphasis is placed upon the unknow-

---

6. A J. FESTUGIÈRE, *La Révélation d'Hermès trismégiste*, Vol. IV: *Le Dieu Inconnu et la gnose* (Paris, 1954), ch. 6.

ability of God. In the *Apocryphon of John*, for example, God is presented not only as invisible and imperishable, beyond quality, perfect and
without needs, immeasureable, and undifferentiated, unnameable and
therefore indescribable, but he is also infinite and incomprehensible;
and in the *Gospel of Truth*, he is repeatedly called the illimitable,
inconceivable one[7]. The more graphic *Bythos* or *Depth* of Ptolemaic
Gnosticism expresses the same idea. Sophia's *hybris* was a desire to
know what is incomprehensible (Ireaneus, *Adv. haer*. 1.1.1; 1.2.2.).
Two questions can be asked. Where did Gnosticism get the idea from? Is
there any possibility that Neoplatonism and later orthodox Christian
theology reached the conclusion that God trancends knowledge through
Gnostic influence?

To give a clear answer to these questions is as difficult as it is to
produce a theory of Gnostic origins. At a time when scholarship was
dominated by the theory of the History of Religions School that Gnosticism was derived from Iranian religion, Norden argued that God's
incomprehensibility was not a genuinely Greek idea, but was an adaptation of oriental mysticim in a syncretistic age — so confirming the
suspicion of some scholars that Plotinus and the Neoplatonists came
under eastern influence. E.R. Dodds[8], however, showed that Plotinus
based his teaching upon certain Platonic texts and the case for indige-
nous Platonist development was further argued by A.J. Festugière (*Le
Dieu Inconnu*). Three passages in Plato are of particular importance :

> In the *Symposium* (210e - 211b; Festugière, 79ff), absolute
> beauty is described as beyond time, change, relativity, definition
> or *knowledge*. In the *Parmenides* (142a; Dodds, 311), we read
> that the One "is not named, nor defined, nor conjectured, nor
> *known*, nor sensed...", and this text was understood to refer to the
> Supreme God by the Neopythagoreans as early as the First
> Century A.D. And the passage in the *Seventh Letter* (341 c-d;
> Dodds, 311): "it cannot in any way be expressed in words like
> other studies, but is suddenly born in the soul, as light that is
> kindled by a leaping spark, and thereafter nourishes itself", was
> interpreted by Plotinus as meaning that the One is unknowable
> except by a mystical union with it which is incommunicable.

---

7. R.M. GRANT, *A Gnostic Anthology* (London, 1961) provides convenient translations of both these documents: see pp. 70-71 and 146-161.
8. E.R. DODDS, *Proclus, The Elements of Theology* (Oxford, 1963),
Appendix I.

Thus Plato himself suggested to Plotinus that the One is beyond knowledge (*Enneads* 5.3.12ff.); and in Proclus, the word ἄγνωστος is closely associated with ἄρρητος (*Elements* Prop. 123, 162), a word we have already found firmly entrenched in the Platonist tradition. Platonist teaching was clearly amenable to development of a more transcendent doctrine than previously outlined, though for much of its history, that development did not take place. The reason for this was the fear of likening God to non-being or matter; for in the *Sophist* (238c), non-being is described as "incomprehensible and inexpressible (ἄρρητον) and unspeakable and irrational (ἄλογον, i.e., not subject to rational discourse)"; and Numenius reflects a common Platonist view when he argued, "If matter is infinite (ἄπειρος), it is unlimited (ἀόριστος); if it is unlimited, it is irrational (ἄλογος); if it is irrational it is unknown (ἄγνωστος)[9]". Incomprehensibility was the outcome of irrationality and infinity, which were characteristics attributed to formless matter. In the case of God, therefore, there was usually an appeal to the possibility of intuition by the mind, even when it was admitted that God's indescribability implied that he is hard to know and certainly not knowable by the normal processes of naming, defining, representing or categorising. Indeed, Numenius describes ways of knowing God with the mind exactly like the Middle Platonists[10], and yet asserts that Plato said he was totally unknown[11]. Thus he admirably reflects a basic tension in the Platonist tradition, though claiming himself to be a Neopythagorean.

The interesting thing about Numenius, however, is that he clearly knew something about Judaism[12]; and while God's incomprehensibility was a possible development within Platonism, the texts of Hellenistic Judaism feature this idea more prominently. It is doubtful whether Wolfson[13] was right when he argued that the doctrine of God's incomprehensibility entered the Platonist tradition through Philo, for even though Philo is our earliest evidence for the idea, direct Philonic influence on mainstream Platonism seems extremely unlikely[14]. Yet

9. NUMENIUS. *Fragments* (ed. E. Des Places; Paris, 1973): 4a (13 Leemans); cf. PROCLUS. *Elements* Prop. 11.

10. Frg. 2 (11 Leemans).

11. Frg. la-c (9a-b; 32 Leemans).

12. Frg. 17 (26 Leemans).

13. H. A. WOLFSON. *Philo* (Cambridge, Mass., 1947), vol. 2, ch. 11.

14. Daniélou also assumes that Middle Platonism came under the influence of Judaism *Gospel Message and Hellenistic Culture* (London/Philadelphia, 1973); but cf. John DILLON. *The Middle Platonists* (London, 1977) 144.

Norden was certainly right in noting that this idea is more obviously to be found in the writings of Jews like Philo and Josephus, and texts where there is the most striking development of these doctrines, namely the Hermetic writings and the literature of Gnosticism, are now thought to have come under the influence of Judaism as well as Hellenistic philosophy. If Judaism in general and Philo in particular had little influence upon mainstream Platonism, both certainly affected Christian philosophy; and it is the congruence of Platonic and Hellenistic-Jewish motifs which contributed to the Christian understanding of God. The fact that Jews never pronounced God's name, never made images of him, and used scriptures which asserted that the greatest prophet of all had no direct confrontation with God, "for no one can see God and live", undoubtedly contributed to this "negative" Jewish theology. Words emphasising God's otherness and incomparability seem to have been particularly characteristic of Hellenistic Judaism, and so entered Christian tradition: God is unapproachable (ἀπρόσιτος), untraceable (ἀνεξιχνίαστος) and inscrutable (ἀνεξερεύνητος)[15]; so he is incomprehensible (ἀκατάληπτος). Not surprisingly many of the terms of Hellenistic Judaism and of philosophy overlapped, and in Christian tradition they tended to be amalgamated, as previously in Philo, so as to point to a more ultimate transcendence than the mainstream Platonist tradition suggested. Thus God came to be regarded as beyond human understanding, as well as beyond human language.

3. The apophatic tradition in Christian writings.

In Gregory's *Second Theological Oration,* many of the terms of apophatic theology make their appearance: the divine is incorporeal (ἀσώματον) and therefore infinite (ἄπειρον), unlimited (ἀόριστον), without shape (ἀσχημάτιστον), untouchable (ἀναφής) and invisible (ἀόρατον); he is unbegotten (ἀγέννητον), without beginning (ἄναρχον), unchangeable (ἀναλλοίωτον),imperishable (ἄφθαρτον); he is the One who is "incomposite and incomparable by nature" But none of these nagative terms, Gregory argues, tells us what he *is* in his being and hypothesis; their opposites, corporeal, mortal, begotten and so on, may be used of a man, a horse or a cow, but we need to know

15. 1 Tim 6:16; Rom 11:33; Ephes 3:8; + LXX, Philo, Josephus.

54

what the subject is in order to present these objects clearly to the mind. Eunomius' claim to define God as *agennetos*, and so to know his Being, is therefore a false claim. God's Being is beyond our grasp and comprehension (ἄληπτος καὶ ἀπερίληπτος).

In using these negative terms Gregory was drawing upon a tradition of Christian theology reaching right back to the early apologists, who had not been slow to adopt a philosophical inheritance which so admirably suited their purposes[16]. On the one hand, Christians had quickly adopted the refined theism of philosophy to characterise the God they proclaimed as the one being to whom worship should be offered; on the other hand, Christian apologists emphasised the criticisms of anthropomorphism produced by earlier Greek philosophy. However, as a result of adopting these two intellectual traditions, Christians were driven into a defensive position in respect to the anthropomorphisms of the Old Testament. This problem pervades the works of Origen. He is not by any means an isolated case, but he is an interesting one in that he was obliged to deal with the problems in two quite different contexts. In the first place he was confronted with the problem in his exegesis of scripture, where he found it necessary to allegorise not only God's hands and face, but also his wrath and his repentance[17] — for emotions and change are alike foreign to the nature of God as Origen conceived him. Secondly, Origen faced the criticism and ridicule of the pagan Celsus for whom the bibical narratives made an identification of the Christian God with the Supreme Being incredible *(Contra Celsum* 4.13,71,72). ''God-talk'' which uses personal language of the divine bristles with difficulties for the Greek intellectual tradition, and those difficulties were fully acknowledged by an intellect as fine as that of Origen. Origen was certainly aware that to speak of God reacting to or intervening in the affairs of men was distinctly problematical. Neither pagan nor Christian philosophers took traditional religious language ''literally''; but it suited their convenience to accuse each other of doing so.

---

16. Typical passages will be found as follows: ARISTIDES. *Apology* 1.1; JUSTIN. *Apology* 2.6; *Dialogue* 114, 127; TATIAN. *Ad Graecos* 4.1.2; ATHENAGORAS. *Legatio* 10.1; THEOPHILUS. *Ad Autolycum* 1.3.4. For discussion see G.L. PRESTIGE. *God in Patristic Thought* (London, 1936); R. M. GRANT. *The Early Christian Doctrine of God* (Charlottesville, 1966).

17. E. g. *Hom. in Jer.* 18.6. For discussion see R. P. C. HANSON. *Allegory and Event* (London, 1959), especially ch. 8.

The problem of anthropomorphism is still at issue in Gregory's time; for in the *Second Theological Oration,* Gregory replies to the objection that Spirit, Fire, Light, Love, Wisdom, Righteousness, Mind, Reason and so on, are all intelligible descriptions of the First Nature by saying that none of these can we envisage without corporeal associations *(Orat.* 28.13):

> How do you conceive of mind? Is it not that which is inherent in something not itself, and are not its thoughts, silent or uttered, its movements? ...And Justice and Love, are they not praiseworthy dispositions... making us what we are and changing us as colours do bodies? (His point is that mind as we know it is contained, moves, and is subject to change and interaction, while justice and love are mere qualities of something else.) Must we not leave all these things, (he continues,) and look at the Deity absolutely...? What then is this subtle concept (μηψανή — mental contrivance), which is (built out) of these (notions) and yet is not them...? For every rational nature longs for God and for the First Cause, but is unable to grasp him.

The radical rejection of anthropomorphism meant that the problem of religious language certainly did not go unrecognised. In fact Christian theology has proved incurably anthropomorphic, and one suspects that some of the problems with religious language today are related to the fact that Christian theism has tended to replace the apophatic tradition with a kind of refined and sophisticated anthropomorphism; for God is usually regarded as in some sense personal. The problems of that kind of theology were patently obvious to the Greek intellectual tradition, and Christian theologians affected by this tradition could not avoid recognising that religious language is not like ordinary language. To some extent this was even imparted to the masses in the effect it had on liturgical language, where apophatic terms heightened the sense of God's mystery and were a constant corrective to the highly anthropomorphic language predominantly found in scripture and in expressions of the Christian Gospel[18].

For Gregory, however, the prime object was to discredit Eunomius, and simply to reassert the traditional negative theology was not suffi-

---

18. F.E. BRIGHTMAN, *Liturgies Eastern and Western* (Oxford, 1896) 1. 310, 322, etc.

cient for his purposes. Eunomius too inherited the traditions of apophatic theology, indentifying God as the single, absolute One which is invisible, without size or form, incomposite, undifferentiated and unchangeable. The problem was that Eunomius thought that God's identification as the First Cause meant that his nature was definable in terms of the negative attribute *agennetos;* and that God's unitary simplicity implied two things, first that any secondary being, like the Son, must be totally unlike Him, and secondly that definition and knowledge of God was not merely possible but simple. An already observed tension within the apophatic tradition itself became polarised in the Eunomian debate: on the one hand, God was regarded as beyond the senses but known to the mind; on the other hand, he was conceived as infinite and incomprehensible, though known indirectly through his works. Gregory takes the latter position; Eunomius the former.

The Alexandrians, Clement and Origen, provide a good illustration of the typical lack of clarity to be found among Christian thinkers before the Eunomian debate. In the *De Principiis* (1.1.6; 2.4.3; 4.4.9-10), God is identified as incorporeal substance of Mind, invisible because he has no shape, size or color, but perceived by intellectual beings through their kinship with him. Yet even so Origen states that God is incomprehensible and immeasurable. In what sense then does he understand these words? Origen explains that God is incomprehensible to the human mind because "he is far and away better than our thoughts about him"; for "our mind is shut up within bars of flesh and blood and rendered duller and feebler by reason of its association with material substances" (1.1.5). In fact Origen has picked up an idea found in Albinus alongside the insistence that God is Known by the mind (*Didaskalikos* 10), and indeed this explanation is the one later offered by Gregory in our passage from the *Second Theological Oration*. God's incomprehensibility does not mean that the mind cannot ultimately comprehend him, but that it cannot until purified and released from earth. But Origen also suggests that "no created mind can... possess the capacity to understand all", and that even intellectual natures purified of the flesh, though they acquire a good deal of knowledge, cannot comprehend everything (*De princ.* 4.3.14; cf. *Comm. in Jn.* 19.6.37). Is this a hint that Origen may have recognised that God's being is in principle incomprehensible? Hardly, for Origen in fact denied God's infinity on the grounds that this would mean he was by nature incomprehensible — even incomprehensible to himself (*De princ.* 2.9.1). Festugière has argued that God's incomprehensibility was admitted in the Platonist tradition in the sense that God is beyond the normal processes of reason and definition; but though incomprehensible to reason, he was not regarded as in principle unknowable since he may be grasped by the direct intuition of the mind after a process of purification (*Le Dieu Inconnu*, Ch. 6). On the whole, Origen's thought moves firmly within this Middle Platonist tradition[19], though his suggestion was to be developed more radically by the Cappadocians.

Philo had argued that God was incomprehensible in his essence, and only known indirectly through his works[20]; this suggests a different sense of the word "incomprehensible". Further hints of a more profound understanding of God's incomprehensibility are to be found in Clement of Alexandria. In an important discussion in *Stromateis* 5.12.81-82[21], Clement repeats familiar texts from Plato and many Middle Platonist axioms:

> the first principle of everything is hard to find; ...how could that be spoken of which is neither genus, nor differentia, nor species, nor individual, nor number, and on the other hand is neither accident nor that to which an accident pertains; ...he is not understood by scientific demonstration, for this depends on prior and more readily known principles, and there is nothing prior to the Unoriginated.

But Clement also accepted that the logic of the *Parmenides* was right when it passed from indivisibility, formlessness and namelessness to infinity:

> Therefore it is infinite, not merely in the sense that one cannot give an exhaustive account of it, but in the sense that one cannot analyse it into parts and that it has no limit and is therefore without form or name.

Clement thus seems to acknowledge God's inexpressibility and incomprehensibility in a way more radical than that of most Middle Platonism

---

19. Cf. J. WHITTAKER, "ἐπέκεινα νοῦ καὶ οὐσίας", *Vigiliae Christianae*, 23 (1969) 91-104, for ambivalence in Origen and other Middle Platonists.

20. PHILO, *Leg. alleg.* 1.91; *Post.* 169. Cf. JOSEPHUS, *Contra Apionem* 2. 167; ARISTIDES, *Apology* 1.1; JUSTIN, *Apology* 2.6. For discussion and references to Aristotle, see FESTUGIÈRE, *Le Dieu Inconnu*, ch. 1.

21. For discussion see E.F. OSBORN, *Clement of Alexandria* (Cambridge, 1957).

58

which did not easily accept the idea of infinity into its understanding of God; for, as we have seen the concept was firmly attached to the formlessness of matter. As far as our evidence goes, both Philo and Clement, probably under the influence of the Neopythagoreans, made more of this aspect of the argument of the *Parmenides* than their Middle Platonist contemporaries[22]. Yet even they do not seem to have deduced from such a radical understanding of God's 'unlikeness' that knowledge of him becomes impossible even for purified and perfected intellectual beings.

In Gregory's *Orations*, we can detect a growing awareness of the extent of God's incomprehensibility. In the *Second Theological Oration* (28), Gregory largely follows the position of Origen in that he explains God's incomprehensibility as the result of impurities and deficiencies of the human mind, especially in its incarnate state; he has, however, adopted the distinction between essence and existence, claiming that God's works give us knowledge of the latter, though his essence remains incomprehensible to us. By *Oration* 38.7-8, however, his understanding of incomprehensibility seems to have advanced further:

> The divine nature is infinite and hard to understand; and all that we can comprehend of him is his infinity — granted that one may assume that because his nature is simple, he is therefore either wholly incomprehensible or perfectly comprehensible.

He goes on to speak of the mind having no resting place as it seeks to contemplate the ''depth above'', affirming again that God is infinite and it is impossible to get to the end of him. Thus Gregory seems to suggest that God's Being is incomprehensible because there is no possibility of completely comprehending something that is infinite; God's incomprehensibility is no longer attributed to the inadequacies of the imperfect mind, but to God's very Being.

Such a radical assertion of God's incomprehensibility is reminiscent of the extreme statements of Gnosticism. Throughout most of the orthodox tradition it had been overlayed by the Platonist confidence that once the mind was sufficiently purified, it would know God through its likeness to him. Where then did Gregory get it from? Gregory's imme-

---

22. S.R.C. LILLA, *Clement of Alexandria* (Oxford, 1971) 206: but see J. WHITTAKER (note 19).

diate source seems to have been the *Contra Eunomium* of his friend,
Gregory of Nyssa. E. Mühlenberg has made a largely convincing case
that the latter Gregory was the first philosopher-theologian to use the
idea of infinity in a positive sense, and that it was in the context of the
debate with Eunomius that this notion was fully developed[23]. Mühlenberg dismissed the hints in writers like Philo and Clement too cavalierly,
I think, but it is certainly true that God's incomprehensibility is more
consistently grounded in the infinity of his Being, and more positively
developed as a central theological concept in Gregory of Nyssa's works
than in any earlier writer.

Gregory's *Contra Eunomium* contains more explicit discussion of the
problem of religious knowledge and religious language than any other
patristic treatise, except perhaps for Clement's *Stromateis*. Gregory
asserts the utter unlikeness of the infinite creator and finite creatures, so
that no intuition of God's being is possible through realising one's
kinship with him[24]; and he insists that the traditional negative terms
suggesting that no rational discourse can give an account of God, and
that no analysis or definition is possible of an infinite being, means that
complete knowledge of God is logically impossible. He thus takes
Clement's assertions to their logical conclusion. God has no limit or
boundary; he cannot be compared with anything else; so he is inconceivable. This is not simply due to the disabilities of human reasoning, but
it is a feature of God's very Being.

> The simplicity of true faith assumes God to be what he is, namely,
> incapable of being grasped by any term or any idea or any other
> device of our apprehension remaining beyond the reach not only
> of the human but of the angelic and of all supramundane intelli-
> gence, unthinkable, unutterable, above all expression in words,
> having but one name that can represent his proper nature, the
> single name being "above every name"[25].

Thus the apophatic tradition reached its epitome and the possibility
both of religious language and of religious knowledge was denied. The
denial was partly philosophical: there is no logic common to ordinary

---

23. E. MÜHLENBERG, *Die Unendlichkeit Gottes bei Gregor von Nyssa* (Göttingen,
1966).

24. E.g. *Contra Eunomium* 1.373-4 (JAEGER 1. 132); 1.446ff. (JAEGER 1. 156ff.) denies
the possibility of analogy on the basis of likeness; 2.67ff. (JAEGER 1. 245).

25. *Contra Eunomium* 1.683 (JAEGER, 1.222); cf. 2.586 (JAEGER, 1. 397).

60

language and language used of the divine. But it was also partly religious: a God worthy of worship is beyond comparison with anything derivative from him. Gregory Nazianzen already recognises the latter point in his *Second Theological Oration* when he asks how is God "worshipable" if he is circumscribable[26]. If God is God, he cannot be pinned down. Chrysostom too when he preached against the Eunomian position stressed not merely the philosophical basis of apophatic theology but the religious awe inspired by one beyond speech or knowledge[27]. The possibility of religious language has thus been denied not just in the context of modern empirical scepticism, but as an assertion of the profoundest religious faith. However, the nearest precedent to Gregory of Nyssa's position is to be found in the Gnostic Basilides, who wrote "the truly ineffable is not ineffable but above every name which is named"; and even spoke of the non-existent God making a non-existent universe out of the non-existent (Hippolytus, *Ref.* 7.20-21). Certainly it is ironic that Gregory attributed to God all the characteristics attributed by Plato to non-being (*Sophist,* 238c) — perhaps after all the logic of Gregory's position was a denial of the existence of God.

II. THE REENTRY OF RELIGIOUS LANGUAGE.

The *Second Theological Oration* (28.31) concludes that the nature of the First Being surpasses the power of mind (νοῦ κρείττων); yet in the following discourses, Gregory is able not only to give a detailed account of his Trinitarian God and relationships within the Trinity, but also to discuss many names given to God, particularly to the Second Person of the Trinity. Does he give us any clue as to how he is able to use religious language when his previous discussion suggests that it is impossible?

The only explicit clue in Gregory's theological orations is his statement that God is not known in his essence but in his attributes (*Orat.* 30.17):

> The divine cannot be named... For no-one has ever breathed the whole air, nor has any mind located or language contained the

---

26. *Orat.* 28.7; cf. GREGORY of NYSSA, *Contra Eunomium* 3.109ff. (JAEGER, 2. 40ff.).

27. CHRYSOSTOME, *Sur l'incompréhensibilité de Dieu* (Sources Chretiennes, ed. R. Flacelière; Paris 1957).

Being of God completely. But sketching his inward self from his outward characteristics, we may assemble an inadequate, weak and partial picture. And the one who makes the best theologian is not the one who knows the whole truth, for the chain (of the flesh) is incapable of receiving the whole truth, but the one who creates the best picture, who assembles more of Truth's image or shadow, or whatever we should call it.

It is on this basis that Gregory proceeds in the following paragraphs to list significant names of the Godhead and of each person within it, distinguishing names which are of God's essence and names which are "relative" to his creatures.

Gregory was not, of course, the first to be faced with the problem of speaking about the unspeakable. The problem had long since arisen in the Platonist tradition. Platonism recognised three ways of knowing or speaking about God, namely synthesis, analysis and analogy. According to Origen *(Contra Celsum* 7.42-44), Celsus quoted the famous saying from the *Timaeus* and then added:

You see how the way of truth is sought by seers and philosophers, and how Plato knew that it is impossible for all men to travel it. Since the reason why wise men have discovered it is that we might get some conception of the nameless first Being which makes him manifest, either by synthesis with other things, or by analytical distinction from them, or by analogy, I would like to teach that which is otherwise indescribable...

Albinus *(Didaskalikos* 10) explains the three ways for us: synthesis means building up a picture starting from the beauty of physical objects, going on to the beauty of the soul, from there to the beauty of customs and laws, and on to the vast ocean of the beautiful, so proceeding to the good, lovable and desirable (an example taken straight from the *Symposium); analysis* means successive abstractions, just as we get to the concept of a point by removing the idea of surface and then that of line; the way of analogy means the kind of thing Plato did when he used the simile of the sun in the sixth book of the *Republic.* In this way, the Platonist tradition asserted the possibility of knowing God, and a more popular account of a similar process is to be found in Maximus of Tyre *(Dissertationes* 11. 7-9). The way of analysis clearly produces the apophatic theology discussed in the previous section, but is counterbalanced by constructive processes of enlarging as well as purifying human experience so as to reach an intuitive grasp (sometimes regarded as a mystical union) with the divine. Underlying these ways is the assumption that man in his intellectual being is akin to God; by comparison with our knowledge of physical entities, God is unknown and indefinable, but kinship with him makes possible a cumulative process of overcoming the restrictions of the physical world so that the intellect achieves an immediate rather than discursive knowledge of him. This account derives, I suggest, from the need for an epistemology rather than some kind of mystical experience, yet the Platonist tradition certainly spoke of purification and of a process closer to religious devotion than to a logical exercise.

The earlier Christian Platonists knew of these approaches to the problem, but were not entirely satisfied with them. Thus, Clement accepts the way of analysis (*Strom.* 5.11.71):

> Abstracting from the body all physical attributes, taking away from it the three dimensions of space, we arrive at the conception of a point having position; from which if we abstract position, there is the concept of unity.

As in other Platonist writings, the way of analysis, or the *via negativa* produces the radical apophatic theology discussed in the last section: "We know not what he is, only what he is not". Origen (*Contra Celsum* 7.42-44) quotes Celsus' description of the three ways, and admits in reply that what Plato has to say is impressive and that it is probable that knowledge of God is beyond the capacity of human nature, but Origen was less inclined to radical apophatic theology than Clement. Neither of them make much positive use of the three ways. Rather they introduce a quite different factor which enables them to speak of God positively — namely the revelation of God through the incarnate Logos.

> We affirm (says Origen) that human nature is not sufficient in any way to seek for God and find him in his pure nature, unless it is helped by God who is the object of the search... (Plato) does not say that he is indescribable and nameless, but that although he can be described it is only possible to declare him to a few... (God is seen; for) "he who has seen me has seen the Father". (God is not known by synthesis, analysis or analogy, but) by a certain divine grace... by God's kindness and love to man...

Earlier (*Contra Celsum* 6.65ff.) too in reply to Celsus' claims that God is unattainable by reason and unnameable, Origen had already asserted that God is comprehended through his Logos and that it is possible by names (in fact, those revealed in scripture) to show something of his attributes so as to give an idea of his character. It is not philosophy but revelation and grace which makes religious knowledge and so religious language possible. The contrast between the philosopher's hopeless search for God and the Christian's revealed access to him was becoming commonplace in Christian apologetic literature, but Clement could put the Christological claim in a more obviously philosophical framework (*Strom.* 4.25.156):

> The divine then being indemonstrable, is not the object of knowledge, but the Son is Wisdom and Knowledge and Truth and whatever else is akin to these, and so is capable of demonstration and definition. All the powers of the divine nature gathered into one complete the idea of the Son... He is not then absolutely one as unity, nor many as divisible, but one as all in one.

Clement is utilising the Platonic distinction between a simple unity, a one, and a composite untity, a one-many; for Clement, God is the transcendent One, but the Logos is the composite One-Many, the ontological link between the One and the multifarious creation to which he gives unity. This being is knowable, but he is also the image of the One, and therefore the one through whom some knowledge of the transcendent God is revealed. The way of analysis may be counterbalanced by "casting ourselves into the greatness of Christ" (*Strom.* 5.11.71); for the unknown is known by divine grace. Clement gives further philosophical backing to the Christian way of knowing the incomprehensible divine by a careful evaluation of the epistemological value of faith, building up his discussion on the basis of both Platonist and biblical precedents (*Strom.* 2.2.4-6.31; 10.46-12.55)[28].

Thus the notion of divine revelation also provided justification for the Christian claim to religious knowledge. The Logos of God was not simply identified with the person incarnate in Jesus, but with revelation in the word of scripture and in the works of creation. Thus, scripture and tradition supplied possible "names" of God, all of which could be regarded as revealed by the Logos; and further attributes could be adopted from philosophy, since the best philosophy was plagiarised

---

28. For discussion see LILLA, *Clement*, 118ff.

from Moses and so was equally derived from the revealing activity of the Logos (e.g. *Strom.* 2.5.20ff.; 5.14.89ff.).

But what exactly was the status of the names? In what sense could such language be regarded as descriptive of or corresponding to the reality it sought to express? For Clement (*Strom.* 5.4.20-10.66; 12.82), all religious truth was to be found in prophecies and oracles spoken in enigmas; the mysteries were not conveyed to all and sundry, but only to certain people after certain purifications and previous instructions. He points out that symbols are characteristic of Egyptian religion, the mysteries and Pythagoreanism, and that in the Old Testament the tabernacle and its furniture have mystical meanings. Plato composed myths which should be interpreted allegorically; myriads of enigmatical utterances by poets and philosophers are to be found. So it is proper that the "barbarian philosophy" should prophesy obscurely and by symbols. The truth of scripture comes through a veil; we need an interpreter and guide. The language of scripture is only an expression of the inexpressible God in a very indirect way, and the problem of religious language is closely connected with the problem of exegesis. Yet Clement is confident that somehow the hidden mysteries have been unlocked; for the key is Christ. The true Gnostic inherits an unwritten tradition by which he comprehends what is incomprehensible to others; for nothing is incomprehensible to the Son of God. Through his incarnation, faith has become knowledge, and the solution of riddles and enigmas. The gnostic is taught by Christ to become like God and so to know him. However in the last analysis, Clement's religious ideas are negative. His God is the One, above change and passion, his Christ a virtually docetic revelation of this static God, and his ideal Christian (gnostic) an ascetic trying to emulate such a being. Clement is not really attempting to find a basis for a religious language which has any life to it. He regards the traditional language of the Church as allegorical and symbolic, and the reality of God remains elusive and abstract. The One is "without form or name, and if we name it, we do not do so properly, even in terming it the One, or the Good,... or God, or Creator,... etc. We speak not as supplying his name, but out of helplessness (ἀπορία) we use good names, so that the mind has these for support and does not wander after others". At bottom, the *via negativa* has obscured more positive use of religious language, and Clement is remarkably close to his contemporaries who accepted Homer by removing through allegory the anthropomorphic elements and so the dramatic impact of the poem[29].

Origen, though sharing many of Clement's philosophical presuppositions, was perhaps more successful in providing a basis for religious language. For, recognizing the parallel between the Logos-in-scripture and the Logos-in-flesh he spoke of both as divine accommodation to the conditions of fleshly existence. Thus religious language, while recognised to be inadequate, was grounded in God's character and activity. The scriptural "names" of God may need interpretation, and Origen is the master of allegorical exegesis, but they cannot be dismissed as wholly misleading. Indeed, Origen delights in listing the fascinating array of attributes and titles which scripture gives to the Logos (e.g. *Comm. in Jn.* 1.22; *Contra Celsum* 6.65); for these names are indicative of his loving accommodation to mankind, just as the names of God himself show something of his attributes and character. For Origen, the problem was not quite so acute, since he clearly stated that God was knowable, at least to spiritual beings; in Jesus Christ as much as possible of that knowledge was made available to men in their present incarnate state. Ultimately it seems, Origen allowed the Gospel of a loving God to modify the God of Platonist philosophy (Grant, *Doctrine of God*, 29ff.); he accepted that God's loving care for his creatures was real, however anthropomorphic the idea, simply because of the evidence of divine accommodation to the condition of men. Religious language, like the incarnation, could thus serve as the flesh in which truth was clothed and partially hidden; but the veil was not totally opaque.

Thus it was that Gregory inherited a tradition which dwelt upon the attributes and names of God as indications of his being, as a basis for religious language which was not totally misleading. This tradition he assumed. He also inherited the assumption that the incarnation was the basis of religious knowledge. But it was precisely this assumption which was threatened by the Arian controversy, as many of the chief protagonists realised. Athanasius repeatedly asked how Christ could be the revelation of the Father if he was not truly his Son and entirely one with him in his being; but it was Gregory's friend, Gregory of Nyssa, who came closest to grappling with the profound problem raised by the

---

29. For discussion of Hellenistic and Christian allegory, see R.M. GRANT, *The Letter and the Spirit* (London, 1957).

Arian-Eunomian debate, and so with the difficulties of the relationship between religious language and that to which it refers. What was the problem he faced?

Up to the time of Arius, the prevailing assumptions of Christian theology were those of the Platonist tradition, expressed in more or less sophisticated form. The ultimate transcendent God was linked with creation through a hierarchy of being which in varying degrees shared a certain kinship with the divine. The Logos was at the apex of this hierarchy, linked, as Clement had explained, with the one transcendent God in his oneness and with the multifarious creation through his many aspects and activities. Thus he fulfilled the same functions for religious knowledge as the ways of synthesis, analysis and analogy, emodying both the difference and likeness between creator and creature. For this ontological, indeed epistemological, structure to work, the Logos had to remain poised between the transcendent God and everything else. Arius, however, destroyed the hierarchy by focussing attention upon the utter unlikeness of creature and creator, an emphasis certainly present in scripture as well as implicit in the *via negativa,* but not so far allowed to disrupt the continuous chain of Being. Arius in effect raised the question where the line between God and his creation was to be drawn across this hierarchical triangle, answered it by placing the Logos firmly on the side of creation, and so destroyed the possibility of genuine revelation of God in the incarnation, or genuine knowledge of God based upon man's kinship with the divine. The orthodox reaction was not to deny the existence of the line, but to re-draw it, so that the Logos was placed on the divine side; but that solution also destroyed the hierarchy, made the problem of Christology intractable, and undermined the account so far offered of the basis of religious knowledge and religious language; for now the Logos as well as God was defined as transcending human comprehension. The consequences of this development and the new theological structures it produced are to be seen most clearly in Gregory of Nyssa, who more than any other, recognised that the radical distinction between creator and creature rendered the traditional accounts of religious knowledge unusable.

Gregory's answer to the problem seems to have been two-fold: in the first place, he grounded all religious knowledge in God's will to make himself known; in the second place, he established on this basis a symbolic theology through which some degree of theological knowledge was made possible (Mühlenberg, *Die Unendlichkeit Got-*

tes). These two points may be clarified by examining his treatment of "names", a recurring theme in the works against Eunomius .

Gregory basically believed that "reason supplied us with but a dim and imperfect comprehension of the divine nature; but nevertheless the knowledge that we can gather from the names which piety allows us to apply to it, is sufficient for our limited capacity"[30].

1. *The names are inadequate and humanly contrived expression.*

Gregory grounds his theory of religious language in a general theory of language: all language depends upon created human speech and the existence of different languages is a clear indication that God allowed men the freedom to invent and develop linguistic expression[31]. This means that no human language is God-given, not even Hebrew[32]. Gregory, because of his high doctrine of God's transcendence, has come close to recognising the cultural relativity of scripture, and he certainly asserts that the names of God are the work of human thought and conception. Gregory does not hesitate to speak of the vast range and variety of nomenclature devised by man, and he thinks men "have a right to such word-building"[33]. "We allow ourselves the use of many diverse appellations in regard to him, adapting them to our point of view. For whereas no one suitable word has been found to express the divine nature, we address God by many names, each by some distinctive touch adding something fresh to our notions of him — thus reaching by a variety of nomenclature to gain some glimmerings for the comprehension of what we seek"[34]. Gregory realised that man creates his own conceptions of God.

2. *The names are not arbitrary, but are grounded in the prior existence and activity of God.*

The inventive activity of man is not independent of a prior reality: "we do not say that the nature of things was of human invention but only

---

30. *Contra Eunomium* 2.130 (JAEGER, 1. 263).
31. 2.200ff; 246-250; 284; 406 (JAEGER, 1. 283; 298-9; 310; 344).
32. 2.260-61 (JAEGER, 1. 302).
33. 2.148 (JAEGER, 1. 298).
34. 2.145 (JAEGER, 1. 267).

their names''[35]. Likewise religious language is grounded in what man perceives of God's operations[36]: through contemplation of the works of God, certain peculiar and appropriate names are derived. Creation and scripture guarantee that the names of God are more than a figment of the human imagination; for creation and scripture are expressive of God's will and God is truth. They provide an adequate though limited means of communication, like the gesture and signs used in communicating with the deaf[37]. Though he has to accommodate himself to the limitations of human perception, God cannot be a party to deception[38]. So when scripture honours the only-begotten with the same names as the Father, it must imply that he shares the dignity and honour of the Godhead. Furthermore, if the Word of God names God the Father, he must eternally and unchangeably have been Father, and therefore must have had a Son[39]. The names have sufficient grounding in reality to form a basis for theological argument.

3. *The names cannot be totally misleading, but they do have to be interpreted by indicating the similarities and differences between their application to human beings and to the divine.*

"There is a similarity of names between things human and things divine, revealing nevertheless underneath this sameness a wide difference in meanings''[40]. For example, "We think of man's generation one way; we surmise of the divine generation in another''; for in the case of divine generation, the mind has to reject notions of sex and passion, of time and place, and think simply of the Son as being eternally derived from the Father. So wide is the gulf between creator and creature, finite and infinite, that different attributes or names have to be associated together in order to correct one another. But Eunomius' attempt to treat all titles of the Logos, including Son of God, as metaphorical will not do[41]. Even though "the infinity of God exceeds all the significance and

---

35. 2.283 (JAEGER, 1. 310); cf. 2.171 (JAEGER, 1. 275); God is not a concept of mind.

36. 2.149-154 (JAEGER, 1. 268-70); cf. 2.12ff. (JAEGER, 1. 230).

37. 2.417-21 (JAEGER, 1. 348-9).

38. 2.325 (JAEGER, 1. 321).

39. 2.15 (JAEGER, 1. 231); cf. 1.556, 591ff. (JAEGER, 1. 187, 196ff). *Refutatio Confessionis Eunomii* 7 (JAEGER, 2. 315).

40. 1.620-633 (JAEGER, 1. 205-208); 3.76-7 (JAEGER, 2. 30-31).

41. 2.294ff (JAEGER, 1. 313ff); cf. 3.128-9 (JAEGER, 2. 46-7).

comprehension that names can furnish''[42], if such names are truly predicable of God, they should be understood in their most natural and obvious sense, though with a heightened and more glorious meaning[43].

4. *The names do not all have the same status; some refer to God absolutely and some are relative, and theological discourse can only proceed by distinguishing these senses.*

In a number of passages[44], this kind of distinction is made: "God is called Father and King and other names innumerable in scripture. Of these names, some can be pronounced absolutely... like immortal etc.; others express his service towards something, like Helper, Champion, Rescuer... Some are both absolute and relative, like God or good." Gregory makes use of this distinction when he insists that Fatherhood is an absolute not a relative term: "Son of the Father" must be distinguished from "Shepherd", "Light", "Resurrection", etc. This discussion easily slips into a traditional Christological pattern with a tendency to assign the former kind of terms to Christ's Godhead and the latter to his Manhood; thus the rhetorical use of Christological paradoxes, so characteristic of Christian preaching and liturgy, is grounded in an attempt at logical distinctions. The whole point of the exercise was to clarify the status and therefore the theological usefulness of the symbols implied by the names. The kind of thing they wanted to say was that God is absolutely Father of the Son, but not absolutely our Father[47]. They were attempting to distinguish degrees of symbolic usage in religious language — from the purely metaphorical to a closer approximation to truth. Hence this analysis of the status of names and also the somewhat tedious effort to explain in what respects the names are and are not applicable. If this analysis strikes us as somewhat arbitrary, that does not detract from the fact they recognised the need for a critical evaluation of the symbols used in religious language.

---

42. 3.110 (JAEGER, 2. 41).
43. 3.87ff, 135ff (JAEGER, 2. 33ff, 48ff).
44. 1.570ff (JAEGER 1. 190ff); 2.130ff (JAEGER, 1. 263-4); 3.131ff. (JAEGER, 2. 47ff). Cf. GREGORY NAZIANZEN, *Orat.* 18 (Masson, 135ff).
45. 2.558 (JAEGER, 1. 389).
46. 3. 131ff (JAEGER, 2. 47ff.). Cf. GREGORY NAZIANZEN, *Orat.* 30.20ff.
47. 1.570ff (JAEGER, 1. 190ff.).

5. The names can provide a positive theological language by indicating a variety of attributes without endangering the transcendent unity of God's nature.

Gregory's discussion appears in the context of Eunomius' attempt to reduce the names to one essential definition entirely expressive of God's Being. Gregory counters this by insisting that no name provides a definition, all are simply attributes[48], and all are necessary to express different aspects of the total infinite reality beyond our grasp: "while the divine nature is simple... and cannot be viewed under any form of complex formation, the human mind...in its inability to behold clearly the object of its search, feels after the unutterable Being in diverse and many-sided ways, and never chases the mystery in the light of one idea alone"[49], and "because in such cases there is no appropriate term to be found to mark the subject adequately, we are compelled by many and differing names... to divulge our surmises as they arise within us with regard to the deity"[50].

Statements of this kind take us back to the passage of Gregory Nazianzen with which we began this section. The two Gregories adopted earlier traditions, but in a new theological setting they concluded that theology can only produce a partial picture of divine reality. The meaning of religious language can only be made clear by endless qualifications. But through the attributes revealed by God's will, some grasp and advance in understanding is made possible. The biblical narratives, treated imaginatively rather than literally, can become luminous of a divine reality beyond human expression; and the complete incarnation of one who was by nature totally transcendent was the crown of God's loving accommodation to men and the triumph of sheer grace which made possible man's assimilation to God. The possibility of religious language was located not in man's natural kinship to the divine, but in God's will to create and redeem; and the symbolic character of religious language was no longer confined to allegorical exegesis but was fully recognised in formal theology. It is likely that the epistemological questions at issue were more important for this deve-

---

48. 1.587ff (JAEGER, 1. 195ff.).
49. 2.475 (JAEGER, 1. 364-57).
50. 2.577 (JAEGER, 1. 394-5).

lopment than the mysticism so long presumed to be the basis of Gregory Nyssen's theology[51]. The Eunomian debate forced him to face the question how we can speak about an unutterable being, or know an incomprehensible God.

III. Religious Language and its User

If God is beyond the grasp of human comprehension, then the normal processes of human logic are inapplicable; as Gregory Nazianzen says (*Orat.* 30.17), "the best theologian" is not the one who can give a complete logical account of his subject, but the one who "assembles more of Truth's image or shadow". The one best able to do this will need special qualities of perception, and it is not unimportant that the first of Gregory's theological orations (*Orat.* 27) is devoted to the character of the true theologian.

In this discussion, Gregory draws upon two traditions: on the one hand, he picks up the moral contrast between those who just talk and those who act, a contrast which reflects the scriptural insistence on doing God's word and not just saying, "Lord, Lord"; on the other hand he utilises the catch-phrases of philosophers condemning sophists, criticising the clever tricks of logicians who perform acrobats with words, twisting absurdity into apparently reasonable syllogisms. Heretics are accused of priding themselves on their eloquence and delighting in the antitheses of knowledge falsely so-called (a phrase reminiscent of the earlier battle with the gnostics); they make theology cheap by disputations in the market-place and at the dinner-table. Throughout the works against Eunomius, the other Gregory also confronts his opponent with the charge that his theology is confined to false syllogisms and quibbling sophistries; his eloquent phrases and rhetorical rhythms are the product of fussy conceit; his claim to have mastered God by the powers of human reason is nothing short of blasphemous; he has been misled by the pretensions of philosophy. By contrast, the true theologian, according to the *First Theological Oration,* must qualify by meditation, by purification of soul and body, and by genuine concern about the subject.

---

51. The case is argued by Mühlenberg (*Die Unendlichkeit Gottes*), for the *Contra Eunomium;* and is developed in relation to the Vita Moysis by R.E. Heine, *Perfection in the Virtuous Life* (Patristic Monograph Series, 2; Philadelphia, 1975).

A hostile listener is incapable of receiving what the true theologian has to say; he is bound to misunderstand it. For what the true theologian has to impart is strictly speaking incommunicable, and the reward of both moral and intellectual purification. The need for purification has deep roots, of course, in the Pythagorean and Platonist traditions, and was reinforced in Christian literature by the scriptural stress on morality as the way of response and access to God; it had reached profound Christian expression in Clement of Alexandria's description of the true gnostic. The description of the true theologian is rooted in a tradition, and conventional polemic also supplied the motifs for characterising the obnoxious heretic.

Yet these traditional elements should not blind us to a significant point about religious language which is being recognised. Just as modern discussions of language have drawn attention to the importance of the language user and his intellectual, social and cultural context, so Gregory and his friend have come close to recognising that the language of theology may have different meanings depending upon who is using it and how it is being used. Ultimately religious language is grounded in a *Sitz im Leben* outside which it is inevitably distorted. It is the *Sitz im Leben* of religious language which permits the use of traditional, biblical and paradoxical expressions, for in their proper context, these symbolic utterances are grasped by the attuned imagination. The attitude of worship, the activity of contemplation and devotion to a particular life-style contribute to developing the necessary faculties for perception of meaning in what is meaningless according to the normal functioning of human logical categories. For the Gregories, the *Sitz im Leben* was the orthodox tradition of the holy catholic and apostolic church. This tradition was their safeguard against arbitrariness in exegesis or analysis of theological meanings. The heretic, they assumed, had put himself outside the moral and spiritual context in which theological language could be properly understood.

But their condemnation of this particular heretic was also closely related to the theological problems examined in the last two sections. According to the Gregories, Eunomius' principal error was to imagine that God could be defined, that a complete analysis of the divine nature was possible by using human reason. How easy it was to link this particular theological position with blasphemous pride and relate the epistemological question to the whole moral and religious life! It was natural to suggest that Eunomius dragged Aristotelian syllogisms into a field of study to which they were totally inapplicable, and so condemn him for distorting the biblical revelation with philosophy. But the fundamental conflict was not between Christianity and philosophy; nor was it between a revived Aristotelianism and a Christianised Platonism. It was a conflict within an intellectual tradition made up of all these elements, a conflict involving different evaluations of the status of religious language. For Eunomius, religious language, though often utilising metaphors, ultimately had some objectivity since God's Being was definable; the consequence of his position would be to regard theology as an objective science available to all reasonable men. For his opponents, however, religious language referred only obliquely to its object, and yet not all theological language was merely metaphorical; the theologian therefore had to operate within the context and rules of this particular "language-game". Religious language could never be completely accurate but must be symbolic; it is therefore in need of constant correctives, and can only be appreciated in its proper *Sitz im Leben* by a person totally committed and prepared by moral and intellectual purification. Such a position never implied the absence of the object to which religious language referred — simply the impossibility of access to it, and the importance of sympathetic awareness in gaining some faint glimmering of this incomprehensible reality. The theologian is one who is sensitive to "disclosure situations".

In this brief concluding section, a process of natural drift has shifted some of the terminology used from that of the ancients to that of our contemporaries — for it should be clear by now that there are points of similarity as well as difference in the two intellectual traditions. I do not wish to pretend that there are patristic solutions to the problems of modern theology — our self-consciously pluralistic world has become too sceptical of appeals to a unique special revelation to accept such an idea as a basis for religious epistemology, and the fragmentation of Christendom into a welter of differing groups has rendered impracticable an appeal to the catholic orthodox tradition as guaranteeing Truth. What I do suggest, however, is that there are patristic counterparts to some problems of modern theology and some of what they have to say is extremely suggestive. A persistent conundrum is the relationship between the logic of scientific explanation and the logic of theological discourse. A persistent defence of religious language is based upon the need for insight — for the response of *faith* — in order to appreciate its meaning and to grasp in some measure both how religious language

74

functions and to what object it refers. A suggestive direction is provided by the patristic denial of anthropomorphism and consequent recognition of the entirely symbolic character of religious language[52]. But how are the symbols to be evaluated? By what criteria are they to be classified. and interpreted? These are questions worthy of further exploration[53].

---

52. Since this paper was written, Joseph C. McLELLAND's *God the Anonymous* (Patristic Monograph Series, 4; Philadelphia, 1976) has reached me. A more detailed account of the relevant material in Philo, Clement and Origen will be found in that work, and a somewhat different theological assessment.

53. Note the important book by David BURREL, *Analogy and Philosophical Language* (Yale, 1973).

INDEX

Abraham: XIX 68
Adam: I 24; III 112; XIX 62–4, 66–8
*Address to young men on how they might
    profit from pagan literature*: IV 188
Adrianos: V 121–2
aesthetics: I 10; IV 187
Albinus: XX 50, 56, 61
Alexandrian: *xii*; I 30; IV 189; V 120, 123;
    VII 424; XI 292–3, 295, 297, 303;
    XIV 5; XX 56
allegory: II 350; III 107, 111; VI 103, 110–12,
    116–17; IV 182–3, 193; V 120,
    122–3; VII 432; XI 291–2, 297, 299,
    303; XII 113; XIII 267, 270;
    XIV 6, 11, 15; XVIII 346; XIX 60;
    XX 54, 70
anagnōsis: IV 187
anagōgē: XIII 271
anakephalaiōsis: XIX 61, 62
anamnēsis: X 173
angels: I 7, 23
animal: I 20
anthropology: *xi*; I 11, 25, 29; XVII 2, 5, 7,
    10, 12, 17, 19; XVIII 335–6, 343,
    347; XIX 60, 62, 64
anthropomorphism: XX 54–5, 65, 74
Anthrōpotokos: XIX 55
Antiochene: *xii*; II 350; IV 184, 189–90,
    195–6; V 120–21, 123–4; VI 113,
    115–16; XI 292–3, 297–8, 303;
    XIII 279; XIX 65
apatheia: I 20; XVII 3
aphthartos: XIX 60
Apollinari[u]s: I 17, 18, 30
apologetic: I 18; XIV 4; XVI 142; XX 45, 54
apologists: XX 48
apophatic: *xii*; XX 48, 51, 53, 55, 58–9, 62, 64
Apostolic Constitutions: VIII 105, 107, 109,
    114; X 161–9, 171–2
Apostolic Fathers: VIII 106; X 162
Apostolic Traditions: X 162, 173
Apuleius: XX 50
Arian: VIII 110; XII 102, 106, 108, 111;
    XIV 4; XVI 140, 151; XVII 2;
    XVIII 343; XX 65
Arian Controversy: VII 422; XI 292;
    XVIII 342, 343, 348

Aristophanes: IV 189
Aristotelian: XX 72
Aristotle: I 18, 21, 30; IV 183; XX 46–7,
    49–50
Arius: III 107, 111; VII 422, 427, 429;
    XI 300–301; XII 102, 107; XX 66
Artemis: XIX 70
ascetic: I 20
Athanagoras: XII 103–5; XVI 141;
    XVII 9–10, 13, 15; XVIII 340
Athanasius: III 107, 111–12; XI 301; XII 107,
    109–13, 115; XIV 7; XVI 147;
    XVIII 342; XIX 61, 72; XX 65
    Contra Gentes - De Incarnatione:
        III 111–12
atheism: XVII 6; XVIII 345
atonement: *ix*; I 8; III 107, 110, 112–13
atreptos: XIX 60
Augustine of Hippo: *xii*; XIV 1; XVI 147;
    XVII 2; 15–16, 18; XVIII 335–9,
    343–348; XIX 61
    Confessions xii: XIV 1
Aulen, G.: III 107, 112
autobiography: XIV 13, 15; XVIII 336

baptism: XIX 69–70, 73
barbarism: XV 200, 202
Barnard L.W.: XVII 9
Barr, James: VI 105
Barth, Karl: XVI 146
Barthes, R.: VII 426; VIII 108
Basil of Caesarea: I 1–2; IV 188; X 159–62,
    167, 173; XIV 4, 7; XVII 5;
    XVIII 344–5, 348
    Homilies on the Hexaemeron: I 1
Basilides: XVI 147–50; XX 60
Bauckham, R.: XVII 1
beautiful, the: I 9; XVII 7; XVIII 345; XX 50
Behr, John: XVIII 342
Bible: I 10–11, 23–6, 29–31; IV 184;
    VII 423, 429; VIII 106; XI 293, 304;
    XII 110–12, 115; XIII 267, 276;
    XIV 6–7, 9, 11–12; XV 201–2;
    XVI 139, 144, 151; XVII 1, 7;
    XVIII 342–3; XIX 57, 60–61, 64;
    XX 63, 69
Bigg, C.: XIII 266